Fundamentals *of* **FORTRAN** *for Management*

Fundamentals of **FORTRAN** *for Management*

ROY AGELOFF
University of Rhode Island

RICHARD MOJENA
University of Rhode Island

WADSWORTH PUBLISHING COMPANY, INC.
Belmont, California

Library of Congress Cataloging in Publication Data

Ageloff, Roy, 1943-
  Fundamentals of FORTRAN for management.

  Includes index.
  1. FORTRAN (Computer program language)
I. Mojena, Richard, joint author. II. Title.
QA76.73.F25A34   001.6′424   78-27731
ISBN 0-534-00710-4

Data Processing Editor: H. Michael Snell

Editorial production services by Cobb/Dunlop Publisher Services, Inc.

About the Cover: The cover of this book began as a black and white photograph of a tape library. The color was computer-generated through a high-resolution video camera, and the resulting image was converted to a 35mm transparency.

Printed in the United States of America

      4   5   6   7   8   9   10   –   83   82   81   80

To Hilda and Fran,
with love

Preface

This textbook is designed for students in business administration, economics, and public administration. Its breadth of applications and nontechnical orientation also may make it appropriate for students in education, the humanities, and the social sciences. No prerequisites are required, other than basic high school mathematics. The combination of features described below distinguishes this book from others in the field.

Informal writing style reflects student orientation. Formal academic manual prose is discarded in favor of a style that more nearly reflects the conversational, classroom approach. We believe this facilitates the learning of a technical subject by nontechnical students, and livens up the subject.

Emphasis on meaningful applications and uses of the computer. We sacrifice some degree of scope in the FORTRAN language in order to devote space to applications and uses of the computer. Applications include those relating to information processing and those relating to analytic decision making (modeling). They are described in a wide variety of contexts, including the traditional areas in the private sector (for example, marketing, finance, production, personnel, accounting, etc.) and the emerging areas in the public sector (health care delivery, emergency response systems, allocation of public resources, and so on).

Table 0.1 summarizes and references the 114 applications programs described in the book through examples and exercises. This table clearly illustrates our philosophy that problems should be presented in an evolutionary context. As new material is learned, many examples and exercises improve upon previous versions of the same problem. This approach not only is pedagogically sound but also is consistent with the evolutionary nature of program design in the "real world."

Chapter 13 describes three extensive applications using the case method of

TABLE 0.1   *Page References for Applications Programs*

Information Processing

student billing   28, 48, 52, 89, 98, 99, 101, 104, 106, 128, 161, 203, 310, 341, 349, 369, 372, 376

bank savings account   56, 171

temperature conversion   58, 84, 119

depreciation   59, 85, 180, 332

coded data—traffic court fines   108

rate schedule   112, 193, 261, 331

property tax assessment   122, 261, 331

telephone company billing   123, 331

personnel benefits budget   124, 332

affirmative action search   125, 300

alphanumeric distribution—Interstate Commerce Commission   178, 261

sales forecasts   180

aging retail customer accounts   181, 332

placement service—a file search   183, 295

credit billing   184, 332

checking account report   186, 333

payroll   188, 333, 355

SAT scores by class   199, 252

finding minimum value   209

mailing list   217, 295

sales pay report   218

student fee bill   218, 333

electric bill   220, 333

installment loan   221, 334

analysis of bank deposits   227

table look-up—life insurance premium   246

sorting   254, 298

crime data summary   261, 334

revenue sharing   262

exam grading   263, 334

text processing   264

Humpty Dumpty Sat   281

financial report   286

income tax   289

computerized matching   295

questionnaire analysis   295, 334

personnel salary budget   296, 334

interactive airline reservation system   297

Fortune 500 sort   298

cross tabulations   300

affirmative action statistics   306

ARMS (Automated Repair and Maintenance System)   386

Analytic Decision Making

marketing   58, 84, 120

manufacturing   58, 85, 120

blood-bank inventory   58, 85, 121

forecasting population growth   59, 85, 122, 350

bracket search algorithm   126, 362

break even analysis   206, 213

police car replacement   223

personnel selection—a combination problem   224, 362

automobile rental decision   315, 330

mean of one-dimensional array   322

replacement problem   382

inventory simulation   394

study popularized by graduate programs in business administration. These cases are designed as capstone programming assignments using a proven technique that simulates reality more effectively than end-of-chapter programming assignments.

Extensive examples and exercises. The learning of FORTRAN is greatly facilitated by numerous and carefully designed examples and exercises. More than forty *complete* programs are illustrated within the book; almost half of these are accompanied by program flowcharts. Exercises are found both within chapters (Follow-up Exercises) and at the end of chapters (Additional Exercises). The book has 323 exercises, many with multiple parts. The chapters on programming (Chapters 2–11) average better than 31 exercises per chapter.

Follow-up exercises serve to reinforce, integrate, and extend preceding material. This feature gives the book a "programmed learning" flavor without the regimentation of such an approach. Additionally, we have found that they create an excellent basis for planning many classroom lectures. Answers to selected follow-up exercises are provided at the end of the textbook.

The chapter-end exercises offer opportunities for review and the development of new programming problems. Examples and exercises are framed in business, economic, and public sector scenarios to interest and motivate the student. Exercises are ordered from least to most difficult. The more difficult exercises are designed to challenge the good student, and are identified by a double asterisk. Solutions to all exercises are given in the *Instructor's Manual*.

Evolutionary approach. Coverage of programming proceeds from simple to difficult, with the student running a complete program by the end of Chapter 3. By design, the pace of Chapters 2–4 builds slowly, to encourage confidence and to develop a sound foundation. Necessarily, this approach discards the complete treatment of a topic in one place. For example, transfer of control is broken up into Chapters 4 and 7, and I/O is specifically discussed in Chapters 2, 5, 6, 7, 8, and 9.

In addition, many sample programs and exercises are introduced early, and then improved and expanded in later chapters as new features of the FORTRAN language are presented.

Treatment of I/O. We believe that programming logic and structure should be emphasized prior to the tedious effort of learning I/O with FORMATs. In keeping with this belief, we have utilized unformatted I/O and have placed the first chapter on transfer of control (Chapter 4) prior to the first chapter on FORMATs (Chapter 5).

To meet the needs of those instructors who do not share our belief, or who do not have a compiler that allows unformatted I/O, we have included programs with simple FORMATs in Chapters 2 and 3 and have designed Chapters 4 and 5 as independent modules; that is, the sequence 1–3,5,4,6,7. . . can be followed. This is not a perfect solution in that unformatted I/O statements appear in other chapters; however, such statements should not prove detrimental to the learning of the topics in the non-I/O chapters.

In effect, this treatment of I/O allows advocates of either approach to proceed without hindrance.

Common errors. The necessary process of debugging is time consuming, frustrating, and difficult to master by beginning programmers. In our experience, students commit certain programming errors more commonly than others. Accordingly, the book features sections on debugging procedures and common errors at the end of *each* programming chapter, beginning with Chapter 3 and ending with Chapter 10.

Batch and time sharing. Since the computer systems at institutions of higher education vary, we illustrate both batch and time-sharing approaches to computing. Time sharing is given more than a superficial treatment in keeping with its increased use in universities, governmental agencies, and companies.

To accommodate both batch and time-sharing users, most programs and discussions of FORTRAN are independent of processing environments. For example, we consciously use the term input record instead of card, and we avoid the use of comments within programs, since time-sharing systems differ in their methods of identifying comment lines. Most sample programs, however, include comments or descriptions along the right margin.

Where appropriate (Chapters 3, 6, and 11) we design programs for either batch or time-sharing environments. This allows us to describe features of each system. In general, however, the book can be used without bias by either batch or time-sharing users. Better yet, as in our own treatment of programming, it can be used by courses that require exposure to both processing environments.

ANSI X3.9-1966 FORTRAN is the basis for the FORTRAN material, but selected features of FORTRAN 77, WATFIV, and time-sharing versions of FORTRAN are covered.

Structured programming. Chapter 11 introduces top down design, modular programming, pseudocode, control structures, and selected structured FOR-TRAN commands. This material follows the standard FORTRAN material for two reasons: (1) it can be omitted without loss of continuity and (2) it delays the discussion of additional statements in FORTRAN, which first gives the student ample opportunity not only to become "expert" prior to seeing new features of FORTRAN but also to appreciate the features offered by these approaches.

A book on programming and problem solving, not a programming manual. We believe that a FORTRAN course in the management and social sciences should be much more than just a course that teaches the FORTRAN language. It should teach the *process* of programming as a creative activity, from conceptualization of the problem to implementation of the computer program.

Our emphasis on applications, examples, and exercises is in keeping with this belief. Additionally, we give structure to the programming process by introducing a four-step procedure in Chapter 2 that incorporates top down design principles.

A programming course also should broaden a student's perspective. Accordingly, Chapter 1 overviews the field more thoroughly than the typical introductory chapter, and Chapter 12 includes a discussion of other programming languages.

Acknowledgments

We wish to express our deep appreciation to many who have contributed to this project: to Mike Snell, our editor, for unflagging encouragement, support, and expert advice; to Jenny Sill, for liaison par excellence; to Warren Rogers, Chairman, Department of Management Science, and Richard R. Weeks, Dean, both of the University of Rhode Island, for consistent administrative help; to Diane Marcotte, for overseeing the preparation of hundreds of copies of the manuscript for class testing; to our students, who suffered through "ditto" copies of the manuscript, yet managed to teach us something about teaching; to our reviewers, Aaron H. Brown, Memphis State University, Betty J. Brown, University of Tennessee, Harrison S. Carter, Georgia Southern College, Donald Chand, Georgia State University, Paul Cheney, Texas Tech University, Asad Khailany, Eastern Michigan University, Thomas J. Murray, University of Missouri-St. Louis, and John E. Nixon, University of Nevada, Las Vegas, who provided invaluable corrections and suggestions for subsequent revisions; to Chip Hatfield, for a thorough, patient, and skilled probing of examples and exercises; to Richard Perreault and Niel Prescott, for help with the manuscript and "grunt" work on the *Instructor's Manual;* to Fran Mojena, for her skill, patience, and steadiness in typing through several drafts of the manuscript, while claiming that she actually learned something; and to our immediate families, who remained cheerfully supportive in spite of our frequent absences.

January, 1979   ROY AGELOFF
Kingston, Rhode Island   RICHARD MOJENA

Contents

CHAPTER 1

Orientation

The electronic computer is one of humankind's foremost technological inventions; for good or for bad, its presence affects each of us, and its future holds even more potential to affect our lives.

This chapter is an orientation to the course you are about to take. We first define the computer and discuss its impact. Thereafter we provide a relatively complete, nontechnical overview of what makes up a computer system and a preview of how to communicate with the computer. Finally, we outline how you will benefit from this course.

If you are warm-blooded and living in the twentieth century, then we suspect that you are curious about the computer. By the time this course is over we hope that we (together with your instructor) will have helped you translate that curiosity into a continuing, productive, and rewarding experience.

1.1
WHAT IS A COMPUTER?

A **computer** can be defined most generally as *a device which is capable of manipulating data to achieve some task*. Given this definition, adding machines, cash registers, gasoline pumps, and electronic calculators all qualify as simple computers. The machine we usually think of as a computer, however, can be identified by three significant characteristics.

Characteristics of Electronic Computers

1. Great speed
2. Large storage capability
3. Ability to execute stored instructions

The great speed of today's computers is a direct result of miniaturization in solid-state electronics. To give you a rough idea of the speed capabilities of large electronic computers, consider the following estimates. One minute of computer time is equivalent to approximately 6700 hours of skilled labor by a person using a calculator. In other words, a person using a calculator would take one hour to accomplish what a computer can accomplish in less than one hundredth of a second. In fact, the electronic transfers within computers are so fast that computer designers use a basic unit of time equal to one billionth of a second (called a *nanosecond*)—quite a feat when you consider that the basic unit of time for us mortals is one second.

A second significant characteristic of electronic computers is their capacity to store large amounts of data and instructions for later recall. In other words, much like the human brain, the computer has "memory." For example, academic computers at medium to large universities can store several million characters of data in primary storage and hundreds of millions of characters in secondary storage.

Finally, an electronic computer is different from other computing devices by its ability to store a program in memory. By this we mean that the computer can execute a set of instructions without interference from human beings. This characteristic makes the computer efficient: it can do its thing automatically while we do something else. Of course, the computer cannot completely do without us, but more about that later.

Computer Classifications

To further narrow the definition of an electronic computer, we make the following distinctions: analog versus digital computers and special-purpose versus general-purpose computers.

The **analog computer** manipulates data by measuring continuous physical processes such as temperature, pressure, and voltage. The fuel injection system of an automobile, for example, deals with physical processes as it regulates fuel/air ratio in the carburetor based on engine speed, temperature, and pressure; the gasoline pump converts the flow of fuel into price (dollar and cents) and volume (gallons to the nearest tenth). Not surprisingly, therefore, analog computers are used primarily to control such processes. For example, analog computers now control the production of products such as steel and gasoline, provide on-board guidance for aircraft and spacecraft, regulate the peak energy demands of large office buildings or factories, and monitor the vital life signs of patients in critical condition.

As a strict computational device, however, the analog computer lacks the precision one needs with counting. Place yourself in the role of a computer which has the task of adding the numbers 1 and 2. Your props are a ruler, pencil, paper, and a jar of beads. You might proceed with your task as follows: first, you take out one bead from the jar and place it on the paper; next, you take out two beads from the jar and place them on the paper; finally, you count the number of beads you have on the paper. *Exactly* three, right? Now, be an analog computer. With pencil, paper, and ruler, draw a line one inch in length; next, draw a two-inch line at the end of the one-inch line you drew earlier; now measure the length of this overall line. Is your line exactly three inches long? Not really, only *approximately three,* for the accuracy of your answer depends on the precision of the scale on the ruler, the steadiness of your hand, the acuteness of your eyesight, and the sharpness of your pencil point. When it comes to calculating, the counting approach based on beads is more accurate than the approach based on measurement.

You will be using the **digital computer,** which operates by counting digits. This type of computer manipulates data (numbers in our decimal system, letters in our alphabet, and special characters) by counting binary (two-state or 0-1) digits. **Hybrid computers** which combine the features of digital and analog computers have been designed for certain types of applications, such as the analysis of aircraft designs which are tested in wind tunnel experiments.

We have been classifying computers by how they process data, but we can also classify them according to their function. **Special-purpose computers** are designed to accomplish a single task, whereas **general-purpose computers** are designed to accept programs of instruction for carrying out tasks from different users. For example, one special-purpose computer has been designed strictly to do navigational calculations for ships and aircraft. The instructions for carrying out this task are built into the electronic circuitry of the machine so that the navigator simply keys in data and receives the answer. On the other hand, a general-purpose computer used by a corporation might accomplish tasks relating to the preparation of payrolls and production schedules and the analyses of financial, marketing, and engineering data all in one day. Similarly, the academic computer you are about to use might run a management simulation one minute and analyze the results of a psychology experiment the next minute, or it might even accomplish both of these tasks (and more) concurrently.

In general, compared to the special-purpose computer, the general-purpose computer has the flexibility of satisfying the needs of a variety of users, but at the expense of speed and economy. In this textbook, we will focus strictly on the *digital, general-purpose computer.*

1.2
IMPACT OF THE COMPUTER

Since the first sale of an electronic computer in 1951, the computer industry has grown to such an extent that by the mid-1970's it had generated over $75 billion in sales and provided at least 700,000 jobs. The computer has revolutionized the operations of many governmental agencies, private enterprises, and public institutions, and many experts agree that the computer industry is a "young child" if not still an "infant." In this section we present a brief historical sketch of the development of the computer, provide you with a sample of computer applications, and end with an assessment of the computer's impact.

Historical Sketch

Many conceptions and inventions dating back to the early nineteenth century were necessary precedents to the development of the computer. The first digital, general-purpose computer was completed in 1944 when Howard Aiken at Harvard University designed the **Mark I** to generate mathematical tables. Unlike electronic computers, the Mark I was a mechanical computer that operated by a system of telephone relays, mechanized wheels, and tabulating equipment. By current standards, it was *very* large, *very* unreliable, *very* slow, and *very* limited in its scope of applications. In 1946 the team of J. W. Mauchly and J. P. Eckert, Jr., from the University of Pennsylvania, completed the first *electronic* computer. This computer was named **ENIAC,** for the intimidating title <u>E</u>lectronic <u>N</u>umerical <u>I</u>ntegrator <u>A</u>nd <u>C</u>alculator. Essentially, ENIAC was an electronic version of Mark I, in which vacuum tubes replaced the function of telephone relays; this replacement resulted in an increase of computing speed by a factor of nearly 200. Commissioned by the U.S. Army, it did an incomparable job (for the times) of generating artillery trajectory tables.

UNIVAC I (<u>Uni</u>versal <u>A</u>utomatic <u>C</u>omputer), developed by Remington (now Sperry) Rand in 1951, was the first commercial computer. Unlike its predecessors, it computed using binary arithmetic and allowed the storage of instructions in internal computer memory. During this **first-generation** period computers were developed by RCA, Philco, GE, Burroughs, Honeywell, NCR, and IBM. The first computer to achieve dominance in the industry was the IBM 650, which became the commercial leader during the period 1954–1959. These first-generation machines used vacuum tubes, required air conditioning, had relatively small amounts of internal memory, and were slow by today's standards.

Subsequent generations of computers resulted in dramatic reductions in *size* and relative *cost* and increases in *speed, reliability,* and the capacity for *storage.* **Second-generation** computers during the period 1959–1965 replaced the vacuum tubes of the first-generation computers with transistors. The most widely used second-generation computers were the IBM 1620, the IBM 1401, and the IBM 7094.

The **third-generation** computers (1965–1970) that followed made use of the emerging field of microelectronics (miniaturized circuits) which increased the packing densities of transistorized circuits by a factor of 100. The third-generation computers were more reliable, faster, and more sophisticated than earlier computers. They also had the ability to handle several programs concurrently (multiprogramming), resulting in a more efficient use of the computer. The most prominent family of computers in this generation was the IBM System/360.

During the 1970s, a series of refinements and improvements to third-generation machines were marketed. These computers utilized large scale integrated circuitry (LSI) and other microminiaturization features, resulting in further reductions in size and power requirements compared to earlier computers. Another significant development in the 1970s was the use of small (in physical size and memory capacity), inexpensive, yet powerful computers referred to as **minicomputers** and **microcomputers.** The use of minicomputers is common in small to medium companies, colleges, hospitals, governmental agencies, and other organizations. Microcomputers, which are smaller than minicomputers, currently are marketed by consumer retail outlets such as Radio Shack. Their use in small organizations and homes is expected to increase dramatically in the next decade.

Applications in the Management and Social Sciences

The computer represents a revolutionary technological tool for extending our applied capabilities. It has been especially prominent in the management and social sciences for information processing and analytic decision making, as illustrated in Table 1.1. The diversity of the sample applications listed in the table should give you an idea of the increasing influence of computers. Users of the computer include all facets of our society: individuals, private organizations such as industrial companies and banks, and public institutions such as hospitals, universities, and governmental agencies.

Originally the management and social sciences used the computer for very basic information processing, such as updating customer accounts, preparing payrolls, and generating status reports on personnel, sales, production, and inventories. Although these automated approaches were more effective than hours of "hand-crunching" effort by an "army" of clerks, they failed to integrate adequately the sources and uses of information in complex organizations. Today, users are calling for the design and implementation of **management information systems (MIS)** that can integrate and aggregate timely information for use by management in their decision-making activities.

In recent years, managers and social scientists have increasingly emphasized analytic or scientific decision making. For example, disciplines such as **operations research** and **management science** develop and apply quantita-

TABLE 1.1   *Sample Applications of the Computer in the Management and Social Sciences*

Information Processing

Preparation of payroll and billings
Maintenance of inventory information
Maintenance of customer accounts
Technical processing of reference information by media and public libraries
Calculation of income taxes by the IRS
Maintenance of student records by universities
Maintenance of flight and reservation information by airlines
Cataloguing of blood supplies by regional blood banks
Maintenance of checking accounts by banks
Editing and reproduction of typed manuscripts
Maintenance of criminal records by the FBI
Maintenance of property tax records by a municipality
Budgeting by organizations and individuals
Recording of monetary distributions by state and federal welfare agencies

Analytic Decision Making

Statistical analysis of census data
Production scheduling and inventory control
Medical diagnosis
Financial assessment of real estate investments by developers
   and individuals
Management of financial portfolios
Location of fire stations in an urban area
Simulation of economic decay in a city
Dietary meal planning in institutions
Statistical forecasting
Educational planning and school bus scheduling
Design of airway and highway traffic systems
Determination of advertising media mix
Transportation schedules
Planning, scheduling, and controlling complex projects (such as construction
   of a submarine, office building, or sports stadium)

tive techniques (mathematics, probability, statistics) to help solve problems faced by managers of public and private organizations.

The second part of Table 1.1 gives you an idea of the types of problems that lend themselves to analytic techniques. In many cases the data required for these quantitative approaches to decision making are best provided by an MIS, which effectively integrates our two broad classes of applications.

Inevitably, the following question is asked: Can computers think? The computer cannot think in the usual sense, for it can accomplish only what people instruct it to accomplish through written programs of instruction. It is best at solving problems that are well structured; that is, problems whose solutions can be determined on a step-by-step basis which is quite explicit. Problems that require ill-defined or spontaneous actions to cope with complex or entirely new situations do not lend themselves as well to computer solution. For example, an executive can reorganize a company better than a computer; a composer writes music better than a computer; a chess master plays better chess than a computer; and an inventor is more capable of inventing than a computer.

As scientists come to better understand thinking processes behind creativity, adaptation, and judgment, programs of instruction for solving ill-structured problems will improve. This area of research, called **artificial intelligence,** has made some progress as computers have been programmed to compose music, play chess, prove theorems, and solve puzzles. Success, however, has been limited, and future progress in this area is uncertain.

Assessment

Any task that can be performed by a general-purpose, digital computer can also be performed by a human being (given unlimited time). Of course, when it comes to the amount of data that can be stored and the speed with which these data can be manipulated, the computer is in a class by itself. In effect, therefore, the computer magnifies our own capacities. This results in both advantages and disadvantages, which we now summarize.

ADVANTAGES

1. *Power of analysis and technological advancement.* The computer can accomplish massive amounts of scientific calculation in a short span of time and can control complex processes such as steel making, automatic guidance of spacecraft, and air-ground traffic control.
2. *Career opportunities.* The computer upgrades the skill requirements of jobs and creates new career opportunities both for labor and management; the current (and projected) supply of skilled people in this area is far short of demand.
3. *Information needs.* As the society becomes more complex (and the individuals become more numerous), the computer provides a means to satisfy society's information needs.
4. *Level of service.* The computer provides faster and better quality of service to members of society; examples include airline reservation systems, health care delivery systems, bank accounts, and preregistration of classes for university students.
5. *Cost savings to society.* The computer results in a more efficient delivery of services when used in applications where it is more productive than alternative approaches.

DISADVANTAGES

1. *Mistakes*. A survey of the public showed that 34 percent of those surveyed had a problem because of the computer;[1] billing problems account for the majority of reported mistakes insofar as the public is concerned; in recent years, however, channels of communication for correcting errors have been improved; *the source of such mistakes is typically traced to computer personnel, rather than to the computer equipment.*

2. *Legalities*. Invasion of privacy and safeguards to programs of instruction and data have become major issues of national concern; the increasing centralization of files which contain information about individuals requires the legal protection of accuracy and confidentiality; computer crime has been one of the fastest rising categories of crime; examples of such crimes include the $2 billion Equity Funding Corporation swindle of the early 1970s, bank embezzlements which average $500,000 per swindle, and the "kidnapping" of computer data tapes for ransoms.[2]

3. *Regulatory problems*. Federal and state agencies have an increasing problem in regulatory issues relating to computer product pricing policies, protection of copyrights and patents, and quality of data transmission over phone lines.

4. *Job displacement*. The creation of new jobs by the computer has resulted in the displacement of old jobs, a result which is typical of all new technologies (automobiles, airplanes, electricity, and so on); inevitably this causes psychological trauma, social displacement, and economic deprivation for the affected segment of the population.

5. *Dependence*. Our increasing dependence on the computer raises philosophical and practical issues regarding security; for example, backup systems are needed in airport traffic control should the main computer become disabled; and duplicate copies of critical data files should be maintained in case the original files are destroyed.

On balance, the positive aspects of the computer far outweigh its negative aspects. As with all new technologies, however, those in positions of responsibility must strive toward correcting existing problems and, more importantly, toward preventing potential problems.

1.3
ORGANIZATION OF A COMPUTER

Figure 1.1 should give you a "feel" for the makeup of a digital, general-purpose computer. As you can see, six components have been identified by the nature of their functions. Before describing each of these components, however, we define two terms which we use often.

---

[1] "A National Survey of the Public's Attitude Toward Computers," available from *Time Magazine,* Rockefeller Center, New York, NY.
[2] See, for example, Don Parker, *Crime by Computer,* New York: Scribner's, 1976.

FIGURE 1.1   *Functional Organization of a Digital, General-Purpose Computer*

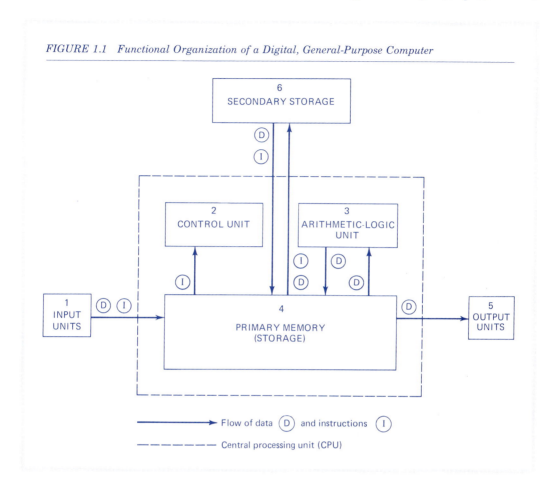

An **instruction** represents a specific task for the computer to accomplish. For example, the following represents three instructions:

1. Read and store the name of a student and the grades received for the school term.
2. Calculate and store the grade point average.
3. Print the student's name and grade point average.

Data represent facts or observations which the computer is to input, manipulate, and/or output. In the above example, the student's name, grades, and grade point average all represent data.

Input Units

The input function of the computer brings data and instructions from the "outside world" to the computer's memory. To accomplish this transfer process the data and instructions must be converted into a "machine-readable" input

TABLE 1.2   *Input Units and Input Media*

MEDIUM	CORRESPONDING INPUT UNIT
Punched card	Punched card reader
Punched paper tape	Paper tape reader
Optical characters	Optical character reader (OCR)
Magnetic ink characters	Magnetic ink character reader (MICR)
Magnetic tape	Tape drive
Magnetic disk	Disk drive

medium. The more commonly used **input media** are punched cards, magnetic tapes, magnetic disks, punched paper tape, optical characters, and magnetic ink characters.

These media require **data preparation devices** to convert data from source documents (bills, invoices) to the desired medium. For example, the **keypunch machine** is a data preparation device for converting data on source documents to punched cards; a **key-to-tape machine** transfers data from source documents to magnetic tapes.

Data, once in machine-readable form, are transferred to the computer through an **input unit.** This device "reads" the coded data on the input medium and converts it into electrical impulses which are transferred to the memory unit of the computer. For example, the holes in a punched card are sensed by a **punched card reader** and converted to appropriate electrical signals which are submitted to the computer's memory for storage.

Table 1.2 lists some input units which are used with specific input media.

By the way, MICR units are used by banks to process checks, and OCR units are widely used by universities for processing student records and grading exams.

Data and instructions also may be entered into a computer through **online terminals.** The terminals are connected directly to the computer (the meaning of online) by either cable or telephone lines. Terminals have a keyboard for entering data and instructions, and either a visual display (video) screen or teleprinter for output.

In general, a computer system will have more than one input unit. The mix of input units in any one computer system, however, will depend on factors such as cost, the amount of data to be processed, and the method by which data originate.

Central Processing Unit (CPU)

Input and output devices are part of the computer system, but they are not generally considered the "computer"; rather they are *peripheral* to the computer. The **central processing unit** (CPU), consisting of primary memory, control unit, and arithmetic-logic unit, is what most professionals think of as *the* computer.

The **primary (internal) memory** unit of the computer stores instructions and data. Sometimes this unit is called **core storage,** because in some computers primary memory is made up of thousands of "doughnut" shaped magnetic cores strung like beads on wire. More recent computer models use **semiconductor memory** where the basic memory component is the silicon chip. These units are cheaper, faster, and more compact than core memory.

Regardless of the technology which is used to construct memory units, primary memory consists of storage locations which have numerical designations called addresses. Figure 1.2 represents a means of visualizing the storage locations of primary memory. Each storage location is assigned a number **(address)** that is used to reference the location whenever the item of data stored within that location **(contents)** is to be accessed. For example, in Figure 1.2, an employee's rate of pay, $3.75, is stored in location 1 and the number of hours worked by that employee, 36, is stored in location 2.

The storage capacity of computer memory may be expressed in terms of the number of characters (bytes) that can be stored. By a **character** or **byte** we mean a letter, numerical digit, comma, plus sign, and so on. Because of the way memory units are constructed, storage capacity is usually expressed as some multiple of 1024, where the number 1024 is represented by the letter K. For example, if memory capacity is quoted as 64K, then internal memory has the capacity to store 65,536 (that is, 64 × 1024) characters of data. Primary memory units usually range in storage capacity from 4K to 8000K.

Data stored in primary storage are transferred to the **arithmetic-logic unit** whenever processing of data is required. Basic arithmetic operations such

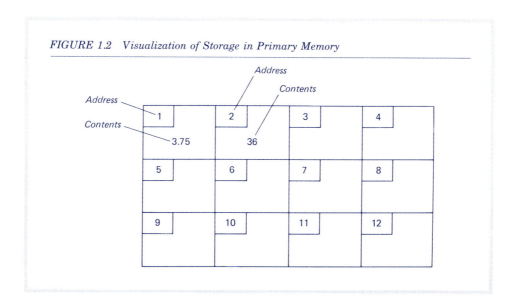

FIGURE 1.2   *Visualization of Storage in Primary Memory*

as addition, subtraction, multiplication, and division are performed within the arithmetic-logic unit. In addition, logical operations such as comparison of values can be made. This capability permits the testing of various conditions, for example, whether an employee is entitled to receive overtime pay.

The **control unit** of a computer directs the operation of all other units associated with the computer, including peripheral devices (input/output units). The control unit obtains instructions from primary memory, interprets these instructions, and then transmits directions to the appropriate computer components. For example, suppose the instruction "read and store student's name and grades" is obtained from memory and interpreted by the control unit; the input unit would be directed to read these data into memory. The next instruction might be "calculate and store the grade point average"; the control unit would direct the memory unit to provide the arithmetic-logic unit with the data; then the arithmetic-logic unit would be directed to perform the calculations and to transmit the result to primary memory.

Interestingly, current technology can place an entire CPU on a single silicon chip that is less than one quarter of an inch square. These so-called **microprocessors** are as effective as small second-generation computers in terms of calculating and storage capabilities. In effect, a microprocessor that you can balance on the tip of your finger is equivalent to an early 1960's computer with a CPU as large as an office desk.

Output Units

The function of an **output unit** is exactly opposite that of an input unit; that is, an output unit receives data from the computer in the form of electronic signals and converts these data into a form which can be used by either humans or computers. The list below summarizes output units; of these, most likely you will use line printers and online terminals.

Line Printers.   If output of data is meant for human "consumption," then the line printer is used. The **line printer** illustrated in Figure 1.3 is capable of printing 2000 lines per minute, each line having up to 132 characters. Picture yourself standing in front of such a printer. At 65 lines per page, you would see approximately 31 pages of printed output whiz by you in the time span of one minute.

Online Terminals.   If you are using either a video or teleprinter terminal as an input unit, then most likely you are using the terminal as an output unit. This is convenient, but compared to a line printer the speed of output is slow. Many computer systems, however, allow input through terminals and output on line printers, a feature which is advantageous if a particular job requires a high volume of output.

Other Output Units.   Other output devices include **magnetic tape drives,** which have both read (input) and write (output) capabilities using the magnetic tape medium; **paper tape units,** some of which can be attached to remote, online terminals for the purpose of both input from and output to punched paper tape; **magnetic disk drives,** which allow both input from and output to magnetized disks which resemble a stack of LP phonograph records; **card punch units,** which allow output onto punched cards; and **voice response units,** which process verbal output. Voice response units, by the way, have been used by telephone companies for many years. Without realizing it, you might have listened to the computer give you someone's new telephone number.

Secondary Storage

Secondary storage (auxiliary or **external storage)** is memory that is housed outside the central processing unit. Instructions and data not currently in use are kept on secondary storage and read into primary storage when needed. Magnetic tapes, disks, drums, and data cells are used for secondary storage. Compared to primary storage, secondary storage has greater capacity at less cost, but the amount of time it takes to access data is greater.

1.4
COMMUNICATING WITH
THE COMPUTER

If we wish to solve a problem using a computer, we must communicate our instructions to the computer through a language. A **language** can be defined as patterns that have meaning. To a computer, these patterns are electronic; to a human being, they are symbolic (letter, numbers, punctuation). Unfortunately, no computer can understand any of the some 4000 languages practiced by peoples earthwide. It was necessary, therefore, to invent **computer languages** for the express purpose of person-machine communication. These can be classified into the three categories shown below. The designation **high-level** refers to a computer language which is far removed from the patterns "understood" directly by the computer. A **low-level** language, therefore, deals with patterns which are more nearly compatible with the electronic patterns of the machine.

1. Procedure and problem- oriented languages	High-level languages
2. Assembly languages	⇑
3. Machine languages	Low-level languages

Procedure and Problem-
Oriented Languages

Any language can be distinguished from any other language by its **syntax,** that is, by the rules for arranging a specified set of symbols into recognizable patterns. You will be communicating your instructions to the computer using a language called **FORTRAN.**[3] This is one of many so-called **procedure-**

---

[3] This stands for <u>FOR</u>mula <u>TRAN</u>slation. It was originally developed by IBM in the 1950s.

FIGURE 1.3A   *Functional Components of a Computer System (IBM 370). Courtesy of IBM.*

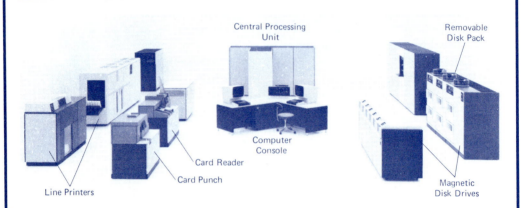

FIGURE 1.3B   *IBM 059 Keypunch Machine. Courtesy of IBM.*

FIGURE 1.3C   *NCR 798-401 Video (CRT) Terminal. Courtesy of NCR.*

FIGURE 1.3D   *Xerox 1760 Typewriter Terminal. Courtesy of Xerox Corporation.*

FIGURE 1.3E IBM 3505 Card Reader Unit. Courtesy of IBM.

FIGURE 1.3F IBM 3420 Magnetic Tape Drive. Courtesy of IBM.

FIGURE 1.3G IBM 3211 Line Printer. Courtesy of IBM.

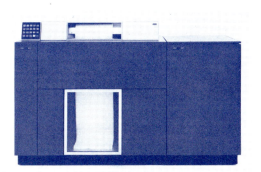

FIGURE 1.3H An integrated circuit. Courtesy of IBM.

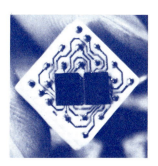

oriented languages. In general, these computer languages are easily understood by us humans (after some education, of course) and are *machine-independ-
ent,* which means that they can be used across a wide variety of computers.
FORTRAN is the most popular high-level language used for solving algebraic
or scientific-type problems. By this we mean that FORTRAN is an excellent
language for solving the types of problems which we described earlier as
"analytic decision making." Moreover, FORTRAN can be used for "information
processing" applications as well, although **COBOL** (**CO**mmon **B**usiness **O**ri-
ented **L**anguage) is a more suitable language for such applications.

Problem-oriented languages usually refer to a set of high-level languages which have been developed for solving certain special-purpose problems, such as the simulation of traffic flows in a city or the computer editing of
newspaper articles. These and other high-level languages are discussed more
fully in Chapter 12.

A **computer program** *is a complete set of instructions written in a computer language for solving a specific problem.* Table 1.3 illustrates and describes
a FORTRAN program having exactly six statements. **Statement** is another

TABLE 1.3   *FORTRAN Program for Calculating and Printing the Balance ($) Due a
University Based on a Student's Tuition and Fees*

FORTRAN PROGRAM	HOW THE COMPUTER EXECUTES EACH INSTRUCTION (AND WHAT IT MEANS IN ENGLISH)
CREDIT = 15.	Store a value of 15. as the contents of a storage location addressed or identified as CREDIT. (The 15. represents the number of credits taken during the school term.)
TUIT = CREDIT*100.	Multiply the contents of the storage location known as CREDIT by 100. and store this result in the location called TUIT. [In other words, the tuition is the number of credits (15) times the cost per credit ($100), or $1500.]
BALDUE = TUIT + 250.	Take the contents of the address known as TUIT, add 250., and store this result in the address known as BALDUE. (The balance due the university is tuition plus $250 in fees, or $1750.)
WRITE(6,*) BALDUE	Print the contents of the address known as BALDUE. (The number 1750 is printed by either the line printer or the online terminal.)
STOP	Stop processing this program.
END	This instruction defines the end of the program.

term for instruction. In the next chapter, we will examine this program in detail (so don't be concerned about it, yet).

Assembly and Machine Languages

Each type of computer has associated with it an assembly language and a machine language. An **assembly language** is specifically designed for a particular type of computer; hence, it can accomplish more detailed tasks for that computer than could a high-level language. Such a language, however, requires more specialized training for persons who would use it. In other words, it is more difficult for us to learn an assembly language than to learn a high-level language. Another disadvantage of assembly languages is that they vary from one computer type to another. Thus, if we were restricted to programming only in assembly languages, we would need to learn a new assembly language for each computer type we might use—and worse yet, every computer program which was written for one computer would have to be rewritten for use on another computer.

After all this, you might be surprised to learn that computers do not directly "understand" either high-level or assembly languages! Computers understand only machine language. An instruction in **machine language** is written in binary form as a series of 0s and 1s, as this scheme conforms to the needs of the electronic circuitry in binary computers. Needless to say, programming in machine language is impossibly tedious, which is one reason why high-level languages were developed.

The Compiler

How is it possible for the computer to understand the FORTRAN program which you write? Well, each computer manufacturer provides the means for that computer to translate your FORTRAN-language program into an equivalent program in machine language. This translation of a high-level language into its equivalent machine language is accomplished by a computer program called a **compiler.** In other words, the compiler acts as the language interpreter between you and the computer, much as a foreign language interpreter would translate from English into, say, Spanish.

Each manufacturer of a general-purpose computer provides its own FORTRAN compiler. Most FORTRAN compilers conform to a standard form of FORTRAN developed by the American National Standards Institute (ANSI); however, some manufacturers may also provide certain extensions of **ANSI FORTRAN** which differ from the prescribed standard.

While on the subject of compilers, some years ago the University of Waterloo in Ontario developed a compiler dubbed **WATFOR** (for <u>WAT</u>erloo <u>FOR</u>tran). This compiler was designed explicitly for student use; its outstanding features were speed of compilation, certain simplifications in the FORTRAN language, and outstanding error diagnostics. The huge success of this compiler prompted the development of an improved successor called **WATFIV.** Since we expect many of you will be using the WATFIV compiler, we have included some of its FORTRAN features where appropriate.

1.5
COMPUTER SYSTEMS

Your interactions with the computer involve much more than a simple communication between you and the CPU. In fact, you will be dealing with a comprehensive computer system.

Hardware and Software

The **computer system** is a collection of related hardware and software. As the name implies, **hardware** refers to the physical equipment: input/output (I/O) units, CPU, secondary storage, and other specialized machinery. The term **software** refers to computer programs, procedures, and specialized aids that contribute to the operation of a computer system. In general, software is classified as either systems software or applications software.

Systems software is a term for programs which are designed to facilitate the use of hardware. The **operating system** of a computer (supplied by the computer manufacturer) is the most important piece of systems software. This software, which is often called the "manager," "monitor," or "supervisor," consists of a number of specialized programs for operating the computer efficiently. Among others, the following important functions are performed by the operating system:

1. Scheduling the sequence of jobs within the computer[4]
2. Supplying the appropriate compiler
3. Allocating storage for programs and data
4. Controlling input and output operations
5. Performing "housekeeping" chores, such as accounting for the amount of CPU time used by each user

Applications software denotes programs which are written in either high-level or assembly languages to solve specific types of problems. These programs are normally developed "in-house" (by the organization's systems analysts and programmers) to process applications such as payroll, inventories, billing, and accounts receivable.

Many computer manufacturers and independent software companies prepare generalized applications packages ("canned" software) for widely used applications. The cost of these packages range from a few hundred dollars to amounts in excess of one-hundred thousand dollars. For example, the MRP (materials requirement planning) package provided by IBM is designed to assist a manufacturing company in managing its labor force, machines, materials, and money; Information Associates, Inc., has developed a package called "Students Records System" for generating class rosters, grade reports, and student transcripts; and SPSS (statistical package for the social sciences) and BMD (biomedical) are two statistical packages widely used by researchers. By

---

[4]Each computer program which is to be run (executed) is called a "job."

the way, the types of programs that you will be writing in your computer class are examples of applications programs.

Batch versus Time-Shared Processing

The specific configuration of hardware and software in a computer system is determined by the needs of that organization. Two of the more common environments in academic institutions are batch processing and time-shared processing.

Batch Processing.   Those of you who will be punching programs on cards most likely will be submitting jobs by the "batch" method. After you have punched your program onto cards, you will submit your job to the computing center personnel in order to have your program compiled and executed. In this mode of operation, programs are grouped and executed at the computing center according to job priorities established by computing center personnel. In some batch environments, each program is run serially, that is, one program at a time. In more sophisticated systems, with **multiprogramming** capabilities, several programs may be executed "simultaneously" under the control of the operating system. In either case, it may take from a few minutes to several hours before the results of your program are available to you. When you pick up your job at the computing center, errors may exist. These errors must be identified, corrected, and the job must be resubmitted. This cycle continues until you are satisfied with the results.

Time-Shared Processing.   Many of you will be introduced to computers within a "time-sharing" environment. In a time-sharing environment many users working at online terminals have "simultaneous" utilization of the computer system. In this mode of processing jobs, you will send data and instructions to the computer via terminals, and the computer responds within seconds. This dialogue between you and the computer continues until you complete the task on which you are working. Thus you code, execute, and correct programs at a terminal that is connected directly to the computer. While sitting at a terminal you may believe you have the computer to yourself. Actually, you and others who use terminals are sharing the computer's CPU in rotation under the control of the operating system (thus the term "time-sharing").

Many of today's computer systems are hybrid in that they include two or more processing environments. For example, the computer systems in many medium to large universities include both batch and time-shared processing. Many of these same systems also feature **remote batch,** whereby *you* can submit your own jobs to the card reader and receive your results at a line printer in a location which is removed from the computer center; and **batch interface,** whereby you can bypass the use of cards altogether by entering your program at a terminal into the batch "stream" and receiving your output on either the line printer at the computer center or the online terminal.

Which system is best for you depends on many factors, some of which we list here.

1. **Turnaround time** is usually less for time sharing than for batch processing. By turnaround time we mean the time between submission and completion of a job.

2. The *process of correcting programs* is more convenient by time sharing than by batch processing, for two reasons. First, in time sharing, it can all be done in one place. In other words, you submit your job, get results, and make corrections all at the terminal in one sitting. Second, time-sharing systems have powerful *editing* capabilities for making changes in programs. For example, if you have to change the same letter in each of 20 different lines in a program, then you must repunch each of 20 cards in the batch approach. In time sharing, a single command may automatically make the 20 changes in your internally stored program.

3. *Direct interaction* between person and machine is facilitated by time sharing. This is useful for many types of analyses and decision processes which require the user to make a sequence of decisions based on feedback from the computer. For example, a computer program which simulates factors such as levels of world population, pollution, energy consumption, depletion of natural resources, and per capita income can be used interactively by government officials to answer "What if . . . ?" types of questions. (Such a program does exist!)

4. Jobs which require *many computations* are best handled by batch processing. This is because time-shared jobs must wait their turn for CPU time. For example, a job which requires, say, 60 minutes of CPU time would reside at least 60 minutes within the computer in a batch environment, but may take several hours to complete in a relatively busy time-sharing environment. By the way, your jobs will probably use less than 1 second of CPU time.

5. Jobs which require *large amounts of input or output* also are best run in a batch environment. For example, a job which prints 30 pages of output may take 1 minute on a line printer and 120 minutes on a teleprinter terminal which prints 30 characters per second.

1.6
BEFORE YOU LEAP

Before you "leap" into your course in FORTRAN, we offer some objectives for you to ponder, and some advice which we believe is sound.

Objectives

By now we should have convinced you that the computer is used increasingly as an indispensable tool for clerical purposes, to satisfy information needs, and to make decisions. Moreover, according to a survey which is already outdated, 49 percent of the public have had a job requiring either direct or indirect contact with a computer, 15 percent feel that their current job requires some knowledge of the computer, and 7 percent state that their job requires working directly with computers.[5] Given current trends these percentages will increase dra-

---

[5] "A National Survey of the Public's Attitude Toward Computers," *op. cit.*

matically in coming years. In fact, the job market in computer-related fields looks quite promising for years to come.[6]

What does all of this mean to you? Well, we feel that if you do not accomplish the two objectives stated below, then you are shortchanging what will prove to be a very relevant part of your education.

Objective 1.   Achieve a modest level of programming and problem-solving skills.

Objective 2.   Acquire a basic knowledge of computer concepts, uses, and limitations.

The first objective is intended to develop your ability to access, utilize, and exploit the computer for the purpose of more effectively analyzing problems and making decisions, both in subsequent academic courses which you take and in your career. The second objective should serve to dispel the mystique and misconceptions surrounding computers—and to aid you in feeling "comfortable" and operating effectively in a computerized environment.

Advice

Some of you have a great aptitude for the material which follows. We hope you will get "turned on" to do fine things in this field. Others of you are less inclined to readily absorb this type of material. If you feel that you are in the latter category, then you should take the following advice seriously.

1.   Pay close attention to *written detail*. The computer is not very permissive. For example, if you spell REID instead of READ, the computer will not understand.
2.   Pay close attention to *logical detail*. The computer is a machine. Therefore, you must tell it what to do in rather precise detail which is broken down into logical steps.
3.   Develop *good habits*. Work consistently (not constantly!). Try to rely on others as little as possible, in order to sharpen your own inherent problem-solving skills. Try to solve the "Follow-up Exercises"—before looking up answers in the back of the book.
4.   Be *patient*. Don't get frustrated by your mistakes. Don't get angry at the computer if it breaks down (after all, it also works hard). Finally, give yourself time. Our years of teaching this course shows that many students take about 6–8 weeks before the material crystallizes.

Exercises

1.   Can you define the following terms?
     computer   paper tape unit
     analog computer   card punch unit
     digital computer   voice response unit

---

[6] Estimates by the Bureau of Labor Statistics show over 50,000 annual new openings for programmers and systems analysts.

hybrid computer
special-purpose computer
general-purpose computer
minicomputer
microcomputer
MIS
operations research
management science
artificial intelligence
instruction
data
input media
data preparation devices
keypunch machine
key-to-tape machine
input unit
punched card reader
online terminal
CPU
primary or internal memory
core storage
semiconductor memory
address
contents
byte
character
arithmetic-logic unit
control unit
microprocessor
output unit
magnetic disc drive
magnetic tape drive

secondary storage
language
computer language
procedure-oriented language
problem-oriented language
FORTRAN
COBOL
high-level language
low-level language
assembly language
machine language
syntax
computer program
statement
compiler
ANSI FORTRAN
WATFIV
computer system
hardware
software
systems software
applications software
operating system
manager
monitor
supervisor
batch processing
time-shared processing
multiprogramming
remote batch
batch interface
turnaround time

2. Identify and briefly discuss the three outstanding characteristics of electronic computers.

3. Identify two broad areas of computer applications in the management and social sciences. Give a sample application in each area.

4. Cite some advantages and disadvantages of the widespread use of computers. (Don't necessarily restrict yourself to what we said.)

5. Sketch the organization of a digital, general-purpose computer. Briefly describe the functions of each component.

6. Briefly describe the functions of the operating system.

7. Briefly describe the functions of the compiler.

8. Compare batch and time-shared processing with respect to various criteria.

9. How are you doing?

CHAPTER 2

Fundamentals of FORTRAN

This chapter will show you how to write a computer program and provide you with some fundamentals of the FORTRAN language. By the end of this chapter, you will be able to write a complete (although simple) FORTRAN program; by the end of the next chapter, you will be able to run such a computer program on either a batch or a time-sharing system.

2.1
STEPS IN WRITING
COMPUTER PROGRAMS

As you might recall from Chapter 1, a **computer program** is a complete set of instructions written in a computer language; its purpose is to solve a problem which has been defined by the programmer. This problem is solved when the computer program is executed in a logical sequence by the computer.

Writing a computer program involves the following four steps:

1. Analyzing the problem
2. Preparing the flowchart
3. Coding the problem
4. Debugging the computer program

Analyzing the Problem

You must first determine what information you need to solve your problem. Our approach is to specify:

1. A general statement (in prose) which describes the nature of the problem that is to be solved
2. The data you will provide to the computer
3. The output you want to receive as the solution to your problem
4. A description of the computations and logical processes the computer must perform to convert the provided data to the output data

Preparing the Flowchart

A **flowchart** is a drawing portraying (1) the means of providing data to the computer, (2) the required output data, and (3) the logical and arithmetic steps required to solve the problem. It has two primary uses: to help you write the computer program by serving as a "blueprint" and to document the logic of the computer program for future review.

Flowcharts use specific symbols to represent different activities and a written message within each symbol to explain each activity. Table 2.1 shows the flowcharting symbols we will use in this textbook, and Figure 2.1 on page 27 illustrates a sample flowchart. At this point don't worry about flowcharting technique. The art and style of constructing flowcharts will be demonstrated often by example in the chapters to come.

TABLE 2.1 *Flowcharting Symbols*

SYMBOL	MEANING
	Indicates the start or end of the program.
	Indicates when an input or output operation is to be performed.
	Indicates calculations or data manipulation.
	Represents the flow of logic.
	Represents a decision point or question that requires a choice of which logical path to follow.
	Connects parts of the flowchart.
	Indicates a preparation step, as in describing a DO loop (Chapter 7).
	Indicates a predefined process or step where the details are not shown in this flowchart, as in calling a subprogram (Chapter 10).

Coding the Problem

Coding is the translation of your problem-solving logic from the flowchart into a computer program. In other words, you use the flowchart as a guide for writing your instructions to the computer.

The computer language that your instructions are to be written in must be decided by this step in the procedure. (The same flowchart can be used with any computer language.) In our case, we will use ANSI FORTRAN and certain variations available on the WATFIV compiler. The (relative) ease of learning FORTRAN and its excellent mathematical capabilities are two reasons for the widespread usage of this language. Advantages and disadvantages associated with using other high-level languages are discussed in Chapter 12.

Start out by writing your code on either a regular sheet of paper or on special paper called FORTRAN **coding form.** After you are reasonably sure your program is correct, place the code on the appropriate input medium for your system. As a beginning programmer you will most likely use either a keypunch for punched cards or a computer terminal. Details on these procedures are presented in Chapter 3.

Debugging the Computer Program

You will often write programs that fail to run or run improperly. (It happens to all of us.) **Debugging** is the process of locating and correcting errors, or "getting out the bugs." Types of bugs and methods for correcting them are illustrated in the next chapter.

EXAMPLE 2.1   Student Billing Problem

Let's follow the four program-writing steps using a specific example: Suppose that State College is in the process of converting its student billing system from a manual to a computerized system.

The total student bill at State College is made up of charges for tuition and fees. The tuition charge at the College varies depending on the number of credits in which a student is enrolled. The present charge is $100 per credit. Fees include an activity fee, union fee, and health fee amounting to $250.

The College is beginning work on the computer program for this problem; it has decided to use Noah Arrowsmith, who has enrolled for 15 credits, as a test case for the program. Here is the process you should use in writing a program for this situation.

Step I.   Analyzing the Problem

1. *Problem statement*
   The purpose is to develop a program for processing student bills at State College. The program calculates and prints the balance due from a student given data for number of credits, cost per credit, and cost of fees.
2. *Provided data*
   a.   Cost of tuition per credit ($100)
   b.   Cost of fees ($250)
   c.   Number of credits in which Noah Arrowsmith is enrolled (15)
3. *Data output*
   Balance due the State College
4. *Computations and logical processes*
   a.   Multiply the number of credits in which Noah Arrowsmith is enrolled (15) by the cost of tuition per credit (100) to determine the tuition charge.
   b.   Add the tuition charge to the fees (250) to determine the balance due the college.

Figure 2.1   Flowchart for Computing Balance Due

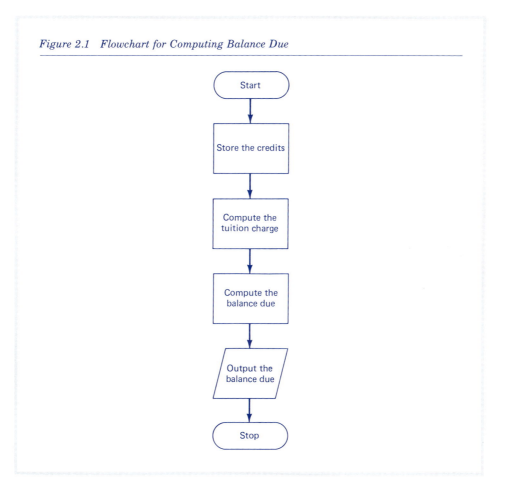

Step II.   Preparing the Flowchart

Figure 2.1 is a flowchart showing the steps necessary to determine a student's total amount owed. The flowchart breaks down the problem into several steps:

1.   Store the number of credits in a memory location.
2.   Calculate tuition.
3.   Calculate balance due the college.
4.   Print the output.

Note that this flowchart uses only the first four symbols in Table 2.1. The other symbols are introduced in later chapters, as your programming becomes more sophisticated.

In general, a flowchart must indicate a "Start" and must have at least one "Stop." The flow generally runs from top to bottom and from left to right. As an option, you can use arrowheads to indicate the direction of flow, which is our preference.

Although this flowchart is rather simple, and you may be tempted not to use it for such a simple problem, *we strongly suggest that you get in the habit of using flowcharts now.* As programs become more complex, you will find flowcharts increasingly helpful for coding the problem.

Step III.   Coding the Problem

Version A: Output Without FORMAT	Version B: Output With FORMAT	Comments
CREDIT = 15.	CREDIT = 15.	Assign the value 15. to a memory location named CREDIT.
TUIT = CREDIT*100.	TUIT = CREDIT*100.	Compute the tuition. (The * represents multiplication.)
BALDUE = TUIT + 250.	BALDUE = TUIT + 250.	Compute the balance due.
WRITE(6, *) BALDUE	WRITE(6, 50) BALDUE 50 FORMAT(1X, F7.2)	Print the balance due. (In version A, * does not mean multiplication; we will explain later.)
STOP	STOP	Stop execution of the program.
END	END	The last FORTRAN instruction in the program.

Note the correspondence between each program and the flowchart in Figure 2.1. For simple programs, this correspondence is *almost* one-for-one; that is, each symbol in the flowchart (except for "Start") will have a corresponding instruction in the program. As problems grow in length and complexity, however, the number of symbols in the flowchart will be less than the number of instructions in the program, for two reasons:

1. Symbols can be used to summarize related groups of instructions in a program. For example, "Compute the tuition charge" and "Compute the balance due" in Figure 2.1 can be combined into a single rectangle which reads "Compute the tuition charge and the balance due."
2. Not all instructions need be represented in a flowchart. For example, the FORMAT and END instructions are not depicted in the flowchart of Figure 2.1. Flowcharts need only represent what we call executable instructions. We take up this topic later in the chapter.

Either one or both versions of the program will be relevant to you, depending on your computer system and on the preferences of your instructor. At this point, you need not worry about the exact meaning of each instruction in either program, for we will discuss it further throughout the chapter; however, the programs should make some sense to you.

Step IV.   Debugging the Computer Program

This program contains no errors. In Chapter 3, however, we purposely introduce errors to illustrate their nature, detection, diagnosis, and correction.

2.2
ELEMENTS OF FORTRAN

Six basic elements describe the structure of the FORTRAN language. These are briefly described here for the purpose of perspective and are elaborated upon in the remainder of this chapter and other chapters.

1.   Character Set

Forty-six characters can be used in FORTRAN: twenty-six alphabetic characters (the letters of the alphabet), ten numeric characters (the digits 0 through 9), and ten special characters (plus sign, minus sign, asterisk, slash, equal sign, left parenthesis, right parenthesis, comma, decimal point, and blank space). Some versions of FORTRAN also allow the dollar sign and the apostrophe as special characters. These characters represent the most fundamental element of the language, since they are used to construct the other five elements.

2.   Data Representation

Data are represented within programs by the use of variable names and constants. These we discuss fully in Section 2.3.

3.   Key Words

Certain words, called **key words,** are used either to describe an operation which is to be performed by the computer or to communicate certain information to the computer. WRITE, FORMAT, STOP, and END are key words in the programs of Example 2.1. We introduce other key words throughout the remainder of the book.

4.   Function Names

Certain operations can be performed by using what are called **function names.** For example, we can use SQRT to take square roots and ALOG10 to find base-ten logarithms. These and other functions are discussed in Chapter 10.

5. *Expressions*

These are combinations of variable names, constants, function names, and special characters. They are used to express either arithmetic calculations or logical comparisons, or both. For example, CREDIT*100. is an arithmetic expression in the program of Example 2.1. We introduce arithmetic expressions in Section 2.5 and logical expressions in Chapter 4.

6. *Instructions*

An **instruction,** also called a **statement,** either directs the computer to perform a specific task or declares certain information which the computer needs. FORTRAN statements are combinations of characters, variables, constants, key words, function names, and expressions. Thus they utilize the first five elements of FORTRAN. The version B program in Example 2.1 contains seven statements. We introduce the various types of FORTRAN statements in Section 2.4 and discuss them in detail throughout the book.

2.3
FORTRAN VARIABLES
AND CONSTANTS

Historically, a programmer accessed an item of data by finding its numerical address on a long and tedious list showing which item of data was stored at which address location. Now, however, programmers can use symbolic names rather than numbers to reference memory locations in a way that communicates the nature of the contents. For example, BALDUE in the student billing program is a symbolic name that clearly indicates that the balance due the college is stored in this location, as opposed to, say, address location 0003, which would tell us nothing about what is stored at this address.

In FORTRAN a symbolic name is called a **variable name.** A variable name, therefore, identifies a location in memory where a particular item of data is stored (found). The student billing program used three variables: TUIT, which represents "tuition charge"; CREDIT, which represents "number of credits in which the student is enrolled"; and BALDUE, which represents "balance due the college." In choosing a variable name, you can use a combination of letters and/or numbers; however, it is best to choose meaningful names to help you remember what values you are storing in the memory locations.

FORTRAN has three rules for forming a variable name:

1. A variable name must have six characters or less.
2. The first character of a variable name must be a letter.
3. The remaining characters can be letters, digits, or a combination of both. No special characters such as plus (+), slash (/), asterisk (*), or comma (,) are permitted. Although blanks may be used within variable names, they generally are not used because of the potential for misunderstanding.

EXAMPLE 2.2

The following list illustrates both acceptable and unacceptable variable names in FORTRAN.

Variable Name	Comment
ACCOUNT	Unacceptable. One too many characters.
ACCT	Acceptable.
1EXAM	Unacceptable. Does not begin with a letter.
EXAM1	Acceptable.
X + Y	Unacceptable. Special character not allowed.
XPY	Acceptable.
MALESEX.	Unacceptable. Too many characters and use of period.
M SEX	Acceptable, but not recommended.
MSEX	Acceptable.

Follow-up Exercise

1. Tell whether each of the following variable names is acceptable or unacceptable. If a name is unacceptable, indicate why.

   a. X
   b. IX
   c. 3Y
   d. Y3
   e. AGE/35
   f. AGE35
   g. SUM∗
   h. PROFITS
   i. PROFIT
   j. SET-UPCOST
   k. SU COST
   l. SUCOST

Integer and Real Variables

Two types of numeric values can be stored in memory locations: integer values and real values. **Integer values** are whole numbers with no decimal point, such as 25, 175, -42, or 24; **real values** are numbers with a decimal point, such as 25.3, -7.26, 1234567., or 24.0.

The distinction between real and integer values is necessary because the computer stores integer values differently from real values. Moreover, this distinction allows certain advantages and efficiencies, which we will discuss later.

Because both integer and real values can be stored in a memory location, the computer needs to know which type of value (integer or real) a particular location is going to hold. You will indicate which type of value the memory location holds by your selection of a variable name.

To tell the computer you wish to store an integer value, you must select a variable name beginning with a letter I through N; the variable is referred to as an **integer variable.** For example, INDEX, MONEY, and NUMBER are storage locations in which integers are stored.

If you begin a variable name with the letters A through H or O through Z,

you are telling the computer to store real values, and the variable is called a
real variable. $\underline{R}$ATE, $\underline{P}$AY, and $\underline{B}$ALDUE are all examples of real variables.

Constants

Not all data in a computer program need to be stored in memory locations
which are referenced by variable names. In some situations you will need to use
a constant (unchanging) value, such as the constant π in the computation πr^2.
In this case, you would write the number 3.141593 directly into a FORTRAN
program.

In the student billing program the instruction

BALDUE = TUIT + 250.

consists of two real variables, BALDUE and TUIT, and the constant 250. The
values stored in the variable may change whenever the computer executes an
instruction, but the quantity 250. is not subject to change.

A **constant**, therefore, represents a fixed unvarying quantity that does not
change during the execution of a program. As with variables, FORTRAN
makes a distinction between integer and real constants. An **integer constant**
represents a whole number and does not include a decimal point. For example,
in the instruction

KOUNT = KOUNT + 1

the "1" is an integer constant. A **real constant** is one that contains a decimal
point. For example, "250." in the student billing program is designated a real
constant.

FORTRAN does not allow the use of a comma in a constant. For example,
the constant 25,000 would provoke an error from a FORTRAN compiler; it
would have to be written as 25000.

Follow-up Exercises

2. Identify each of the following as integer constant, real constant, or unacceptable
    constant:

a. 5,000	d. −.05	g. 7.351
b. 5000	e. 0.05	h. 7,351
c. 5000.	f. 0.050	i. 7351

3. Identify each of the following as an integer variable, real variable, or unaccept-
    able variable.

a. YEAR	e. AGE
b. NYEAR	f. JAGE
c. K	g. 72P
d. XK	h. P72

TABLE 2.2   Types of **Executable** Instructions

TYPE	ACTIVITY
1. Assignment	Computes and/or stores data.
2. Output	Causes output device to print stored data.
3. Input	Causes input device to accept data for storage.
4. Stop	Causes the control unit to stop execution.
5. Transfer of control	Alters the sequence of execution in the program.

2.4
FORTRAN INSTRUCTIONS

The instructions in a FORTRAN program can be classified as those which are executable and those which are not executable. An **executable instruction** is one which causes activity within the CPU during execution of the program. Table 2.2 indicates five types of executable instructions and the activities they represent.

We discuss the assignment statement in the next section and simple versions of input and output statements later in this chapter. Transfer of control is introduced in Chapter 4 and continued in Chapter 7.

As illustrated in Example 2.1, the stop instruction is written as

STOP

This statement terminates the execution of a program and should be included as part of every program. Typically, you will place this statement just before the END statement, although it can be placed elsewhere in the program should it make sense to do so.

A **nonexecutable instruction** is used to provide or declare certain information to the CPU during compilation of the program. In Example 2.1, the statement

END

is a nonexecutable instruction which defines the last physical line in a FORTRAN program. It simply tells the compiler that this is the last instruction of the program. Once this instruction is compiled, execution of the program begins, providing that rules of the FORTRAN language have not been violated.

Don't forget to include the END statement in every program you write.[1]

The FORMAT statement in Example 2.1 is another nonexecutable instruction. When this instruction is translated by the compiler, we have declared certain information to the computer relating to input/output tasks. We discuss this more fully later in the chapter, and in great detail in Chapters 5 and 6.

2.5
ASSIGNMENT STATEMENTS

An **assignment statement** is used (1) to perform and store calculations, (2) to assign a constant to a storage location, or (3) to transfer the contents of one storage location to another. In the student billing program of Example 2.1, the instruction

    BALDUE = TUIT + 250.

is an example of an assignment statement. This statement adds the value stored in TUIT to the constant 250. and stores the result in the storage location named BALDUE.

Structure

In more general terms, the assignment statement in FORTRAN is structured as follows:

variable name = arithmetic expression

On the left-hand side of the equal sign, a single variable identifies a storage location in internal computer memory. The right-hand side of the equal sign is referred to as the arithmetic expression. An **arithmetic expression** may

TABLE 2.3   *Arithmetic Operation Symbols*

OPERATION SYMBOL	ARITHMETIC OPERATION
+	Addition
−	Subtraction
/	Division
*	Multiplication
**	Exponentiation (raise to a power)

---

[1]The latest version of ANSI FORTRAN, called FORTRAN 77, treats the END statement as an executable statement having the same effect as the STOP statement.

TABLE 2.4   *Three Types of Assignment Statements*

variable name = arithmetic expression	
TYPE	ILLUSTRATION
Variable = Constant	VOL = 5000.
Variable = Variable	COST = MONEY
Variable = Combination of constants and variables separated by operation symbols	PROF = 7.*VOL − COST

consist of a single constant, a single variable, or a combination of constants and variables separated by arithmetic operation symbols.

An **arithmetic operation symbol** indicates the type of computation that is desired. Five symbols are used in the FORTRAN language to indicate the type of arithmetic operation, as described in Table 2.3.

Table 2.4 illustrates the three possible types of (or uses for) assignment statements. In the first illustration the real constant 5000. is placed in the storage location identified by VOL. In the second case, the contents of the storage location called MONEY are copied by the storage location called COST. Note, however, that this transfer is electronic; that is, whatever is in MONEY remains there, but whatever was in COST gets replaced by whatever is in MONEY. Finally, the third illustration places the computational result of 7.*VOL − COST in the storage location called PROF. This means that the contents of COST will be subtracted from seven times the contents of VOL and the result will be stored in PROF.

You should very carefully note the meaning of the equal sign (=) in FORTRAN. It means "place the value indicated by the arithmetic expression on the right in the storage location indicated by the variable on the left." Because of this meaning, an assignment such as

$$I = I + 1$$

makes sense in FORTRAN but not in algebra. Note that each time this statement is executed by the computer, the content (value) of I gets increased by 1. In other words, this statement instructs the computer to "add 1 to the contents of I and place this result in I." This type of statement is used quite often in FORTRAN programs for the purpose of "counting," as you will see in the chapters which follow.

Finally, we should mention that *two operation symbols must never appear adjacent to one another,* as this would cause a syntax error.[2] Can you reason why?

---

[2]Note that ** is treated as a single operation symbol for exponentiation.

EXAMPLE 2.3

In the student billing program of Example 2.1, three assignment statements were used:

    CREDIT = 15.
    TUIT = CREDIT*100.
    BALDUE = TUIT + 250.

In the first assignment statement the expression is a single constant; hence the value 15. is simply stored in the memory location named CREDIT, as indicated below:

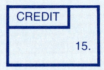

The second statement instructs the computer to multiply the constant 100. by the contents of the memory location named CREDIT, and to store the result in the memory location TUIT. After this calculation, the memory locations appear as follows:

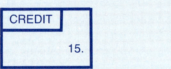   

The third instruction tells the computer to add the constant 250. to the contents of the memory location TUIT, and to store the result in the memory location BALDUE. After this calculation, the memory locations appear as follows:

      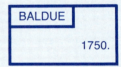

Follow-up Exercises

4. Identify what is wrong with each of the following assignment statements:
    a. B + C = A
    b. D = 4.* − X
    c. 5. = AGE
    d. X = Y = 5.3

5. Consider the following sequence of instructions
    A = 37./C
    B = A + 1.6
    D = B**2
    and the current contents of the specified storage locations given below:

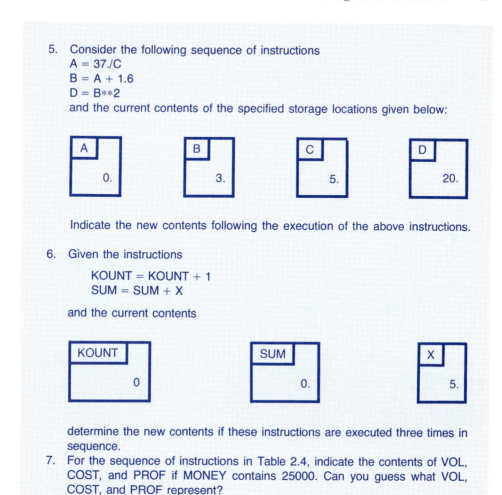

A	B	C	D
0.	3.	5.	20.

Indicate the new contents following the execution of the above instructions.

6. Given the instructions

        KOUNT = KOUNT + 1
        SUM = SUM + X

and the current contents

KOUNT	SUM	X
0	0.	5.

determine the new contents if these instructions are executed three times in sequence.

7. For the sequence of instructions in Table 2.4, indicate the contents of VOL, COST, and PROF if MONEY contains 25000. Can you guess what VOL, COST, and PROF represent?

Integer and Real Arithmetic Expressions

There are two **modes** of arithmetic expressions in FORTRAN: integer and real. An expression is an **integer expression** if it consists of an integer constant (a number that has no decimal point), or an integer variable (the first character of the variable name begins with I, J, K, L, M, or N), or a combination of integer constants and integer variables. The right-hand sides of the following assignment statements are examples of integer expressions:

    NUM   = 50
    KOUNT   = KOUNT + 1
    INVEST = MATERL + LABOR
    MONEY   = NUMSLD*ITMCST + 5000

An integer expression performs integer arithmetic; that is, the results will be integer values. Awareness of this is particularly important in *integer division,* where an integer quantity is divided by another integer quantity. In this case, the "whole number" portion of the result is retained and the fractional portion is lost. This procedure is called **truncation;** the result is not rounded, as illustrated next.

EXAMPLE 2.4

As universities become more cost conscious, computer programs to calculate costs of educating different majors are under development.

A computer program might include the assignment statement

MTCPS = MATHCT/NUMBER

where MTCPS represents the "cost per student for the Math Department," MATHCT represents the "total cost for the Math Department," and NUMBER represents the "number of majors in the Math Department."

If 150175 is stored in MATHCT and 100 is stored in NUMBER, then 1501 will be stored in MTCPS. Note that the numerical result is not rounded up to 1502; rather, the fractional value (.75) is truncated, since MATHCT/NUMBER is an integer expression.

An expression is a **real expression** if it consists of a real constant (a decimal point is part of the number), a real variable (first character begins with A through H or O through Z), or a combination of real constants and real variables. The right-hand sides of the following statements are examples of real expressions:

```
BALDUE = TUIT + 250.
CREDIT = 15.
PAY    = HOURS*RATE
WAGE   = PAY
```

A real expression performs real arithmetic. That is, the result will be a real number.

EXAMPLE 2.5

A student received an 85 and a 94 on two exams. The average can be found by using the following arithmetic statements:

```
SUM = EXAM1 + EXAM2
AVG = SUM/2.
```

If EXAM1 has the value 85. and EXAM2 has the value 94., then SUM has the value 179.0 and AVG the value 89.5.

If integer and real variables or constants are combined in an expression, then the expression is known as a **mixed-mode expression.** The following are examples of mixed-mode expressions:

Mixed-Mode Expression	Comment
TOTAL/2	TOTAL is a real variable and 2 is an integer constant.
50.5*I	I is an integer variable and 50.5 is a real constant.
ASSETS + LIAB	ASSETS is a real variable and LIAB is an integer variable.

As a programmer you must pay very close attention to mixed-mode expressions for two reasons. First, the compiler on your system may not allow mixed-mode expressions. If it does not, then your program will not be executed. Many compilers, however, do allow mixed-mode expressions and will treat them as follows: integer variables or constants will be converted to real mode during the computations, and the final result will be a real value; however, the exact value of the final result may differ from computer to computer, depending on the sequence of computations. In general, *it is good programming practice to avoid mixed-mode expressions,* since the process of conversion is inefficient and follows complicated rules.[3]

A second reason for you to pay close attention to the use of mixed-mode expressions is that you may get an undesirable result. To illustrate, the cost per student in Example 2.4 is actually $1501.75. If truncation is undesirable for a particular computation, then real expressions should be used.

In our definitions of integer, real, and mixed-mode expressions we omitted one complicating factor. *Any expression (positive or negative) may be raised to a (positive or negative) integer power, but only (positive) real expressions may be raised to real powers.* Study the examples at the top of page 40 to make sure you understand this condition.

Finally, we note some other items of interest.

1. When truncation is of no concern, integer arithmetic is preferred to real arithmetic because it is faster.
2. In some applications truncation is desirable, as we illustrate later in the book.
3. For many computers, the maximum number of digits retained in integer arithmetic is ten; the maximum number of *significant* digits in real arithmetic is generally seven, although certain nonexecutable statements (which we do not treat in this book) can increase this figure.

---

[3]FORTRAN 77 allows mixed-mode expressions. See Section 11.7.

Expression Raised to a Power	Comment
X**K	Real expression (X) may be raised to integer power (K); X is simply multiplied by itself a total of K times. For example, if 5. is in X and 3 is in K, then the result is 5. × 5. × 5., or 125.
J**8	Integer expression (J) may be raised to integer power (8). J is multiplied by itself eight times.
J**8.	Considered mixed mode. Treatment depends on computer system.
K**X	Considered mixed mode. Treatment depends on computer system.
(−4.)**L	Use of parentheses causes treatment of 4. as a negative number. This is permissible since the power is integer. If 2 is in L, then the result is (−4.) × (−4.), or 16. If 3 is in L, then the result is −64.
A**3.	This is permissible if A stores a positive value.[4]
(−A)**3.	This is not allowed since the expression is negative (assuming A stores a positive value) and the power is real.[5]

EXAMPLE 2.6

Consider the sequence of instructions

    J = X/2.
    Y = 2*J
    I = .4*Y

where the real number (5.) is in the storage location labeled X. After the execution of these statements, the storage locations for J, Y, and I would contain the following values:

Thus, the computation (X/2.) yields the real number 2.5, but this is truncated to the integer number 2 for storage in the location for integer variable J. (Note that a decimal point does not appear in the storage location for J.) The computation (2*J) yields the integer number 4, but this is stored as the real number 4. because Y is a real variable. Finally, the computation .4*Y gives the real number 1.6, which is truncated and stored as the integer number 1 because I is an integer variable.

Finally, note that *it is permissible for the variable to the left of the equal sign to differ in mode from the arithmetic expression to the right of the equal sign.* The mode of this variable simply determines the mode of the value stored.

---

[4]Whenever a real power is used, the computer uses logarithms in the evaluation. In this case it would find the antilog of 3log(A).
[5]The computer attempts to evaluate this as the antilog of 3log(−A), but the log of a negative number is undefined.

Follow-up Exercises

8. Fill in the contents for

after the following statements are executed.

C = 5*L − L/2
K = C − 10.2

9. Identify any mixed-mode expressions and correct them by appropriately modifying the constants.
    a.   CABE − 100
    b.   5.*K − 1
    c.   7**Q
    d.   (−7.)**Q
    e.   Y**2

Arithmetic Hierarchy

Computers do arithmetic on only two numbers at a time (pairwise arithmetic). Therefore, an arithmetic expression involving several computations must be computed in a certain sequence.

In FORTRAN the sequence for performing arithmetic operations is

First: All exponentiation is performed.
Second: All multiplication and division is completed.
Third: All addition and subtraction is performed.

We illustrate this so-called **arithmetic hierarchy** through examples.

EXAMPLE 2.7

The calculation of amount due for tuition and fees in the student billing program of Example 2.1 can be combined into one assignment statement. The statement would look like this.

    BALDUE = 250. + CREDIT*100.

If CREDIT has a value of 15., then 1750. is stored in BALDUE. This value is arrived at through the following steps:
    First, CREDIT is multiplied by 100. because multiplication is completed before addition. The result is 1500.
    Second, 250. is added to 1500. The result is 1750.

EXAMPLE 2.8   Marketing Problem

The Product Manager for Prangles Potato Chips, a competitor of Pringles, wishes to determine the area of the top which would be required of a super-economy-size cylindrical container of radius 5 inches. As you might recall, the area of a circle is computed by using the formula $area = \pi r^2$, where r is the radius. This can be written in FORTRAN as

AREA = 3.141593*RADIUS**2

If the variable RADIUS has the value 5., then 78.53982 is stored in AREA. This result is achieved as follows:

First, RADIUS is raised to the second power because exponentiation is performed before multiplication. The result is 25.

Second, 3.141593 is multiplied by 25. The result is 78.53982.

Left-to-Right Rule

The exact order of computation when two or more operations are at the same level of arithmetic hierarchy will differ depending on the complexity of the arithmetic expression and the particular computer system. If you avoid intricate mixed-mode expressions, however, then *the computational result will be consistent with a left-to-right scan of the arithmetic expression,* as the following examples illustrate.

EXAMPLE 2.9

The percentage of business students relative to the university enrollment is calculated using the following assignment statement:

PERCT = BUS/UNIV*100.

If 1000. is stored in BUS and 5000. is stored in UNIV, then 20. is stored in PERCT. The value of 20. is determined by the following sequence:

First, BUS is divided by UNIV because division and multiplication are at the same level, so that operations are from left to right. The result is 0.2.

Second, 0.2 is multiplied by 100. The result is 20.

Note that the left-to-right rule prevents the wrong sequence of first multiplying UNIV by 100. (giving 500000.) and then dividing this result into BUS (giving 0.002 for PERCT).

EXAMPLE 2.10   Manufacturing Problem

The daily cost in dollars (c) of operating a small manufacturing firm is described by the equation

$$c = u^3 - 6u^2 + 250$$

where *u* represents the number of units produced by the firm per day. The equivalent assignment statement in FORTRAN is

    COST = UNITS**3 − 6.*UNITS**2 + 250.

If UNITS has the value 20., then 5850. will be stored in COST. The value 5850. is determined as follows:

First, UNITS is raised to the third power because exponentiation is the first operation performed, and UNITS**3 appears to the *left* of UNITS**2. The result is 8000.

Second, UNITS is raised to the second power. The result is 400.

Third, 6. is multiplied by 400. because multiplication is performed before addition and subtraction. The result is 2400.

Fourth, 2400. is subtracted from 8000. because the subtraction operation is found to the left of the addition operation. The result is 5600.

Fifth, 250. is added to 5600., giving 5850.

Use of Parentheses

The insertion of parentheses within arithmetic expressions changes the order of computation according to the following rules:

1. The operations enclosed within parentheses are computed before operations not included in parentheses.
2. Parentheses may be embedded inside other parentheses in complicated expressions.
3. The innermost set of parentheses contains the computations done first.

We might note that within parentheses themselves the hierarchy and left-to-right rules apply.

EXAMPLE 2.11   Temperature Conversion

Conversion of temperatures from Fahrenheit to Celsius is a procedure you should become accustomed to as the United States converts to metric measurements. The appropriate formula is

$$Celsius = \tfrac{5}{9}\,(Fahrenheit - 32)$$

In FORTRAN the formula is written

    CEL = 5./9.*(FAHREN − 32.)

If 212. is stored in FAHREN, then 100.0000 will be stored in CEL according to the following steps:

First, 32. is subtracted from FAHREN because this operation is enclosed in parentheses. The result is 180.

Second, 5. is divided by 9. because the division operation is found to the left of the multiplication operation. The result is 0.5555556.

Third, 0.5555556 is multiplied by 180. The result is 100.0000.

Note: dividing 5 by 9 actually gives the irrational number 0.555555555 . . . , that is, the 5s never end. We expressed the result to 7 significant digits according to item 3 on page 39. When this 7-digit number is multiplied by 180, the precise result is 100.000008, which we have expressed to 7 digits as 100.0000.

Follow-up Exercises

It is very important that you pay close attention to hierarchy, left-to-right, and parentheses rules when you are writing FORTRAN expressions. Inattention to these rules is a leading cause of logic errors. The following exercises emphasize this point.

10. In Example 2.11, what would be stored under CEL if the assignment statement were as follows?

CEL = 5./9.*FAHREN − 32.

11. Indicate what would be stored in A for each of the following, given that 3. is in B and 2. is in C:
a. A = (4. + B**3 − C)*C**2
b. A = (4. + B**(3. − C))*C**2
c. A = (4. + B**(3. − C))*(C**2)
d. A = 9./B*C + 5./C
e. A = 9./(B*C) + 5./C
f. A = 9./B/C + 5./C
g. A = 9./B*(C + 5.)/C

12. Write FORTRAN arithmetic expressions for each of the following algebraic expressions. Do not mix mode.

a. x^{i+1}
b. $x^i + 1$
c. $s^2/(p − 1)$
d. $(x − a)^2/(p − 1)$
e. $(y − 3^{x-1} + 2)^5$
f. $(7 − x)^{1/2}$
g. $\sqrt{(x − a)^2/(p − 1)}$

2.6
INPUT/OUTPUT (I/O)
WITHOUT FORMATS

In this section we present some simple input and output statements which do not require you to indicate the format of how data are to appear on cards or on printed pages. Learning I/O with the use of formats requires a fair amount of concerted effort. We believe that your efforts at this time are best spent in writing and running simple programs; hence, we now present the simplest (unformatted) versions of I/O statements and defer a complete treatment of formats to Chapters 5 and 6. Unfortunately, there is one disadvantage to this approach: ANSI FORTRAN does not recognize I/O without formats.[6] If you have access to a compiler which translates unformatted I/O, such as the WATFIV compiler and compilers on time-sharing systems, then this section is relevant to you; otherwise, you should go on to Section 2.7.

The WRITE Statement

The WRITE statement transfers the contents of the specified storage locations (variables) to a designated output device such as a line printer or terminal. This enables you to observe the results of the program.

The general form of an output statement without formats is

> **WRITE(***output unit number,*****)** *list of variables*

where "output unit number" refers to a specific output unit such as a line printer or terminal; the asterisk identifies this output statement as **unformatted** or **list-directed** and the "list" contains variable names (separated by commas) in the same sequence as the desired contents which are to be output.[7]

In the version A program of Example 2.1, the output statement

    WRITE(6,*)BALDUE

serves to transfer the contents of the memory location identified as BALDUE either to a line printer in a batch system or to a terminal in a time-sharing system, depending on what system you are using.[8] When this statement is executed, the value printed will be 1750.

The "list" in the WRITE statement may also contain more than one variable, separated by commas. For example, to print the number of credits, the tuition, and the balance due, the WRITE statement in Example 2.1 is modified as follows:

    WRITE(6,*) CREDIT,TUIT,BALDUE

When this statement is executed by the computer, the following printout would result:

    15.   1500.   1750.

Note that the output appears on one line; that the sequence of numbers in the output corresponds to the sequence of variables in the list; and that each number contains a decimal point, since each variable in the list is a real variable.

---

[6] FORTRAN 77 allows I/O without formats, as described in this section.
[7] Some time-sharing systems may not accept this specific form of the WRITE statement. Ask your instructor.
[8] The number "6" is specific to selected IBM equipment; the output unit number may be different for your system, so ask your instructor.

Depending on which compiler you are using, the output of real variables might be expressed in **E-notation** or **scientific notation.** For example, the above line of output might appear as follows:

0.15E 02   0.15E 04   0.175E 04

Thus, the first number is equivalent to 0.15×10^2, or 15.; the second number is 0.15×10^4, or 1500.; and the third number is 0.175×10^4, or 1750.

Follow-up Exercises

13. Indicate how you think the output would appear if the following three WRITE statements were to be used in place of the one above:

        WRITE(6,∗) CREDIT
        WRITE(6,∗) TUIT
        WRITE(6,∗) BALDUE

14. In WATFIV, an alternative to the WRITE statement is the PRINT statement

> **PRINT,** *list of variables*

At this point, an advantage of the PRINT statement over the WRITE statement is *its ability to print literals, or textual matter.*[9] For example, when the statement

    PRINT, 'THE BALANCE DUE IS', BALDUE

is executed the printout would appear as follows:

    THE BALANCE DUE IS   1750.

a. What print statement would be necessary for the output below?

    THE NUMBER OF CREDITS IS   15.

b. What print statement would be necessary for the output below?

    CREDITS = 15.   BALANCE DUE = 1750.

15. For each of the following write the appropriate equivalents. (*Note:* the E-notation equivalent always begins with 0.)

Number		E-notation
a.	0.32×10^8	0.
b.	3.2×10^7	0.
c.	32×10^6	0.
d.	-3.2×10^7	0.
e.	45.76×10^{-6}	0.
f.		0.134E−05
g.		−0.56E 35

---

[9]The list-directed WRITE statement in FORTRAN 77 includes the option of printing literals. See Section 11.7.

The READ Statement

You need to make an important distinction between your computer program (that is, the instructions that tell the computer what to do) and your **input data** (that is, the data that you want processed through an input device). For example, a business firm has data on the number of hours worked and the rate of pay for each employee. The firm has recorded these data on an appropriate input medium such as cards or magnetic tape, and uses these to compute each employee's pay. The hours worked and rate of pay for each employee are considered input data; the FORTRAN instructions to determine each employee's pay represent the computer program.

In the student billing program of Example 2.1, three items of data were provided: cost of tuition per credit ($100), cost of fees ($250), and number of credits (15). By definition, these are not input data, since they represent constants in the computer program. For example, the assignment statement

    CREDIT = 15.

was used to store 15. in CREDIT and the 100. and 250. were incorporated in the assignment statements

    TUIT = CREDIT*100.

and

    BALDUE = TUIT + 250.

The READ statement is an alternative approach to storing data in memory locations and *is preferred to the assignment statement whenever data have a high likelihood of changing values each time the program is executed.* The READ statement enables the computer to transfer the data from some source, such as punched card or terminal, to the appropriate storage locations in computer memory.

A general form of the **unformatted (list-directed) READ statement** is

READ(*input unit number,****)** *list of variables*

where the "input unit number" refers to a specific input unit such as a card reader or a terminal; the asterisk identifies this input statement as unformatted; and the "list" contains variable names (separated by commas) in the same sequence as distinct items of data which are to be entered into memory.[10]

---

[10]Some time-sharing systems may not accept this form of the READ statement. Ask your instructor.

EXAMPLE 2.12   Student Billing Problem Continued

We can rewrite the version A program in Example 2.1 using the READ instruction as follows:

```
READ(5,*) ID, CREDIT
TUIT = CREDIT*100.
BALDUE = TUIT + 250.
WRITE(6,*) ID,BALDUE
STOP
END
```

Note that two input variables have been specified: ID (for student identification number) and CREDIT. Also, ID is to be printed along with BALDUE.

Assume that Noah Arrowsmith's ID (7581) and number of credits (15.) are either on a punched card for batch processing or to be typed at the terminal for time-shared processing. (Just how we do this is a topic in the next chapter.) The READ instruction activates the appropriate input unit and transfers the values on the input medium to the memory locations ID and CREDIT.[11] After the READ instruction is executed, the memory locations appear as

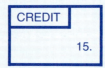

The use of a READ statement for ID and CREDIT is preferred to the use of assignment statements, since the values of ID and CREDIT will change for each student that is processed. If a READ statement were not used, then the assignment statements would have to be changed for each student, which is both cumbersome and more costly than the use of input data.

Follow-up Exercises

*16.   Change the program in Example 2.12 by treating the "cost of tuition per credit" (CPC) and the "cost of fees" (FEES) as input variables. Use a single READ statement for all input variables. Is it preferable to treat CPC and FEES as input variables? Explain.

17.   Some compilers (for example, WATFIV) allow the following list-directed READ statement:

> **READ,** *list of variables*

Answer the preceding exercise using this version of the READ statement.

---

[11]The number 5 for the input unit number in the READ statement is specific to selected IBM equipment; it refers either to a card reader in a batch system or to a terminal in a time-sharing system. The input unit number may be different for your system, so ask your instructor.
*Answers to exercises marked with a single or double asterisk are not given at the end of the text. Ask your instructor for these answers.

2.7
INPUT/OUTPUT (I/O) WITH FORMATS

This section is a brief introduction to FORMAT statements for those of you who will not be using unformatted I/O. Our purpose here is for you to become familiar with the basic I/O of integer and real variables. In other words, you will be able to run your programs using simple I/O. For you to become skilled in this topic will require a fair amount of effort, as you will see in Chapters 5 and 6.

The WRITE Statement

The following statements are used for output in version B of the student billing program in Example 2.1:

```
    WRITE(6,50) BALDUE
50 FORMAT(1X,F7.2)
```

This WRITE statement says "print the contents of BALDUE using output unit number 6 according to the layout indicated in the FORMAT statement numbered 50." The number 6 refers to a line printer in the batch system we use. Your instructor will give you the appropriate number for your system. The number 50 is called a **statement number.** In this instance, the statement number allows us to pair the WRITE statement with the appropriate FORMAT statement. In general, a statement number can be any positive integer up to five digits.

The layout of the print line is described by the codes or specifications within the parentheses of the FORMAT statement. The "1X" tells the line printer or terminal to go down the page one line (single space) before printing the value in BALDUE. For now, you should always start an output FORMAT with this 1X code. The "F7.2" describes the exact appearance of the 1750. (the value in BALDUE) on the print line:

First, note that the "7" in F7.2 specifies the total number of print spaces (columns) which is to be used for printing the value of BALDUE. Second, the ".2" in F7.2 tells the computer that you want this value expressed to two digits to the right of the decimal place. Finally, the "F" in F7.2 is the letter used for the output of a real variable.

Now consider the following statements:

```
    WRITE(6,75) ID,BALDUE
75 FORMAT(1X,I6,F9.0)
```

Assume that ID represents "student identification number" and has 7581 for its contents. The following will be printed when this WRITE statement is executed:

	1	2	3	4	5	6	7	8	9	10	11	12	13	14	15	16	17	18	19	20
1		7	5	8	1							1	7	5	0	.				
2																				
3																				
4																				
5																				
6																				

You should note the following:

1. The statement number for the FORMAT statement is 75, which must match with the number used in the WRITE statement.
2. The output of ID is described by the I6 specification and the output of BALDUE by the F9.0 specification.
3. ID is an integer variable, which requires that its output specification must contain the letter I as in I6. The "6" in I6 says that six columns are to be used for the printout of 7581, the value in ID. Note that the 7581 is "right-justified" (printed to the extreme right) in the six columns.
4. The "9" in F9.0 says to print the value in BALDUE nine columns *over* from the printout of ID. Thus 1750. is printed up-against (right-justified on) column 15. Note that the "0" in F9.0 specifies that no places are to be printed to the right of the decimal point.

Follow-up Exercises

18. For each part, state the appropriate WRITE and FORMAT statements for the printout of ID and BALDUE.

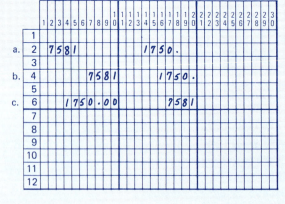

19. For each part, state the appropriate WRITE and FORMAT statements for the printout of ID, BALDUE, CREDIT, and TUIT.

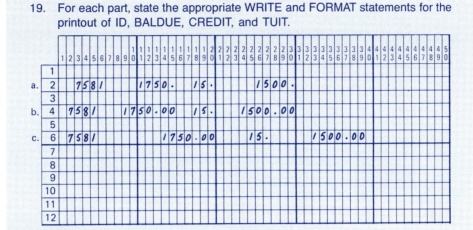

20. A new line is printed each time a WRITE statement is executed. Describe the exact appearance of printout for the following:

```
        WRITE(6,15) ID
    15 FORMAT(1X,I6)
        WRITE(6,25) BALDUE
    25 FORMAT(1X,F9.0)
```

The READ Statement

You need to make an important distinction between your computer program (that is, the instructions that tell the computer what to do) and your **input data** (that is, the data that you want processed through an input device). For example, a business firm has data on the number of hours worked and the rate of pay for each employee. The firm has recorded these data on an appropriate input medium such as cards or magnetic tape, and uses these to compute each employee's pay. The hours worked and rate of pay for each employee are considered input data; the FORTRAN instructions to determine each employee's pay represent the computer program.

In the student billing program of Example 2.1, three items of data were provided: cost of tuition per credit ($100), cost of fees ($250), and number of credits (15). By definition, these are not *input* data, since they represent constants in the computer program. For example, the assignment statement

        CREDIT = 15.

was used to store 15. in CREDIT and the 100. and 250. were incorporated in the assignment statements

        TUIT = CREDIT*100.

and

        BALDUE = TUIT + 250.

The READ statement is an alternative approach to storing data in memory locations and *is preferred to the assignment statement whenever data have a high likelihood of changing values each time the program is executed.* The READ statement enables the computer to transfer the data from some source, such as punched card or terminal, to the appropriate storage locations in computer memory.

EXAMPLE 2.13   Student Billing Problem Continued

We can rewrite the version B program in Example 2.1 using the READ statement as follows:

```
      READ(5,20) ID,CREDIT
   20 FORMAT(I6,F7.0)
      TUIT = CREDIT*100.
      BALDUE = TUIT + 250.
      WRITE(6,25) ID,BALDUE
   25 FORMAT(1X,I6,F9.2)
      STOP
      END
```

This READ statement says "transfer the values of ID and CREDIT from input unit number 5 to the storage locations for ID and CREDIT according to the layout indicated by the FORMAT numbered 20." The number 5 refers to a card reader in the batch system we use. Your instructor will give you the appropriate number for your system. Note that the statement number 20 within the parentheses of the READ statement matches the statement number associated with the input FOR-MAT.

The layout of the values for ID (7581) and CREDIT (15.) on the input medium (a punched card in this case) is described by the specifications within the parentheses of the FORMAT statement. You should carefully note the following:

1. The I6 specification is paired with ID and the F7.0 specification is paired with CREDIT.
2. The I-specification is used for integer variables and the F-specification is used for real variables.
3. The 1X specification is not used at the beginning of an *input* FORMAT statement. It is used only for *output* FORMAT statements.
4. The "6" in I6 tells the computer that the value of ID is found right-justified in the first six columns of a card. Thus the number 7581 would appear in columns 3 through 6 of the data card.
5. The "7" in F7.0 tells the computer that the value of CREDIT is found in the *next* 7 columns (columns 7 through 13) of the data card, as follows:

Column in Data Card

1 2 3 4 5 6 7 8 9 10 11 12 13 . . .

7581 15.

The value 15. can be placed *anywhere* in columns 7 through 13, as long as we include the decimal point. The use of a decimal point for the input of real numbers causes the computer to ignore the ".0" part of the F7.0 specification. Procedures for working with this fractional part of the F-specification are detailed, so for now just use ".0". Using F7.0, we can still input fractional values. For example, if the number of credits is 9.5, then the data card could be prepared as follows:

Column in Data Card

1 2 3 4 5 6 7 8 9 10 11 12 13 . . .

7581 9.5

Again, the real number can be placed anywhere in columns 7 through 13, *as long as you include the decimal point.* Data card preparation and placement are illustrated in the next chapter, so don't worry about the exact details now.

6. After the READ instruction is executed, the memory locations appear as shown:

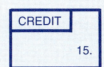

The use of a READ statement for ID and CREDIT is preferred to the use of assignment statements, since the values of ID and CREDIT will change for each student that is processed. If a READ statement were not used, then the assignment statements would have to be changed for each student, which is both cumbersome and more costly than the use of input data.

Follow-up Exercises

21. Use the data 7581 for ID and 15. for CREDIT and describe the input record for each of the following FORMATs:
     a. 20 FORMAT(I4,F3.0)
     b. 20 FORMAT(I10,F10.0)
22. Explain why the following FORMAT will not work.
         20 FORMAT(I3,F2.0)
*23. Change the program in Example 2.13 by treating the "cost of tuition per credit" CPC and the "cost of fees" FEES as input variables. Use a single READ statement for all four input variables. The values for ID, CREDIT, CPC, and FEES are to appear in columns 1–5, 6–10, 11–20, and 21–28 of a data card, respectively.
      Is it preferable to treat CPC and FEES as input variables? Explain.

2.8
DECLARATIVE STATEMENTS

The FORTRAN language has a number of statements which can be used to declare certain information about variables to the compiler. These statements are nonexecutable and are collectively labeled **declarative statements.** Of the many available, we present three particularly useful ones in this section.

REAL Statement

The statement

> **REAL** *list of variables*

explicitly informs the compiler that the variables in the list are to be treated as real variables. For example,

    REAL I, LOAD, NARC

causes the compiler to treat the variables I, LOAD, and NARC as if they were real variables. In other words, the fact that they begin with letters in the range I through N is not used by the compiler to determine mode. Thus, these variables will store real numbers and will be treated by the computer as real variables in assignment and I/O statements.

The use of the REAL statement is recommended whenever it is convenient for naming variables. For example, if LOAD represents the weight of a truck in tons, then we wish this variable to be real. LOAD is more descriptive than, say, XLOAD as the variable name. So we select LOAD rather than XLOAD as the variable name and use the REAL statement to ensure that it is treated as a real variable.

You need to *place REAL statements at the beginning of a program, prior to all DATA, FORMAT, and executable statements.*

INTEGER Statement

The statement

> **INTEGER** *list of variables*

explicitly informs the compiler that the variables in the list are to be treated as integer variables. For example,

    INTEGER   YEAR, AGE

causes the compiler to treat YEAR and AGE as integer variables. This means that YEAR and AGE will store integer numbers and will be treated as integer variables in assignment and I/O statements. The fact that they begin with letters other than I through N is ignored in determining mode.

The INTEGER statement is recommended whenever it improves the description of variable names. For example, if AGE is to store whole numbers only and is to be used only in integer arithmetic, then it should be treated as an integer variable. The name AGE is more descriptive than, say, JAGE, so we select AGE and use the INTEGER statement to ensure integer mode.

As with REAL statements, you must *place INTEGER statements prior to all DATA, FORMAT, and executable statements.* It doesn't matter, however, whether REAL comes before INTEGER, or vice versa, when both statements are used in the same program.

DATA Statement

The short form of the DATA statement is given by

> **DATA** *list of variables/list of constants/*

For example,

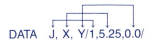

DATA   J, X, Y/1,5.25,0.0/

is a *nonexecutable* statement which declares to the compiler that J is to store 1, X is to store 5.25, and Y is to store 0.0. This statement has the same effect as

    J = 1
    X = 5.25

and

    Y = 0.0

Both approaches are termed **initialization** of variables; however, there is an important difference which should not escape you: The DATA statement initializes when the program is *compiled* and the assignment statements initialize when the program is *executed*.

We recommend using the DATA statement whenever the initialized variable does *not* need to be reinitialized to its former value during the execution of the program. We illustrate this condition in Chapter 4.

The DATA statement must be placed following any INTEGER and REAL statements, but before FORMAT and executable statements.

Follow-up Exercise

24. Modify the student billing program of Example 2.1 such that CREDIT is initialized by a DATA statement and all variables are treated as integer.

2.9
ONE MORE SCENARIO

To complete your introduction to fundamentals of FORTRAN we present one more problem scenario for which we write a complete FORTRAN program.

Suppose that we have $1000 to invest in a savings account which yields interest of 0.015 ($1\frac{1}{2}$ percent) per quarter (every three months). If we deposit the

$1000 now, then one quarter from now we have our original $1000 plus $15 interest (1000 × 0.015), or a total of $1015. This calculation can be written as follows:

$$1015 = 1000 + 1000 \times (0.015)$$
$$= 1000 \times (1 + 0.015)$$

Now, consider how much we would have two quarters from now: the $1015 at the end of the first quarter plus the new interest of $15.22 on this amount (1015 × 0.015), or a total of $1030.22. In other words,

$$1030.22 = 1015 + 1015 \times (0.015)$$
$$= 1015 \times (1 + 0.015)$$

But we already know that

$$1015 = 1000 \times (1 + 0.015)$$

Thus,

$$1030.22 = 1015 \times (1 + 0.015)$$
$$= 1000 \times (1 + 0.015) \times (1 + 0.015)$$
$$= 1000 \times (1 + 0.015)^2$$

Do you see an emerging pattern? In general, if A represents our accumulated funds, N represents the number of quarters into the future, P represents the principal we start off with, and R represents the quarterly interest rate, then

$$A = P \cdot (1 + R)^N$$

EXAMPLE 2.14   Bank Savings Account

Today's banks have computerized virtually all computational aspects dealing with savings and checking accounts, mortgages, loans, and investments. This example illustrates a simple program for determining accumulated funds in a savings account.

Step I.   Analyzing the Problem

1. *Problem statement*
   To develop a savings account program for determining accumulated funds given the principal, quarterly interest rate, and number of quarters.
2. *Data input*
   a.   Principal (P)
   b.   Quarterly interest rate (R)
   c.   Number of quarters (N)
3. *Data output*
   Accumulated funds (A) and the data which were input
4. *Computations and logical processes*

$$A = P \cdot (1 + R)^N$$

Step II.   Preparing the Flowchart
See Figure 2.2.

FIGURE 2.2   *Flowchart for Bank Savings Account Problem*

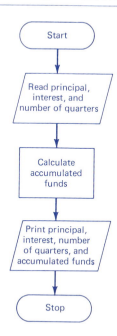

Step III.   Coding the Problem

I/O without FORMATs	I/O with FORMATs

```
READ(5,*) P,R,N
A = P*(1. + R)**N
WRITE(6,*) P,R,N,A
STOP
END
```

```
   READ(5,95) P,R,N
95 FORMAT(F10.0,F10.0,I5)
   A = P*(1. + R)**N
   WRITE(6,96) P,R,N,A
96 FORMAT(1X,F10.2,F10.4,I5,F10.2)
   STOP
   END
```

Step IV.   Debugging the Computer Program

We defer this step (and the running of the program) to Section 3.2 in the next chapter.

Follow-up Exercises

25. Why is it best to use a READ statement rather than an assignment statement for storing appropriate values of P, R, and N?

26. If 1000. is stored in P, 0.015 in R, and 2 in N, then describe the print line for the program which uses an output FORMAT.

Additional Exercises

27. Define the terms below. For each, include FORTRAN rules for its use and state its purpose or function.

flowchart	arithmetic operation symbol
coding	integer expression
coding form	real expression
debugging	mixed-mode expression
FORTRAN character set	truncation
key words	arithmetic hierarchy
function names	unformatted (list-directed) READ statement
variable name	unformatted (list-directed) WRITE statement
instruction	E-notation
statement	input data
integer variable	formatted WRITE statement
real variable	formatted READ statement
integer constant	FORMAT statement
real constant	statement number
executable instruction	declarative statements
nonexecutable instruction	REAL statement
STOP	INTEGER statement
END	DATA statement
arithmetic expression	initialization
assignment statement	

28. **Temperature Conversion.** Write a program which accepts degrees Fahrenheit as input and outputs degrees Celsius. (See Example 2.11.) Don't forget to specify the first three steps in the four-step procedure. *Note:* Input data for this problem are provided in Exercise 8 of the next chapter.

29. **Marketing Problem.** Consider the scenario in Example 2.8. Suppose that each top costs C dollars per square inch of surface and X containers are needed. Write a computer program which determines the total cost of X containers. Treat RADIUS, C, and X as input variables. Don't forget to specify the first three steps in the four-step procedure. Note: Input data for this problem are provided in Exercise 9 of the next chapter.

30. **Manufacturing Problem.** Consider the scenario in Example 2.10. Suppose that all units produced can be sold at a constant price of $100 per unit. Noting that daily revenue is price times the number of units produced and sold in one day and that daily profit is daily revenue less daily cost, write a program which calculates daily profit. Treat UNITS as an input variable, and print the daily revenue, daily cost, and daily profit. Don't forget to specify the first three steps in the four-step procedure. *Note:* Input data for this problem are provided in Exercise 10 of the next chapter.

31. **Blood-Bank Inventory Problem.** Decision making relating to the management of physical inventories is an established area in the management sciences which in recent years has been applied increasingly in semiprivate and public organizations.

Suppose that whenever a hospital replenishes its supply of a certain type of blood, it orders from a regional blood bank the amount indicated by the following formula:

$$Q = \sqrt{2 \cdot C \cdot D/H}$$

where Q is the number of pints of blood to order, C is the administrative and shipping cost (in dollars) of placing the order, D is the average weekly demand (usage) for this type of blood, and H is the cost (dollars per pint per week) of refrigerating the blood.

Also, it can be shown that the cost per week of this inventory policy is given by the formula

$$CPW = \sqrt{2 \cdot C \cdot H \cdot D}$$

where CPW is the expected cost (dollars) per week. Write a computer program which inputs values of C,H, and D, and determines how much blood to order and the cost of such a policy. Don't forget to specify the first three steps in the four-step procedure. *Note:* Input data for this problem are provided in Exercise 11 of the next chapter.

32. **Forecasting Population Growth.** In recent years, the prediction of world population levels into the next century has been a concern of many political, environmental, and agricultural planners. The following equation can be used to predict future levels of world population:

$$p = c \cdot [1 + (b - d)]^n$$

where p is the predicted level of future population, b is the birth rate, c is the current level of population, d is the death rate, and n is the number of years into the future.

Write a FORTRAN program that can be used to predict future population level given the current level, the birth rate, the death rate, and the number of years into the future as input data. Don't forget to specify the first three steps in the four-step procedure. *Note:* Input data for this problem are provided in Exercise 12 of the next chapter.

33. **Depreciation Problem.** The concept of depreciation plays a prominent role in the financial accounting of organizations which report profits and pay taxes. Write a program to calculate the amount of depreciation *in the first year* for a capital asset (building, automobile, machine, and so on) using

a. *The straight-line method.* This method uses the following formula to determine depreciation in any given year:

$$\text{Depreciation} = \left(\begin{array}{cc}\text{Cost of} & \text{Salvage value} \\ \text{asset} & \text{of asset}\end{array}\right) \cdot \left(\frac{1}{\text{Life of asset}}\right)$$

b. *The double-declining balance method* (a method used to increase the amount of depreciation in early years). This method uses the formulas:

$$\begin{array}{c}\text{Book value} \\ \text{of asset}\end{array} = \left(\begin{array}{c}\text{Cost of} \\ \text{asset}\end{array}\right) - \left(\begin{array}{c}\text{Accumulated depreciation} \\ \text{from all preceding years}\end{array}\right)$$

$$\text{Depreciation} = \left(\begin{array}{c}\text{Book value} \\ \text{of asset}\end{array}\right) \cdot (2) \cdot \left(\frac{1}{\text{Life of asset}}\right)$$

Input data for the program should include cost, salvage value, and life of the asset. Output should include the depreciation in the first year by each method. Note that accumulated depreciation should be initialized to zero for this calculation. Don't forget to specify the first three steps of the four-step procedure. *Note:* Input data for this problem are provided in Exercise 13 of the next chapter.

CHAPTER 3

Running the Complete Computer Program

By now you should have written on paper at least one program from the problems at the end of the last chapter, which, presumably, you are impatient to run on the computer. In this chapter we give you that opportunity by describing and illustrating procedures for running FORTRAN programs in batch and time-sharing environments.

3.1
RUNNING A FORTRAN PROGRAM
IN A BATCH ENVIRONMENT

Punched Cards

Computer programs run in a batch environment may use punched cards to transmit both the computer program and the input data to the computer.

The **punched card** illustrated in Figure 3.1 has 80 columns. Each column is capable of holding one character (a digit, a letter, or a special character). Rectangular holes punched in specific positions on the card represent a code of the different characters. Observe that a single hole is used for numbers (0–9), two holes for letters (A–Z), and one, two, or three holes for special characters.

As mentioned in Chapter 1, a **keypunch machine** is used to enter characters onto a punched card. Your instructor should give you a brief introduction on operating the type of keypunch available to you. Then, find a keypunch machine, and try your hand at it. Really, it's easy.

The Card Deck

To submit a FORTRAN program to a batch environment you need to prepare a **card deck,** which generally consists of four different types of punched cards:

1. Cards for FORTRAN instructions
2. Cards for comments
3. Cards for control
4. Cards for data

Each of these uses the standard 80-column punched card, but differs with respect to subject matter, purpose, and layout.

FIGURE 3.1   *Punched Card Illustrating FORTRAN Character Set*

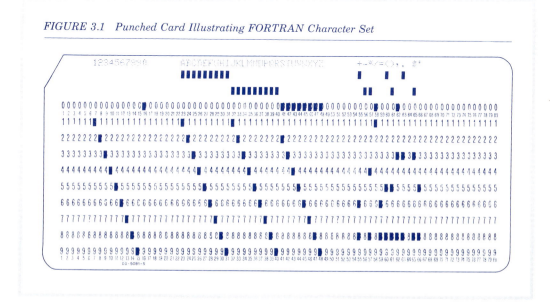

Instruction Cards. Each FORTRAN instruction is punched on one or more cards according to a prescribed set of rules which specify how the instruction is to be placed on the punched card. Figure 3.2 summarizes these rules, and Figure 3.3. illustrates the appearance of the FORTRAN **instruction cards** within the card deck for the student billing program of Examples 2.12 and 2.13. Notice that each instruction (except for the statement number in the program of part b) must be punched anywhere between column 7 and column 72 inclusive. At this point, you should begin each statement in column 7, which avoids wasted space and is visually appealing. Later, we will show you how certain indentations further improve the appearance of a program.

FIGURE 3.2   *Rules for Placement of FORTRAN Instruction on Punched Card*

Columns On Punched Card	Use	Explanation
1–5	Statement number field	These may contain an unsigned, nonzero, integer constant that serves as a statement number.
6	Continuation field	This is used when a statement is too long to fit on the preceding card. Any character other than a blank or zero in column 6 identifies this card as a continuation of the preceding card.
7–72	Statement body	These contain the FORTRAN statement, except for the statement number.
73–80	Identification/ sequence field	These are used either to identify a particular program or to sequence cards within the program so that if cards are dropped, the deck can be reordered correctly. The contents of this field are ignored by the compiler.

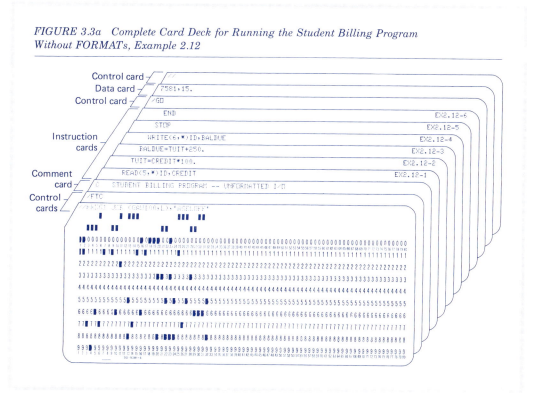

FIGURE 3.3a   *Complete Card Deck for Running the Student Billing Program Without FORMATs, Example 2.12*

Those of you using I/O with FORMATs need to use statement numbers, as illustrated in part b of Figure 3.3. The "15" and the "25" are punched in columns 4 and 5, although they could have been punched anywhere in the first five columns.

The continuation field described in Figure 3.2 is not utilized by either one of these programs, since no statement is too long for one card.

Finally, in columns 73 through 80 of Figure 3.3a we have identified each instruction card as EX2.12- (which is our abbreviation for Example 2.12) and sequenced each card as 1, 2, . . . , 6). Likewise, we have filled in columns 73 through 80 of each instruction card in the program of Figure 3.3b. The use of this identification/sequence field is optional; in most cases, you probably will not use it.

Have you been wondering about the *use of blank spaces in FORTRAN instructions?* With one exception which we discuss in Chapter 5, the compiler ignores blank spaces. For example, you need not be concerned about the number of blank spaces: between ID and CREDIT in the READ list; around equal signs and operation symbols in assignment statements; and around and between the enclosed parentheses in READ and WRITE statements. Use blank spaces simply to improve readability. It's even permissible to embed blank spaces within keywords, such as ST OP, but we don't recommend it since it detracts from readability.

Comment Cards.   The card which has a C punched in column 1 is known as a **comment card.** Thus the comment card in Figure 3.3a identifies this program as "Student Billing Program—Unformatted I/O"; the comment card in Figure 3.3b identifies this program as "Student Billing Program—Formatted I/O."

Comment cards are useful for documenting programs. This means that they can be used to describe programs, identify sections of programs, explain logic, and define variables. In fact, the entire description under Step I in the four-step procedure is best represented by comment cards at the beginning of a program. *You can place these cards anywhere within the set of instruction cards, as they are ignored by the compiler. Also, all 80 columns of the comment card can be used.*

Control Cards.   **Control cards** supply information to the operating system regarding user identification number, user name, expected processing time, programming language, and other factors.

Control cards are *not* part of the FORTRAN language; moreover, the specific control cards necessary to run a program vary from computer center to computer center. All computer centers, however, require the use of control

FIGURE 3.3b   *Complete Card Deck for Running the Student Billing Program with FORMATs, Example 2.13*

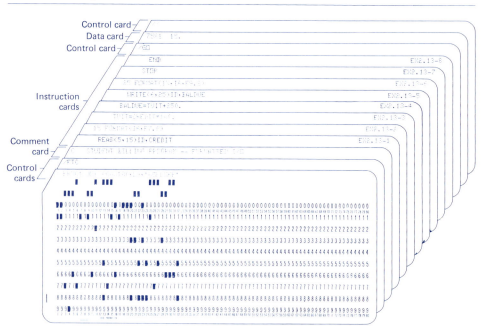

cards; otherwise, the essential information they supply would not be available for the operating system to do its job. *Your instructor will provide you with additional information concerning the control cards for your computer center.*

Data Cards. Typically, computer programs are designed to "read" data from an external source such as punched cards. For example, in the program of Figure 3.3, the data for ID and CREDIT are not part of the FORTRAN program. Instead, the program contains a READ instruction to transfer the student data from a punched card to computer memory. In general, cards which contain data for processing by a READ statement are called **data cards.**

The placement of data on a punched card does not follow the rules specified for placing a FORTRAN instruction on a punched card. *Data may be punched in columns 1 through 80.*

Data cards must physically follow the instruction cards which make up the entire FORTRAN program, since the instruction cards must be processed first by the card reader in order for the program to **compile.** If the program compiles without errors, then the computer begins **executing** or "running" the program; that is, it carries out your executable instructions in the same sequence given by the cards. *Each time the computer executes a READ statement, a new data card is processed.*

Unformatted I/O. For the program in Figure 3.3a, the unformatted READ statement contains a list of two variables: ID and CREDIT; hence, the single data card contains the two items 7581 and 15., separated by a comma. If the single READ statement were to be replaced by the statements

```
READ(5,*) ID
READ(5,*) CREDIT
```

then two data cards would be required: one with the number 7581 and another with the number 15.

Formatted I/O. In the program with FORMAT statements, the two data items for ID and CREDIT must appear on one data card according to the layout indicated by the FORMAT numbered 15. Thus the I6 specification for the integer variable ID requires that the data item 7581 be placed right-justified in the first six columns (columns 3 through 6) of the data card; the F7.0 specification for the real variable CREDIT requires that the data item 15. be placed *anywhere* in the *next* seven columns of the same data card (columns 7 through 13). If the following READ/FORMAT statements had been used

```
    READ(5,15) ID
15 FORMAT(I6)
    READ(5,20) CREDIT
20 FORMAT(F7.0)
```

then two data cards would be required: one with the number 7581 in columns 3 through 6 and another with the number 15. anywhere in columns 1 through 7.

The general setup for a card deck is depicted by Figure 3.4. Once again, however, we remind you that the nature and placement of control cards is specific to each system.

Process of Running the Program

Figure 3.5 describes the process of running a FORTRAN program in a batch environment. Figure 3.6 illustrates **computer printouts** when the card decks of Figure 3.3 are submitted to an IBM 370/155 computer. In this case, the WATFIV compiler was used.

In general, computer printouts have three distinct segments, assuming errors are absent:

1. Technical matter
2. Listing
3. Output

FIGURE 3.4   *Card Deck for Running a Batch Program*

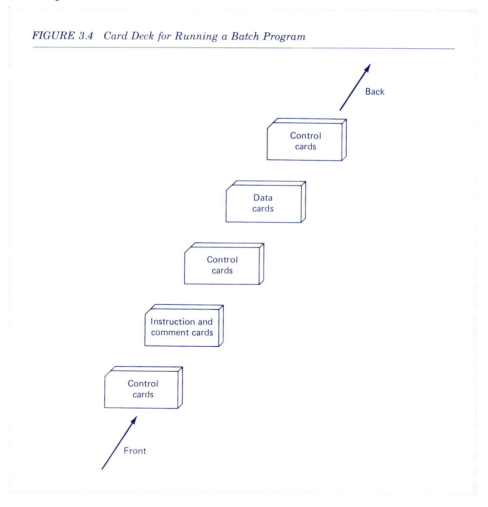

FIGURE 3.5   *Process of Running a FORTRAN Program in a Batch Environment*

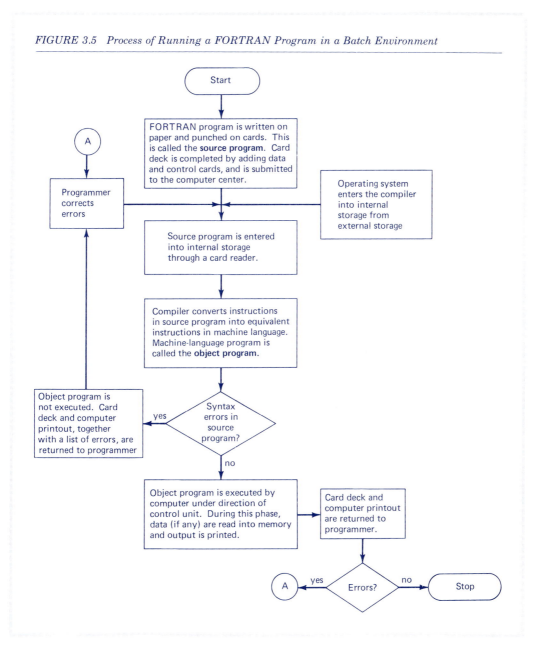

Technical matter includes the technical information on control cards and other information, such as amount of memory and CPU time which has been utilized. For example, the unformatted program in Figure 3.6a used 312 characters ("bytes") of internal storage and 0.10 second of CPU time; the formatted program in Figure 3.6b used 376 characters of internal storage and 0.13 second of CPU time. The **listing** is a printed copy of the FORTRAN program. This is simply a convenience which is especially useful when you are debugging or modifying a program. The **output** is printed matter based on the execution of WRITE statements in the program. In this example, the output is simply the ID number (7581) and the balance due ($1750.00).

Finally, note that the input data which are punched on data cards do not directly appear anywhere on the computer printout. These data can be printed out only through the use of WRITE statements, which is what we did with ID.

FIGURE 3.6a   *Computer Printout for Card Deck of Figure 3.3, Unformatted Version*

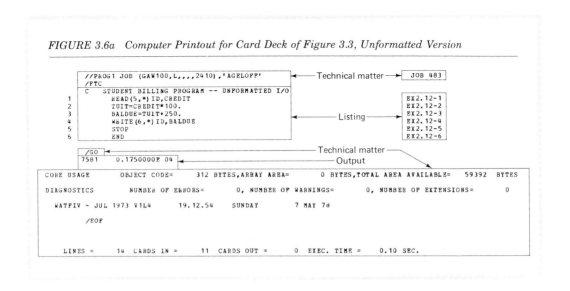

FIGURE 3.6b   *Computer Printout for Card Deck of Figure 3.3, Formatted Version*

Follow-up Exercise

1. For your particular batch system, prepare and submit a card deck for the following:
   a. The program in Figure 3.3. Use 543 for ID and 18. for CREDIT. Confirm that your output is correct by hand calculation. Repeat for an ID number of 70105 and 12 credits. Include four new comment cards immediately following the existing comment card. These comment cards define the variables ID, CREDIT, TUIT, and BALDUE.
   b. The program in Example 2.14. Use 1000. for P, 0.015 for R, and 4 for N. Confirm that your output is correct by hand calculation. Repeat for the same P and R but change N to 20. Include five comment cards at the beginning of the program. The first identifies the program as a BANK SAVINGS PRO-GRAM and the next four define the variables P, R, N, and A.

3.2
RUNNING A FORTRAN PROGRAM IN A TIME-SHARING ENVIRONMENT

FORTRAN programs which are run in a time-sharing environment are similar to those which are run in a batch environment. You should, however, be aware of some differences:

In time sharing you enter your program via a terminal, whereas in batch you enter the program using punched cards.

In time sharing the output comes back to you at the terminal; in batch your output is visually produced on a line printer.

In time sharing the time between submitting a program and receiving the results is almost instantaneous; in batch this "turnaround time" could run anywhere from a few seconds (if remote job entry is used) to hours.

System Commands

In time sharing you communicate with the computer by entering your program at a terminal, through which information is transmitted over either a phone line or a cable to the computer. To interact with the operating system when you are at the terminal requires the use of a set of commands called **system commands.**[1] Among other things, system commands allow you to run the program, list the program, and save the program for future recall. Therefore, when you run programs in a time-sharing environment, you will have a set of system commands to learn in addition to the FORTRAN instructions.

Unfortunately, system commands are not universal, which means that they differ from one time-sharing system to another. *Your instructor, therefore, must provide you the system commands which are specific to your system.*

---

[1] These commands are the time-sharing counterpart of the control language on control cards in a batch system.

Work Area versus Secondary Storage Area

The first step in using a time-sharing system is "signing-on." This means that you must type your assigned identification (user) code which is then validated by the operating system. If your identification code is acceptable, then the operating system assigns you a portion of memory which we call the **work area.** In fact, each user currently utilizing the time-sharing system is assigned a separate work area. The purpose of the work area is to store both FORTRAN instructions and values for variable names.

Once you "sign-off" a time-sharing system, the program in your work area is "erased." For this reason, each user of a time-sharing system also has an assigned **secondary storage area** (usually magnetic disk) which is often called a **library.** The secondary storage area allows you to save programs that you prepare in your work area for recall at a later date. In other words, your library saves you the trouble of having to retype programs that you previously entered into your work area.

In addition to storing programs, libraries also store data that can be used as input to programs. A set of data stored in this manner is called a **data file.** The creation and processing of data files is different for each time-sharing system, so we omit the topic in this book. Its use, however, is quite important. Ask your instructor if data files will be used in your course.

Illustration

In this section we illustrate a time-sharing run on IBM's CALL-OS system. The program used is Example 2.14. In what follows below, boxed segments indicate the computer run and marginal notes describe the corresponding boxed segment. To clearly point out the interactions between the user and the computer, all information typed by the computer is underlined; information typed by the user is not underlined.

ON AT 13:16 USER NUMBER,PASSWORD--GAR101,MO READY	Entry of identification code for signing-on. *Note:* Each time you finish typing, you must depress the carriage return key on the terminal.
ENTER FORTRAN READY	System command for using FORTRAN compiler.
10 READ(5,*) P,R,N 20 A = P*(1. + R)**N 30 WRITE(6,*) P,R,N,A 40 STOP 50 END	Entering program into work area.
NAME EX214 READY	System command for naming program as EX214.

RUN	System command which first compiles and then executes the program.
?1000.,.015,4	Computer executes READ statement, and stores 1000. for P, .015 for R, and 4 for N.
1000. 0.150000E-01 4 1061.36	Output of P,R,N,A. Note use of E-notation.
STOP CPU TIME 0.07 SECS.	End of execution and amount of utilized CPU time.
SAVE READY	System command for electronic transfer of program from work area to library.
CLEAR READY	System command for erasing program from work area. (Program is still in your library.)
RUN NO PROGRAM PRESENT	Confirmation that program is no longer in work area.
LOAD EX214 READY	System command for electronic transfer of program from library to work area.
LIST	System command to list program in work area.
10 READ(5,*) P,R,N 20 A = P*(1. + R)**N 30 WRITE(6,*) P,R,N,A 40 STOP 50 END	Listing of program in work area. Programs need not be listed to be run.
RUN ?1000.,.015,20	
1000. 0.150000E-01 20 1346.82 STOP CPU TIME 0.07 SECS.	Rerun of program for each new set of data input. Program takes 0.07 second to compile and execute.
OFF	System command for signing-off.
OFF AT 13:22 CPU TIME... 0 SEC. CONNECT TIME... 6 MIN.	Time of day, total CPU time for entire session, and total time terminal was "connected" to computer system.

Line Numbers.   Note that, as the FORTRAN program is entered on the terminal, each instruction is preceded by a **line number.** These numbers, which typically run from one to five digits in length, are used to sequence time-shared programs. After a program is entered and before it is executed, the operating system rearranges the instructions in the work area from lowest to highest number. In other words, the instructions can be entered "out of order," but the computer executes in the desired sequence according to the line numbers. This feature makes it convenient to insert instructions into an existing program. For example, suppose we inadvertently omit the WRITE statement in the above illustration and realize this once the END statement has been typed. We can simply "insert" the WRITE statement by typing it after the END statement and giving it a line number which numerically falls between the line numbers of the assignment statement and the STOP statement (between 20 and 40). Also note that we have incremented line numbers by 10, that is, each line number changes by 10. This allows room to insert new instructions at a future point in time, should it be necessary to do so. Finally, a minimum of one blank space must separate your instruction from your line number.

Other System Commands.   The system commands which we have illustrated represent a small subset of the some 40 commands available for a typical system. For example, powerful commands exist for making either editorial or debugging changes which are far superior to the process of making changes in a batch environment. Also, please note that, unless the time-sharing system you are about to use is a CALL-OS system, the system commands for your system will differ from those described here. Your instructor will provide you with the details.

Compilation versus Execution.   As you know from Chapter 1, a high-level language such as FORTRAN first must be translated or compiled into the machine language of the computer. This process is known as **compilation.** If rules of the FORTRAN language have not been violated, then the operating system instructs the control unit of the computer to execute or "run" the program. **Execution** means that the computer carries out your executable instructions in the sequence indicated by your line numbers.

Data Input.   Did you notice the method of data input that we used? When the control unit executes the READ statement, a question mark (?) is printed at the terminal. At this point we can enter the appropriate data corresponding to the variable list in the READ statement. The unformatted READ statement in line 10 contains a list of three variables: P, R, and N; hence, following the question mark, we type the three corresponding data items given by 1000., .015, 4. After typing the last data item, we depress the carriage return key on the terminal. This act completes the execution of the READ statement, which results in the storage of 1000. for P, .015 for R, and 4 for N.

Each time the computer executes a READ statement, a new data line is requested (a new question mark is printed in our case). For example, if the single READ statement were to be replaced by the statements

    READ(5,*) P
    READ(5,*) R
    READ(5,*) N

then data input would appear as follows:

    ? 1000.
    ? .015
    ? 4

Other methods of data input exist, depending on the system. Again, your instructor will provide the details.

Blank Spaces.   The compiler ignores blank spaces within FORTRAN instructions, with one exception which we discuss in Chapter 5. For example, you need not be concerned about the number of blank spaces: between P, R, N in the READ list or P, R, N, A in the WRITE list; around equal signs (=) and operation symbols in assignment statements; and around and between the enclosed parentheses in READ and WRITE statements. Use blank spaces simply to improve readability. It's even permissible to embed blank spaces within key words, such as WRI TE, but we don't recommend it since it detracts from readability.

Comment Lines.   Suppose we insert the following line just before the READ statement in our time-shared program:

    05   "   BANK SAVINGS PROGRAM

This is known as a **comment line.** In this case it documents the name of the program within the program itself. Comment lines are for "human consumption," which means that they are meant for human eyes to describe programs, identify sections of programs, explain logic, and define variables. In fact, the entire description under Step I in the four-step procedure is best represented by comment lines at the beginning of a program. Comment lines are ignored by the compiler; they are simply listed along with the program. How does the compiler distinguish a comment line from a FORTRAN instruction? In the above case, the quotation marks (") two spaces over from the line number identify this line as a comment line. *The method of identifying comment lines, however, differs from system to system.* Ask your instructor how comment lines are specified on your time-sharing system.

Continuation Lines. Occasionally, a FORTRAN instruction will be too long to fit on one line, which means that it must be continued on the next line. The method of accomplishing this differs from one system to another, so ask your instructor.

Follow-up Exercises

2. Answer the following based on the illustration above.
   a. How much money do we end up with after four quarters when we start with $1000 and earn interest at 6 percent per year compounded quarterly?
   b. After five years?
3. For your particular time-sharing system, run the following:
   a. The program of Example 2.12 on page 48. Use 543 for ID and 18. for CREDIT. Confirm that your output is correct by hand calculation. Repeat for an ID of 70105 and 12 credits. Include five comment lines at the beginning of the program. The first comment line states STUDENT BILLING PROGRAM. The next four comment lines define the variables ID, CREDIT, TUIT, and BALDUE. List your program.
   b. The program in our illustration above. Use 1000. for P and .015 for R, but successively change N as follows: 4, 8, 12, 16, 20, 40. Include four new comment lines following the existing comment line. These should define the variables P, R, N, and A. List your program.

3.3
DEBUGGING PROGRAMS

Debugging is the process of detecting and correcting errors. Much of your time, in fact, will be spent on this process. To help you along, we now define general types of errors, illustrate each in both batch and time-sharing environments, and indicate how you go about debugging such errors.

Error Detection and Correction

Any programming error can be classified into one of the following three categories:

1. Syntax error
2. Execution error
3. Logic error

A **syntax error** occurs when a FORTRAN instruction violates a rule of the FORTRAN language. When you make this type of error, your program will fail to run, and the compiler will identify the incorrect instruction by an appropriate diagnostic message. Thus syntax errors are detected by the compiler during the compilation of the program. If a syntax error is found, then it follows that the program never enters the execution phase.

Common syntax errors at this point in your programming development include the following:

1. Typing error, as when STOP is typed as STAP.
2. Variable name which exceeds the allowable number of characters (six for ANSI FORTRAN standards). *Note:* A separate error message will be printed for each statement which contains this variable name.
3. Imbalance between the number of left parentheses and the number of right parentheses in an arithmetic expression.
4. Missing equal sign (=) in an assignment statement.
5. Arithmetic expression to the left of the equal sign in an assignment statement.
6. For those of you using punched cards, a violation of the rules for placing a statement on a card, as when the key word END is punched within the first six columns of a card.
7. For those of you using FORMATs, a mismatch between the statement number indicated in the READ or WRITE statement and the statement number labeling the FORMAT statement. For example,

```
    WRITE(6,10) A
 15 FORMAT(1X,F8.0)
```

would result in an "unreferenced statement number" or "missing format statement" error message, since the FORMAT labeled 10 is not found.

Once you determine the exact nature of your syntax error (with the help of the error messages), you simply replace the incorrect instruction with a syntactically correct instruction.

Your program begins executing only after it is free of syntax errors. Unfortunately, a second type of error can occur after the compilation phase: An **execution error** is one that takes place during the execution of your program. Typically, when an execution error is encountered, an error message or code is printed and the computer terminates execution. Common execution errors include the following:

1. Wrong I/O device number in READ and WRITE statements
2. Incorrect data input, as when a letter is typed for numeric data input

3. End-of-file condition, as when the computer attempts to execute a READ statement and a data item is not provided
4. Improper numeric condition during the evaluation of an arithmetic expression; for example, you might attempt to divide by a variable which has zero in its storage location, or you might attempt to raise a negative real number to a power

Generally, it is more difficult to determine the exact location and nature of an execution error than of a syntax error, for several reasons: execution errors tend to be system-dependent; execution error messages may be more ambiguous than syntax error messages in locating and diagnosing errors; the cause of an execution error may be due to faulty program logic, which is related to the third category of errors.

If your program runs but gives you unexpected, unwanted, or erroneous output, then you may assume that a **logic error** exists. Common logic errors include the following:

1. No output. Did you forget to include WRITE statements?
2. Wrong numeric results.
   a. Are the input data correct?
   b. Are the arithmetic expressions and assignment statements correct? In particular, check the sequence of arithmetic calculations within arithmetic expressions.
   c. Is the program logic correct? For example, are the statements in proper sequence?
   d. Have any statements been omitted?
3. Incorrect I/O formats. If you're using FORMAT statements, then you're open to a multitude of errors. We discuss these in detail in Chapters 5 and 6.

Here is some emphatic advice: *Just because your program runs (that is, you get results) does not mean your program is correct—check your results for logic errors against a set of known results.* We cannot overemphasize the importance of this advice. In Step IV of the four-step procedure, *always* test your program under varying conditions using a set of test data for which you already know the correct results.

In your efforts to debug execution and logic errors, you might try the following **classic debugging techniques:**

1. **Roleplaying the computer.** Pretend that you're the computer and begin "executing" your program line by line. As you do this, enter data into boxes

that represent storage locations. You will be surprised at how many errors you can find this way. Really. You should do this with every program you write.

2. **Mirror or echo printing.** To check your data input for errors, place a WRITE statement immediately after each READ statement. The paired READ and WRITE statements must have identical variable lists. Once you have confirmed that the input data are correct, remove these WRITE statements.

3. **Diagnostic WRITE (trace) statements.** Place temporary WRITE statements at strategic points in your program. These should print the values of important variables as the calculating sequence evolves. In other words, these WRITE statements provide you intermediate results which may be helpful in tracing what, where, and when something went wrong. When the error is corrected, remove these WRITE statements.

4. **Programming technique.** You will avoid many errors if you carefully develop the first three steps of our four-step procedure. Get in the habit now.

5. **Experience.** Learn by your mistakes. Experience is a classic teacher.

6. **Attitude.** Debugging can be fun. Finding errors and correcting them can be a very satisfying experience. Perhaps you will become the greatest debugging sleuth in computer history.

Batch Environment

Figure 3.7 shows listings for versions of the student billing program which purposely incorporate syntax, execution, and logic errors. The syntax error messages are those given by the WATFIV compiler.[2]

Unformatted Version, Figure 3.7a. The compiler has printed several syntax warnings and error messages. Note that each message is printed immediately following the incorrect line of instruction.

Line 1.   READ misspelled as REED.
Line 2.   No syntax error.
Line 3.   Arithmetic expression to the left of the equal sign.
Line 4.   No syntax error.
Line 5.   No syntax error.
Line 6.   END was punched in columns 1–3 instead of columns 7–9. Note

---

[2] It's also possible to make an error in preparing your control cards, in which case your program will not be executed. **Control card errors** are specific to the system you're using, so carefully review the instructions you received for preparing control cards.

FIGURE 3.7a *Illustration of Syntax Errors, Unformatted Version*

```
        //PROG1 JOB (GAW100,L,,,,2410),'AGELOFF'                         JOB 481
        /FTC
        C STUDENT BILLING PROGRAM -- UNFORMATTED I/O
    1           REED(5,*)ID,CREDIT
***ERROR***  UNDECODEABLE STATEMENT
    2           BALDUE = TUIT - 250.
    3           CREDIT * 100. = TUIT
***ERROR***  ILLEGAL QUANTITY ON LEFT OF EQUALS SIGN
    4           WRITE(6,*) ID,BALDUE
    5           STOP
    6     END
**WARNING**  BLANK CARD ENCOUNTERED
***ERROR***  INVALID CHARACTERS IN COL 1-5. STATEMENT NUMBER IGNORED.PROBABLE CAUSE:STATEMENT PUNCHED
             TO LEFT OF COLUMN 7
**WARNING**  MISSING END STATEMENT;END STATEMENT GENERATED

        /GO

CORE USAGE        OBJECT CODE=    280 BYTES,ARRAY AREA=      0 BYTES,TOTAL AREA AVAILABLE=   59392 BYTES

DIAGNOSTICS       NUMBER OF ERRORS=      3, NUMBER OF WARNINGS=      2, NUMBER OF EXTENSIONS=        0

   WATFIV - JUL 1973 V1L4      19.12.53     SUNDAY       7 MAY 78

        /EOF


   LINES =    18  CARDS IN =    11  CARDS OUT =     0  EXEC. TIME =    0.15 SEC.
```

FIGURE 3.7b *Illustration of Syntax Errors, Formatted Version*

```
        //PROG1 JOB (GAW100,L,,,,2410),'AGELOFF'                         JOB 477
        /FTC
        C STUDENT BILLING PROGRAM -- FORMATTED I/O
    1           READ(5,15) ID,CREDIT
    2        15 FORMATNI6,F7.0E
***ERROR***  INVALID ELEMENT IN INPUT LIST OR DATA LIST
***ERROR***  UNDECODEABLE STATEMENT
    3           BALDUE=TUIT - 250.
    4           CREDIT * 100. = TUIT
***ERROR***  ILLEGAL QUANTITY ON LEFT OF EQUALS SIGN
    5           WRITE(6,30), ID,BALDUE
    6        25 FORMAT(1X,I6,F9.2)
    7           STOP
    8     END
**WARNING**  BLANK CARD ENCOUNTERED
***ERROR***  INVALID CHARACTERS IN COL 1-5. STATEMENT NUMBER IGNORED.PROBABLE CAUSE:STATEMENT PUNCHED
             TO LEFT OF COLUMN 7
**WARNING**  MISSING END STATEMENT; END STATEMENT GENERATED
***ERROR***  MISSING FORMAT STATEMENT     30 USED IN LINE      5
**WARNING**  FORMAT STATEMENT     25 IS UNREFERENCED

        /GO

CORE USAGE        OBJECT CODE=    352 BYTES,ARRAY AREA=      0 BYTES,TOTAL AREA AVAILABLE=   59392 BYTES

DIAGNOSTICS       NUMBER OF ERRORS=      5, NUMBER OF WARNINGS=      3, NUMBER OF EXTENSIONS=        0

   WATFIV - JUL 1973 V1L4      19.12.47     SUNDAY       7 MAY 78

        /EOF


   LINES =    23  CARDS IN =    13  CARDS OUT =     0  EXEC. TIME =    0.14 SEC.
```

the warning message which is given: since an END statement was not detected, the WATFIV compiler automatically inserts the END statement.

Formatted Version, Figure 3.7b.   The compiler has printed several syntax warnings and error messages. Most of the messages are printed immediately following the incorrect line of instruction. Some, however, refer to "labeling" errors (missing statement numbers), and are printed at the end of the program listing.

Line 1.   No syntax error.
Line 2.   Parentheses in FORMAT statement mistyped. We forgot to depress the shift key on the keyboard.
Line 3.   No syntax error.
Line 4.   Arithmetic expression to the left of the equal sign.
Line 5.   Missing FORMAT statement number 30. The 30 in the WRITE should be changed to 25 or the 25 in line 7 should be changed to 30. (Note the error messages at the end of the program.)
Line 6.   No syntax error; however, statement number 25 is unreferenced, as indicated by the warning message at the end.
Line 7.   No syntax error.
Line 8.   END was punched in columns 1–3 instead of columns 7–9. Note the warning message and the automatic insertion of the END statement by the WATFIV compiler.

The above syntax errors were corrected by repunching a new card for each statement in error and then resubmitting the job. This time the program compiled without syntax errors; however, an execution error was encountered, as illustrated in Figure 3.8. This error occurred because the FORTRAN instructions for the computation of balance due and tuition were placed in the wrong sequence. The assignment statement for BALDUE could not be executed because at this point nothing had been placed in the storage location named TUIT.[3] To correct this error we reversed the order of the two cards and resubmitted the job.

Figure 3.9 illustrates a run with no syntax or execution errors, but with two logic errors. Note that the output for BALDUE is $950, instead of the expected $1750. The first logic error is easily uncovered by the echo print for ID and CREDIT. It appears that the value for ID (7581) was input properly, but 12. instead of 15. was input for CREDIT, which is readily confirmed by examining the data card. The second logic error is identified by noting that the fee of $250 was subtracted rather than added to TUIT in the assignment statement for BALDUE. Correcting these two errors and removing the echo print results in the run illustrated by Figure 3.6.

---

[3] Some compilers initially store zero in all variables. Thus, this error would be a logic error rather than an execution error.

FIGURE 3.8a   Illustration of Execution Error, Unformatted Version

```
        //PROG1 JOB (GAW100,L,,,,2410),'AGELOFF'                          JOB 480
        /FTC
        C STUDENT BILLING PROGRAM -- UNFORMATTED I/O
   1         READ(5,*)ID,CREDIT
   2         BALDUE = TUIT - 250.
   3         TUIT=CREDIT * 100.
   4         WRITE(6,*) ID,BALDUE
   5         STOP
   6         END

        /GO
***ERROR*** VALUE OF TUIT   IS UNDEFINED

        PROGRAM WAS EXECUTING LINE    2 IN ROUTINE M/PROG WHEN TERMINATION OCCURRED

CORE USAGE        OBJECT CODE=    312 BYTES,ARRAY AREA=      0 BYTES,TOTAL AREA AVAILABLE=   59392  BYTES

DIAGNOSTICS      NUMBER OF ERRORS=     1, NUMBER OF WARNINGS=     0, NUMBER OF EXTENSIONS=        0

  WATFIV - JUL 1973 V1L4    19.12.52    SUNDAY      7 MAY 78

        /EOF


  LINES =    15 CARDS IN =    11 CARDS OUT =    0  EXEC. TIME =   0.14 SEC.
```

FIGURE 3.8b   Illustration of Execution Error, Formatted Version

```
        //PROG1 JOB (GAW100,L,,,,2410),'AGELOFF'                          JOB 479
        /FTC
        C STUDENT BILLING PROGRAM -- FORMATTED I/O
   1         READ(5,15) ID,CREDIT
   2      15 FORMAT(I6,F7.0)
   3         BALDUE = TUIT - 250.
   4         TUIT=CREDIT * 100.
   5         WRITE(6,30) ID,BALDUE
   6      30 FORMAT(1X,I6,F9.2)
   7         STOP
   8         END

        /GO
***ERROR*** VALUE OF TUIT   IS UNDEFINED

        PROGRAM WAS EXECUTING LINE    3 IN ROUTINE M/PROG WHEN TERMINATION OCCURRED

CORE USAGE        OBJECT CODE=    376 BYTES,ARRAY AREA=      0 BYTES,TOTAL AREA AVAILABLE=   59392  BYTES

DIAGNOSTICS      NUMBER OF ERRORS=     1, NUMBER OF WARNINGS=     0, NUMBER OF EXTENSIONS=        0

  WATFIV - JUL 1973 V1L4    19.12.49    SUNDAY      7 MAY 78

        /EOF


  LINES =    17 CARDS IN =    13 CARDS OUT =    0  EXEC. TIME =   0.11 SEC.
```

FIGURE 3.9a   *Illustration of Logic Errors, Unformatted Version*

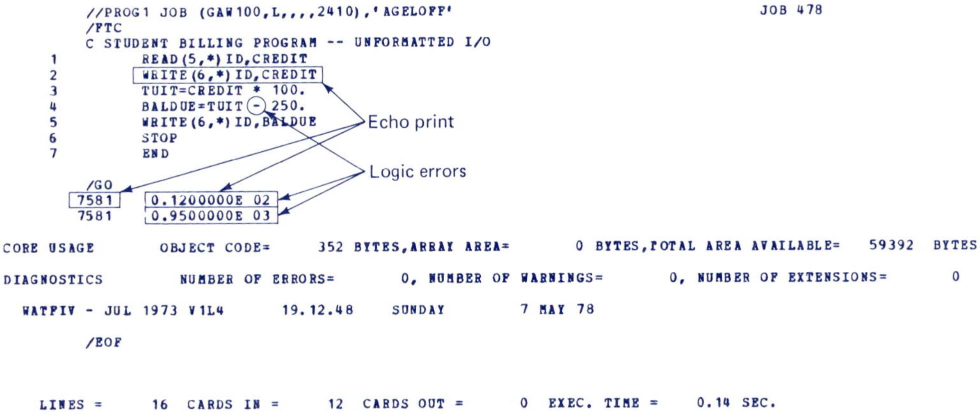

```
        //PROG1 JOB  (GAW100,L,,,,2410),'AGELOFF'                          JOB 478
        /FTC
        C STUDENT BILLING PROGRAM -- UNFORMATTED I/O
    1         READ(5,*) ID,CREDIT
    2         WRITE(6,*) ID,CREDIT
    3         TUIT=CREDIT * 100.
    4         BALDUE=TUIT - 250.
    5         WRITE(6,*) ID,BALDUE        Echo print
    6         STOP
    7         END
        /GO                              Logic errors
        7581    0.1200000E 02
        7581    0.9500000E 03

CORE USAGE       OBJECT CODE=    352 BYTES,ARRAY AREA=     0 BYTES,TOTAL AREA AVAILABLE=   59392  BYTES

DIAGNOSTICS         NUMBER OF ERRORS=       0, NUMBER OF WARNINGS=       0, NUMBER OF EXTENSIONS=      0

   WATFIV - JUL 1973 V1L4       19.12.48    SUNDAY       7 MAY 78

        /EOF


    LINES =     16  CARDS IN =     12  CARDS OUT =     0  EXEC. TIME =    0.14 SEC.
```

FIGURE 3.9b   *Illustration of Logic Errors, Formatted Version*

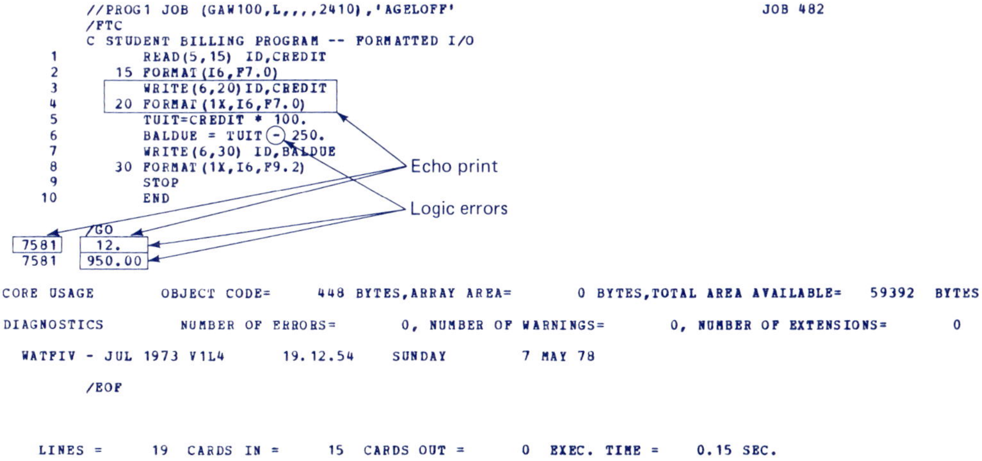

```
        //PROG1 JOB  (GAW100,L,,,,2410),'AGELOFF'                          JOB 482
        /FTC
        C STUDENT BILLING PROGRAM -- FORMATTED I/O
    1         READ(5,15) ID,CREDIT
    2      15 FORMAT(I6,F7.0)
    3         WRITE(6,20) ID,CREDIT
    4      20 FORMAT(1X,I6,F7.0)
    5         TUIT=CREDIT * 100.
    6         BALDUE = TUIT - 250.
    7         WRITE(6,30) ID,BALDUE
    8      30 FORMAT(1X,I6,F9.2)          Echo print
    9         STOP
   10         END
                                         Logic errors
        /GO
    7581    12.
    7581    950.00

CORE USAGE       OBJECT CODE=    448 BYTES,ARRAY AREA=     0 BYTES,TOTAL AREA AVAILABLE=   59392  BYTES

DIAGNOSTICS         NUMBER OF ERRORS=       0, NUMBER OF WARNINGS=       0, NUMBER OF EXTENSIONS=      0

   WATFIV - JUL 1973 V1L4       19.12.54    SUNDAY       7 MAY 78

        /EOF


    LINES =     19  CARDS IN =     15  CARDS OUT =     0  EXEC. TIME =    0.15 SEC.
```

Time-Sharing Environment

In this section we run the savings account program once more, with the exceptions that syntax, execution, and logic errors are purposely included.

ON AT 13:24

USER NUMBER, PASSWORD--GAR101,MO
READY

ENTER FORTRAN
READY

As before.

10 READ(5,*) PRINCIPAL,R,N
20 A = PRINCIPAL + (1. + R)**N
30 WRITE(5,*) PRINCIPAL,R,N,A
40 STOP
50 END

Entry of program with syntax errors in lines 10, 20, and 30; execution error in line 30; and logic error in line 20.

RUN

LINE 10 SYNTAX ERROR
LINE 20 SYNTAX ERROR
LINE 30 SYNTAX ERROR
SEVERE ERRORS EXECUTION INHIBITED

CPU TIME   0.05 SECS.

Execution aborted and lines with syntax errors identified. Programmer realizes that PRINCIPAL exceeds six characters. Note that this single error in naming a variable caused an error message for each line containing this variable.

10 READ(5,*) P,R,N
20 A = P + (1. + R)**N
30 WRITE(5,*) P,R,N,A

Syntax errors corrected by retyping incorrect lines. The new lines replace the old lines in the work area.

RUN

? 1000.,.015,4

LINE 30 INVALID UNIT NUMBER IN I/O STATEMENT

CPU TIME   0.05 SECS.

No syntax errors exist; however, execution error occurred because incorrect output unit number was used in WRITE statement. Computer attempts to execute line 30 but cannot.

30 WRITE(6,*) P,R,N,A

Correction of execution error; new line 30 replaces old line 30 in work area.

```
RUN

? 1000.,.015,4


1000.    0.150000E-01   4   1001.06


STOP

CPU TIME   0.07 SECS.
```

Calculated by hand, the answer for A is $1061.36. The computer, however, prints $1001.06. Since data input is correct, it follows that a logic error must exist within the program.

```
20 A = P*(1. + R)**N
```

Correction of logic error; new line 20 replaces old line 20 in work area.

```
LIST

10 READ(5,*) P,R,N
20 A = P*(1. + R)**N
30 WRITE(6,*) P,R,N,A
40 STOP
50 END
```

Confirmation that program stands corrected.

```
RUN

?1000.,.015,4


1000.    0.150000E-01    4   1061.36


STOP

CPU TIME   0.07 SECS.
```

Correct answer as before.

Note that the compiler will identify syntax errors and the operating system will print execution error messages, but you must identify any logic errors by checking the correctness of the output. In this case, all errors are corrected by simply retyping the entire lines of instruction. All time-sharing systems, however, include specific system commands which greatly facilitate the process of editing programs. Ask your instructor about your system.

One final note: *Anytime you replace an old line with a new line, the replacement is made in the work area, not in you library.* So if you wish to use your corrected program at a later date, you must type the system command that stores the program in your library.

Additional Exercises

4. Define or explain each of the following terms associated with batch environments:

punched card   computer printout
keypunch machine   listing

instruction cards

comment cards

control cards

data cards

card deck

source program

object program

rules for placing instructions,
data, and comments
on punched cards

5. Define or explain each of the following terms associated with time-sharing environments:

system commands

work area

secondary storage area

library

data file

line numbers

comment line

continuation line

6. Define or explain each of the following terms:

execution

compilation

use of the blank character

debugging

syntax error

execution error

logic error

roleplaying the computer

mirror printing

echo printing

diagnostic WRITE

trace statement

7. **Debugging Problem.** Run the program below on your system *exactly* as shown. On the first run let the compiler identify syntax errors and then make the necessary corrections. On the second run let the operating system identify execution errors and then make the necessary corrections. Finish with an error-free run. Use the following data input: First try 4.2 for X and 0. for Y; next try −4.2 for X and 0.1 for Y; finally, try 4.2 for X and 0.1 for Y.

PROGRAM WHICH ADDS, SUBTRACTS, MULTIPLIES, DIVIDES, AND EXPONEN-TIATES TWO NUMBERS

```
    READ(8,*) X,Y
    SUMMATION = X + Y
    SUB = X − Y
    X*Y = MULT
    DIV + X/Y
    EXP = X**Y
    WRITE(10,*) SUMMATION,SUB,MULT,DIV,EXP
    STEP
```

Those of you using FORMATs should replace the READ statement with

```
    READ(8,35) X,Y
35 FORMAT(I5,I5)
```

and the WRITE statement with

```
    WRITE(10,55) SUMMATION,SUB,MULT,DIV,EXP
75 FORMAT 1X,F10.2,F10.2,F10.2,F10.2,F10.2)
```

8. **Temperature Conversion.** Run the program of Exercise 28 in Chapter 2. Determine the degree Celsius equivalents of −10, 0, 32, and 80 degrees Fahrenheit.

9. **Marketing Problem.** Run the program of Exercise 29 in Chapter 2. What is the total cost of 500 thousand container tops, where each top has a radius of 5 inches and costs

$.02 per square inch? What if the cost is $.005 per square inch, all other things being the same?

10. **Manufacturing Problem.** Run the program of Exercise 30 in Chapter 2. How many units should be produced to maximize profit? *Hint:* Try input values of 1, 2, 3, . . . , 10 for UNITS.

11. **Blood-Bank Inventory Problem.** Run the program of Exercise 31 in Chapter 2. How many units of blood should be ordered if it costs $50 to place an order, weekly demand averages 3000 pints, and it costs $.20 per week per pint of blood to refrigerate? How much should be ordered if the refrigeration cost increases to $.30? What is the expected cost per week for each of the above?

12. **Forecasting Population Growth.** Run the program of Exercise 32 in Chapter 2. Predict the earth's population in the year 2000. The population in 1976 was approximately 4 billion.

    a. Assume a birth rate of 0.025 (2.5 percent) per year and a death rate of 0.009 (0.9 percent), both of which are expected to remain constant until the year 2000.

    b. How would your prediction change if the birth rate fell to 0.02? *Suggestion:* Input the 1976 population as a real constant having one digit (that is, as 4.). Why did we make this suggestion?

    c. How many years before the earth's population doubles? Use the birth and death rates given in part a. *Hint:* Try different input values for N and observe the output values for P.

13. **Depreciation Problem.** Run the program of Exercise 33 in Chapter 2. A small business firm has just purchased a car costing $4200. The owners intend to "run the car into the ground" in 4 years, at which time they will be happy to get $200 salvage for the car. How much depreciation is allowed in the first year under the straight-line method? The double-declining balance method? What happens to the amount of depreciation if the life of the asset were 2 years?   8 years?

CHAPTER 4

Introduction to Control Statements

The computer programs up to now have been simple in the sense that the computer executed the instructions sequentially from the first instruction to the last, and then the computer stopped. As you know by now, this "single pass" through the program forces you to run the program separately each time you have new data. The statements in this chapter will allow you to control the flow of execution within the program. These so-called **control statements** not only permit "multiple passes" for processing new data but also greatly improve your ability to solve intricate problems.

4.1 LOOPS USING THE GO TO STATEMENT

The computer can repeat a group of instructions over and over again within a program, without submitting the program each time you have new data. This ability to repeat a series of instructions is called **looping.**

By using looping techniques, you can modify the tuition and fee program written in Chapter 2 to process the bill for all students at State College. Since the same logic for computing the student bill applies to all students, the set of instructions

1. Read ID number and number of credits
2. Compute tuition charge
3. Compute balance due
4. Output ID number and balance due

can be repeated as many times as there are students.

To help you visualize the loop concept look at Figure 4.1, which shows the flowchart for calculating the amount due from each student at State College. Notice that, unlike previous flowcharts, the control of execution is altered by returning to statements which previously had been executed. Before you can incorporate this feature in your programs, however, you need to master two new concepts: statement numbers and the GO TO statement.

FIGURE 4.1   *Flowchart for Tuition Program with Loop*

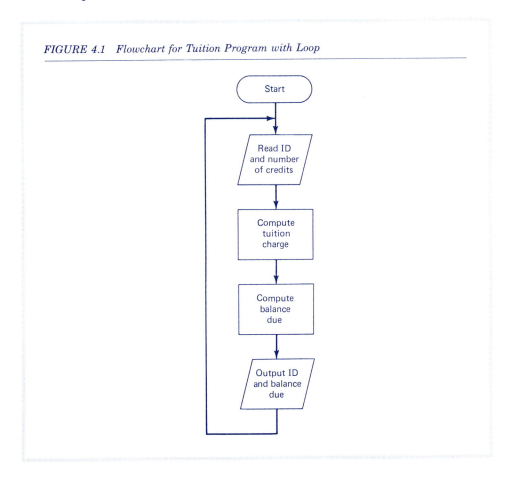

Statement Numbers

A **statement number** is an integer number from 1 to 5 digits long which is assigned to a FORTRAN instruction. For example, in the statement

```
10 READ(5,*) ID,CREDIT
```

the statement number is 10. In this chapter a statement number is used with an instruction that is to be executed outside the normal sequence. Just how this is accomplished will become clear in the next section. Statement numbers also are used for referencing statements associated with input and output, which we take up in the next chapter.

Notice that the statement number associated with a statement appears to the left of the statement. Those of you using cards for your programs can place the statement number anywhere in columns 1–5. Those of you using a time-sharing system must place the statement number between the line number and the instruction, with at least one space on each side of the statement number.[1]

Although you need not assign a statement number to *every* FORTRAN instruction (none of our earlier programs did), you will use several statement numbers in your future programs. One caution to remember here is: *Do not assign the same statement number to more than one FORTRAN instruction in the same program.* Otherwise, a "confused" compiler will send you a syntax error message.

GO TO Statement

The **GO TO statement** causes the computer to interrupt the normal sequential execution of a program and branch (jump or transfer control) to some other executable instruction in the program that is not the next instruction in the normal sequence. This process of breaking the sequential flow of a program is referred to as **branching** or **transfer of control.**

The basic form of the GO TO statement is

GO TO *statement number*

For example, when the statement

```
GO TO 20
```

is executed, transfer of control goes to the statement labeled with statement number 20; that is, the next statement executed is labeled 20.

How do you use the GO TO statement to construct a loop? The GO TO instruction transfers control to the first instruction of the group of instructions you want repeated, where the statement number is used to identify the first instruction of this group.

---

[1]Some time-sharing systems may not use line numbers; instead a statement number is assigned to each instruction.

EXAMPLE 4.1   Student Billing Program with Loop

Let's look at the tuition and fee program to see how the loop is built into the program.[2]

Program	Comments
10 READ(5,∗) ID,CREDIT	Line 1: The values for student ID number (ID) and the number of credits (CREDIT) are read into computer memory.
TUIT = CREDIT∗100. BALDUE = TUIT + 250. WRITE(6,∗) ID,BALDUE	Lines 2–4: *Statements "inside" the loop are indented to improve readability and identification of the loop*
GO TO 10 END	Line 5: Following execution of the GO TO statement, the program returns to statement number 10 (the READ instruction) and the computer again moves sequentially through the program.

Now consider a test run for three students based on the following data:

Student ID	Number of Credits	
101	15.0	First student data
102	12.0	Second student data
103	10.5	Third student data

The output from this program is

101	1750.
102	1450.
103	1300.

∗∗∗Out of data execution error condition∗∗∗

Follow-up Exercises

1. Suppose the GO TO statement in Example 4.1 were rewritten as GO TO 5. What other change would you have to make in the program?
2. Why didn't we insert the STOP statement in Example 4.1?
3. How does this program differ from the example? What would the output look like because of this logical error?

```
      READ(5,∗) ID,CREDIT
   10 TUIT = CREDIT∗100.
      BALDUE = TUIT + 250.
      WRITE(6,∗) ID,BALDUE
   GO TO 10
   END
```

---

[2]Those of you using input/output (I/O) with FORMATs need not be concerned about our use of unformatted I/O in this and other chapters, since our focus in this and other non-I/O chapters is on statements other than I/O statements. This approach has the advantage of simplifying the appearance of programs, thereby eliminating a source of distraction. Just pay attention to the list of variables in READ and WRITE statements.

4.2
LOOPS USING THE
LOGICAL IF STATEMENT

A weakness of constructing a loop by using a GO TO statement is that you have no way of telling the computer when to stop looping.

In the previous example, the computer continues to read in data, computes the amount due, and prints out the results as long as there are student data to process. When no more data are available, an "out of data execution error condition" occurs, which is a "messy" way to terminate a program. (In some systems the error condition occurs and no output may be printed.) We now avoid this shortcoming by introducing a new statement which allows us to construct loops by one of two methods: the counter method and the last-record-check method.

Logical IF Statement

The **logical IF statement** is a FORTRAN instruction that requires the computer to test a condition and then, based on one of two possible results, to take a proper transfer of control action.

The general form of this instruction is

IF (*relational expression***) executable statement**

The relational expression is used to construct the condition that you want tested. The result of this test is either "true" or "false." If the result is true, then the executable statement to the right of the parentheses is executed. If the result is false, however, then the next *executable* statement following the logical IF is executed. In general, the statement to the right of the parentheses can be any *executable* statement, except for another logical IF or a statement which we present later called a DO statement.

EXAMPLE 4.2

A salesperson earns a base salary of $150 plus a 2-percent commission on sales if weekly sales are above $5000; otherwise, no commission is added to the base salary. The statements

```
BASE = 150.
PAY = BASE
IF (SALES .GT. 5000.) PAY = BASE + .02*SALES
   :
   :
```

determine the appropriate pay. The salesperson's base salary of $150 is stored in a variable named BASE and the logical IF statement determines whether or not the salesperson receives the 2-percent commission.

The relational expression "SALES .GT. 5000." represents the condition "sales greater than $5000," where .GT. stands for "greater than." When executed, the logical IF statement tests this condition, giving one of two results: true or false. If in fact the value of SALES is greater than 5000., then the result of the test is true, and the statement

PAY = BASE + .02*SALES

is executed. *Following this execution, control drops to the first executable statement below the IF;* however, if the result of the test is false, then the statement to the right of the parentheses is skipped and control immediately goes to the first executable statement below the IF.

Every **relational expression** takes the form of an arithmetic expression, then a relational operator, and then another arithmetic expression. A **relational operator** indicates a mathematical comparison such as less than, equal to, or greater than. FORTRAN uses six relational operators, as indicated in Table 4.1. *Notice that the periods which surround the letters are part of the relational operator.* To test a condition, you will use one of these relational operators "wedged" between the two arithmetic expressions. As in Chapter 2, arithmetic expressions may consist of a single variable, a single constant, or a combination of variables, constants, and arithmetic operators. As in our previous work with arithmetic expressions, it is good programming practice not to mix mode when coding a relational expression; that is, *the arithmetic expression to the left of the relational operator should be the same mode as the arithmetic expression to the right.*

TABLE 4.1   *Relational Operators in FORTRAN*

MATHEMATICAL COMPARISON	RELATIONAL OPERATOR	MEANING
=	.EQ.	Equal to
≠	.NE.	Not equal to
<	.LT.	Less than
≤	.LE.	Less than or equal to
>	.GT.	Greater than
≥	.GE.	Greater than or equal to

The flowchart symbol ◇ is used whenever a decision or test is made. The test is described within the diamond, and the arrows show the alternative paths that your program may take from that decision point. The symbol ○ indicates transfer of control points in the program.

Example 4.3 further illustrates the use of the logical IF statement for testing conditions within your program.

EXAMPLE 4.3

Flowchart

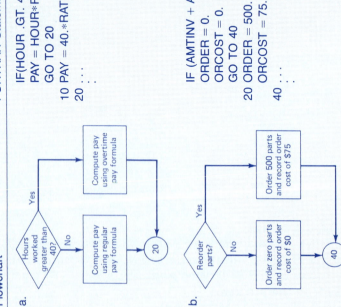

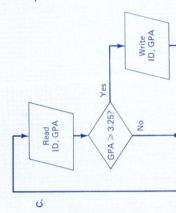

FORTRAN Statements

a.
```
   IF(HOUR .GT. 40.) GO TO 10
   PAY = HOUR*RATE
   GO TO 20
10 PAY = 40.*RATE + (HOUR – 40.)*RATE*1.5
20 . . .
   . .
```

b.
```
   IF (AMTINV + AMTORD .LT. REORD) GO TO 20
   ORDER = 0.
   ORCOST = 0.
   GO TO 40
20 ORDER = 500.
   ORCOST = 75.
40 . . .
   . .
```

c.
```
15 READ(5,*) ID,GPA
   IF (GPA .GE. 3.25) WRITE(6,*) ID,GPA
   GO TO 15
```

Explanation

If the value stored in HOUR exceeds 40., then the statement

$$PAY = 40.*RATE + (HOUR – 40.)*RATE*1.5$$

is executed. If the value stored in HOUR is less than or equal to 40., then the program executes the statement

$$PAY = HOUR*RATE$$

and branches to statement 20, thereby bypassing the overtime calculation.

If the inventory (AMTINV) plus the amount on order (AMTORD) is less than the reorder point (REORD), then the statements

$$ORDER = 500.$$
$$ORCOST = 75.$$

are executed. If the sum of inventory and amount on order equals or exceeds the reorder point, then the statements

$$ORDER = 0.$$
$$ORCOST = 0.$$

are executed.

If the grade point average (GPA) is greater than or equal to 3.25 then the student's ID and GPA are printed, and the computer next executes the instruction GO TO 15. If the GPA is less than 3.25, then the WRITE statement is bypassed, and the GO TO statement is executed.

Follow-up Exercises

4.   Indicate what is wrong, if anything, with the following:

   a.   IF(K.LE.M) GO TO 20
   b.   IF(K .LE. M) GO TO 20
   c.   IF(K. LE .M) GO TO 20
   d.   IF(K LE M) GO TO 20
   e.   IF(Q.EQ.J+L) STOP
   f.   IF(P.GT.Q) END

5.   Indicate whether a true or false condition exists for each relational expression.

   a.   A .LT. B   e.   A + D .GE. B − C
   b.   B .LE. D   f.   B/A .NE. C + D
   c.   C .GT. −58.
   d.   D .EQ. 33.

6.   Generally, it is best to minimize the number of GO TO statements in a program, as their unnecessary use both promotes programs which are difficult to follow by us humans and may increase CPU time.

   a.   Part a of Example 4.3 could have been coded as follows:

```
       PAY = HOUR*RATE
       IF (HOUR .GT. 40.) PAY = 40.*RATE + (HOUR − 40.)*RATE*1.5
   20 . . .
     .
     .
```

   Draw the flowchart segment which is consistent with this code.

   b.   Part a of Example 4.3 also could have been coded as follows:

```
       IF (HOUR .LE. 40.) PAY = HOUR*RATE
       IF (HOUR .GT. 40.) PAY = 40.*RATE + (HOUR − 40.)*RATE*1.5
   20 . . .
     .
     .
```

   Draw the flowchart segment which is consistent with this code.

   *c.   Now look at part b in Example 4.3. Write two alternative codes, the first corresponding to the approach in part a of this exercise and the second corresponding to part b.

   *d.   Discuss pros and cons in comparing these three approaches.

7. Code each flowchart into a segment of a FORTRAN program.

a.

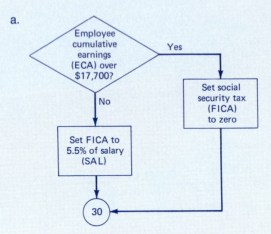

b.

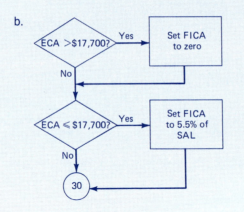

c.

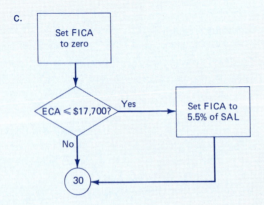

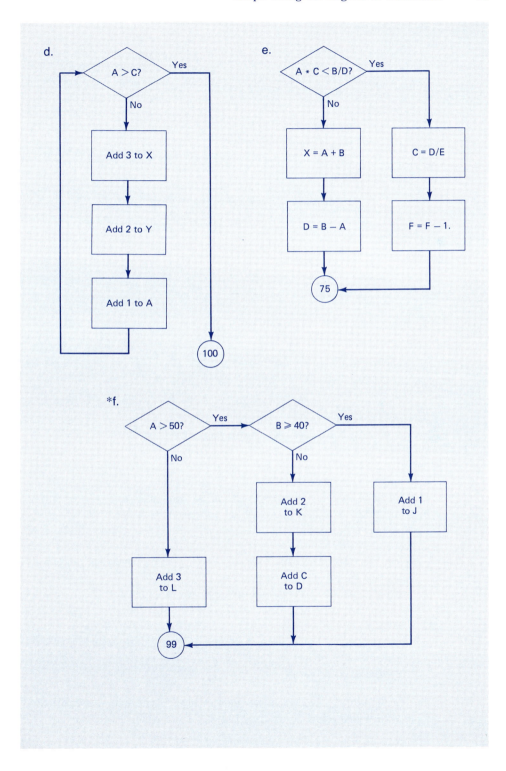

*8. A department store has the following minimum payment policy for its customers. When the balance owed (BAL) is under $50, the customer pays (PAYS) the full balance owed. When the amount owed is $50 or more, the customer pays according to the formula $50 + 10 percent (balance owed − $50). After PAYS is determined, the computer next executes statement number 80. Prepare a flowchart and FORTRAN code which reflect this policy. *Hint:* Several approaches are open to you; see Exercise 6.

9. For each case, indicate the printed values for ISAP and ISOP.

a.   ISAP = 10
      ISOP = 5
      IF (ISAP .NE. 2*ISOP + 1) ISAP = ISOP
      WRITE(6,*) ISAP,ISOP
       :
       :

b.   ISAP = 10
       ISOP = 5
   40 IF (ISAP .LE. ISOP) GO TO 50
           ISOP = ISOP + 1
       GO TO 40
   50 WRITE(6,*) ISAP,ISOP
       :
       :

Loops Using the Counter Method

The **counter method** of looping counts the number of times the loop has been executed and branches out of the loop after the counter reaches some desired number. For example, the flowchart in Figure 4.2 uses the counter method to determine whether or not the test data for the three students in Example 4.1 have all been processed. The computer reads in the data, computes the tuition and balance due, prints out the results, and adds one to a counter. After each pass through the loop the counter is tested to determine whether three loops have been completed. This process is repeated until the counter is greater than three, after which the computer branches out of the loop and stops.

You need to remember four key points in constructing loops by this method.

1. *Initialization.* Before you enter the loop you store an initial value (usually 0 or 1) in a variable you will use as your counter. This process is called **initialization;** it is an action that takes place *before* you enter the loop. Instructions that are part of the initialization phase are executed once, whereas statements within the loop are executed as many times as the loop is processed.

2. *Increment.* Each time the instructions in the loop are executed the counter is **incremented** (increased) by 1.

3. *Test for Loop Termination.* The set of instructions making up the loop is repeated until the counter reaches a value either greater than (when

initialized to 1) or equal to (when initialized to 0) the required number of loops, at which time the computer exits from the loop. (This step compares the counter with a value representing the desired number of loops.)

4. *Body of the Loop.*   The set of instructions that are repeated is called the **body.**

FIGURE 4.2   *Flowchart for Looping by Counter Method*

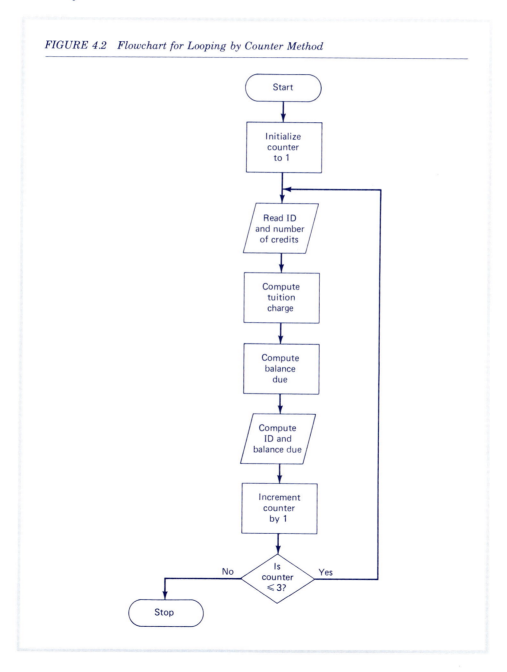

EXAMPLE 4.4 Student Billing Program with Loop
by the Counter Method

Program	Comments
KOUNT = 1	Initialization of counter
10 READ(5,*) ID,CREDIT	
TUIT = CREDIT*100.	
BALDUE = TUIT + 250.	Body of loop
WRITE(6,*) ID,BALDUE	
KOUNT = KOUNT + 1	Incrementing the counter
IF (KOUNT .LE. 3) GO TO 10	Test for loop termination
STOP	
END	

As before, the following test data are used:

Student ID	Number of Credits
101	15.0
102	12.0
103	10.5

The computer processes stored data in the following way.

After initialization:

As data for the first student are processed (first time through the loop):

ID	CREDIT	TUIT	BALDUE	KOUNT
101	15.	1500.	1750.	2

As data for the second student are processed (second time through the loop):

ID	CREDIT	TUIT	BALDUE	KOUNT
102	12.	1200.	1450.	3

As data for the third student are processed (third time through the loop):

ID	CREDIT	TUIT	BALDUE	KOUNT
103	10.5	1050.	1300.	4

The output from this program is:

101	1750.
102	1450.
103	1300.

Usually, *it is good practice to let your counter be an integer variable rather than a real variable;* otherwise, the machine process of real arithmetic may not give exact (whole number) values to your counter, which means that the test condition in the logical IF may not be satisfied when you expect it to be.

Another good programming practice is to represent the total number of times through the loop as a variable rather than a constant. This approach is more general since you don't have to change the program each time the total number of loops changes. The program in Example 4.5 illustrates this approach.

EXAMPLE 4.5 General Approach to Looping by the Counter Method

```
      READ (5,*) LOOPS
      KOUNT = 1
   10 READ(5,*) ID,CREDIT
          TUIT = CREDIT*100.
          BALDUE = TUIT + 250.
          WRITE(6,*) ID,BALDUE
          KOUNT = KOUNT + 1
      IF (KOUNT .LE. LOOPS) GO TO 10
      STOP
      END
```

The input data for this program would appear as follows:

Number of times
through the loop
(or number of
students) ──────────→ 3

```
3 students ──────┐      101      15.0
                 └───→  102      12.0
                        103      10.5
```

Note that the first data item is the total number of times we wish to loop in this run.

Follow-up Exercises

10. If you have data to process on 25 students, how would you modify Example 4.4? Example 4.5?
11. If you initialize the variable KOUNT to zero, how would you change Examples 4.4 and 4.5 to read and process data for three students?
12. What happens in the execution of the program if statement number 10 is KOUNT = 1 instead of READ(5,*) ID,CREDIT?

Loops Using the Last-Record-Check Method

A single data card in a batch system or a single line of input in a time-sharing system is called an **input record.** Terminating a loop using a method called the **last-record check** requires a special record which signals the end of the data. This special record, sometimes called a **trailer record** or **end-of-file record** has a unique number assigned to one of the input variables. By a "unique" number we mean one that would never be part of regular input data. For example, in the student billing program, a student ID number of -99 might serve as a trailer number since normally ID numbers are positive. After each record is read into the computer a test is made to determine whether or not the

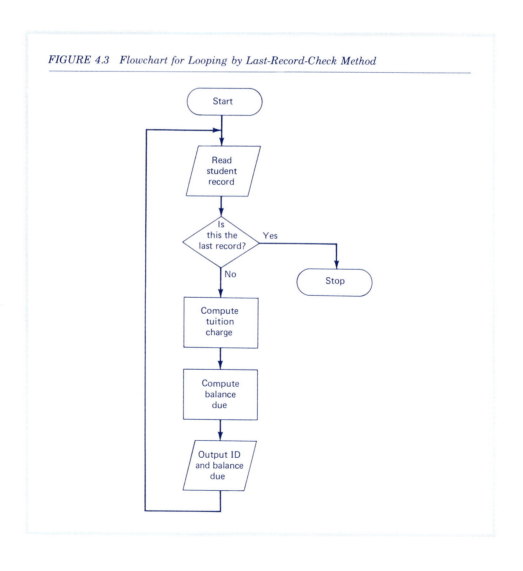

FIGURE 4.3   *Flowchart for Looping by Last-Record-Check Method*

information just read in is the trailer record. If the computer determines that a particular record is the trailer record, then the computer branches out of the loop; otherwise, the computer continues looping. Figure 4.3 illustrates this method for the student billing example.

EXAMPLE 4.6   Student Billing Program with Loop by the Last-Record-Check Method

Program	Comments

```
10 READ(5,*) ID,CREDIT
       IF (ID .EQ. -99) STOP          Testing for the trailer record
       TUIT = CREDIT*100.             Body of loop
       BALDUE = TUIT + 250.
       WRITE(6,*) ID,BALDUE
   GO TO 10
   END
```

The test data using a trailer record would appear as follows:

Student ID	Number of Credits	
101	15.0	First record
102	12.0	Second record
103	10.5	Third record
-99	0.0	Trailer record

The trailer record has the number -99, an arbitrary number, assigned to ID. This record does not represent another student; it is placed at the end of the data to indicate no more data. When the computer reads this record, it has already processed all the student data.

The instruction

IF (ID .EQ. -99) STOP

needs some further explanation. Immediately after reading in the ID number and the number of credits for a given student, the computer checks for the trailer record by testing the value of ID against -99. After the data for the first student are read in, the location ID contains the value 101, which is not equal to -99. Thus the logical expression "ID .EQ. -99" is tested as false. As a result, control drops to the first executable statement below the logical IF, which is to say that the computer next computes tuition, computes and prints the balance due, and returns to statement 10 to read in more data. For the second and third students the same process is repeated; that is, the program again bypasses the stop instruction and executes the next instruction. Finally, when the trailer record is processed, the contents of ID test true against the value -99. As a result, the STOP statement is executed and processing terminates.

Follow-up Exercises

13. If we were to use zero as the student ID number on the trailer record, how would you change the program in Example 4.6?
14. Do you see any problem with placing the test for the trailer record immediately after the WRITE instruction? Why or why not?
15. Do you need a data entry for CREDIT on the trailer record? Does it have to be zero? Explain.
16. Change the program such that CREDIT is used to test the last record.
17. Can you think of two advantages that the last-record-check method has over the counter method at this point in your programming?

Accumulating a Sum

Accumulating and printing sums for one or more variables is a common computation in programming. For example, a payroll program computes gross pay, deductions, and net pay for each employee and also computes the total gross pay, total deductions, and total net pay paid for all employees of a firm. To illustrate how the computer can accumulate a sum, we return to our tuition and fee problem.

EXAMPLE 4.7   Student Billing Program with Sum

The Financial Vice-President of State College needs to know the total amount of money that State College will collect in tuition and fees. Conceptually, we set aside a memory location (that is, assign a variable) which represents the sum. Each time the computer computes the amount owed by a student, the sum is increased by the amount the student owes. In effect the sum can be thought of as a running total whose final value is not known until all the student data are read in and processed. For our test data, the amount due from each student is $1750, $1450, and $1300. As the program is computing, the sum will be:

After the first student,	$0 + 1750 = 1750$;
After the second student,	$1750 + 1450 = 3200$;
After the third student,	$3200 + 1300 = 4500$.

Thus a running total accumulates.

The flowchart in Figure 4.4 illustrates the steps needed to accumulate a sum. In the program below, SUM is the variable which stores the accumulated amount due from all students.

FIGURE 4.4 *Flowchart for Incorporating a Sum in the Loop*

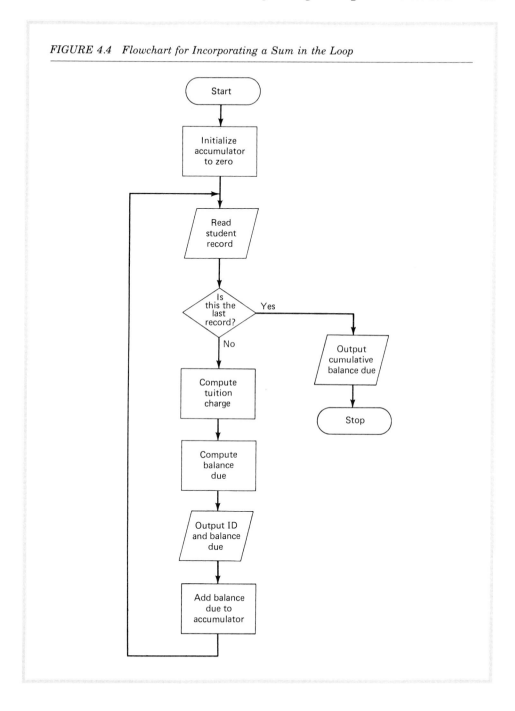

Program	Comments
SUM = 0.	Initialize SUM to zero to be sure zero and nothing else is stored in that memory location.
10 READ(5,∗) ID,CREDIT IF (ID .EQ. −99) GO TO 30	The GO TO statement replaces the STOP statement in the previous program because we must print SUM before stopping.
TUIT = CREDIT∗100. BALDUE = TUIT + 250. WRITE(6,∗) ID,BALDUE SUM = SUM + BALDUE	Each time the computer calculates the balance due for a student, the location for SUM is increased by the value stored in BALDUE.

GO TO 10
30 WRITE(6,∗) SUM
    STOP
    END
	SUM is printed following the loop.

Notice that by placing the instruction

SUM = SUM + BALDUE

within the loop the value stored in BALDUE is added to the value stored in SUM, and the result of the addition is stored in SUM, replacing the value previously stored in SUM.

As the program is executed, the contents of memory locations change in the following way.

After initialization:

After the first student is processed:

After the second student is processed:

After the third student is processed:

Now, the output would appear as follows:

```
101      1750.
102      1450.
103      1300.
4500.
```

Notice that when the trailer number (−99) is read, the computer branches to statement 30 and prints the total amount owed by all students, $4500.

Follow-up Exercises

18. With respect to Example 4.7,

    a. Would the output change if the instructions

           WRITE(6,*) ID,BALDUE

       and

           SUM = SUM + BALDUE

       were reversed?

    b. Would the output change if the instruction

           SUM = SUM + BALDUE

       were placed before

           BALDUE = TUIT + 250.

19. Describe the output if

        30 WRITE(6,*) SUM

    were placed just before the GO TO 10 instruction?

20. Modify the program in Example 4.7 to accumulate and print three sums: cumulative tuition, cumulative fees, and cumulative balance due. *Hint:* you need a separate variable to accumulate each total. Can you think of simplifications in the program which make use of the fact that once you have two of these sums you automatically have the third?

21. Modify the program of Example 4.7 by calculating and printing the average balance due, AVE. *Hint:* You need to add a counter to the loop.
*22. Modify the program in Example 4.7 so the counter method is used to terminate the loop. Also, print the average balance due, AVE, on the same line as the SUM.
23. Modify Example 4.7 by using a DATA statement to initialize SUM to 0., cost per credit (CPC) to 100., and FEE to 250. Discuss pros and cons of this approach versus the approach in the example.

4.3
DECISION MAKING USING
THE LOGICAL IF STATEMENT

In the previous section you learned how to use the logical IF statement to construct a loop in your program. A more common and powerful use of this statement is its application to making choices or decisions. Two examples of choices made by computers in education include the following: The determination of whether a student is part time or full time for the purpose of calculating the appropriate tuition; the determination of whether a student is above or below a grade point average of 3.5 for the purpose of identifying the students on the Dean's List. Other examples were illustrated as part of Example 4.3.

EXAMPLE 4.8   Student Billing Program with Decision

The tuition charges at State College vary depending on whether a student is full time or part time. A full-time student (12 credits or more) pays a fixed amount of $1200. A part-time student (under 12 credits) pays $100 per credit. The fees in either case are $250 per student. The flowchart in Figure 4.5 illustrates the steps necessary for the programming of this problem.

Program	Comments
10 READ(5,*) ID,CREDIT	
IF (ID .EQ. −99) STOP	Test contents of ID for trailer number (−99).
TUIT = 1200.	Set tuition to 1200., assuming a full-time student.
IF (CREDIT .LT. 12.) TUIT = CREDIT*100.	If part-time student, then compute tuition and store in TUIT (the 1200. in TUIT is replaced).
BALDUE = TUIT + 250.	
WRITE(6,*) ID,BALDUE	
GO TO 10	Return to process next student.
END	

FIGURE 4.5   *Flowchart for Student Billing Program with Decision*

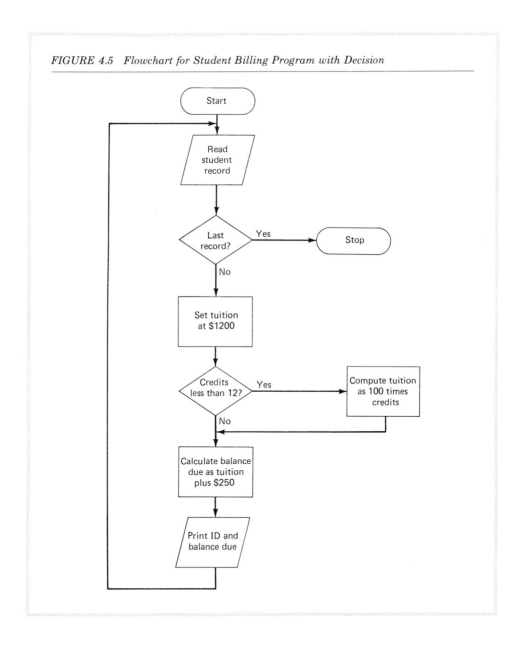

Follow-up Exercise

24. Students sometimes will write the program in Example 4.8 like this:

```
10 READ(5,*) ID,CREDIT
      IF (ID .EQ. −99) STOP
      IF (CREDIT .GE. 12.) GO TO 15
      IF (CREDIT .LT. 12.) GO TO 20
15    TUIT = 1200.
      GO TO 25
20    TUIT = CREDIT*100.
25    BALDUE = TUIT + 250.
      WRITE(6,*) ID,BALDUE
   GO TO 10
   END
```

a. Is anything wrong with this? Explain.
b. Do you see any problem if the statement GO TO 25 is removed from the program? Explain.
c. Can you think of modifications in this program which would make the use of two logical IFs more efficient in terms of the length of the program? *Hint:* Incorporate the calculation of tuition in the logical IFs. Draw the flowchart for your revised program.

EXAMPLE 4.9   Use of Coded Data: Traffic Court Fines

A **code** is the representation of words or groups of words by numbers, letters, or symbols. Codes are used by organizations to provide meaningful identification for descriptions that otherwise would be awkward to store and manipulate.

The student file at State College might record information on the students' sex, residence, and class standing through the use of codes. For example,

The code for sex could be 1 or 2—1 for male and 2 for female.
The code for residence could be 1 or 2—1 for in-state resident and 2 for out-of-state resident.
The code for class standing could be 1, 2, 3, 4—1 for freshman, 2 for sophomore, 3 for junior, and 4 for senior.

The next program illustrates the testing of decisions based on coded data.

Each week the clerk in traffic court summarizes the fines collected for traffic violations by major categories: moving violation and standing violation. The data on each violation include traffic ticket number, traffic violation type (1 = moving; 2 = standing), and amount of fine.

Figure 4.6 is a flowchart which presents the steps necessary to summarize the traffic violations data. In the program below TOTMOV accumulates the total fines collected for moving violations, TOTSTD accumulates the total fines collected for standing violations, ITYPE = 1 when the violation is a moving violation, and ITYPE = 2 when the violation is a standing violation.

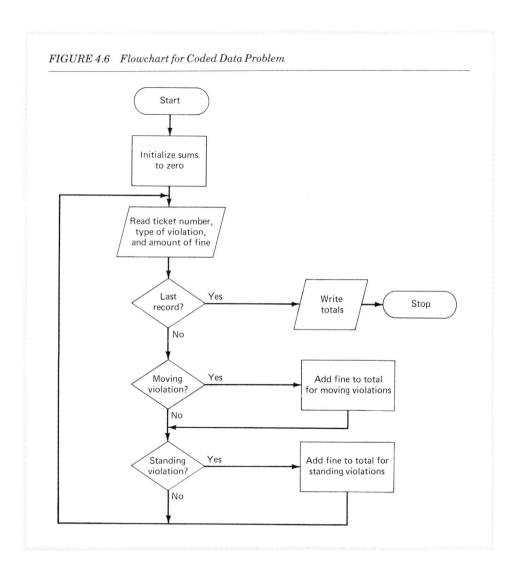

FIGURE 4.6   *Flowchart for Coded Data Problem*

Program	Comments
DATA TOTMOV, TOTSTD/0.,0./	Initialize to zero the variables that accumulate total fines.
10 READ(5,*) NUM,ITYPE,FINE	Read ticket number (NUM), type of violation (ITYPE), and amount of fine (FINE).
IF (NUM .EQ. −99) GO TO 30	Test for trailer record.
IF (ITYPE .EQ. 1) TOTMOV = TOTMOV + FINE	Accumulate fines for moving violations.
IF (ITYPE .EQ. 2) TOTSTD = TOTSTD + FINE	Accumulate fines for standing violations.
GO TO 10	Branch to READ statement.
30 WRITE(6,*) TOTMOV, TOTSTD	Print total fines by category.
STOP	
END	

Follow-up Exercises

25. Indicate the output from the program for the following test data:

Ticket Number	Type of Violation	Fine ($)
1001	1	50
1002	2	15
1003	2	10
1004	1	35
−99	0	0

26. When using codes students sometimes will try a READ statement like

    10 READ(5,*) NUM,IMOVE,ISTAND,FINE

instead of

    10 READ(5,*) NUM,ITYPE,FINE

Do you see a problem with this setup?

FIGURE 4.7 *Alternative Flowchart for Coded Data Problem (Exercise 28)*

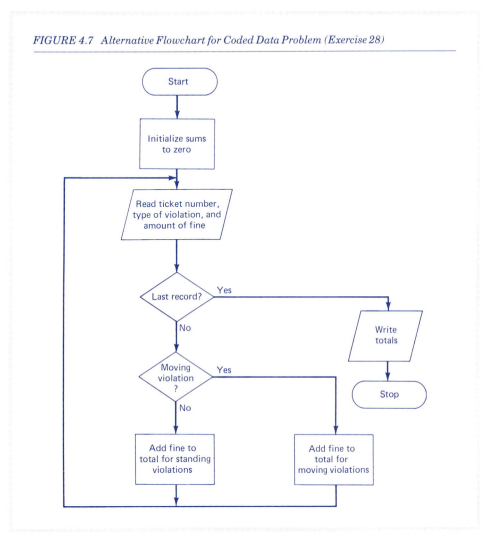

27. What changes need to be made in the program to use the variable TYPE instead of ITYPE, such that TYPE is treated as an integer variable?

*28. The program in Example 4.9 could have been coded according to the flowchart in Figure 4.7. Write a program that is consistent with this flowchart. Compare the merits and demerits of each approach.

*29. **Input Error Detection.** Professional programs generally include logic which tests for errors in the input data. Modify the flowchart and program in Example 4.9 such that immediately after the last-record check, a test for ITYPE greater than 2 is made: if "true" then print NUM, ITYPE, and FINE and branch to read the next record; if "false" then proceed as before.

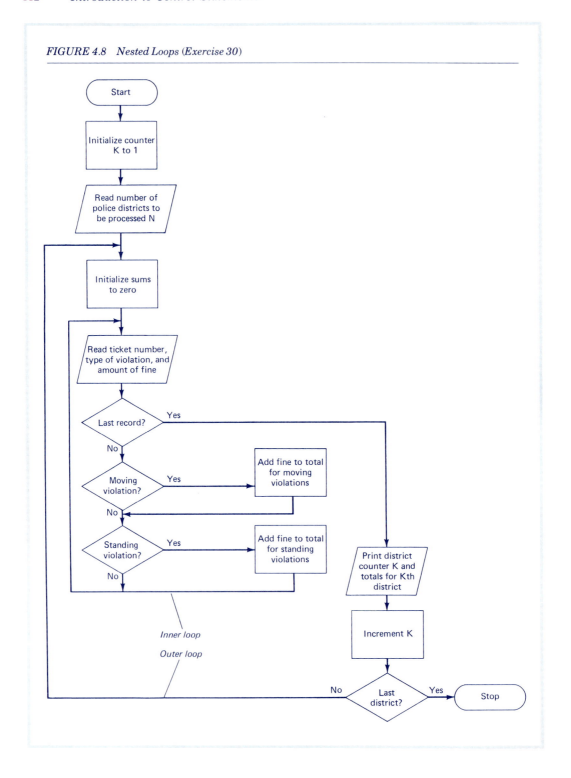

FIGURE 4.8   Nested Loops (Exercise 30)

*30. **Nested Loops.** Modify Example 4.9 to include an "outer" loop for processing N police districts, as illustrated in Figure 4.8. In other words, we wish the program to calculate and print totals for each of N police districts, where the value of N is to be input. The outer loop processes districts and the inner loop accumulates fines within a particular district. These are called nested loops because one loop (inner) is entirely within the other (outer) loop. *Why would it be incorrect to initialize TOTMOV and TOTSTD using a DATA statement?* Roleplay the computer by processing the following data:

Ticket Number	Type of Violation	Fine ($)
1001	1	50
1002	2	15
−99	0	0
2001	2	10
2002	1	35
2003	1	45
−99	0	0

EXAMPLE 4.10   Rate Schedule Problem

The Vice-President of Marketing for Mopups, a fast-selling motorized bike which gets 155 miles per gallon, has determined a new rate schedule for shipments to dealers. To illustrate, an order for 15 Mopups would cost a total of $3690, or $2250 for the first nine Mopups at $250 each plus $1440 for the remaining six Mopups at $240 each.

Size of Order	Marginal Price per Bike ($)
9 or less	250
10–19	240
20–29	225
30 or more	205

The Vice-President heard recently through the company grapevine that a recent college graduate is a "hotshot" programmer. With little effort, the Vice-President found Hotshot under a deck of spilled cards, and wasted no time in assigning a computer program to determine the total price to charge a dealer for a shipment of Mopups. Within an hour, Hotshot returned with the results shown below.

Step I.   Analyzing the Problem

1. *Problem Statement*
   To determine the total price to charge a dealer for a shipment of Mopups based on the size of the order.
2. *Data Input*
   a. Number of dealers that need to be processed (N)
   b. Code number for dealer (NUM)
   c. Size of order (SIZE)

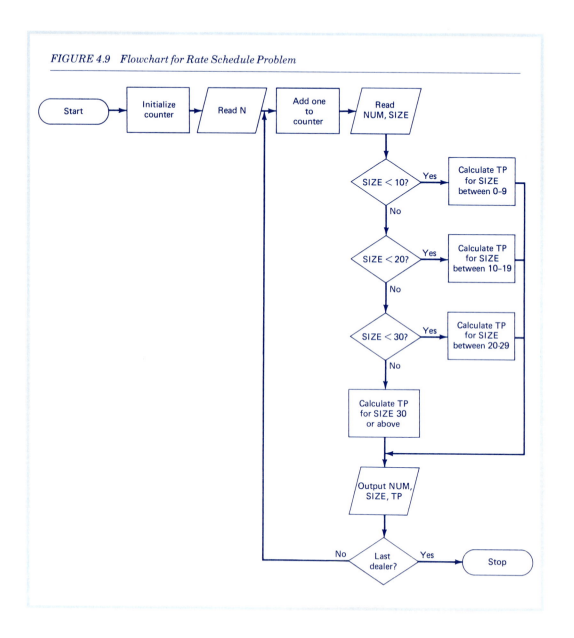

FIGURE 4.9   *Flowchart for Rate Schedule Problem*

3. *Data Output*
   Code number, size of order, and total price (TP) for each dealer.
4. *Computations and Logical Processes*
   Based on rate schedule

Step II.   Preparing the Flowchart

See Figure 4.9.

Step III.   Coding the Problem

```
  K = 0
  READ(5,*)N
5 K = K + 1
      READ(5,*) NUM,SIZE
      IF (SIZE .LT. 10.) GO TO 10
      IF (SIZE .LT. 20.) GO TO 15
      IF (SIZE .LT. 30.) GO TO 20
      TP = 205.*(SIZE − 29.)  + 6900.
      GO TO 25
10    TP = 250.*SIZE
      GO TO 25
15    TP = 240.*(SIZE − 9.) + 2250.
      GO TO 25
20    TP = 225.*(SIZE − 19.) + 4650.
25    WRITE(6,*) NUM, SIZE, TP
   IF (K .LT. N) GO TO 5
   STOP
   END
```

Step IV.   Debugging the Computer Problem

For the test data

```
4
6152    25.
4169    12.
5574    29.
3456    55.
```

the following output should be obtained:

```
6152    25.     6000.
4169    12.     2970.
5574    29.     6900.
3456    55.    12230.
```

   Note 1: Did you notice that the first item of data is the number of times (4) we wish to loop? As the program is written, the number of times we wish to process the loop is treated as a variable (N), which gives the program flexibility in processing. This avoids the necessity of having to change the program each time we wish to process the loop a different number of times.

Note 2: You should carefully relate the logic in the flowchart to the logic in the program. In particular, pay close attention to the method of branching which guarantees one and only one price calculation for each dealer. Also, notice how we branch to the WRITE statement following each TP calculation.

Note 3: To make sure you understand the calculation of TP for each category, you should "handcrank" the test data through the program; that is, you should role-play the computer by "processing" the program using the test input data. In doing so, make sure you confirm the constants (2250., 4650., 6900.) used in the assignment statements. (See Exercise 31.)

Follow-up Exercises

31. For the test data given in Step IV of Example 4.10, write in the successive values that are stored internally for the indicated variables. Assume that a "snapshot" of memory is taken just before the execution of the IF statement at the end of the loop.

			Stored values for		
Loop	N	K	NUM	SIZE	TP
1					
2					
3					
4					

*32. Modify the program so that the overall total (TOT) and average price per order (AVE) for *all* dealers are calculated and printed; that is, find the sum and average of TP. Determine their values for the test data.

33. The program of Example 4.10 could have been written as follows:

```
    K = 0
    READ(5,*) N
  5 K = K + 1
    READ(5,*) NUM,SIZE
    IF (SIZE .GE. 30.) TP = 205.*(SIZE − 29.) + 6900.
    IF (SIZE .LT. 30.) TP = 225.*(SIZE − 19.) + 4650.
    IF (SIZE .LT. 20.) TP = 240.*(SIZE − 9.) + 2250.
    IF (SIZE .LT. 10.) TP = 250.*SIZE
    WRITE(6,*)NUM,SIZE,TP
    IF (K .LT. N) GO TO 5
    STOP
    END
```

Using the test data given in Step IV of Example 4.10, confirm that this program gives correct results. Compare the merits of each approach. Which program do you prefer?

4.4
COMMON ERRORS

Beginning programmers are likely to make at least one of the errors below when applying the material in this chapter. Will you?

1. *Statement Numbers.* Two types of syntax errors seem to occur often here: *multiple* statement numbers and *missing* statement numbers. In the first case, two or more statements have the same statement number. So, as you're writing your program, *make it a habit to scan your existing statement numbers prior to assigning a new statement number.* In the second case, a control statement references a statement number which does not exist. For example, if you have the statement GO TO 50 and no executable statement is labeled 50, then you have a missing-statement-number error. This type of "labeling error" also may occur if you transfer control to a statement which has a syntax error. For example, in the segment

    > .
    > .
    > GO TO 20
    > .
    > .
    > 20 STAP

    the compiler not only will identify the syntax error within statement 20 but also may indicate a second syntax error concerning the statement number. This second error occurs because the first syntax error "masked" the fact that this was statement number 20. In effect you have made only one error but the compiler believes it to be two errors.

    > 20 STOP

    would correct both errors.

2. *Relational Expressions.* The relational expression within the following logical IF statement illustrates one common error and a second possible error:

    > IF (A GT N) N = N + 1

    First, a syntax error would be indicated because GT is not recognized as a relational operator. The correct form is .GT., *so don't forget the periods.* Second, the comparison A to N is a *mixed-mode comparison,* since A is a real variable and N is an integer variable. Some, but not all, compilers will indicate a syntax error here. *It is good programming practice for the arithmetic expression to the left of the relational operator to be consistent in mode with the arithmetic expression to the right.*

3. *Looping an Incorrect Number of Times.* Sometimes you wish to loop a specific number of times but you end up looping either one more or one less than the intended number. This type of logic error usually occurs because

you failed to pay close attention to the relationship between initialization and test of the counter. To illustrate, look at Example 4.4 on page 98. If we had paired the statements

```
KOUNT = 0
    ⋮
IF (KOUNT .LE. 3) GO TO 10
```

then we would have looped four times rather than the intended three. Or if we had paired

```
KOUNT = 1
    ⋮
IF (KOUNT .LT. 3) GO TO 10
```

then we would have looped twice.

4. *Logic Errors.*   A variety of logic errors can occur when designing transfers of control. To illustrate a common logic error, consider the following segment based on the program of Example 4.10 on page 115.

```
    ⋮
    IF (SIZE .LT. 10.) GO TO 10
    IF (SIZE .LT. 20.) GO TO 15
    IF (SIZE .LT. 30.) GO TO 20
    ⋮
10 TP = 250.*SIZE
15 TP = 240.*(SIZE − 9.) + 2250.
20 TP = 225.*(SIZE − 19.) + 4650.
25 WRITE(6,*) NUM,SIZE,TP
    ⋮
```

Now, suppose 5. is stored in SIZE. The first logical IF appropriately transfers control to statement 10, and 1250. is stored for TP; however, TP next is evaluated as 1290. according to statement 15, and finally as 1500. according to statement 20. The WRITE statement prints TP as 1500., which is the incorrect price to charge for five Mopups. This process of roleplaying the computer clearly points out the need for inserting the statement GO TO 25 between statements 10 and 15 and between statements 15 and 20. Do you see why it's unnecessary to insert GO TO 25 between statements 20 and 25?

In some cases it is tedious to uncover your logic error by this roleplaying approach, particularly if many computations are involved. When this is the case, temporary WRITE statements that trace the flow of computations may prove very useful. (Do you remember this technique from Section 3.3?) For example, if we were to insert the statement

```
WRITE(6,*) SIZE,TP
```

between statements 10 and 15 and between statements 15 and 20, then the following output would be observed when 5. is stored in SIZE and 1099 is stored in NUM:

$$\begin{array}{lll} & 5. & 1250. \\ & 5. & 1290. \\ 1099 & 5. & 1500. \end{array}$$

The first two lines of output are the direct result of the trace, and they clearly illustrate the sequence of computations in the program.

Additional Exercises

34. Define or explain each of the following:

control statements
looping
statement number
GO TO statement
branching
transfer of control
logical IF statement
relational expression

relational operator
counter method
initialization
body of a loop
input record
last-record-check method
trailer record
end-of-file record

35. **Temperature Conversion.** Modify the program and flowchart described in Exercise 28 of Chapter 2 (page 58) as follows:

a. Let degrees Fahrenheit be a counter in a loop which calculates and outputs degrees Celsius equivalents. Define initial (FI), terminal (FT), and incremental (FINC) degrees Fahrenheit as input variables. Run the program for the following two sets of input values:

FI	FT	FINC
20.	40.	1.
−30.	120.	5.

For example, your output for the first run should look like this:

	Degrees Fahrenheit	Degrees Celsius
	20.	−6.67
	21.	−6.11
21 rows	22.	−5.56
	⋮	⋮
	40.	4.44

Note that the counter is initialized by FI and that the loop terminates when the counter exceeds FT.

**b. Include an outer loop which processes as many sets of data as desired (two sets for the above input data). If you use the counter method, then define a new input

**Exercises marked with a double asterisk are more difficult than "typical" exercises.

variable L as the total number of times through the outer loop. (See the approach in Example 4.5.) If you use the last-record-check method, terminate your run when −999. is input for FI.

36. **Marketing Problem.** Modify the program and flowchart described in Exercise 29 of Chapter 2 (page 58) as follows:
   a. Let cost per square inch (C) be a counter in a loop which calculates and outputs the total cost. Define initial (CI), terminal (CT), and incremental (CINC) costs per square inch as input variables, along with RADIUS and number of containers (X). Run the program for the following three sets of input values:

CI	CT	CINC	RADIUS	X
0.005	0.100	0.005	5.0	500000.
0.005	0.100	0.005	5.2	500000.
0.010	0.150	0.010	5.2	650000.

   For example, your output for the first run should look like this:

	Cost per Square Inch	Total Cost
	0.005	196349.
	0.010	392699.
20 rows	0.015	589048.
	⋮	⋮
	0.100	3926991.

   Note that the counter is initialized by CI and that the loop terminates when the counter exceeds CT.
   **b. Include an outer loop which processes as many sets of data as desired (three sets for the above input data). If you use the counter method, then define a new input variable L as the total number of times through the outer loop. (See the approach in Example 4.5.) If you use the last-record-check method, terminate your run when a negative value is input for CI.

37. **Manufacturing Problem.** Modify the program and flowchart described in Exercise 30 of Chapter 2 (page 58) as follows:
   a. Let UNITS be a counter in a loop which calculates and prints daily revenue, daily cost, and daily profit. Initialize UNITS to 1 and let it vary as follows within the loop: 1, 2, 3, . . . , UMAX, where UMAX is an input variable that represents the maximum number of units to be considered. Also include PRICE as part of your input. Run the program for the following four sets of data:

UMAX	PRICE
15	80
15	100
15	120
15	140

For example, your output for the first run should look like this:

Units Produced	Daily Revenue	Daily Cost	Daily Profit
1	80	245	-165
2	160	234	-74
3	240	223	17
⋮	⋮	⋮	⋮
15	1200	2275	-1075

Note that the loop terminates after the counter reaches UMAX. Based on your output, how many units should be produced at each price?

**b. Include an outer loop which uses D as the counter. Define initial (DI), terminal (DT), (PT), and incremental (PINC) prices as input variables, along with UMAX. The above input data now appear as follows:

PI	PT	PINC	UMAX
80	140	20	15

The computer now prints all four tables in one run. Note that the computer run terminates after the price counter reaches PT. Just before each table, print the price that corresponds to that table.

38. **Blood-Bank Inventory Problem.** Modify the program and flowchart described in Exercise 31 of Chapter 2 (page 58) as follows:

a. Let the cost of refrigeration (H) be a counter in a loop which calculates and outputs the number of pints to order (Q) and the expected cost per week (CPW). Define initial (HI), terminal (HT), and incremental (HINC) costs of refrigeration as input variables, along with administrative and shipping cost (C) and average weekly demand (D). Run the program for the following three sets of input values:

HI	HT	HINC	C	D
0.20	0.30	0.01	50.	2500.
0.20	0.30	0.01	50.	3000.
0.20	0.30	0.01	50.	3500.

For example, your output for the first run should look like this:

	Cost of Refrigeration	Order Quantity	Cost per Week
	0.20	1118.	223.61
11 rows	0.21	1091.	229.13
	⋮	⋮	⋮
	0.30	913.	273.86

Note that the counter is initialized by HI and that the loop terminates when the counter exceeds HT. Draw conclusions with respect to the behavior of Q and CPW as H and D change.

**b.   Include an outer loop which uses D as the counter. Define initial (DI), terminal (DT), and incremental (DINC) demands as input variables, along with HI, HT, HINC, and C. The above input data now appear as follows:

HI	HT	HINC	C	DI	DT	DINC
0.20	0.30	0.01	50.	2500.	3500.	500.

The computer now prints all three tables in one run. Note that the computer run terminates after the demand counter reaches DT. Just before each table, print the demand that corresponds to that table.

39. **Forecasting Population Growth.** Modify the program and flowchart described in Exercise 32 of Chapter 2 (page 59) as follows:

a.   Let N be a counter in a loop which increments N by 1, calculates P, and prints N, corresponding year (YEAR), and P. Initialize N by defining an input variable called NIN. Exit from the loop when the ratio of predicted population to current population exceeds a desired ratio (DESRAT). Run the program for the following three sets of input values:

C	YEAR	B	D	NIN	DESRAT
4.	1976	0.025	0.009	10	2.
4.	1976	0.025	0.009	25	3.
4.	1976	0.020	0.009	30	3.

For example, your output for the first run should look like this:

	Years into Future	Corresponding Year	Predicted Population
	10	1986	4.688
	11	1987	4.763
35 rows	⋮	⋮	⋮
	43	2019	7.915
	44	2020	8.042

Note that the counter is initialized by NIN and that this loop terminates when the predicted population *exceeds* (not equals) double the current population. Comment on the number of years it takes the current world population to double and triple relative to changes in the birth rate.

**b.   Include an outer loop which processes as many sets of data as desired (three sets for the above input data). If you use the counter method, then define a new input variable L as the total number of times through the outer loop. (See the approach in Example 4.5.) If you use the last-record-check method, terminate your run when a negative value is input for C.

40. **Property Tax Assessment.** The property tax rate in a town is set at an increasing rate according to the following table:

Annual Property Tax Schedule

Value of Property ($)	Tax Rate (%)
Less than 10,000	3
Between 10,000 and 30,000	4
Over 30,000	5

a. Prepare a flowchart and write a program to read in the value of the property, then determine and print the tax charge. Design your program either (1) to process N property values, where N is part of the input data, or (2) to end the loop when a property value of zero or less is input.

Debug your program using the following test input data:

Lot Number	Property Value ($)
613	8,900
975	25,000
152	42,000
1642	37,000
1785	75,000

Your test output should look like this:

Lot Number	Property Value ($)	Tax Charge ($)
613	8,900.	267.
975	25,000.	1,000.
152	42,000.	2,100.
1642	37,000.	1,850.
1785	75,000.	3,750.

b. Modify the program in part a such that it prints the sum of property values and the total tax charge.

41. **Telephone Company Billing.** "Flat rate service" charges for telephone service is a method of billing which includes some fixed amount for the main station (main telephone, switchboard, and so on) plus a variable amount per extension phone in service. Distinctions also are made between residential and business customers according to the table below. PBX (Public Branch Exchange) service uses a switchboard for the main station, off of which extensions can be wired. Centrex service is for large-scale business firms and governmental agencies, which require such a large number of extensions that the telephone switching equipment is located on the customer's premises.

Customer Type	Code	Type of Service	Monthly Flat Rates ($)	
			Main Station	Each Extension
Residential	1	Main phone/extensions	13	3
Business	2	Main phone/extensions	50	10
Business	3	PBX/extensions	150	5
Business	4	Centrex/extensions	500	3

In actual practice, PBX and Centrex include many special features. For example, options include fully automatic equipment versus partly manual equipment, facilities for data transmission, private lines which ring at specific locations when the receiver is picked up (PLs), facilities for foreign exchange (FX), and many others.

To illustrate a calculation, consider a business customer with PBX equipment and 50 extensions. In this case, the monthly flat rate is $400 (or $150 + 50 × 5) which, of course, excludes long distance charges, taxes, and charges due to special features.

a. Prepare a flowchart and write a program which calculates flat rate service charges and outputs customer phone number and charge. Test your program with the following input data:

Customer Phone Number	Code	Number of Extensions
7835132	2	5
7927541	4	400
4458162	4	550
6126148	3	75
7831235	1	0
4452164	1	3
7895849	2	7
7897812	4	730
7922674	1	1
6156513	3	50

Either include a last-record test or use a variable (not a constant) to test your loop for termination.

b. Modify the program in part a to include the calculation and output of the following:
1. Total number of customers by code category
2. Percent number of customers by code category
3. Total charges by code category
4. Overall total charges

42. **Personnel Benefits Budget.** A budget officer for the State Agency of Education is in the process of preparing the personnel budget for the next fiscal year. One phase of this process is to prepare a budget of personnel expenditures paid by the state in addition to salaries. The additional expenditures include the following:

1. *Social Security.* The state contributes 6.13 percent of an employee's salary up to $22,900. No deduction is made for earnings above that amount.
2. *Retirement.* The state contributes 9.6 percent of total salary if the employee belongs to the state retirement plan; 9 percent is contributed by the state if the employee elects a private plan; and nothing is contributed by the state if the employee is not eligible for a retirement plan (for example, employees under 30 years of age are not eligible for a retirement plan).
3. *Group Life Insurance.* The state contributes $1.30 for every $1000 of salary paid to the employee. For purposes of calculation, round every salary to the next highest $1000. For example, a yearly salary of $11,150 results in a $15.60 contribution. (12 × 1.30).

The input for each employee consists of:

1. Social security number
2. Annual salary
3. Code for retirement: 1 = not eligible; 2 = state plan; 3 = private plan

Prepare a flowchart and write a program which outputs each employee's social security number, salary, social security contribution, retirement contribution, group life contribution, and total contribution. After all employees have been processed, print the totals of each budget category (the four contribution columns) for all employees. Use the test data below to debug your program. Either include a last-record test or use a variable (not a constant) to test your loop for termination.

Social Security Number	Salary ($)	Retirement Code
267629765	17,000	2
281424162	19,500	3
454124876	21,300	2
363815421	23,800	1
371654456	22,900	2
265814632	10,750	1
245786541	24,375	2
414623456	15,600	3

43. **Affirmative Action Search.** A personnel file in a large firm consists of the following items:

Employee number	(four-digit number)
Age	(nearest whole number)
Sex	(1 = male, 2 = female)
Marital status	(1 = single, 2 = married, 3 = divorced)
Education	(1 = high school, 2 = some college, 3 = college degree, 4 = masters degree)
Annual salary	(five-digit number)

Note: Trailer number −99 is found in employee number field. The affirmative action officer wants to determine whether there is any difference in salaries paid to males and females of comparable age and education levels.

a. For purposes of this assignment, prepare a flowchart, write a program, and use the test data below to determine the average salary for males under 35 years of age with a masters degree; find the average salary for a similar group of females. Conclusion?

Employee Number	Age	Sex	Marital Status	Education	Annual Salary
1642	50	1	2	3	27,000
4162	25	2	2	4	18,000
3715	29	2	1	2	12,000
5682	27	1	3	4	22,000
6154	40	1	2	4	31,000
4625	35	1	1	2	15,000
7543	41	2	2	4	25,000
6987	32	1	3	4	21,000
5265	38	1	2	3	24,000
7364	30	2	2	4	20,000
8415	28	1	1	4	26,000
6875	21	2	1	4	19,000

**b. Generalize your program such that the affirmative action officer can compare average salaries of males versus females by age category on the one hand and by education on the other. For example, the required input to answer the question in part a would be 35 (for age cutoff) and 4 (for education level). Use this program to answer other interesting questions which might occur to you.

**44. Bracket Search Algorithm. Read Section 2.9 once more. Suppose that we are given *A, P,* and *N* in

$$A = P \cdot (1 + R)^N$$

and we wish to solve for the interest rate *R*. One way to go about this is to divide both sides by *P*, take the *N*th root, and solve for *R*. This algebraic approach gives

$$R = (A/P)^{1/N} - 1.$$

Another approach is to solve for *R* by trial and error. That is, select a test value for *R* and calculate a trial value for *A*. If the trial value for *A* is less than the actual value for *A*, then the trial value for *R* must be increased by some increment. If trial *A* is greater than actual *A*, however, then trial *R* must be reduced by the increment. Each time we "bracket" the actual value of *A*, then the increment can be made smaller and the procedure can be repeated until the desired degree of accuracy is achieved. The following set of calculations illustrates this "bracket search algorithm" for *A* = 1500, *P* = 1000, and *N* = 4:

Trial *R*	Trial *A*	Increment in *R*	Comment
0.2	2074	0.1	Reduce trial *R* since 2074 > 1500.
0.1	1464	0.01	Actual *A* has been bracketed since 1464 < 1500. Increment changed by factor of 10, and trial *R* is increased. We now know that actual *R* is between 0.1 and 0.2.
0.11	1518	0.001	Again actual *A* bracketed. Actual *R* between 0.10 and 0.11.
0.109	1513	0.001	Reduce trial *R*.
0.108	1507	0.001	Reduce trial *R*.
0.107	1502	0.001	Reduce trial *R*.
0.106	1496		Actual *R* between 0.106 and 0.107.

In this case, the algebraic approach gives 0.1066819197. Prepare a flowchart (very important!) and write a program which solves for *R* by the trial-and-error method. To check the result, have the program output the algebraic solution as well. Process the following data:

A	*P*	*N*
1500	1000	4
3000	1000	10
3000	1000	20
100000	20000	20

In each case, terminate the algorithm (calculating procedure) when the increment in *R* drops below 0.00001.

Essentials of Input and Output With Formats

If you are using unformatted input/output (I/O), then presently you are unable to control the exact positioning of data in either input or output. Instead you have delegated that function to the FORTRAN compiler through the use of unformatted or list-directed READ and WRITE statements. If you are using FORMAT statements, then perhaps you feel somewhat unsure, since we have spent little time in their explanation. In either case, this and the next chapter will make you master of your own I/O destiny.

5.1
ON FILES, RECORDS, FIELDS, AND FORMATS

To motivate interest in the topics in this section, we first present a familiar example.

EXAMPLE 5.1   Student Billing Program Revisited

Consider the following version of the student billing program.

```
    WRITE(6,10)
10 FORMAT('1','IDENTIFICATIONbbbbbBALANCE DUE')
    READ(5,15) ID,CREDIT
15 FORMAT(I6,F4.0)
    BALDUE = 100.*CREDIT + 250.
    WRITE(6,20) ID,BALDUE
20 FORMAT('0',I9,F19.2)
    STOP
    END
```

The character b in FORTRAN programs represents a blank space. We use it whenever it is important for you to identify two or more blank spaces. For example, there are five blank spaces between IDENTIFICATION and BALANCE.

If we wish to enter the value 5142 for ID and 16. for CREDIT, then the input data can be represented as follows:

	Input Record	1 2 3 4 5 6 7 8 9 10 11 ...
	1	5142 16

Following the execution of the WRITE statement, printed output would appear as follows:

Column of Printed Output

At this point, don't worry about understanding the mechanics of the above I/O. Just look at the "big picture," realizing that we are now controlling exactly how and where data are to appear on input media and printed lines.

The following classification scheme is useful in helping you understand the mechanics of I/O with FORMATs.

Field. A data item. For example, an employer might maintain data on the employee's name, social security number, rate of pay, number of deductions, and other items. Each of these data is considered a field. In the input data for the student billing example, ID number is a field and number of credits is another field. In the printed output, ID number is a field and the balance due is another field.

Record. A collection of related fields. For example, all of the data items relating to a single employee represent a single record. In the student billing example, the data items pertaining to a single student make up a record. Typically, a single data card or a single line of printed output represents a record.

File. A collection of related records. For example, a "payroll file" contains all the employee pay records; a "student file" contains data on all students.

Figure 5.1 illustrates this relationship among fields, records, and files. Note that each field contains a specific number of characters. For example, in the first input record of the student billing problem, the field for ID is six characters wide (two blanks and the digits 5142) and the field for CREDIT is four characters wide (two blanks and the digits 16), as shown in Figure 5.2.

The **FORMAT statement** is used to specify information about fields on the input record and to describe exactly how printed matter is to appear on the output medium. The general form of the FORMAT statement is given by

$$
\begin{array}{l}
\textit{format} \\
\textit{statement} \;\; \textbf{FORMAT} \left(\begin{array}{l} \textit{carriage} \\ \textit{control} \end{array} \textit{and/or} \begin{array}{l} \textit{field} \\ \textit{specifications} \end{array} \right) \\
\textit{number}
\end{array}
$$

where the "format statement number" is any unsigned integer constant up to five digits which uniquely identifies the FORMAT statement. The items enclosed within parentheses after the key word FORMAT describe the information needed by the computer to read the data or print the output. This information is written in code, called **field specifications,** in order to be brief and precise. In the next three sections, we discuss carriage control features and selected field specifications in detail.

You should note that *the FORMAT statement is a nonexecutable instruction* which simply serves as a reference for READ and WRITE statements. Since the

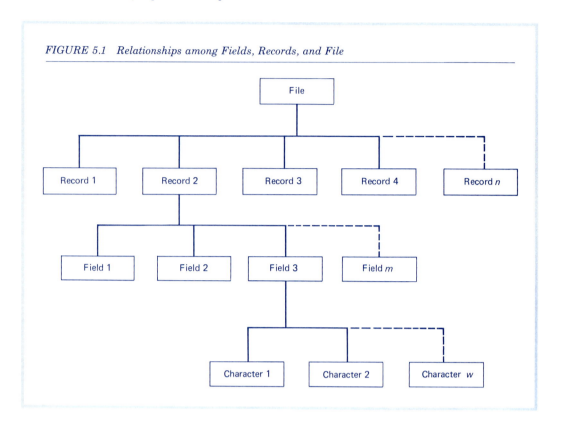

FIGURE 5.1   Relationships among Fields, Records, and File

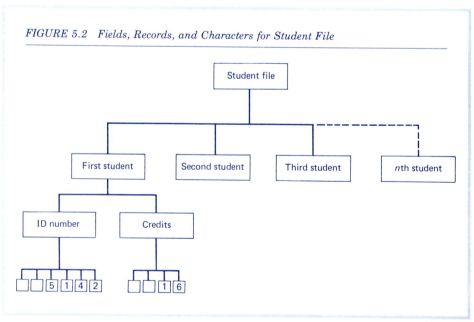

FIGURE 5.2   Fields, Records, and Characters for Student File

FORMAT statement is nonexecutable, it can be placed anywhere in the program prior to the END statement. In fact, many programmers prefer to place all FORMAT statements in a group, either at the beginning or the end of a program.

5.2
INPUT WITH FORMATS

The general form of the READ statement that uses FORMATs is

The "input unit number" is an integer code number which specifies the type of input unit which is to be used to read in your data, such as a card reader or a terminal. In our system we use the number "5" to identify either the card reader or the terminal, although this number varies depending on which computer system your institution is using. The "format statement number" references the FORMAT statement which is to be used by this READ statement. As before, the "list of variables" is a sequence of variable names separated by commas.

Each formatted READ statement in a program must reference a FORMAT statement by number in order to describe the exact appearance of data on punched cards, magnetic disk, terminal input line, or some other medium. In effect, the READ statement fetches a mirror image of the input record, and then the computer partitions this record into fields using the information specified in the associated FORMAT statement.

You should note that *the READ statement directs the reading of a new record from the data file each time the READ statement is executed*. Thus in Example 5.1 only one input record is processed, since the READ statement is executed once each time the program is run.

I-field Specification

The information within parentheses in a FORMAT statement communicates to the computer the mode (integer or real) and maximum width (number of characters) of each field within the record. The following field specification is used to enter data for *integer variables:*

I *width of field*

EXAMPLE 5.2

The following statements were used in Example 5.1:

```
READ(5,15) ID,CREDIT

15 FORMAT(I6,F4.0)
```

For now ignore the variable CREDIT and the F4.0 field specification. In effect, the READ statement tells the computer "to read in the value of ID using input unit '5' according to the FORMAT statement labeled '15'." Again, note that the input unit number is specific to your system. The format number, however, is your choice.

FORMAT "15" tells the computer "the data entry for ID is to be found in an integer field which is six columns in width." In other words, the first specification, I6, has been paired with the first variable in the list, ID. Note that ID is an integer variable; hence, the I-field specification must be paired with it.

Now, look at the input record in Example 5.1. The value that is to be stored in ID is found in the first six columns of the record; however, it is not found just anywhere in the first six columns. It is **right-justified** in, or placed at the extreme right of, the field. This is because *blanks on input are interpreted as zeros.* In other words, if 5142 had been placed in columns 1–4, for example, then 514200 would be stored under ID.

Have you wondered why we chose a field width of six for ID? No special reason, except it cannot be less than four for the given ID number. And, of course, I6 can accommodate numbers up to six digits, if needed. In general, *the choice of field width is equal to the length of the largest data item represented in a particular field.*

EXAMPLE 5.3

Consider the statements

```
READ(5,32) J, K, L

32 FORMAT(I5, I3, I2)
```

and the input record

Column Number

```
123 4 5 6 7 8 9 1011 . . .
76514 82
```

Note that J, K, and L are integer variables, and that they are paired respectively with the field specifications I5, I3, and I2. When this READ statement is executed, the input record is processed by the input unit and values for J, K, and L are stored according to FORMAT "32." In this case, 765 is stored under J, 140 under K, and 82 under L. Right? Alternatively, a zero could have been punched in column 8.

Follow-up Exercises

1. Suppose that I3 is used in Example 5.2 to enter the value of ID, and that 5142 is in columns 1–4 of the input record. What value would be stored in memory for ID?

2. For the statements

        READ(5,3) JACK,JILL,IUP,KHILL
        3 FORMAT(I1, I4, I2, I5)

    and the input record

                        1 2 3 4 5 6 7 8 9 1011121314. . .
                        5   6241984 75

    determine the stored values following execution.

3. Given the input record

                        1 2 3 4 5 6 7 8 9 . . .
                        613042 1

    write the appropriate statements which result in the storage of 613 for K, 420 for M, and 1 for N.

4. Appropriately fill in the input record below if 35 for J, 600 for K, and 3 for L are to be stored using

        READ(5,25) J,K,L
        25 FORMAT(I4,I4,I4)

                        1 2 3 4 5 6 7 8 9 1011121314. . .

F-field Specification

The field specification

> **F** *width of field* **.** *number of digits to right of decimal point*

is used to input values for *real variables*. As with the use of the I-specification, input must be right-justified; however, when the decimal point is included as part of the input, the "number of digits to the right of the decimal point" in the F-specification is overridden and the necessity for right-justification is removed. We now "eliminate" your confusion by example.

EXAMPLE 5.4

Let's go back to the input for Example 5.1:

    READ(5,15) ID, CREDIT
    15 FORMAT(I6,F4.0)

Again, look at the record in Example 5.1 on page 128. The value for ID is read in from the first field given by columns 1–6, as previously discussed. Next, the value of CREDIT is read in using the field specification F4.0, which informs the computer that input for CREDIT is found in a field given by the *next* four columns, or columns 7–10. Note that the number immediately after the "F" indicates the maximum number of characters that the field can contain. The "zero" to the right of the decimal point in the F-specification further tells the computer that the value keyed in for CREDIT has zero places to the right of the decimal point. Thus, the "16" in columns 9 and 10 of the first input record is interpreted appropriately as 16.0. Alternatively, we simply could have punched the number 16. *anywhere* in columns 7–10, as follows:

                    1 2 3 4 5 6 7 8 9 10
                      514216.

This approach of including the decimal point as part of the input causes the computer to ignore the portion of the F-specification which deals with "number of digits to the right of the decimal point." In other words, by directly using the decimal point ourselves, the control unit does not need to "figure out" where the decimal point is to be placed.

   Finally, note that CREDIT and the F-specification agree in *mode,* that is, CREDIT is a real variable and the F-specification is used to inform the computer that the number to be read is to be stored as a real variable.

EXAMPLE 5.5

Study the variations at the top of page 135 based on the following READ/FORMAT statements:

    READ(5,3) P,Q
    3 FORMAT(F10.2,F12.1)

Case a. The use of F10.2 for P causes the computer to right-justify on column 10. The "2" in F10.2 causes the placement of the decimal point two places to the left, or between the digits in columns 8 and 9, as shown.

   The use of F12.1 for Q causes the computer to right-justify 12 columns over from column 10, or on column 22. That is, the field for Q is found in columns 11 through 22. The "1" in F12.1 tells the computer to place the decimal point one place to the left, or between the digits in columns 21 and 22, as shown.

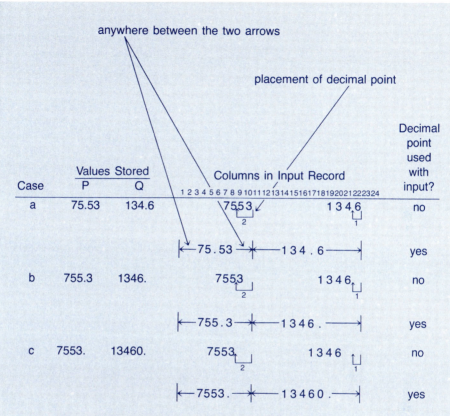

Cases b and c. Notice where the digits 7553 and 1346 have been placed. This shift in columns results in the storage of different values in P and Q.

Now, if we choose to include a decimal point in our input of real numbers, then we can key in the value of P *anywhere* in its field (columns 1–10) and the value of Q *anywhere* in its field (columns 11–22). For the most part, you will find it easier to simply key in the decimal point. When large amounts of data need to be typed, however, it saves space, time, and effort to omit the decimal point.

Follow-up Exercises

5. Indicate how you would have to enter the value 7.553 for P given the same FORMAT statement in Example 5.5. What change would you have to make in the FORMAT statement if you wanted to enter this value without a decimal point?

6. For the statements

       READ(5,105) XJACK,XJILL,UP,HILL
       105 FORMAT(F1.0,F4.1,F2.0,F5.3)

   and the input record given in Exercise 2, determine the stored values following execution.

7. The data item for CREDIT in Example 5.1 is a whole number. Why would it be wrong to use the following?

    ```
         READ(5,15) ID, CREDIT
      15 FORMAT(I6,I4)
    ```

8. Given the input record in Exercise 3, write the appropriate statements which result in the storage of 6.13 for X, 420. for Y and 0.1 for Z.
9. Appropriately fill in the input records below (with and without decimal points as done in Example 5.5) for storage of the indicated values using

    ```
         READ(5,1) COST,NUM,QUANT
       1 FORMAT(F5.2,I5,F5.0)
    ```

	Values Stored in			Columns in Input Record
Part	COST	NUM	QUANT	1 2 3 4 5 6 7 8 9 10 11 12 13 14 15 16 17 18 19 20
a	15.25	45	507.	
b	152.50	450	5070.	
c	1525.00	50	507.4	
d	105.	5	300.0	

10. Consider the following input statements which replace those in Example 5.1:

    ```
       7 FORMAT(I6)
       8 FORMAT(F4.0)
         READ(5,7) ID
         READ(5,8) CREDIT
    ```

    Describe how input records are to be prepared for entering the values for ID and CREDIT. How many input records are needed?
11. More than one READ statement can reference a single FORMAT statement, since the latter is a nonexecutable statement which simply provides information to the control unit. To illustrate, consider the following:

    ```
      10 FORMAT(F5.1,I5)
         READ(5,10) X,J
         READ(5,10) R,K
    ```

    Indicate how the values 73.4 for X, 100 for J, 607. for R, and 3 for K should be placed on input records.
12. The following version of the READ statement is available on most compilers:

    > **READ** *format statement number*, *list of variables*

    Answer Exercise 8 using this version of the READ statement.

X-field Specification

The field specification

> *width of field* **X**

is used in input to skip columns on a record.

EXAMPLE 5.6

Suppose that FORMAT "15" in Example 5.1 is changed as follows:

```
    READ(5,15) ID,CREDIT
 15 FORMAT(I6,5X,F4.0)
```

On input, the value of ID is found right-justified in columns 1–6, then the input unit skips the next five columns (7–11), and finds the value for CREDIT right-justified in columns 12–15.

The input record would look like this:

```
1 2 3 4 5 6 7 8 9 1011121314 15
   5142            1 6
```

You might ask, why would columns 7–11 contain blanks in the first place? Why not begin the next field in column 7? We agree. Blank fields in input records necessarily represent wasted space and effort. You should design input records efficiently. Generally, the X-specification is used within input FORMATs to skip fields that contain data not needed in the current analysis, as the following exercises illustrate.

Follow-up Exercises

13. In Example 5.6, suppose that the input record contains ID in columns 1–4, the student's name in a field given by columns 5–24, the home address in columns 25–71, and the value of CREDIT right-justified in columns 72–75. We wish to read in only ID and CREDIT. Appropriately change the FORMAT statement.
14. You're given an input record with the following layout:

Column	Contents	Variable Name
1–9	Social security number	ISSN
22–45	Name	NAME
46–47	Age	AGE
48	Marital status	MAR
49	Sex	ISEX
50–57	Salary (to two decimal places)	SALRY
58–80	Blank	—

Construct the READ and FORMAT statements necessary to read AGE, ISEX, and SALRY.

5.3
OUTPUT WITH FORMATS

Output from the computer often requires precise column-by-column and line-by-line control. The control of printing is accomplished by pairing WRITE statements with corresponding FORMAT statements.

The general form of the WRITE statement which uses a FORMAT statement is

The "output unit number" is an integer code number which specifies the output unit which is to be used. In many systems, this number is "6" for either the line printer in batch processing or the terminal in time-shared processing, although it varies depending on what computer you're using. The "format statement number" identifies the FORMAT statement which is to be used by this WRITE statement. As before, the list of variables is a sequence of variable names separated by commas.

As in the case of the READ statement, *a new record (line) is processed each time the WRITE statement is executed.* For example, the WRITE statement which outputs ID and BALDUE in Example 5.1 is executed once; hence, the result is one record (printed line) of output for these variables. Incidentally, the maximum length of a printed line usually varies between 80 and 132 characters, depending on the output unit.

Carriage Control

If you are using a line printer or a terminal, carriage control is the first item of information that you need to communicate through your FORMAT statement. To illustrate what we mean, consider yourself as the control unit and a typewriter as the line printer. Now, suppose you have just finished typing the last character on some line. You need to make a decision as to what to do next, don't you? In other words, should the carriage stay on the present line (as when you underscore words)? Should the carriage go down the page one line before typing (single space) or two lines (double space)? Should you go to the top of a new page? Just as you must make these simple decisions when you type, so too must you inform the printer how the vertical spacing is to appear.

In FORTRAN we control the carriage or line by using the **carriage control characters** indicated in Table 5.1. You communicate your carriage control desires to the computer by enclosing one of these characters within single quotation marks at the beginning of each FORMAT statement (just after the left parenthesis).

TABLE 5.1 *Control of Carriage**

CARRIAGE CONTROL CHARACTER	EFFECT ON CARRIAGE
+	Do not advance before printing (hold the line).
Blank space	Advance one line before printing (single space).
0	Advance two lines before printing (double space).
1	Go to the top of a new page.

* Some time-sharing systems may not utilize all of these characters; others may use different characters. Ask your instructor.

If your system does not allow the use of single quotation marks, then you may have to use one of the following options for controlling the carriage: use 1H+ instead of '+' for holding the line; use 1Hb or 1X instead of 'b' for single spacing;[1] use 1H0 instead of '0' for double spacing; use 1H1 instead of '1' for going to the top of a new page.

EXAMPLE 5.7

Consider the following statements:

```
    WRITE(6,10) J,X
10 FORMAT('0',I5,F10.4)
```

When the WRITE statement is executed, FORMAT "10" is used as reference. This FORMAT instructs the carriage to "advance or go down the page two lines from your current position before printing the contents of variables J and X." If a blank had been inserted within the quotation marks, then the carriage would have advanced one line before printing the values of J and X; that is, the values of J and X would have been printed on the next line. Alternatively, a plus sign character within the quotation marks would have resulted in output on the line where the carriage currently stands; and the number 1 would have caused the carriage to go to the top of a new page before printing out the values of J and X.

Textual Matter

The output of textual matter such as word labels, report titles, column headings, table headings, or sentences can be conceptualized as a set of characters which are "strung" together in some meaningful fashion. For example, the statement "I LOVE FORTRAN 4" is textual matter consisting of a "string" of

---

[1] Again, b is our symbol for denoting a blank space.

16 alphanumeric characters (including blanks). By an **alphanumeric character** we mean any allowable character in the FORTRAN character set, such as a letter, a numeric digit, a blank, a slash, and so forth.

The terms **string constant, literal constant,** or **character string** refer to a sequence of alphanumeric characters which is to be output exactly (literally) as it appears in the FORMAT statement. Within FORMAT statements, *most compilers allow the identification of string constants as those characters which are enclosed in single quotation marks (apostrophes).* If your compiler does not allow the use of quotation marks, then you must see Exercise 18.

EXAMPLE 5.8

In the tuition program of Example 5.1 we used the statements

        WRITE(6,10)
    10 FORMAT('1','IDENTIFICATIONᵇᵇᵇᵇᵇBALANCE DUE')

First, note that variables need not be included in the list of a WRITE statement. In this case, we only need to control the carriage and to output labels. Second, note that the carriage control character is itself a string constant, since it is enclosed in quotation marks. Alternatively, this FORMAT could have been written as

    10 FORMAT('1IDENTIFICATIONᵇᵇᵇᵇᵇBALANCE DUE')

which incorporates carriage control into the main string constant.

In either case the carriage control character causes the carriage to go to the top of a new page. Next, the labels indicated by the string constant are printed exactly as they appear in the FORMAT statement, as shown in the output of Example 5.1 on page 128.

Follow-up Exercises

15. Suppose that the printer has just finished printing line 20 and that the statement

        WRITE(6,15)

     is to be executed next. Write the appropriate FORMAT statement to print the label "HAL SPEAKS"

     a. At the beginning of line 20.
     b. At the beginning of line 21.
     c. At the beginning of line 22.
     d. Starting in the fifth print position (column) of line 22.
     e. Starting at the beginning of the first line on the next page.

16. Indicate exactly how the output would appear when the following is executed while the carriage is at the beginning of line 1:

    ```
     9 FORMAT(' STUDENT')
    10 FORMAT(' ID')
    11 FORMAT(' NUMBER')
       WRITE(6,9)
       WRITE(6,10)
       WRITE(6,11)
    ```

17. Write down the necessary statements such that at the beginning of a line which is double spaced from the preceding line of output, the computer prints

    THE ANSWER =

    Hint: Print the underscore character with a second set of WRITE and FORMAT statements which hold the line. *Note:* Some systems may not allow the underscore character.

18. String constants also can be output through the use of a **Hollerith field specification:**

    > *width of field* **H** *string constant*

    Thus,

        20 FORMAT('0','MY NAME IS')

    would be written as

        20 FORMAT(1H0,10HMY NAME IS)

    Note that the *width of the field must be exactly equal to the number of characters in the string constant,* which is 10 in this case.
    Rewrite FORMAT "10" in Example 5.8 using the Hollerith field specification. What is the disadvantage of this approach?

19. Another version of an output statement for line printers which is available on many compilers is

    > **PRINT** *format statement number*, *list of variables*

    Rewrite the statements in Examples 5.7 and 5.8 using this output statement.

I-field Specification

As in input, the output of integer variables requires the use of the specification

> **I** *width of field*

In this case output is automatically right-justified when it appears on the line. If the number to be output does not fill the field, then the left position of the field is padded with blanks. Also, you should note that the output of a negative integer requires a print position for the negative sign, which means that you should take this into consideration in specifying the field width. The plus sign for a positive integer is not printed, however.

EXAMPLE 5.9

The following statements were used in Example 5.1:

```
      WRITE(6,20) ID,BALDUE
 20 FORMAT('0',I9,F19.2)
```

For now, ignore the variable BALDUE and its F19.2 specification. When this WRITE statement is executed, the carriage of the printer first goes down the page two lines from its current position, as specified by '0'. Now, look at the output in Example 5.1 on page 128. Earlier the printer output the column headings "IDENTIFICATION" and "BALANCE DUE" on line 1 at the top of a new page; hence, the value for ID is printed on line 3, right-justified in the field given by columns 1–9.

EXAMPLE 5.10

Study the following program and its output:

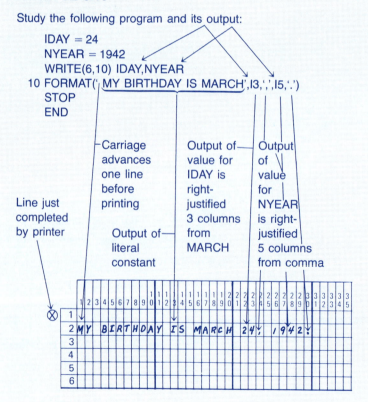

EXAMPLE 5.11

Consider the statements

        WRITE(6,3) K
     3 FORMAT(' ',I4)

and the following variations:

| | Output Columns |
Contents of K	1 2 3 4 5 ...
705	705
−705	−705
7050	7 050
−7050	* * * *
215305	* * * *

The last two cases each indicate that **format overflow** has occurred; that is, the field I4 is of insufficient width to handle the five characters in −7050 and the six characters in 215305. If K is not expected to exceed six characters, including a negative sign, then I6 should be used here.

In the above examples of format overflow, asterisks (∗) were printed in the field which overflowed. Not all systems, however, print asterisks when overflow occurs. Some systems simply print the rightmost characters which fit in the field (7050 and 5305 in the above illustrations), while other systems print some other character to indicate overflow.

Follow-up Exercises

20. Test out how format overflow occurs in your system by writing a short program which causes the overflow conditions illustrated in Example 5.11.

21. Indicate the exact output for the following program, where the input record reads:

            Column
         1 2 3 4 5 6 7 8 9 ...
         10756−401

        10 FORMAT(I2,I3,I4)
        15 FORMAT('1','M=',I4,' N=',I5)
        20 FORMAT('0','ᵇᵇᵇᵇL=',I3)
           READ(5,10) L,M,N
           WRITE(6,15) M,N
           WRITE(6,20) L
           STOP
           END

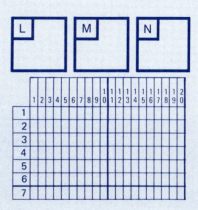

*22.   Indicate the appropriate WRITE and FORMAT statements for the following desired output:

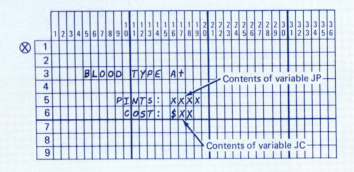

F-field Specification

The field specification used for the output of *real variables* is identical to that used for input:

F *width of field.number of digits to right of decimal point*

As with the output of integer variables, the output of real variables is right-justified. To reduce the likelihood of format overflow, care must be taken in specifying widths of sufficient size. A rule of thumb to keep in mind is that the width of the field to be used for printing the contents of a variable must be large enough to include positions for the decimal point and the sign (only the minus sign is printed), in addition to the digits. For example, if -52.1 is stored in ANS, then the field specification F5.1 is the smallest field width that will avoid format overflow. We illustrate these situations by examples which follow.

EXAMPLE 5.12

This example is a continuation of Example 5.9, which you should quickly read once more. The F19.2 specification causes the value of BALDUE to be printed to two decimal places right-justified in a 19 column field immediately to the right of the field for ID. Thus, on page 128, the value for BALDUE (1850.00) is printed in columns 22–28.

EXAMPLE 5.13

Consider the variations shown below for output of various values for the real variable B using different F-field specifications and the statements

```
    WRITE(6,8) B
  8 FORMAT('0',Fw.d)
```

Case	Contents in Memory for B	Fw.d	Printed Output 1 2 3 4 5 6 7 8 9 . . .
a	735.	F6.0	735.
b	735.	F6.2	7 3 5 . 0 0
c	735.	F5.2	* * * * *
d	−735.	F6.0	−735.
e	66.318	F8.3	66.318
f	66.318	F8.2	66.32
g	66.318	F8.1	66.3
h	.14	F7.2	0.14
i	.14	F4.2	0 . 14
j	.14	F3.2	* * *
k	−.14	F4.2	* * * *
l	−.14	F5.2	−0 . 14
m	−.14	F5.3	* * * * *
n	−.14	F6.3	−0 . 140
o	0.	F7.2	0.

These cases illustrate some points worth remembering.

1. If the number is negative, then the negative sign appears immediately to the left of the number (cases d and l); however, positive numbers do not appear with a plus sign.
2. For fractional numbers less than one, most computers print a leading zero, as in cases i and l. If the value is exactly zero, however, many computers will print blanks to the right of the decimal point (case o).
3. Format overflow occurs when the field width is of insufficient size. See cases c, j, k, and m. These conditions are respectively corrected by cases b, i, l, and n. Overflow would not occur for cases k and m if the computer suppresses the leading zero.
4. The computer *rounds the output* to the specified number of decimal positions when the number of decimal positions in the field specification is less than the actual number of decimal digits stored in the variable. See cases f and g.
5. When the number of decimal positions specified in Fw.d is greater than the decimal digits stored in the variable, the trailing positions are filled with zeros. See cases b and n.

Follow-up Exercise

23. Fill in the following table for the output of a real variable.

Case	Contents	Fw.d	Printed Output 1 2 3 4 5 6 7 8 9
a	−.1074	F6.4	|
b	−.1074	F7.4	|
c	−.1074	F9.4	|
d	.1074	F6.4	|
e	3764.	F9.1	|
f	3764.16	F9.1	|
g	3764.16	F9.0	|
h	3764.16	F9.3	|
i	3764.16	F6.3	|
j	3.105		3.1
k	3.105		3.1050

X-field Specification

The field specification

width of field **X**

inserts blanks in the line to be printed. Also, it can be used to single space the carriage.

EXAMPLE 5.14

Consider the following desired headings:

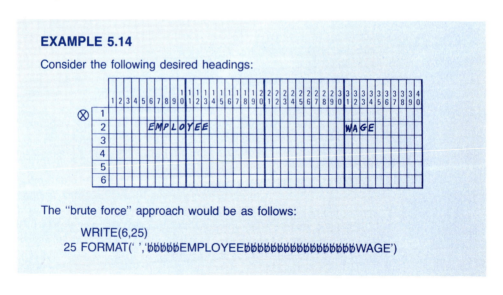

The "brute force" approach would be as follows:

```
     WRITE(6,25)
  25 FORMAT(' ','ƀƀƀƀƀEMPLOYEEƀƀƀƀƀƀƀƀƀƀƀƀƀƀƀƀƀƀWAGE')
```

A more efficient and less painful approach would be

        WRITE(6,25)
     25 FORMAT(' ',5X,'EMPLOYEE',17X,'WAGE')

Note that the carriage control signal given by the blank string constant ' ' communicates single spacing. The same effect can be achieved by using 1X, since this also is interpreted as a blank. Thus, FORMAT "25" could have been written

     25 FORMAT(1X,5X,'EMPLOYEE',17X,'WAGE')

or even more efficiently as

     25 FORMAT(6X,'EMPLOYEE',17X,'WAGE')

where it is understood that the first X is used for carriage control and the next 5 Xs are used for spacing.

Follow-up Exercises

24. In the preceding example, write the appropriate statements for printing on the next line the word NAME centered under EMPLOYEE and the word WEEKLY centered under WAGE.

*25. Indicate the appropriate WRITE and FORMAT statements for the following desired output. Use the X-specification for all blanks.

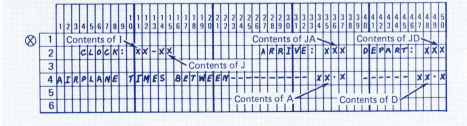

5.4
I/O PITFALLS

In our years of teaching FORTRAN, and in our own early efforts in learning FORTRAN "long" ago, we have witnessed time and again certain I/O errors which occur commonly.

Pitfall 1: Unaligned Output. Output which is other than trivial involves careful planning. For example, if you have to output table headings and values for several variables, then *before writing your FORMAT statements you can save yourself some grief by outlining your output on a sheet of plain paper, quadrille paper, or print chart.* To illustrate, consider the following layout:

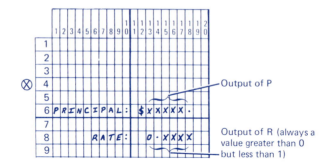

This layout was done *before* the following WRITE/FORMAT statements were written.

```
35 FORMAT('0PRINCIPAL: $',F6.0)
40 FORMAT('0',5X,'RATE:',F8.4)
   WRITE(6,35) P
   WRITE(6,40) R
```

You should confirm that these two FORMATs exactly correspond to this output plan.

Pitfall 2: Forgetting about Carriage Control in Output FORMATs.   If your output is to either a line printer or a terminal, the computer expects a carriage control character whether you like it or not. If you remember to specify carriage control in your output FORMAT, then you are in charge; otherwise, the printer will "ripoff" a column from your first field specification. For example, the statements

```
   WRITE(6,3)
 3 FORMAT('RESULT')
   WRITE(6,4) J
 4 FORMAT(I3)
```

where 23 is stored for J in memory would yield the following output:

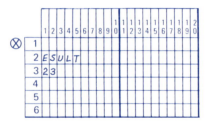

Before the string constant 'RESULT,' carriage control was not specified; hence the printer uses the R for carriage control and prints out "ESULT." Again, carriage control is omitted in the second FORMAT. So the printer takes the first column of the field specification I3 and prints the 23 right-justified in column 2 instead of column 3.

Pitfall 3: Inconsistency of Mode between the I/O Variables and the Corresponding Field Specifications.   Do you see anything wrong with the following?

```
    WRITE(6,7) K,Q
  7 FORMAT(1X,F5.0.I10)
```

In this case the integer variable K is mismatched in mode with the real specification F5.0. Also, the real variable Q is mismatched with the integer specification I10. This type of error is insidious, as many compilers will not identify the error. Instead of getting either a syntax error or an execution error, you get a "junk" number printed; that is, the number which is printed will be in the proper form according to the specification, but its value will be incorrect.

Try writing and submitting a short program which assigns, say, 15 to K and 6.5 to Q, and use the WRITE and FORMAT statements above. What happens on your system?

Pitfall 4: Insufficient Field Width for Numeric Output.   Some students misinterpret how the F-specification determines the width of a field. For example, a beginning student may use a field specification of F5.2 to output a value such as 1050.25. The student adds the width of the field (5) and the number of decimal digits (2) which are noted in the F-specification and concludes, erroneously, that seven characters can be printed—not so. Only five characters can be printed. Thus, 99.99 is the largest value that can be printed with a F5.2 specification. Values larger than this would cause format overflow (see Examples 5.11 and 5.13). What does your computer print when overflow occurs?

Additional Exercises

26. Define or describe each of the following terms:

field	X-field specification
record	carriage control characters
file	alphanumeric character
FORMAT statement	string constant
field specifications	literal constant
right-justification	character string
I-field specification	format overflow
F-field specification	

Section I.

For those who were assigned Chapter 5 before Chapter 4: Revise the output for the problems at the end of Chapters 2 and 3 as indicated below.

27. Exercise 8, Chapter 3 (page 84 Exercise 28, Chapter 2 (page 58)

```
XXX. DEGREES FAHRENHEIT IS THE SAME AS XXX.X DEGREES CELSIUS
```

28. Exercise 9, Chapter 3 (page 84) Exercise 29, Chapter 2 (page 58)

```
TOTAL COST IS $XXXXXXX.
```

29. Exercise 10, Chapter 3 (page 85) Exercise 30, Chapter 2 (page 58)

```
              UNITS    = XX
DAILY REVENUE = $XXXXX
      DAILY COST   = $XXXXX
DAILY PROFIT = $XXXXX
```

30. Exercise 11, Chapter 3 (page 85) Exercise 31, Chapter 2 (page 58)

```
IF YOU ORDER XXXX. UNITS OF BLOOD

THEN THE EXPECTED COST PER WEEK IS $XXX.XX
```

31. Exercise 12, Chapter 3 (page 85) Exercise 32, Chapter 2 (page 59)

```
IN 1976 POPULATION = XX.XXX (BILLION)
     BIRTH RATE = .XXX
     DEATH RATE = .XXX
IN XXXX POPULATION = XX.XXX (BILLION)
```
Note that this is now treated as a variable

32. Exercise 13, Chapter 3 (page 85) Exercise 33, Chapter 2 (page 59)

```
            COST = $XXXXX.XX
SALVAGE VALUE = $XXXXX.XX
        LIFE = XX YEARS
    FIRST YEAR DEPRECIATION BY STRAIGHT-LINE METHOD = $XXXXX.XX
FIRST YEAR DEPRECIATION BY DOUBLE-DECLINING METHOD = $XXXXX.XX
```

Section II.

For those who have studied Chapter 4: Revise the output for the problems at the end of Chapter 4 as indicated below.

33. Exercise 35 (page 119)

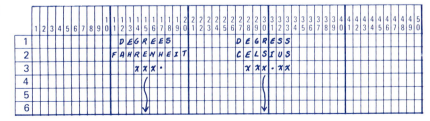

34. Exercise 36 (page 120)

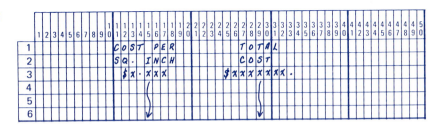

35. Exercise 37 (page 120)

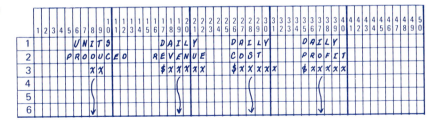

36. Exercise 38 (page 121)

37. Exercise 39 (page 122)

38. Exercise 40
    (page 122)

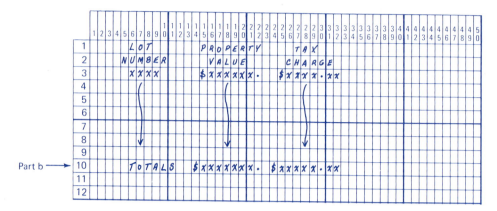

39. Exercise 41
    (page 123)

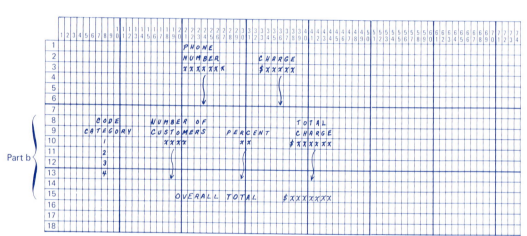

40. Exercise 42
    (page 124)

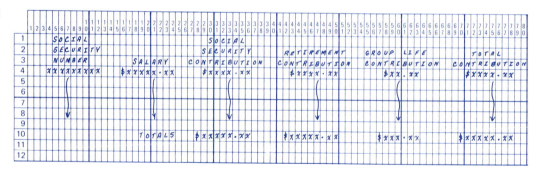

41. Exercise 43
    (page 125)

1	AGE UNDER XX; EDUCATION LEVEL = X
2	
3	AVERAGE SALARY:
4	
5	MALES = $XXXXX.
6	FEMALES = $XXXXX.

CHAPTER 6

Additional Input/Output Features

By now you should have a growing sense of confidence in your ability to design programs which solve meaningful problems. Specifically, you can design loops, incorporate transfer of control logic, control positioning of numeric I/O, and print textual matter.

This chapter further enhances your I/O programming skills by including the processing of nonnumeric data, I/O within loops, and additional FORMAT options.

6.1
ALPHANUMERIC DATA

For simplicity we have presented programs where the input and output data were numeric (look at any previous program). This is unrealistic for many management problems. A record often contains both alphabetic fields and numeric fields. For example, the "student file" at State College also would contain fields for name, address, city, state, zip code, and telephone number. These are considered **alphanumeric fields.**

Alphanumeric data, as opposed to numeric data, include not only numeric digits but also letters and special characters. As with numeric data, alphanumeric data are classified in terms of constants and variables. In Section 5.3, alphanumeric constants were called string or literal constants. In this section, we illustrate how a variable is used to input, store, manipulate, and output alphanumeric data. These so-called **alphanumeric, string,** or **literal variables** utilize alphanumeric fields of the type described in the student file example above. The I/O of alphanumeric data is accomplished by the field specification

A*width of field*

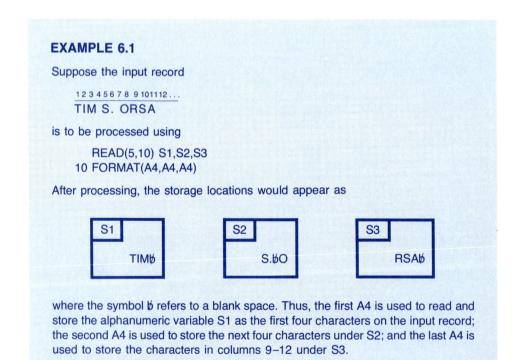

EXAMPLE 6.1

Suppose the input record

123456789101112...
TIM S. ORSA

is to be processed using

READ(5,10) S1,S2,S3
10 FORMAT(A4,A4,A4)

After processing, the storage locations would appear as

S1   S2   S3

TIM⌀   S.⌀O   RSA⌀

where the symbol ⌀ refers to a blank space. Thus, the first A4 is used to read and store the alphanumeric variable S1 as the first four characters on the input record; the second A4 is used to store the next four characters under S2; and the last A4 is used to store the characters in columns 9–12 under S3.

The statements

    WRITE(6,15) S1,S2,S3
    15 FORMAT(21X,A4,A4,A4)

would print the above stored alphanumeric data as

which is an exact reproduction of the input record.

Unfortunately, the choice of field width for the A-specification is somewhat complicated. Computer systems store a maximum number of characters per storage location, where the maximum is determined by the machinery itself and sometimes by the mode designation (integer or real) on the variable. For example, IBM 360–370 systems store a maximum of four alphanumeric characters per storage location regardless of the mode. The simplest approach is to find out the maximum number of characters per storage location for your system and to use this number as your field width in the A-specification. In Example 6.1 three memory locations were needed since the alphanumeric data were twelve characters in length, and we assumed each memory location could hold a maximum of four characters.

Follow-up Exercises

1. Suppose an input record contains an employee's first name in columns 1–8 and last name in columns 9–20. Write the READ and FORMAT statements to enter these data. If you wanted the output line to contain last name (columns 1–12) followed by a comma, a blank space, and then the first name (columns 15–22), what would your WRITE and FORMAT statements look like? Use the alphanumeric variables, NAM1, NAM2, etc., and assume that the computer stores a maximum of four characters per storage location.
2. You're given an input record with the following layout:

Column	Variable	Type of Data	Contents
1–11	SS1,SS2,SS3	Alphanumeric	Social Security Number (for example, 267-61-9814. *Hint:* Use A3 to input SS3.)
12–31	N1,N2, . . .	Alphanumeric	Name
32–33	JAGE	Numeric	Age (for example, 37)
34	MS	Alphanumeric	Marital status (M = married, S = single, O = other. *Hint:* Use A1 to input MS.)
35	SEX	Alphanumeric	Sex (M = male, F = female. *Hint:* Use A1 to input SEX.)
36–42	SAL	Numeric	Salary (to two decimal places; for example, 1534275 would be a salary of $15342.75)
42–80	Blank		

Develop READ and FORMAT statements to enter these data. Assume that the computer stores a maximum of four alphanumeric characters per storage location.

If your field width specification for alphanumeric data is more or less than the maximum number of characters allowed in a storage location (as in Exercise 2), then you will have to pay close attention to the following procedures.

Procedure 1. On *input, if you use a field width less than the maximum number of characters that can be stored in a memory location,* only the number of characters specified in the A-specification are read in (the *leftmost* characters) and blanks are inserted to fill up the memory location. On *output,* only the *leftmost* characters in a storage location are output; the remaining characters are ignored.

EXAMPLE 6.2

Sometimes a program to read in last names is written like this:

```
      READ(5,10) N1,N2,N3,N4,N5,N6,N7
   10 FORMAT(A1,A1,A1,A1,A1,A1,A1)
      WRITE(6,20) N1,N2,N3,N4,N5,N6,N7
   20 FORMAT(5X,A1,A1,A1,A1,A1,A1,A1)
```

For the input record

<u>1 2 3 4 5 6 7 ...</u>
BRANDON

the execution of the READ statement results in the following storage, where we assume a computer which stores a maximum of four characters per storage location regardless of mode:

The output appears as follows:

ƀƀƀƀBRANDON

While this approach works, it does use an excessive number of storage locations; where memory is limited, it should be avoided.

Follow-up Exercise

3. Consider a system where the maximum number of characters is four (regardless of mode) and the input record is given by

    <u>1 2 3 4 5 6 7 8 ...</u>
    CAP NEMO

    a. If we use

    READ(5,10) P,Q,M,N
    10 FORMAT(A3,A2,A1,A2)

    what do the storage locations contain following execution?

    b. If we use

    WRITE(6,15) P,Q,M,N
    15 FORMAT(1X,A3,A2,A1,A2)

    what does the output look like?
    c. If we change statement 15 to

    15 FORMAT(1X,A2,A2,A1,A1)

    how would the output appear?

Procedure 2. On *input,* if you use a *field width greater than the maximum number of characters that can fit in the memory location,* only the *rightmost* part of the field is stored. On *output,* blanks fill up the leftmost part of the field (the characters printed are *right-justified* in the field).

EXAMPLE 6.3

Some students forget about this procedure and write the following program to read in a person's name found in columns 1–12:

```
      READ(5,10) NAME
10 FORMAT(A12)
      WRITE(6,20) NAME
20 FORMAT(1X,A12)
```

For the sample input record

```
1 2 3 4  5 6 7 8 9 10 11 12 ...
HILDA ALLRED
```

the memory location (assuming four-character storage) contains

following execution. The output appears as

ƀƀƀƀƀƀƀƀLRED

As you can see from the preceding examples, it is considerably easier to use the maximum number of characters per storage location (max) in your A-specification. All you need to do is find out what max is for your system and whether or not the mode of an alphanumeric variable affects max. In general, however, you are relatively safe using A4 consistently with real alphanumeric variables regardless of the system. This is because max is at least four for real variables on most systems. In effect, then, you would be using Procedure 1, which at worst, would waste some storage space.

Follow-Up Exercises

4. Consider the input record

```
1 2 3 4 5 6 7 8 ...
CAP NEMO
```

If we use

        READ(5,8) R,Q
        8 FORMAT(A5,A3)

then what would the four-character storage locations contain?

Describe the output if we use

        WRITE(6,9) R,Q
        9 FORMAT(1X,A5,A3)

5. Unformatted input of alphanumeric variables is allowed on some systems. For example, using

        READ(5,*) R,S

    in a time-sharing system where the maximum number of characters per storage location is four regardless of mode would result in the following input for the record shown in Example 6.2:

        ?'BRAN','DON'

    Try this approach on your system. Does it work? What is the disadvantage of this approach?

6. **Character Statement.** Some versions of FORTRAN (for example, WATFIV) allow the programmer to use a declarative statement for alphanumeric variables. The statement

> **CHARACTER** *variable name∗number of characters in storage, . . .*

not only identifies string variables but, more importantly, also specifies the number of characters that are to be stored in this address. For example,

        CHARACTER S∗12,N∗7,NAME∗12

instructs the compiler that 12 alphanumeric characters are to be stored in S, 7 in N, and 12 in NAME. This is quite convenient for two reasons. First, the process of naming string variables is less tedious. For example, S replaces S1, S2, and S3 in Example 6.1; N replaces N1, N2, . . . , N7 in Example 6.2; and NAME allows us to use a single variable for all 12 characters in Example 6.3.

Second, by setting the field width in the A-specification to the number of characters in storage, I/O processing is simplified. Thus, referring to Example 6.1, the execution of

READ(5,10) S
10 FORMAT(A12)

stores the following in S:

Similarly, the execution of

WRITE(6,15) S
15 FORMAT(21X,A12)

gives the same output illustrated in Example 6.1. As is true of other declarative statements (REAL, INTEGER, DATA), *the CHARACTER statement must precede the first executable statement in the program.*
a.   Describe the storage location and output for NAME in Example 6.3 if NAME is declared as 12 characters in a CHARACTER statement.
b.   Rework Exercise 2 by utilizing a CHARACTER statement for Social Security number (SSN), name (NAME), marital status (MS), and sex (SEX).

6.2
I/O WITHIN LOOPS

You are already familiar with this topic through your work in Chapter 4. Here we consolidate I/O within loops by using a familiar example. As you study the example, keep the following in mind:

1.   Any WRITE statements that print table headings must precede the loop for the table.
2.   A READ statement within a loop is executed as often as the number of loops. This means that a new input record is required each time the READ statement is executed. Typically, entire files are processed by a single loop.
3.   A WRITE statement within a loop is executed as often as the number of loops. A new output line is printed each time the WRITE statement is

executed. Thus, the executions of a WRITE statement within a loop result in a "table-like" appearance of printed output.

4. Any WRITE statements that summarize data in a table must follow the loop that prints the table.

**EXAMPLE 6.4   Student Billing Program with Some
"Bells and Whistles"**

```
            SUMT = 0.
            SUMBD = 0.
            WRITE(6,90)
            WRITE(6,92)
        10  READ(5,94) NAME1,NAME2,NAME3,ID,CREDIT
            IF (ID .EQ. −99) GO TO 20
            TUIT = 1200.
            IF (CREDIT .LT. 12.)TUIT = 100.∗CREDIT
            BALDUE = TUIT + 250.
            WRITE(6,96) NAME1,NAME2,NAME3,ID,TUIT,BALDUE
            SUMT = SUMT + TUIT
            SUMBD = SUMBD + BALDUE
            GO TO 10
        20  SUMFEE = SUMBD − SUMT
            WRITE(6,98) SUMT,SUMFEE,SUMBD
            STOP
        90  FORMAT('1',21X,'TUITION AND FEE REPORT')
        92  FORMAT('0',4X,'NAME',4X,'IDENTIFICATION',3X,'TUITION',
        1           6X,'FEE',4X,'BALANCE DUE')
        94  FORMAT(A4,A4,A4,I6,F4.1)
        96  FORMAT('0',A4,A4,A4,I9,F15.2,5X,'250.00',F11.2)
        98  FORMAT('0',19X,'TOTALS',F11.2,F11.2,F11.2)
            END
```

Continuation when using cards → (braces pointing to lines 92, 1, 94)

For the input records given by

Column

```
1 2 3 4  5 6 7 8 9 1011121314151617181920212223 . . .
FC MEYER          5142 16
RH MEYER          6245 185
AA ARISTOTLE       322  9
PP ERUDITE        3164 12
JJ AIDS           1969  6
                   −99
```

printed output would appear as follows:

```
                              1111111111222222222233333333334444444444555555555566 6
           1 2 3 4 5 6 7 8 9 0 1 2 3 4 5 6 7 8 9 0 1 2 3 4 5 6 7 8 9 0 1 2 3 4 5 6 7 8 9 0 1 2 3 4 5 6 7 8 9 0 1 2 3 4 5 6 7 8 9 0 1 2
 1                                      TUITION AND FEE REPORT
 2
 3         NAME        IDENTIFICATION    TUITION       FEE       BALANCE DUE
 4
 5  FC  MEYER          5142              1200.00      250.00      1450.00
 6
 7  RW  MEYER          6245              1200.00      250.00      1450.00
 8
 9  AA  ARISTOTLE      322                900.00      250.00      1150.00
10
11  PP  ERUDITE        3164              1200.00      250.00      1450.00
12
13  JJ  AIDS           1969               600.00      250.00       850.00
14
15                     TOTALS            5100.00     1250.00      6350.00
16
17
```

Follow-up Exercises

7. Roleplay the computer by processing the input records in the example. Carefully confirm the exact placement of output. As you do this, fill in the contents in memory for the following addresses.

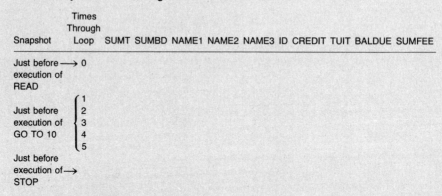

Snapshot	Times Through Loop	SUMT	SUMBD	NAME1	NAME2	NAME3	ID	CREDIT	TUIT	BALDUE	SUMFEE
Just before execution of READ →	0										
Just before execution of GO TO 10	1 2 3 4 5										
Just before execution of STOP →											

8. Modify the program to include:
   a. Underlining under the table headings from column 1 to column 60 (if your system does not allow the underscore character, then use the minus sign).
   b. Underlining between the last row in the table and the row which gives totals from column 29 to column 58.
   c. A dollar sign ($) in columns 29, 41, and 51 of each row of the table.
   d. A dollar sign in columns 27, 39, and 49 in the TOTALS row.

*9. **Input Error Detection.** Modify the program to test for errors in the input data for CREDIT. Specifically, if the number of credits is less than 1 or greater than

21, then instead of the regular row in the table, the student's name, ID, and number of credits should be printed as follows:

Columns 61–72	Columns 73–80	Columns 81–86
Name	Identification number	Number of credits to one decimal place

Once this error condition is printed, processing should continue with the next student. Include a flowchart.

6.3
OTHER FORMAT OPTIONS

Several other format field specifications are available in FORTRAN besides those we have discussed. For example, field specifications exist for the output of real numbers with exponents and real numbers having double precision (or 15 digits of storage rather than the usual 7), for the option of working with tabs (much like a typewriter), and others.

Besides additional field specifications, FORTRAN also offers certain useful format options, three of which we present next.

Repeat Factor

A **repeat factor** is an unsigned integer constant which appears immediately in front of a field specification which is to be repeated.

EXAMPLE 6.5

In the statements

```
      WRITE(6,10)A,B,C,J,K
   10 FORMAT('0',F10.2,F10.2,F10.2,I5,I5)
```

A, B, and C each are to be output using F10.2, and J and K each use I5. This FORMAT can be simplified considerably using repeat factors for each group:

```
                                    repeat factors
   10 FORMAT('0',3F10.2,2I5)
```

Slash

Often we want to use a single FORMAT to describe the appearance of more than one line of output. A slash in the FORMAT statement causes the output record (line) to be terminated.

A series of consecutive slashes has the effect of producing blank lines on the page. The number of blank lines will be one less than the number of consecutive slashes if the slashes are in the middle of the FORMAT statement; however, the number of blank lines will be equal to the number of slashes appearing at the very beginning or end of the FORMAT statement.

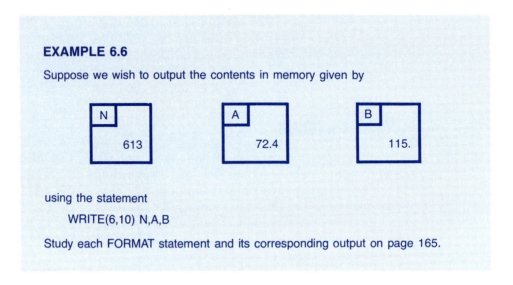

EXAMPLE 6.6

Suppose we wish to output the contents in memory given by

using the statement

    WRITE(6,10) N,A,B

Study each FORMAT statement and its corresponding output on page 165.

To summarize the use of slashes for output: n slashes in the middle of the FORMAT statement cause $n - 1$ blank lines to be printed, where *the first slash is used to return the carriage to the beginning of the current line*. When n slashes are used at the beginning or the end of the FORMAT statement, however, n blank lines are printed. In the case where slashes appear at the end, the first slash is again used to return to the beginning of the current line, after which $n - 1$ blank lines by the remaining slashes plus one additional blank line by the right parenthesis are printed. Note that, in general, *the right outer parenthesis causes the identical behavior of a slash.* The same conclusions can be drawn about records on input. Note, however, that *on output the control unit looks for carriage control following the last slash in a sequence of slashes at the beginning or middle of the FORMAT statement.*

**Inner Parentheses

Are you ready for this? Parentheses may be used within the outer parentheses of a FORMAT statement. The items within a set of inner parentheses make up what we call a **group.** These groups may be nested to a depth of two, at most. The combination of pairing repeat factors with groups is a very powerful feature in output FORMAT statements, which we illustrate next.

**Sections marked with double asterisks include material that is of above average difficulty.

Case	FORMAT Statement	Output	Comment
a.	10 FORMAT(1X,I5/'0',2F8.1)	Row 2: 613 Row 4: 72.4 115.0	The 1X brings carriage to line 2 for printing of N. The slash terminates line 2, *which brings carriage back to beginning of line 2.* The '0' brings carriage to line 4 to print A and B.
b.	10 FORMAT(1X,I5//1X,2F8.1)	Row 2: 613 Row 4: 72.4 115.0	The first slash terminates line 2 and the second slash terminates line 3. The 1X brings the carriage to line 4. Result identical to case a.
c.	10 FORMAT(1X,I5///1X,2F8.1)	Row 2: 613 Row 6: 72.4 115.0	Compared to case b, the two additional slashes cause lines 4 and 5 to be terminated as well.

d.	10 FORMAT(1X,I5/1X,F8.1/1X,F8.1)	Row 2: 613 Row 3: 72.4 Row 4: 115.0	This case is identical to but more efficient than
			
			    WRITE(6,10) N
			10 FORMAT(1X,I5)
			    WRITE(6,11) A
			    WRITE(6,11) B
			11 FORMAT(1X,F8.1)

e.	10 FORMAT(//5X,'PAYROLL REPORT'/1X, 'IDENTIFICATIONᵇᵇPAY')	Row 4: PAYROLL REPORT PAY Row 5: IDENTIFICATION	The first slash brings carriage to line 2 and the second slash to line 3. The first X out of 5X brings carriage to line 4. The last slash brings carriage to beginning of line 5. *The right parenthesis brings carriage to line 6.*

EXAMPLE 6.7

In part d of Example 6.6, the statement

    10 FORMAT(1X,I5/1X,F8.1/1X,F8.1)

could have been written as

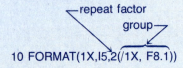

    10 FORMAT(1X,I5,2(/1X, F8.1))

If the repeat factor had been 15, for example, then you should really appreciate the efficiency of this approach.

To illustrate another convenience due to grouping, try to determine what the following statements accomplish before reading on:

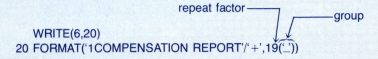

    WRITE(6,20)
    20 FORMAT('1COMPENSATION REPORT'/'+',19('_'))

First, the carriage goes to the top of a new page. Next, the heading, COM-PENSATION REPORT is printed in columns 1–19 of line 1. The slash then causes the carriage to return to the beginning of line 1. The '+' causes the carriage to remain on line 1, after which nineteen underscore characters are printed immediately under the heading. Do you realize what would be required without the use of the repeat factor and inner parentheses? A string constant with nineteen underscore characters.[1]

Follow-up Exercises

*10. Rework Exercise 25 in Chapter 5 on page 147 using options in this section.
*11. Rework Exercise 22 in Chapter 5 on page 144 using options in this section. Underscore the heading BLOOD TYPE A+.
 12. Indicate an appropriate FORMAT statement for

        READ(5,25) A,B,C,D,E

      where three input fields for A, B, and C of ten columns each are on the first input record and two input fields for D and E of five columns each are on the next input record. Each variable is to be entered to two decimal places.
 13. Determine the FORMAT statement for

        WRITE(6,30) A,I,B,J,C,K,D,L

---

[1]If the underscore character is not available in your system, then you can underline using the minus sign character; however, instead of holding the carriage just before underlining, you should single space to the next line (use 1X or ' ' instead of '+' for carriage control).

which results in output of twelve column field widths all on one print line at the top of a new page. Output real variables to one decimal place and insert a percent sign (%) immediately after the output of each real variable. Use inner parentheses.

14. Describe output for each of the following.

WRITE(6,3) M,N

In each case the carriage is currently on line 20.
a. 3 FORMAT(1X,I5,10(/)1X,I5)
b. 3 FORMAT(10(/)1X,2I5)
c. 3 FORMAT(1X,2I5,10(/))
d. 3 FORMAT(1X,6('*'),2I5,2X,6('*'))
**e. WRITE(6,3) K,L,M,N
   3 FORMAT(1X,2(/1X,2(10X,I5)))
   where the contents of M and N are given above and

15. Indicate what is wrong with each of the following:
a. 3 FORMAT(1X,I5//I5)
b. 3 FORMAT(///2I5)
c. 3 FORMAT(1X,I523X,I5)
**d. 3 FORMAT(1X,(4(I5,I3,2(4X,F5.0))))

6.4
IMBALANCE BETWEEN LIST
AND SPECIFICATIONS

In our work so far in this chapter, the number of variables in the list of a READ or WRITE statement has equaled (balanced) the number of *corresponding* field specifications in the FORMAT statement. FORTRAN allows imbalance between these two numbers for greater flexibility.

**Exercises marked with double asterisks are more difficult than other exercises. Answers to these are not given in the back of the text. Ask your instructor for answers.

Less Variables in List than Corresponding Specifications in FORMAT Statement

In this case the following procedure is adopted by the processor: The variables in the list are processed and leftover specifications in the FORMAT statement are ignored.

EXAMPLE 6.8

Given the statements

        READ(5,8) A,B
      8 FORMAT(F5.1,F10.2,I5)

F5.1 is used to read in A, F10.2 is used to read in B, and I5 is simply ignored. Then why have I5 in the first place you ask? Perhaps because some other READ statement such as

        READ(5,8) X,Y,J

also is used in the program, which allows us to get by with one FORMAT.

More Variables in List than Corresponding Specifications in FORMAT Statement

For this situation the procedure states: Variables in the list are processed until the specifications in the FORMAT statement are exhausted, after which the record is terminated; the scan of the FORMAT statement is repeated as many times as needed until all variables are processed. If inner parentheses are present, then repeat scans begin with the *rightmost* group, including the repeat factor which may be present.

EXAMPLE 6.9

Suppose we wish to output the contents in memory given by

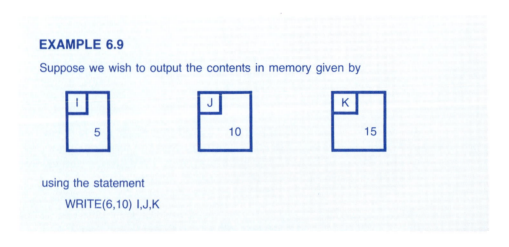

using the statement

        WRITE(6,10) I,J,K

Study each FORMAT statement below and its corresponding output.

Case	FORMAT Statement	Output	Comment

a. `10 FORMAT(1X,I5)`

```
          1111111111222
 1234567890123456789012
     5
    10
    15
```

FORMAT is scanned three times from the beginning. Note the use of carriage control for each scan.

b. `10 FORMAT(1X,2I5)`

```
          1111111111222
 1234567890123456789012
     5   10
    15
```

First scan prints contents of I and J. Second scan prints contents of K.

c. `10 FORMAT(' CODES',I5)`

```
          1111111111222
 1234567890123456789012
 CODES   5
 CODES  10
 CODES  15
```

Three scans.

**d. `10 FORMAT(' CODES'/(1X,I5))`

```
          1111111111222
 1234567890123456789012
 CODES
     5
    10
    15
```

Three scans. First prints label and contents of I. Second and third print J and K, respectively. Note how scans beyond the first reset to rightmost group, or nearest left parenthesis from end of scan.

**e. `10 FORMAT(' CODES'/2(1X,I5))`

```
          1111111111222
 1234567890123456789012
 CODES
     5   10
    15
```

Two scans. First prints label, I, and J. Second prints K. Note reset at repeat factor.

**f. `10 FORMAT(' CODES',2(1X,I5))`

```
          1111111111222
 1234567890123456789012
 CODES    5    10
    15
```

Two scans.

Follow-up Exercises

16. Describe input records:

        READ(5,12) A,B,L,C,D
     12 FORMAT(2F5.0,I10)

17. Fill in the output:

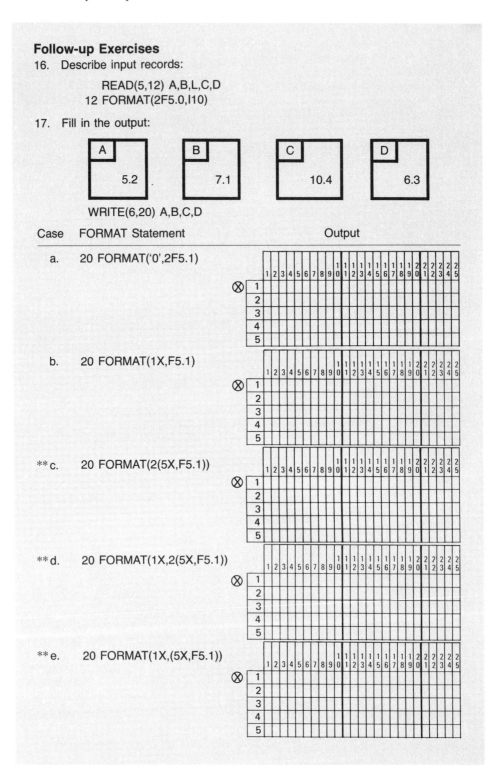

        WRITE(6,20) A,B,C,D

Case   FORMAT Statement

a.   20 FORMAT('0',2F5.1)

b.   20 FORMAT(1X,F5.1)

**c.   20 FORMAT(2(5X,F5.1))

**d.   20 FORMAT(1X,2(5X,F5.1))

**e.   20 FORMAT(1X,(5X,F5.1))

6.5
BANK SAVINGS ACCOUNT PROGRAM

We now give you a breather from new material and provide an opportunity for you to consolidate what you have learned. Study once more the savings bank account program of Example 2.14 on page 56.

In this section we modify the previous version: first, by incorporating I/O with formats; second, by designing an inner loop which automatically calculates and prints accumulated funds over a specified range of quarters; and third, by including an outer loop which allows the user to rerun the model with new data.

Step I.   Analyzing the Problem
   1.   *Problem Statement*
      Bank savings program with two loops: inner loop for printing accumulated funds given principal, interest rate, and quarterly range; outer loop for processing new data
   2.   *Data Input*
      a.   Principal (P)
      b.   Quarterly interest rate (R)
      c.   Lower limit (N1), upper limit (N2), and increment (IN) of quarterly range
      d.   Option for rerunning or terminating the program (K)
   3.   *Data Output*
      P, R, and accumulated funds (A) for each quarter in the range (N)
   4.   *Computations and Logical Processes*
$$A = P \cdot (1 + R)^N$$

Step II.   Preparing the Flowchart. See Figure 6.1. This flowchart illustrates *nested loops,* wherein one loop (the inner loop) lies entirely within another loop (the outer loop).

Batch Version

The accompanying printout on page 173 illustrates Step III (coding the problem) and Step IV (debugging the program) for a run using the WATFIV compiler. Four data cards were used, as follows:

	Column			
1 2 3 4 5 6 7 8 9 10 11 12 13 14 15 16 17 18 19 20 21 22 23 24 . . .				
3000	0 1 5	4	4 0	4
1				
3000	0 2	8	4 0	8
0				

FIGURE 6.1 *Flowchart for Bank Savings Account Program*

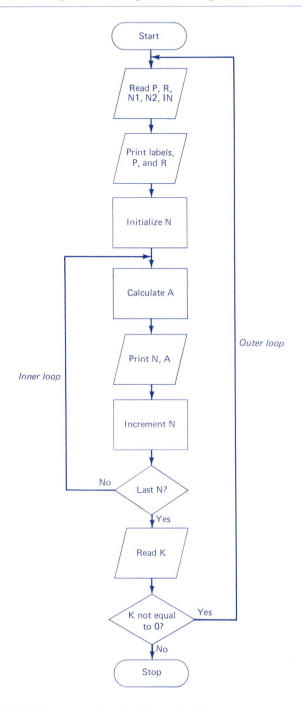

```
        C   PROGRAM DETERMINES ACCUMULATED FUNDS IN A SAVINGS ACCOUNT
        C
        C   VARIABLE KEY:
        C    P=PRINCIPAL
        C    R=QUARTERLY INTEREST RATE
        C    N1=LOWER LIMIT
        C    N2=UPPER LIMIT
        C    IN=QUARTERLY RANGE INCREMENT
        C    A=ACCUMULATED FUNDS
        C
0001      1 FORMAT (F8.2,F7.4,3I3)
0002      3 FORMAT(///'0PRINCIPAL: $',F8.2//6X,'RATE:',
          *        F10.4//' QUARTER    ACCUMULATED FUNDS'/1X,27('-')/)
0003      5 FORMAT (3X,I3,8X,F10.2)
0004      7 FORMAT (I1)
        C
0005     10 READ(5,1) P,R,N1,N2,IN
0006        WRITE(6,3) P,R
        C
        C   INITIALIZE TABLE LOOP COUNTER
        C
0007        N=N1
        C
        C   BEGIN TABLE LOOP
        C
0008     20    A=P * (1. + R)**N
0009        WRITE(6,5) N,A
        C
        C   INCREMENT TABLE LOOP COUNTER
        C
0010        N= N + IN
        C
        C
0011        IF(N .LE. N2) GO TO 20
        C
        C   INPUT AND TEST FOR OUTER LOOP-- IF K=0, THEN TERMINATE RUN
        C
0012        READ(5,7) K
0013        IF(K .NE. 0) GO TO 10
0014        STOP
0015        END
```

```
PRINCIPAL: $ 3000.00

    RATE:    0.0150

QUARTER   ACCUMULATED FUNDS
--------------------------

    4         3184.08
    8         3379.44
   12         3586.80
   16         3806.88
   20         4040.46
   24         4288.37
   28         4551.50
   32         4830.77
   36         5127.19
   40         5441.77


PRINCIPAL: $ 3000.00

    RATE:    0.0200

QUARTER   ACCUMULATED FUNDS
--------------------------

    8         3514.96
   16         4118.30
   24         4825.21
   32         5653.47
   40         6623.89
```

Follow-up Exercises

18. How much money is in the savings account after two years at an interest rate of 1.5 percent per quarter? At 2 percent per quarter? Confirm these figures using an electronic calculator. How much better off are you after ten years under the higher interest rate?
19. Confirm that the I/O in the computer run is consistent with the I/O indicated by READ, WRITE, and FORMAT statements in the program.
20. Modify the program to:
    a. Read the name of the customer in columns 25–44 of each data card.
    b. Print the customer's name in the first 20 columns of a line double spaced above the printout of PRINCIPAL.
21. Can you think of a way to eliminate N1 from the program without altering the values that are stored for N?

Time-Sharing Version

Step III.   Coding the Problem

```
 1 FORMAT(F6.0,F7.4,3I3)
 2 FORMAT('0PLEASE ENTER PRINCIPAL, RATE,'/
          '   BEGINNING QUARTER, ENDING QUARTER,'/
          '   AND INCREMENT'/)
 3 FORMAT(///'0PRINCIPAL: $',F6.0//6X,
          'RATE:',F8.4//'0QUARTERbbbACCUMULATED FUNDS'
          /1X,27('–')//)
 4 FORMAT(3X,I3,8X,F10.2)
 5 FORMAT('0DO YOU WISH TO RUN AGAIN? 0=NO, 1=YES')
10 WRITE(6,2)
   READ(5,1) P,R,N1,N2,IN
   WRITE(6,3) P,R
   N = N1
20 A = P*(1. + R)**N
   WRITE(6,4) N,A
   N = N + IN
   IF (N .LE. N2) GO TO 20
   WRITE(6,5)
   READ(5,*) K
   IF (K .NE. 0) GO TO 10
   STOP
   END
```

Step IV.   Debugging the Computer Program.   The initial test run of this program on a time-sharing system is shown below. To distinguish easily between the computer printout and the user's typing, the latter is underlined.

PLEASE ENTER PRINCIPAL, RATE,
BEGINNING QUARTER, ENDING QUARTER,
AND INCREMENT

?3000.   .015   4 40   4

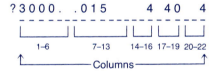

PRINCIPAL: $ 3000.

   RATE: 0.0150

QUARTER	ACCUMULATED FUNDS
4	3184.08
8	3379.44
12	3586.80
16	3806.88
20	4040.46
24	4288.37
28	4551.50
32	4830.77
36	5127.18
40	5441.77

DO YOU WISH TO RUN AGAIN? 0=NO, 1=YES
?1

PLEASE ENTER PRINCIPAL, RATE,
BEGINNING QUARTER, ENDING QUARTER,
AND INCREMENT

?3000.   .02   8 40   8

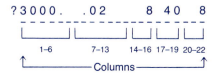

PRINCIPAL: $ 3000.

   RATE: 0.0200

QUARTER	ACCUMULATED FUNDS
8	3514.96
16	4118.30
24	4825.21
32	5653.47
40	6623.89

DO YOU WISH TO RUN AGAIN? 0=NO, 1=YES
?0

STOP
TIME 0.24 SECS.

Note 1: Some programs used on time-sharing systems are termed **interactive** because of the person-machine communication, which is facilitated by a program which is "conversational." The design of conversational programs requires that each READ statement be preceded by a WRITE statement which prints a description of the input that is to follow. Thus, the string constants in FORMAT "2" are printed just before the inputs of P, R, N1, N2, and IN. Similarly, the string constant in FORMAT "5" is printed immediately before the input of K.

Note 2: In time sharing, the use of FORMAT statements for input at the terminal usually is more tedious than list directed (unformatted) input. For example, the list-directed input given by

?3000.,.015,4,40,4

eliminates the need for spacing and keeping track of columns.

Note 3: The excessive lengths of FORMATS "2" and "3" require continuation lines. In this program, the method of continuing a line has been omitted purposely, as time-sharing systems differ in their methods. Those of you using a time-sharing system should ask your instructor how to continue a statement which is too long for one line.

Follow-up Exercises

22. How much money is in the savings account after two years at an interest rate of 1.5 percent per quarter? At 2 percent per quarter? Confirm these figures using an electronic calculator. How much better off are you after ten years under the higher interest rate?

23. Confirm that the I/O in the computer run is consistent with the I/O indicated by READ, WRITE, and FORMAT statements in the program. Indicate the changes needed in the program to place two blank lines between the last line of the accumulated funds portion of the output and the question: DO YOU WISH TO RUN AGAIN ? 0 = NO, 1 = YES. Also include one blank line between the question and your answer to the question.

24. Modify the program to:
    a. Read the name of the customer in columns 1–20 of an input line which precedes each line of input for P, R, N1, N2, N. Also, print appropriate conversation just before the input of customer name.
    b. Print the customer's name in the first 20 columns of a line double spaced above the printout of PRINCIPAL.
    c. Eliminate N1 from the program without altering the values that are stored for N.

**25. Modify the program such that K is treated as an alphanumeric variable. In response to the question "DO YOU WISH TO RUN AGAIN?" the user now responds YES or NO instead of 1 or 0. If the user responds YES, then go back to statement 10. If the user responds NO, then stop execution. If the user inputs something other than YES or NO, then go back to the WRITE statement that prints the question. In the logical IF statement, K now must be compared to another variable which stores a legitimate response (YES or NO). Use the following DATA statement to store these legitimate responses:

    DATA RES1,RES2/'YES','NO'/

or

    DATA RES1,RES2/3HYES,2HNO/

6.6
I/O PITFALLS

Pitfalls 1–4: A Review.   The most common I/O errors are:

1. Unaligned output
2. Forgetting about carriage control in output FORMATs
3. Inconsistency of mode between the I/O variables and the corresponding field specifications
4. Insufficient field width for numeric output

You should review the detailed discussion of these pitfalls in Section 5.4 on page 147 once more.

Pitfall 5: Alphanumeric Data Fields.   Pay careful attention to Procedures 1 and 2 in Section 6.1 when the field width in your A-specification differs from the maximum number of characters allowed in a storage location of your computer. Example 6.3 on page 158 illustrates a very common error.

Pitfall 6: Slashes.   Pay close attention to the effect of slashes in FORMAT statements. Remember that n slashes at the beginning or the end of a FORMAT cause the printing of n blank lines. In the middle of a FORMAT, however, n slashes cause the printing of $n - 1$ blank lines.

Also, *don't forget to specify carriage control following the last slash in a sequence that appears at the beginning or the middle of output FORMATs.* For example, suppose 3 is stored in J and 500 is stored in K and we use the following statements:

    WRITE(6,1) J,K
    1 FORMAT(1X,I1//I3)

We would get the following output:

Column

Row	1	2	3	4	5	6	7	8	9	10	11	12	13	14	15	16	17	18	19	20
1																				
2	3																			
3																				
4	0	0																		

In this case, carriage control was not specified following the second slash, so the printer "rips off" the first position in the field for carriage control, effectively leaving 00 for the output of 500. The statement

    1 FORMAT(1X,I1//1X,I3)

would give the desired output:

Column

Additional Exercises

26.   Define or explain the following:

alphanumeric fields	use of repeat factor
alphanumeric data	use of slash
alphanumeric variable	use of inner parentheses
string variable	imbalance between variable lists
literal variable	and FORMAT specifications
A-specification	nested loops

27.   **Alphanumeric Distribution: Interstate Commerce Commission.** The Interstate Commerce Commission (ICC) routinely receives written complaints regarding illegal, fraudulent, and other unsavory business practices. Below is a test file which stores the type of complaint (code 1, 2, or 3) in column 1 and the state (abbreviation) where the complaint originated in columns 3 and 4.

Column on Input Record

```
  1 2 3  4 5 6 7 8 9 ...
  1  OH
  1  R I
  3  C A
  2  F L
  3  M A
  1  M A
  2  N Y
  3  C A
  4  G A
  2  C A
  1  P A
  3  N Y
  1  C A
  2  N J
  1  N Y
  1  M D
  2  T X
  1  L A
  2  M I
  5  I L
  1  + +
```

Design a flowchart and write a program which inputs this test file and prints the following:

```
          1 1 1 1 1 1 1 1 1 1 2 2 2 2 2 2 2 2 2 2 3 3 3 3 3 3 3 3 3 3 4 4 4 4 4 4 4 4 4 4 5
  1 2 3 4 5 6 7 8 9 0 1 2 3 4 5 6 7 8 9 0 1 2 3 4 5 6 7 8 9 0 1 2 3 4 5 6 7 8 9 0 1 2 3 4 5 6 7 8 9 0
 1  **ERROR ON RECORD NUMBER 9    INVALID CODE = 4
 2  **ERROR ON RECORD NUMBER 20   INVALID CODE = 5
 3
 4
 5      **SUMMARY BY CODE**
 6
 7      CODE   FREQUENCY   PERCENT
 8
 9        1        8          44
10        2        6          33
11        3        4          22
12                18          99
13
14
15      **SUMMARY BY STATE**
16
17      STATE   FREQUENCY   PERCENT
18
19        CA       4          36
20        MA       2          18
21        NY       3          27
22        OH       1           9
23        RI       1           9
24                11          99
```

Part a { rows 5–12 }
Part b { rows 15–24 }

a. First, check your input data for accuracy. A valid complaint code is a 1, 2, or 3; any other number in this field is invalid. Then determine the frequency and percentage of complaints by type of complaint.

b. In addition to the output in part a, output the frequency and percentage of complaints by state. (This version of the program prints a summary for only five states. In actual practice we would treat all 50 states.)

Hint: Use a DATA statement to store the abbreviations for these five states. For example, California (CA) would be stored as follows:

    DATA S1/'CA'/

or

    DATA S1/2HCA/

Thus, the variable S1 stores the following in memory:

Now, suppose we let S represent the input variable for state. The statement

IF (S .EQ. S1) K1 = K1 + 1

counts the number of complaints from California. OK? Note that the last-record check is based on encountering ++ for state abbreviation.

28. **Sales Forecasts.**   Design a flowchart and write a program which calculates and prints sales forecasts by quarters for future years based on current sales and projected annual growth rate. For example, if currently we are at the end of the second quarter in the year 1980 and sales this quarter were $1.2 million with a projected growth rate of 2 percent per quarter, then forecasts through 1982 should appear as follows:

```
        **SALES FORECAST**

CURRENT YEAR    QUARTER     SALES
        1980        2     $ 1.200M

  YEAR  QUARTER    SALES
  1980        3    1.224
  1980        4    1.248
  1981        1    1.273
  1981        2    1.299
  1981        3    1.325
  1981        4    1.351
  1982        1    1.378
  1982        2    1.406
  1982        3    1.434
  1982        4    1.463
```

Note that the next forecast is always the last forecast increased by the growth rate.
a.   Run your program for the following two sets of input data:

Product Name	Current Year	Current Quarter	Current Sales	Growth Rate	Years into Future
OUIJA BOARD	1980	2	1.20	.02	2
STARTREK CHARM	1981	4	0.85	.05	4

Note that the sample output is based on the first set of input data.
b.   Input the name of the product (up to 16 characters) as part of the input record and print the main heading as

SALES FORECAST FOR name of product

beginning in column 1.
c.   Design your program so that you have an outer loop for processing product forecasts. Terminate the loop either by the counter method or the last-record-check method.

29. **Comparison of Depreciation Methods.**   Read Exercise 33 in Chapter 2 (page 59) and Exercise 13 in Chapter 3 (page 85). In this problem we wish to print a "depreciation

schedule" over the life of the asset. For the automobile which costs $4200, lasts four years, and has a salvage value of $200, the following output is desired:

```
                    DEPRECIATION SCHEDULES

A.  STRAIGHT LINE METHOD
B.  DOUBLE DECLINING BALANCE METHOD

          DEPRECIATION      ACCUMULATED        BOOK
   YEAR      EXPENSE        DEPRECIATION       VALUE
A.
    1       1000.00          1000.00          3200.00
    2       1000.00          2000.00          2200.00
    3       1000.00          3000.00          1200.00
    4       1000.00          4000.00           200.00
B.
    1       2100.00          2100.00          2100.00
    2       1050.00          3150.00          1050.00
    3        525.00          3675.00           525.00
    4        262.50          3937.50           262.50
```

a. Prepare a flowchart and write a program which outputs depreciation schedules for the following assets:

Asset	Cost ($)	Life (Years)	Salvage Value ($)
Car	4,200	4	200
Kidney machine	200,000	10	500
Building	75,000	40	0

Cost and salvage value should be input to two decimal places in a field ten columns wide; life should be input in a field two columns wide.

Draw conclusions which compare the effects of these two methods of depreciation. Under what conditions is one method more desirable than the other with respect to the impact on income taxes?

b. Input the name of the asset (up to 16 characters) as part of the input record and print the main heading as

DEPRECIATION SCHEDULES FOR name of asset

beginning in column 6.

c. Design your program so that you have an outer loop for assets. Terminate the loop either by the counter method or the last-record-check method.

30. **Aging Retail Customer Accounts.** Aging of customer accounts requires that the date of the sale be compared with the current date; the difference between these dates is the age of the account. For example, assume the current date is July 1 (182nd day) and a sale was made on February 16 (47th day); then the transaction is 136 days old (183 − 47). Note that 1 must be added to the current date (or 1 must be subtracted from the sale date) in order to compute the correct age.

In the terminology of accounting, this is called "aging accounts receivables." Reports of this type serve a useful purpose in assessing the collection practices and assets of a company.

Output for the report should conform to the following:

			AGED CUSTOMER ACCOUNTS				
				DOLLAR	NUMBER OF	
				AMOUNTS	CUSTOMERS	
OVER 60 DAYS OLD				XXXXX.XX	XXX	
BETWEEN 30-60 DAYS OLD				XXXXX.XX	XXX	
UNDER 30 DAYS OLD				XXXXX.XX	XXX	
TOTALS				XXXXXX.XX	XXXX	

The input for your program includes:

1. Current date (entered as a three-digit number)
2. Customer file consisting of date of sale (entered as a three-digit number—for example, February 16 would be entered as 47, while December 26 would be 360); amount of sale (maximum value of 9999.99)

a. Prepare a flowchart and write a program which produces the report described above. Process the data given below. Check the output from your program after aging the accounts by hand. Current date: July 1. End your loop by using either an appropriate end-of-record test or a counter. If you use the counter method, do not make it specific to these ten records of input data.

Sale Date	Amount of Sale ($)
January 10	310.52
February 20	168.40
March 24	278.29
April 21	125.10
May 5	25.13
May 17	64.79
June 3	37.05
June 13	105.15
June 27	75.98
June 30	44.15

(Assume 28 days in February)

b. Add a new column to the report next to "Number of Customers" which reads "Average Dollar Amounts." This column is computed as "Dollar Amounts" divided by corresponding "Number of Customers" in each category.

c. As part of your input for each record, include the name and address of the customer in an alphanumeric field which is 40 columns wide. Make up your own names and addresses. Before the output of the report on aging accounts receivables, print the name, address, and amount of sale for each customer. (Assume one transaction per customer.)

**d. Enter your input for current and sale dates as four-digit numbers, where the first two digits represent the month and the last two digits the day. For example, April 21 would be entered as 0421. Alternatively, enter the month (4) and day (21) separately. Then, design the logic of your program such that the elapsed time is computed (111 for April 21).

31. **Placement Service: A File Search.** The Placement Office on a college campus is beginning a computerized matching of employers and graduating seniors looking for a job. Each student that registers with the Placement Office provides the following information:

Item	Columns
Name	1–20
Student ID	21–24
Address	25–45
Grade point average (GPA)	50–52
Major (codes 1 to 10)	53
Willing to relocate (1 = no, 2 = yes)	54
Willing to travel (1 = no, 2 = yes)	55

a. A firm is looking for a business major (code = 6) with a GPA of 3.25 or better who is willing to relocate and travel. Search the accompanying Placement Office File and print the name and address of each student that meets the criteria for this job. Include a flowchart with your program.

**b. Generalize your program such that the Placement Office can output the name and address of each student who satisfies criteria which the firm specifies as part of the input. In other words, define variables in your program for (1) desired major, (2) desired minimum GPA, (3) relocation requirement, and (4) travel requirement. Thus, for the criteria in part a, the input for these variables would be 6, 3.25, 2, and 2, respectively. Assume that those students who are willing to relocate or travel would also be willing to accept a job that does not require relocation or travel.

Placement Office File

Name	ID	Address	GPA	Major	Relocate	Travel
Iris Abbot	2119	11 Estell Drive	3.45	6	1	2
Calvin Budnick	3112	Burnside Dorm	2.75	8	2	2
Susan Dent	4112	12 Upper College Rd.	2.50	3	2	2
Ken Driden	4819	RR3	2.85	4	1	1
Flo Further	5811	107 Ocean Rd.	3.00	1	1	2
Ben Lewis	6237	Heath Dorm	3.25	3	1	1
Bella Senate	6331	71 Boston Neck Rd.	3.75	6	1	2
Wally Tenure	6581	15 South Rd.	3.25	8	2	1
Alice Tillitson	8211	97 North Rd.	3.30	6	2	2
Martin Wiener	9112	10 Ballentine	3.70	6	2	1

Test your program by running the following data for inquiries on the above four variables:

(1)	(2)	(3)	(4)
6	3.25	2	1
3	3.00	1	1
8	3.70	2	2

Are you capable of looping for these three inquiries? Or must you run the program again for each inquiry? Time-sharing users can accomplish the former by storing the Placement Office File on disk. Batch users, however, will have to wait until Chapter 9 to handle looping for this problem.

32. **Credit Billing.** Design a flowchart and write a program which prints monthly bills (statements) for Muster Charge, an internationally reknown credit card company. Use the following input data for three customers:

Field	Columns on Input Record
Customer name	1–12
Address	13–40
Credit limit (to zero decimal places)	41–45
Previous balance (to 2 decimal places)	46–51
Payments (to 2 decimal places)	52–57
New purchases (to 2 decimal places)	58–63

```
1 2 3 4 5 6 7 8 9 101112131415 16 1718 192021 22232425262728293031323334 35363738394041424344454647484950515253545556575859606162636465
NAPOLEON B.   19 WATERLOO ST PARIS  FRANCE     800 30000 10000 70000
DUKE WELLY     1 THAMES  AVE   LONDON  GB     1500135070132070 64552
BETSY ROSS    1776 FLAG  ST    BOSTON MA USA 2000   3649   3649   1915
```

Certain conditions must be reflected by the program:

1. The finance charge is 1.5 percent of the difference between the previous month's balance and the payments made since the previous month.
2. The minimum payment due is determined according to one of four results:
   a. If the new balance exceeds the credit limit, then the minimum payment is the difference between the new balance and the credit limit plus 10 percent of the credit limit. Thus, for the first statement (903.00 − 800.00) + 10 percent (800) gives $183.00.
   b. If the new balance is $100 or more and does not exceed the credit limit, then the minimum payment is 10 percent of the new balance. Thus, for the second statement, 10 percent (675.97) gives $67.60.
   c. If the new balance is less than $100, then the minimum payment is set to the new balance (see the third statement).
   d. If the new balance is negative, then the minimum payment is zero.

3. A warning is printed if the credit limit is exceeded by the new balance (Muster Charge doesn't fool around).
4. Printout for each person should take up exactly twelve lines in order to conform to the size of the billing statement. In other words, the printout should appear exactly as illustrated.

Output for these three customers would appear as follows:

```
NAPOLEON B.          PREVIOUS                  FINANCE    NEW            NEW
19 WATERLOO ST       BALANCE  -  PAYMENTS  +   CHARGE  +  PURCHASES  =   BALANCE
PARIS  FRANCE
                      300.00  -   100.00  +    3.00  +     700.00  =     903.00

                                              MINIMUM PAYMENT DUE  =     183.00
**WARNING**
YOU HAVE EXCEEDED YOUR CREDIT LIMIT
CONTROL YOURSELF, OR ELSE...



DUKE WELLY            PREVIOUS                  FINANCE    NEW            NEW
1 THAMES AVE         BALANCE  -  PAYMENTS  +   CHARGE  +  PURCHASES  =   BALANCE
LONDON GB
                     1350.70  -  1320.70  +    .45  +      645.52  =     675.97

                                              MINIMUM PAYMENT DUE  =      67.60






BETSY ROSS           PREVIOUS                  FINANCE    NEW            NEW
1776 FLAG ST         BALANCE  -  PAYMENTS  +   CHARGE  +  PURCHASES  =   BALANCE
BOSTON MA USA
                       36.49  -    36.49  +    0.  +       19.15  =      19.15

                                              MINIMUM PAYMENT DUE  =      19.15
```

5. Terminate your loop when the first four characters of a name are ****. This is accomplished as follows: Use the statement

DATA EOF/'****'/

or

DATA EOF/4H****/

to store the following in memory:

Then use a logical IF statement to test whether or not the first four characters of a name equals EOF.

33. **Checking Account Report.**   Prepare a flowchart and write a program which produces a monthly checking account report for each customer. Checking charges are calculated on the basis of the following information:

1. If the ending balance is less than $200, then the following service charges are assessed: a monthly fee of $.80 plus a charge of $.10 per honored check (withdrawal). No charges are assessed for deposits.
2. If the ending balance is $200 or more, then no service charges are assessed.
3. If a check "bounces" (that is, if the balance were to become negative when the bank attempts to honor a check), then a charge of $5.00 is assessed, and the current balance is reduced by this amount. This charge is made for each check that bounces. Checks that bounce are not honored. In other words, a withdrawal is not made from the account, since the person to whom the check was made out does not get paid. Also the $200 limit does not apply to this bounce charge; that is, if a check bounces, then the $5.00 charge is assessed regardless of the ending balance.

For each bank customer

1. The first line of input data contains four items:
   a.   The bank account number (6 digits)[2]
   b.   Name (20 characters)
   c.   Number of transactions (N), or total number of withdrawals and deposits (2 digits)
   d.   Beginning balance (field width of 8)
2. N lines follow the first line, each line representing a single transaction. If the value is negative, the transaction is a withdrawal; if the value is positive, the transaction is a deposit (field width of 8).

Sample Input

```
1 2 3 4 5 6 7  8 9 1011121314151617 18 192021222324252627282930313233343536373839 40
614275WENDY  BRANDON                    3    741.62
50.75
-125.
-260.50
216422RICHARD R.  WEEKS         4    250.15
-115.
-80.75
100.
-236.80
   -99
```

---

[2]If the bank account number is −99, there are no more customer transactions to be processed.

Sample Output

```
                 BANK STATEMENT
WENDY  BRANDON              614275

BEGINNING BALANCE          741.62

TOTAL  DEPOSITS             50.75
TOTAL  WITHDRAWALS         385.50
CHARGES                      0.

ENDING  BALANCE            406.87



                 BANK STATEMENT
RICHARD  R.  WEEKS         216422


BEGINNING BALANCE         250.15

TOTAL  DEPOSITS           100.00
TOTAL  WITHDRAWALS        195.75
CHARGES                     6.00

ENDING  BALANCE           148.40

**TOTAL  NOT  HONORED**

          236.80
```

Debug your program using the above I/O and the following additional input:

Account Number	Name	N	Beginning Balance	Transactions
make these up.		4	240.00	−50.00
				−35.00
				−175.00
				+200.00
make these up.		7	450.00	−300.00
				−125.00
				+200.00
				−75.00
				−35.00
				+150.00
				−66.00

Before designing your program, make sure you understand the logic by solving these problems by hand. By the way, this is a good program to use diagnostic WRITE statements (traces) for current balance and charges during the debugging phase.

34. **Payroll.**   A small firm recently decided to computerize the payroll process for its hourly employees. The data needed to prepare the weekly payroll are found in the following layout:

Column	Item
1–20	Name
21–25	Employee number
26–27	Number of dependents
28–30	Rate of pay
32–34	Number of hours worked
38–45	Total earnings thus far this year

To determine the pay for each employee, the following facts must be included in your program:

1. Gross pay is defined as pay for regular time plus pay for overtime. Overtime pay is 1.5 times the regular rate for each hour above 40.
2. Social Security tax (FICA) is 6.13% of gross pay. The deduction is made until the employee's cumulative earnings are above $22,900, after which there is no deduction.
3. Deduction for income tax and group health plan are tied to the number of dependents as follows:

Dependents	Income Tax (%)	Group Health ($)
1	22 of gross pay	2.50 per week
2	20	3.60
3	18	5.10
4	16	6.00
5 or more	13	6.50

4. Net pay is defined as gross pay less FICA deduction less income tax deduction less group health deduction.

Prepare a flowchart and write a payroll program to produce a "wage summary report" consisting of a line for each employee; the line contains employee name, hourly rate, hours worked, gross pay, FICA, income tax, group health, and net pay.

After individual figures are printed, the program is to print totals for gross pay, each deduction, and net pay. Include appropriate report and column headings. Be neat! Use the following data to test your program:

Name	Number	Dependents	Rate ($)	Hours	Total Earnings ($)
Al Della Bitta	1940	4	2.50	60	1500.00
Frank Budnick	1942	4	8.25	40	24000.00
Diane Marcotte	2001	1	6.00	45	12300.00
Arun Sanghvi	1776	3	8.00	35	22850.00

Either include a last-record test or use a variable (not a constant) to test your loop for termination.

CHAPTER 7

Additional Control Statements

In this chapter we continue our discussion of control statements by introducing new statements that will allow you to express complex logic and multiple loops more concisely. Moreover, your programs will be easier to code, debug, review, and update.

7.1
COMPOUND LOGICAL
IF STATEMENT[1]

Up to now we have used simple logical IF statements, that is, those that use a single *relational* expression made up of a relational operator (.EQ., .NE., .LT., .LE., .GE., .GT.) wedged between two arithmetic expressions. **Compound logical IF** statements combine two or more relational expressions into a single logical expression. You can accomplish this by using the **logical operators** .AND., .OR., and .NOT. to connect relational expressions. The resulting expression is called a **logical expression.** For example, the relational expression B .GT. A can be combined with the relational expression B .LT. C using the logical operator .AND. as follows:

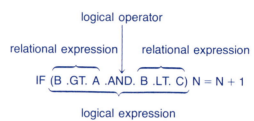

The entire expression within the parentheses is a logical expression which when tested will be either true or false.

Logical Operator .AND.

When using .AND., if the *conditions* (relational expressions) are true, then the logical expression is true, and the statement to the right of the IF statement is executed. If, however, any condition is false, then the statement to the right of the IF is skipped, and control is transferred to the next executable statement in the program.

EXAMPLE 7.1

A salesperson receives a bonus of $250 if monthly sales are above $10,000 *and* if travel expenses are below $1,000. This logic can be written as

```
   .
   .
BONUS = 0.
IF (SALES .GT. 10000. .AND. TRAVEL .LT. 1000.) BONUS = 250.
   .
   .
```

---

[1]Not all FORTRAN compilers allow this form of the logical IF statement.

Logical Operator .OR.

When using .OR., if *any* relational expression is true, then the logical expression is true, and the statement to the right of the IF is executed; however, if *all* the conditions are false, then the statement to the right of the IF is skipped and control is transferred to the next executable statement in the program.

EXAMPLE 7.2

An employer is interested in interviewing students with an economics (code 3) or business (code 7) major. A search routine to find such persons might include the following statement:

    IF (MAJOR .EQ. 3 .OR. MAJOR .EQ. 7) WRITE(6,1) ID,NAME

Logical Operator .NOT.

The logical operator .NOT., unlike .AND. and .OR., is used with only one condition. When .NOT. is used the statement to the right of the IF is executed only if the relational expression is false. In effect, .NOT. reverses the value of the single relational expression. If the relational expression is false, then .NOT. makes the logical expression true. If the relational expression is true, then .NOT. causes a false logical expression.

EXAMPLE 7.3

To count the number of single people (marriage code = 1) who responded to a survey, the following statement can be used:

    IF (.NOT. (MAR .NE. 1)) SINGLE = SINGLE + 1.

This logical IF statement is equivalent to the following:

    IF (MAR .EQ. 1) SINGLE = SINGLE + 1.

Hierarchy

In complex situations you may use more than one logical operator within a single IF statement. For logical expressions of this type the conditions are evaluated in the sequence:

    .NOT.
    .AND.
    .OR.

EXAMPLE 7.4

The logical expression in

IF (I .EQ. J .OR. I .GT. K .AND. AG .LE. 5.) SUM = SUM + AG

is true (SUM = SUM + AG is executed) when the following values are stored:

In this case .AND. is evaluated before .OR., which means that we should focus on the portion given by

I .GT. K .AND. AG .LE. 5.

This logical expression is false for the data given. We are now left with

I .EQ. J .OR. (false expression)

Since the relational expression to the left of .OR. is true, it follows that the entire logical expression is true, so

SUM = SUM + AG

is executed.
    Parentheses can be used to modify the order of evaluation for logical operators. For example, the logical expression within

IF ((I .EQ. J .OR. I .GT. K) .AND. AG .LE. 5.) SUM = SUM + AG

is now false, so

SUM = SUM + AG

is not executed. Now, the first evaluation given by

(I .EQ. J .OR. I .GT. K)

is true, but

(true expression) .AND. AG .LE. 5.

is false since AG is not less than or equal to 5.

EXAMPLE 7.5   Mopups Revisited

To illustrate the use of the compound logical IF within a complete program we rewrite the rate scheduling problem (Example 4.10) on page 113. Observe how the compound logical IF statements make this program more concise and easier to follow than the old version.

Old Version
_____

```
      K = 0
      READ(5,*) N
    5 K = K + 1
          READ(5,*) NUM,SIZE
          IF (SIZE .LT. 10.) GO TO 10
          IF (SIZE .LT. 20.) GO TO 15
          IF (SIZE .LT. 30.) GO TO 20
          TP = 205.*(SIZE − 29.) + 6900.
          GO TO 25
   10     TP = 250.*SIZE
          GO TO 25
   15     TP = 240.*(SIZE − 9.) + 2250.
          GO TO 25
   20     TP = 225.*(SIZE − 19.) + 4650.
   25     WRITE(6,*) NUM,SIZE,TP
          IF (K .LT. N) GO TO 5
          STOP
          END
```

New Version
_____

```
  K = 0
  READ(5,*) N
5 K = K + 1
      READ(5,*) NUM,SIZE
      IF (SIZE .LT. 10.) TP = 250.*SIZE
      IF (SIZE .GE. 10. .AND. SIZE .LT. 20.) TP = 240.*(SIZE − 9.) + 2250.
      IF (SIZE .GE. 20. .AND. SIZE .LT. 30.) TP = 225.*(SIZE − 19.) + 4650.
      IF (SIZE .GE. 30.) TP = 205.*(SIZE − 29.) + 6900.
      WRITE(6,*) NUM,SIZE,TP
  IF (K .LT. N) GO TO 5
  STOP
  END
```

Follow-up Exercises

1. Indicate what is wrong (if anything) for each of the following:

   a. IF (SIZE .GE. 10. .AND. .LT. 20.) TP = 240.*(SIZE − 9.) + 2250.
   b. IF (A*C .EQ. 7.2 .OR. B .EQ. C) GO TO 10
   c. IF (IN .EQ. ON AND COST .LT. REV) WRITE(6,3) NUM

2. Code the following:
   a. If X is less than 2 or greater than 10 then go to statement number 25.
   b. If A is greater than B and C then subtract A from E and store the result in D.

3. Given the stored values

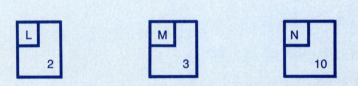

indicate whether or not K is incremented for each of the following:

a.   IF (.NOT. (L .LT. M)) K = K + 1
b.   IF (L .GT. M .AND. M .EQ. N .OR. L .LE. N .AND. M .LT. 4) K = K + 1
c.   IF (L .GT. M .AND. (M .EQ. N .OR. L .LE. N) .AND. M .LT. 4) K = K + 1
d.   IF ((L .GT. M .AND. M .EQ. N .OR. L .LE. N) .AND. M .LT. 4) K = K + 1
**e. IF ((L .GT. M .AND. (M .EQ. N .OR. L .LE. N)) .AND. M .LT. 4) K = K + 1

4.   Code the following flowcharts using compound logical IF statements.
   a.

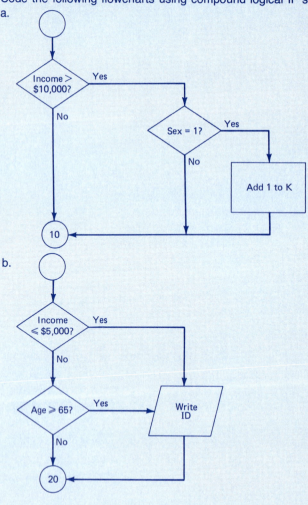

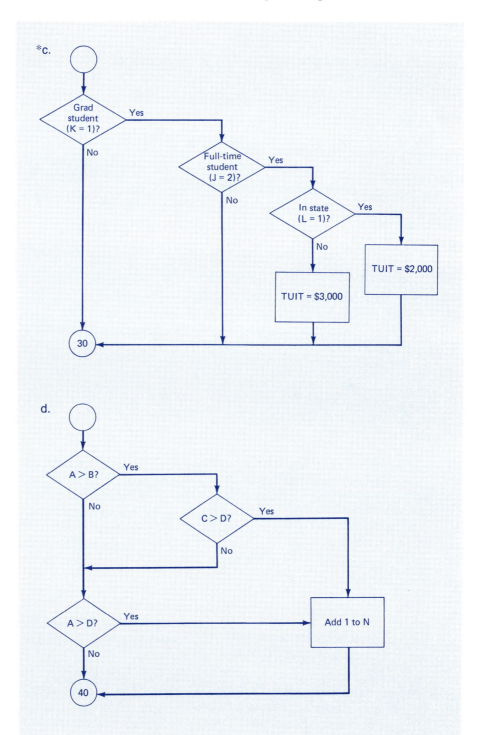

**7.2

ARITHMETIC IF STATEMENT

Another type of IF statement, called the **arithmetic IF,** is used to select up to three alternative paths (the logical IF provides only two paths).

The general form of the arithmetic IF is

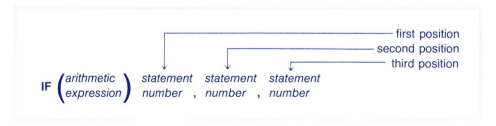

and a specific example is given by

IF (GPA − 3.5) 20,15,10

The computer first evaluates the arithmetic expression, and a value results which is either negative, zero, or positive. Based on this value, the computer then selects the path to which it should branch according to the following procedures:

1. If the value of the arithmetic expression is less than zero (negative), then the program branches to the statement number in the first position following the arithmetic expression. For example, if GPA has a value of 3.1, then the expression GPA − 3.5 is negative and the program branches to statement number 20.
2. If the value of the arithmetic expression is zero, then the program branches to the statement number in the second position following the arithmetic expression. For example, if GPA has a value of 3.5, then the expression GPA − 3.5 is zero and the program branches to statement number 15. We should caution you, however, *that the evaluation of a real arithmetic expression may not give exactly zero (to seven places)*. So, if possible, *avoid the use of real arithmetic expressions when the statement number in the second position is different from the other two statement numbers.*
3. If the value of the arithmetic expression is greater than zero (positive), then the program branches to the statement number found in the third position following the arithmetic expression. For example, if GPA has a value of 3.8, then the expression GPA − 3.5 is positive and the program branches to statement number 10.

In all cases, statement numbers must be associated with *executable* statements; otherwise, an execution error will result. Also, all three statement numbers must be included to the right of the parentheses.

EXAMPLE 7.6   Student Billing Problem

Example 4.4 on page 98 is rewritten below to illustrate the use of the arithmetic IF for two-way branching.

```
      KOUNT = 1
10 READ(5,*) ID,CREDIT
         TUIT = CREDIT*100.
         BALDUE = TUIT + 250.
         WRITE(6,*) ID,BALDUE
         KOUNT = KOUNT + 1
      IF (KOUNT − 3) 10,10,30
30 STOP
   END
```

When KOUNT has the value 2 stored, then IF (KOUNT − 3) is equivalent to IF (2 − 3), the result of which is a negative value. Therefore, the program branches to statement number 10 when the arithmetic IF is executed. When KOUNT has the value 3 stored, then IF (KOUNT − 3) is equivalent to IF (3 − 3), which is a zero value; again the program branches to statement number 10. When KOUNT has the value 4 stored, the statement IF (KOUNT − 3) is equivalent to IF (4 − 3), which is a positive value. Thus, the program branches to statement number 30 and stops.

EXAMPLE 7.7   Mopups Again

The logical IF statements in the old version of Example 7.5 can be replaced by arithmetic IF statements. You should trace through the logic of the program below in order to confirm that it represents the same transfers as before.

```
      K = 0
      READ(5,*) N
 5 K = K + 1
         READ(5,*) NUM,SIZE
         IF (SIZE − 10.) 10,15,11
11       IF (SIZE − 20.) 15,20,12
12       IF (SIZE − 30.) 20,13,13
13       TP = 205.*(SIZE − 29.) + 6900.
         GO TO 25
10       TP = 250.*SIZE
         GO TO 25
15       TP = 240.*(SIZE − 9.) + 2250.
         GO TO 25
20       TP = 225.*(SIZE − 19.) + 4650.
25       WRITE(6,*) NUM,SIZE,TP
      IF (K − N) 5,30,30
30 STOP
   END
```

Recent trends toward improving the readability of programs favor the use of logical IFs over arithmetic IFs. Surely you should agree that either version of the Mopup problem in Example 7.5 is considerably easier to follow than the version in this example. So, unless you have a unique three-way transfer of control, we suggest the use of either logical IFs or the computed GO TO statement discussed in the next section.

Follow-up Exercises

5. Rewrite the program of Example 4.6 on page 101 using the arithmetic IF statement in place of the logical IF statement.
6. Modify the program of Example 7.7 to loop by the last-record-check method; processing terminates whenever a negative or zero value is input for NUM. Use the arithmetic IF statement to test NUM.

7.3
COMPUTED GO TO STATEMENT

The **computed GO TO statement** is another transfer of control statement; it is a multiple transfer statement where control is passed to one of a group of statements based on the value of an integer variable.

The general form of this statement is

$$\textbf{GO TO} \left(\begin{matrix} statement & statement & statement \\ number &, & number, & \ldots, & number \end{matrix} \right), \begin{matrix} integer \\ variable^2 \end{matrix}$$

To illustrate this statement, consider the following two equivalent versions when L has the value 1 or 2:

Version A	Version B
IF (L .EQ. 1) GO TO 20	GO TO (20,15), L
15 K1 = K1 + 1	15 K1 = K1 + 1
.	.
.	.
GO TO 25	GO TO 25
20 K2 = K2 + 1	20 K2 = K2 + 1
.	.
.	.
25 . . .	25 . . .
.	.

Thus, control goes to statement number 20 when the value stored in L is 1 and to statement 15 when the value stored in L is 2.

In general, statement numbers (15 and 20 in this example) are assigned to *executable* statements located within your program. The integer variable (L in the example) must store an integer value (1, 2, 3, etc.) that falls within the

---

[2] The full version of FORTRAN 77 allows any integer expression. Moreover, the comma following the right parenthesis is optional in FORTRAN 77.

range of 1 and the total number of statement numbers within the parentheses. In our example, L must be a 1 or a 2 because there are only two statement numbers within the parentheses. The program branches to the statement number whose *position* within the parentheses corresponds to the *value* of the integer variable. In the example, if L stores a value of 1, then the program branches to the statement number in the first position, or statement 20; if L stores a 2, then the program branches to the statement number in the second position, or statement 15.

If the value of the integer variable is less than one or greater than the total number of statement numbers within the parentheses, then control passes to the next executable statement following the computed GO TO statement.

The computed GO TO statement often is used when a data item has been coded (for example, 1 = freshman, 2 = sophomore, 3 = junior, 4 = senior) and each category requires a different set of calculations, as we illustrate next.

EXAMPLE 7.8 SAT Scores by Class

Every year State College prints a Fact Book which includes SAT scores of students categorized as Freshmen, Sophomore, Junior, and Senior. Figure 7.1 illustrates the flowchart for the program which accomplishes the necessary calculations.

```
      REAL JUN
      DATA K,FR,SOPH,JUN,SEN,TOTF,TOTSO,TOTJ,TOTSR/0,8*0./
      READ(5,*) NOS
   10 READ(5,*) ICLASS,SATVER,SATMTH
      TOTSAT = SATVER + SATMTH
      GO TO (20,30,40,50), ICLASS
   20 FR = FR + 1.
      TOTF = TOTF + TOTSAT
      GO TO 100
   30 SOPH = SOPH + 1.
      TOTSO = TOTSO + TOTSAT
      GO TO 100
   40 JUN = JUN + 1.
      TOTJ = TOTJ + TOTSAT
      GO TO 100
   50 SEN = SEN + 1.
      TOTSR = TOTSR + TOTSAT
  100 K = K + 1
      IF (K .LT. NOS) GO TO 10
      AVGF = TOTF/FR
      AVGS = TOTSO/SOPH
      AVGJ = TOTJ/JUN
      AVGSR = TOTSR/SEN
      WRITE(6,*) AVGF,AVGS,AVGJ,AVGSR
      STOP
      END
```

FIGURE 7.1 Flowchart for Enrollment Distribution Program

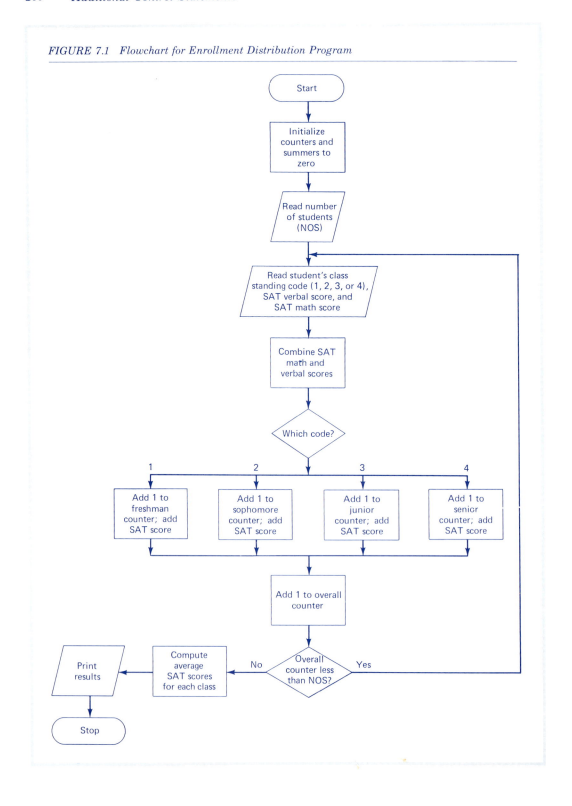

When ICLASS has the value 1, the program branches to the first statement number from the list of statement numbers (statement 20) and increases the counter and accumulates the combined SAT score for freshmen. When ICLASS has the value 2, the program branches to the second statement number from the list of statement numbers (statement 30) and updates the sophomore calculations. Similarly, when ICLASS has the value 3 the program branches to the third statement number (statement 40) and when ICLASS has the value 4 the program branches to the fourth statement number (statement 50).

Note the use of the REAL statement to treat the number of juniors (JUN) as a real variable. The counters were specified as real variables in order to avoid mixing mode when calculating the averages. Finally, note the use of the DATA statement to efficiently initialize counters and summers to zero. The 8*0. means eight zeros.

Follow-up Exercises

7. What is wrong with each of the following?
   a. GO TO (25,20,15) IN
   b. GO TO (20,20,30), ON
   c. GO TO (4,6,8,10,12), K where 6 is stored for K
8. What changes would you make in Example 7.8 if class code is represented by the variable CLASS?
*9. Write a program for the flowchart on page 202 using
   a. logical IFs first;
  **b. arithmetic IFs next; and
   c. the computed GO TO last.
   Which approach do you prefer?

7.4
LOOPS ONCE AGAIN: DO STATEMENT AND CONTINUE STATEMENT

The DO statement facilitates the programming of loops by providing an automatic counter and end-of-loop test. Its general form is given by

		counter			
DO	statement number	(index) variable	= initial value,	terminal value,	incremental value

For example,

    DO 10 KOUNT = 1,3,1

represents a specific DO statement.

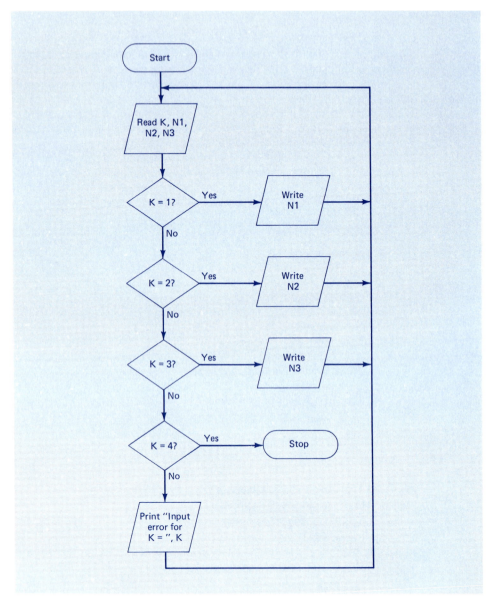

DO-Loop Mechanics

In the DO instruction you must:

1. Indicate the range of the DO statement. The statements which are to be repeated as part of the loop are those executable statements beginning with the statement *immediately following* the DO and ending with the statement specified by the statement number in the DO. These statements are called the **body** or **range** of the DO-loop. Statement number 10 in the

example indicates the last instruction in the loop. Out of convenience, many programmers prefer to specify a dummy statement called the **CONTINUE statement** as the last statement in the loop. In the above example, the DO would be paired with the CONTINUE as follows:

```
          DO 10 KOUNT = 1,3,1
body of   ⌠   ⋮
the loop  ⌡   ⋮
       10  CONTINUE
```

In this case the body of the loop ends with the executable statement which just precedes the CONTINUE statement. Note, however, that the *DO need not be paired with the CONTINUE.* The last statement in the loop can be any executable statement except GO TO, STOP, arithmetic IF, or another DO.

2. Identify the integer variable that represents your counter. The counter in a DO-loop is usually called the **index.** The variable KOUNT is the index in the above example.

3. Specify the initial value of the index. KOUNT in this example is first set equal to 1.

4. Set the terminal value that the index must exceed before your loop is terminated. (KOUNT must exceed 3 before the loop is terminated.)

5. Establish the increment for the index. (KOUNT is incremented or changed by 1 each time the loop is processed.)

EXAMPLE 7.9   Student Billing Program with DO-Loop

In Example 4.4 we illustrated a loop using the counter method. This program can be rewritten using the DO and CONTINUE statements as shown, where both programs produce identical results.

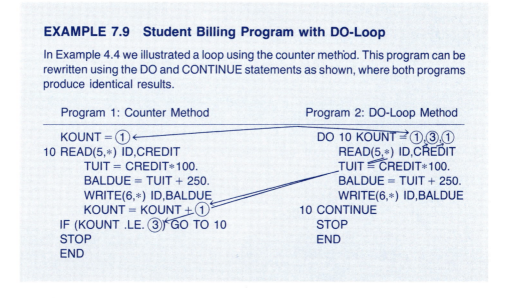

Program 1: Counter Method	Program 2: DO-Loop Method
KOUNT = ①←	DO 10 KOUNT = ①,③,①
10 READ(5,*) ID,CREDIT	READ(5,*) ID,CREDIT
TUIT = CREDIT*100.	TUIT = CREDIT*100.
BALDUE = TUIT + 250.	BALDUE = TUIT + 250.
WRITE(6,*) ID,BALDUE	WRITE(6,*) ID,BALDUE
KOUNT = KOUNT + ①	10 CONTINUE
IF (KOUNT .LE. ③) GO TO 10	STOP
STOP	END
END	

Notice in Program 2 that the body of the DO-loop is within the boundaries of the DO and CONTINUE statements. Thus, these two statements act as "visual brackets" for your loop and improve the readability of your program. As before, we indent the body of the loop to make it stand out.

When the DO statement is executed the first time, the index in the DO statement is set equal to the initial value (KOUNT set equal to 1). Then the computer reads in the data, computes tuition and amount due, and prints the results. At the end of the loop, when the computer executes 10 CONTINUE, the following happens:

1. The index (KOUNT in this example) is incremented by the incremental value specified in the DO statement (1 is the increment in this example).
2. The index is tested to determine if it exceeds the terminal value defined in the DO statement. If the value stored in KOUNT does not exceed the terminal value (3 in this example) the computer returns to the first executable statement following the DO statement (not the DO statement itself).
3. When the index (KOUNT) reaches a value greater than the terminal value (KOUNT is 4), the statement following the last statement in the DO-loop is executed (in this case STOP).

Thus, the DO-loop method of Program 2 works exactly like the counter method of Program 1. Note, however, that the index, increment, and test instructions are automatically built into your loop through the use of the DO statement. This makes Program 2 shorter than Program 1 by one statement (two statements if we had eliminated the CONTINUE and placed the 10 in front of the WRITE). Also, pairing the CONTINUE with the DO makes the loop stand out visually. For these reasons, the *DO-loop method is preferred to the counter method of looping.* Finally, you should realize that the DO statement itself is not part of the loop. It simply defines the features of the loop.

Additional Procedures

Here are some additional procedures to keep in mind when using the DO statement:

1. The variable used as the index must be an integer variable. For example, KOUNT, I, J, and NUM are all acceptable.
2. The initial, terminal, and incremental values must be either positive, integer constants, or integer variables which take on positive values. For example,

       DO 10 KOUNT = 1,3,1
       DO 15 KOUNT = 2,MAX,3
       DO 3 I = M,N,IN

   are all acceptable.
3. If the increment is not specified, then it is assumed to be equal to 1. For example,

       DO 50 J = 1,N

   is treated the same as

       DO 50 J = 1,N,1

4. There is no standard notation for specifying a DO-loop in a flowchart. One common approach is to use the hexagon-shaped symbol to define the start of

FIGURE 7.2   *Flowchart Illustrating DO-loop*

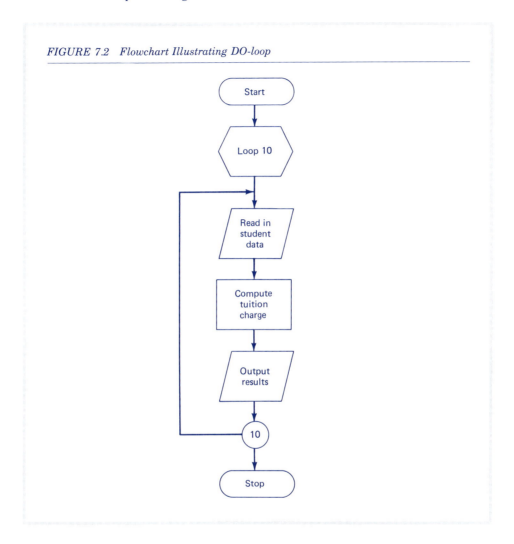

the loop and the circle symbol to indicate the end of the loop. Figure 7.2 illustrates this approach for Program 2 in Example 7.9. Note that the loop returns to the first executable statement following the DO statement, not to the DO statement itself. Alternatively, the flowchart for the counter method can be used, as illustrated in Figure 4.2 on page 97.

EXAMPLE 7.10   Break Even Analysis

Break even analysis is a common tool in the management sciences for assessing the profitability of a new product. In this example we describe this type of analysis within the context of our four-step procedure.

Step I Analyzing the Problem

1. *Problem Statement*
   To determine break even volume and a table of total revenue, total cost, and total profit for an automobile manufacturer given the wholesale price (cost to the dealer), number of cars manufactured and sold (volume), fixed cost (such as tooling, administrative, utilities), and variable cost of manufacturing each car (such as materials and labor). Break even volume is defined as the number of cars that need to be sold so that total profit is zero (total cost is exactly offset by total revenue).

2. *Data Input*
   a. Name of car (MOD1,MOD2), eight-character maximum
   b. Wholesale price of car (PRICE) in thousands of dollars
   c. Fixed cost (FC) in millions of dollars
   d. Variable cost per car (VC) in thousands of dollars

3. *Data Output*
   a. Input data: MOD1, MOD2, PRICE, FC, VC
   b. Break even volume (BE) in thousands of cars
   c. Table of number of cars manufactured and sold (NUM) in thousands, total revenue (TR) in millions of dollars, total cost (TC) in millions of dollars, and total profit (TP) in millions of dollars

4. *Computations and Logical Processes*
   a. $BE = \dfrac{FC}{PRICE - VC}$
   b. $TR = PRICE \times NUM$
   c. $TC = FC + VC \times NUM$
   d. $TP = TR - TC$

   For example, if the dealer must pay $4 thousand for each car, if the fixed cost is $75 million, and if the variable cost is $3 thousand per car, then BE = 75 thousand cars, TR = $300 million, TC = $300 million, and TP = $0 million. In the output table, NUM is to run from 95 percent of BE to 105 percent of BE, to the nearest thousand cars.

Step II Preparing the Flowchart
See Figure 7.3

Step III Coding the Problem

```
      READ(5,1) MOD1,MOD2,PRICE,FC,VC
      BE = FC/(PRICE - VC)
      WRITE(6,3) MOD1,MOD2,PRICE,FC,VC,BE
      M = .95*BE + .5
      N = 1.05*BE + .5
      DO 20 NUM = M,N
         CARS = NUM
         TR = PRICE*CARS
         TC = FC + VC*CARS
         TP = TR - TC
         WRITE(6,5) NUM,TR,TC,TP
   20 CONTINUE
      STOP
```

```
  1 FORMAT(2A4,3F6.3)
  3 FORMAT('1',11X,'BREAK EVEN ANALYSIS'/'0',8X,
    'MODEL:b',2A4/9X,'PRICE:b$',F7.3,'bTHOUSANDS'/
    4X,'FIXED COST:b$',F7.3,'bMILLIONS'/1X,
    'VARIABLE COST:b$',F7.3,'bTHOUSANDS'/4X,
    'BREAK EVEN:',F9.3,'bTHOUSAND CARS'//11X,
    'TOTAL',7X,'TOTAL',7X,'TOTAL'/1X,
    'CARS',5X,'REVENUE',6X,'COST',8X,'PROFIT'/
    '+',40('—')/)
  5 FORMAT(1X,I3,1X,3F12.3)
    END
```

Step IV   Debugging the Computer Program

For the input record

```
1 2 3 4 5 6 7 8 9 10 11 12 13 14 15 16 17 18 19 20 21 22 23 24 25 26 . . .
ZAP2001    4      7 5          3
```

we should get the following output:

Row	Content
1	BREAK EVEN ANALYSIS
3	MODEL: ZAP2001
4	PRICE: $ 4.000 THOUSANDS
5	FIXED COST: $ 75.000 MILLIONS
6	VARIABLE COST: $ 3.000 THOUSANDS
7	BREAK EVEN: 75.000 THOUSAND CARS
9	TOTAL TOTAL TOTAL
10	CARS REVENUE COST PROFIT
12	71 284.000 288.000 -4.000
13	72 288.000 291.000 -3.000
14	73 292.000 294.000 -2.000
15	74 296.000 297.000 -1.000
16	75 300.000 300.000 0.000
17	76 304.000 303.000 1.000
18	77 308.000 306.000 2.000
19	78 312.000 309.000 3.000
20	79 316.000 312.000 4.000

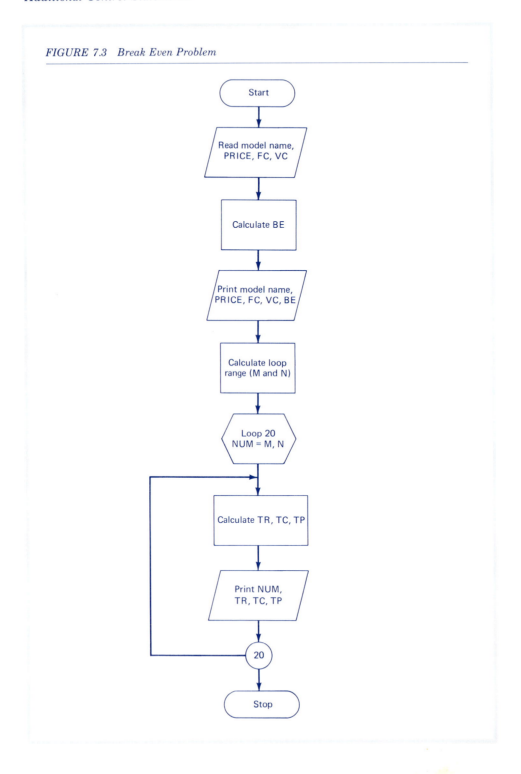

FIGURE 7.3 Break Even Problem

Follow-up Exercises

10. Roleplay (pretend to be) the computer by processing the given input data. Specify contents for the following storage locations:

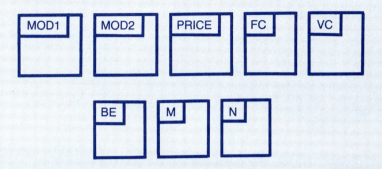

As you go through the program, fill in the following table for the first three values of NUM when the "snapshot" of memory is taken just before the execution of the CONTINUE statement:

NUM	CARS	TR	TC	TP

Don't forget to confirm the input and output FORMATs.

11. Explain why we add .5 to the calculations of M and N. Why were those variables specified as integer? Why do we use the variable CARS?

12. Modify the program such that the lower percentage (95 percent in the example) and upper percentage (105 percent in the example) are treated as input variables PLOW and PUP. Also, let the loop increment be input variable INC. Why might these changes be desirable?

**13. Based on the definition of BE, derive the formula given for BE.

14. Rewrite the program in Example 7.8 by using a DO-loop.

EXAMPLE 7.11 Finding the Minimum Value

The Department of Health, Education and Welfare (HEW) has a data file which includes the per capita income (that is, total income divided by total number of people) for each standard metropolitan statistical area (SMSA) in the country. An administrator wishes to determine the SMSA code which has the smallest per capita income (PCI). The following program illustrates the determination of this minimum (PCIMIN) and its associated SMSA code (SMAMIN).

```
        INTEGER SMSA,SMAMIN
        PCIMIN = 1000000.
        READ(5,*) N
        DO 20 J = 1,N
            READ(5,*) SMSA,PCI
            IF (PCI .GE. PCIMIN) GO TO 20
            PCIMIN = PCI
            SMAMIN = SMSA
 20     CONTINUE
        WRITE(6,*) SMAMIN,PCIMIN
        STOP
        END
```

Follow-up Exercises

15. Draw a flowchart for the preceding program. Check the logic of the flowchart and program by roleplaying the computer through the following input data:

    5
    1472, 5165.
    4165, 7860.
    2134, 6350.
    0415, 4293.
    3147, 5415.

    What does N represent? Indicate the successive stored values for each of the following:

J	SMSA	PCI	PCIMIN	SMAMIN

    Why do we initialize PCIMIN to any arbitrary large value?

**16. Modify the program to find and output the largest PCI (PCIMAX) and its associated SMSA (SMAMAX), in addition to PCIMIN and SMAMIN. Draw a new flowchart.

5. The index, initial, terminal, and incremental values should not be redefined within the DO-loop. For example, the replacement of

    SMAMIN = SMSA

by

    J = SMSA

in the program of Example 7.11 is not allowed since this interrupts the normal manner in which J is changing according to the DO statement. Note, however, that *the index can be utilized within the loop, provided it is not redefined.* In Example 7.10, the index NUM is used both in the assignment statement

CARS = NUM

and in the WRITE statement

WRITE(6,5) NUM,TR,TC,TP

6. Branching within the loop is allowed, as illustrated by Example 7.11, when control is transferred to statement 20 in bypassing the assignment statements for PCIMIN and SMAMIN. *Transfers within the loop directly to the DO statement, however, are either not allowed or result in an infinite loop (depending on the compiler).*

7. Transferring control out of a DO-loop before it terminates naturally is permissible; however, *branching into the body of a DO-loop from the outside is not allowed.* For instance, placing the statement GO TO 20 just before STOP in Example 7.11 is illegal.

8. Unnatural or forced exits from the DO-loop (before the index achieves its terminal value) cause the current value of the index to be retained. Otherwise, the value of the index may or may not be retained following the DO-loop, depending on the system. For example, the value of J in Example 7.11 or the value of NUM in Example 7.10 may be undefined following the DO-loop.[3]

Follow-up Exercises

17. Identify errors in each of the following:

    a.   DO 15 X = 1,N,−2
          :
          :

          CONTINUE
    b.   DO 70 L = 1,M
              L = L**2
              M = M − 1
          :
          :

          70 CONTINUE
    c.   10 DO 20 I = 1,N,4
          15   IF(I/4 .GT. K) GO TO 10
                 WRITE(6,*) I
          20 CONTINUE
              K = K + 10
              GO TO 15

[3]FORTRAN 77 considerably relaxes many of the DO-loop procedures, as described in Section 11.7 on page 353.

18. What value gets printed for K?

a.   DO 30 K = 1,50
            L = K**2 + 5
            IF (L .GT. 15) GO TO 40
        30 CONTINUE
        40 WRITE(6,*) K
            ⋮

b.   DO 30 K = 1,50
            ⋮
        30 CONTINUE
            WRITE(6,*) K
            ⋮

**19. Modify Example 7.10 as follows:
a. Let the index in the DO statement run from 1 to 500 in increments of 2.
b. Exit from the loop when total profit first exceeds 10 percent of total cost.
Include a revised flowchart.

Nested DO-Loops

DO-loops are said to be **nested** when one DO-loop lies entirely within another DO-loop, as illustrated below.

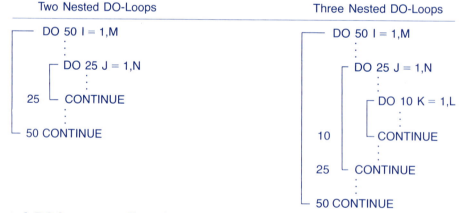

Nested DO-loops are allowed to end on the same statement, *but may not crossover.*

EXAMPLE 7.12 Break Even Analysis with Nested DO-Loops

A better design of the program in Example 7.10 would include an outer loop for processing K sets of input data.

```
    READ(5,7) K
    DO 40 I = 1,K
        READ(5,1) MOD1,MOD2,PRICE,FC,VC
        BE = FC/(PRICE − VC)
        WRITE(6,3) MOD1,MOD2,PRICE,FC,VC,BE
        M = .95*BE + .5
        N = 1.05*BE + .5
        DO 20 NUM = M,N
            CARS = NUM
            TR = PRICE*CARS
            TC = FC + VC*CARS
            TP = TR − TC
            WRITE(6,5) NUM,TR,TC,TP
20      CONTINUE
40 CONTINUE
    STOP
  1 FORMAT (as before)
  3 FORMAT (as before)
  5 FORMAT (as before)
  7 FORMAT(I2)
    END
```

Follow-up Exercises

*20. Run this break even program for the following data:

Model Name	Price ($)	Fixed Cost ($ million)	Variable Cost ($)
ZAP2001	4000	75	3000
ZAP2002	5000	80	3500
ZAP2003	9000	81	6000

What is the value of K?

21. Modify the program in Example 7.12 so that
   a. Only one CONTINUE is used.
   b. No CONTINUE is used.

*22. Solve Exercise 30 in Chapter 4 (page 112) using nested DO-loops. For each district read in M, where M is the number of fines to be processed.

7.5
COMMON ERRORS

The variety of topics in this chapter promotes fertile ground for errors. If you look out for the following common errors, you will be a happier programmer.

1. Logical IF Statements. Don't forget that the periods are part of relational and logical operators. If we write

    IF (I .GT. J AND I .LT. K) GO TO 10

then a syntax error has been committed: having omitted the periods around AND causes the compiler to "think" that J AND I is the variable JANDI. This in itself does not cause a syntax error. The syntax error is provoked when the compiler next encounters the relational operator .LT. instead of a logical operator. This is illegal since the relational expression on the left must be connected by a logical operator to any relational expression on the right.

Do you see what's wrong with the following?

    IF (I .GT. J .AND. .LT. K) GO TO 10

The relational expression on the right is incomplete. We have a tendency to do this because of the way we would state this decision verbally: "If I is greater than J and less than K." To avoid a syntax error it must be written as follows:

    IF (I .GT. J .AND. I .LT. K) GO TO 10

Finally, pay attention to hierarchy when using more than one logical operator. Reread Example 7.4 and make sure you understand the answers to Exercise 3.

2. Computed GO TO Statement. Three errors are common here: first, forgetting the comma after the right parenthesis;[4] second, using a real variable instead of an integer variable to represent code values; third, assigning a value to the code variable which falls outside the range given by 1, 2, . . ., number of statement numbers within the parentheses. The first two are syntax errors and the third may result in a logic error since control defaults to the first executable statement following the computed GO TO.

3. DO-Loops. A lot can go wrong here.

    a. *Improper DO parameters*

DO 50 P = X, Y, Z   ——Real variables may cause syntax errors.

DO 50 J = 1., 10,   ——Real constants may cause syntax errors.

DO 50 I = 0, 10

DO 50 I = 10, 0, -1   Each of these nonpositive constants may cause a syntax error.

---

[4]As mentioned earlier, FORTRAN 77 compilers allow the omission of this comma.

b. *Improper index treatment*

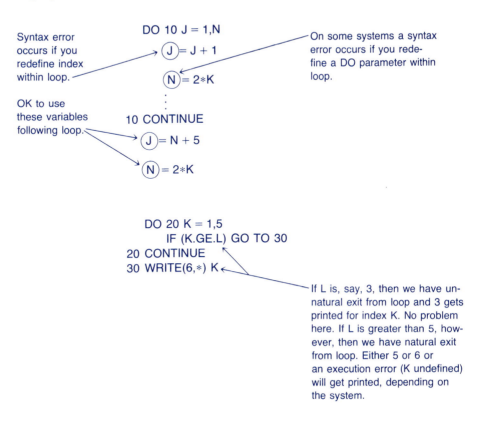

Syntax error occurs if you redefine index within loop.

On some systems a syntax error occurs if you redefine a DO parameter within loop.

```
DO 10 J = 1,N
    J = J + 1
    N = 2*K
        .
        .
10 CONTINUE
    J = N + 5
    N = 2*K
```

OK to use these variables following loop.

```
DO 20 K = 1,5
    IF (K.GE.L) GO TO 30
20 CONTINUE
30 WRITE(6,*) K
```

If L is, say, 3, then we have un-natural exit from loop and 3 gets printed for index K. No problem here. If L is greater than 5, how-ever, then we have natural exit from loop. Either 5 or 6 or an execution error (K undefined) will get printed, depending on the system.

c. *Improper transfers*

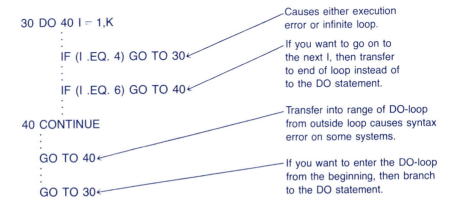

```
30 DO 40 I = 1,K
        .
        .
    IF (I .EQ. 4) GO TO 30
        .
        .
    IF (I .EQ. 6) GO TO 40
        .
        .
40 CONTINUE
        .
        .
    GO TO 40
        .
        .
    GO TO 30
```

Causes either execution error or infinite loop.

If you want to go on to the next I, then transfer to end of loop instead of to the DO statement.

Transfer into range of DO-loop from outside loop causes syntax error on some systems.

If you want to enter the DO-loop from the beginning, then branch to the DO statement.

Consider the following version of Example 7.8 on page 199.

```
        REAL JUN
        DATA K,FR,SOPH,JUN,SEN,TOTF,TOTSO,TOTJ,TOTSR/0,8*0./
        READ(5,*) NOS
        DO 100 K = 1,NOS
            READ(5,*) ICLASS,SATVER,SATMTH
            TOTSAT = SATVER + SATMTH
            GO TO (20,30,40,50), ICLASS
   20       FR = FR + 1.
            TOTF = TOTF + TOTSAT
  100       CONTINUE
   30       SOPH = SOPH + 1.
            TOTSO = TOTSO + TOTSAT
  100       CONTINUE
   40       JUN = JUN + 1.
            TOTJ = TOTJ + TOTSAT
  100       CONTINUE
   50       SEN = SEN + 1.
            TOTSR = TOTSR + TOTSAT
  100 CONTINUE
        AVGF = TOTF/FR
        AVGS = TOTSO/SOPH
        AVGJ = TOTJ/JUN
        AVGSR = TOTSR/SEN
        WRITE(6,*) AVGF,AVGS,AVGJ,AVGSR
        STOP
        END
```

Syntax error due to repetition of statement numbers. Change these to GO TO 100.

d. *Improper nesting.* Watch out for crossovers like the following:

```
        DO 50 I = 1,L
        DO 40 K = 1,N
            .
            .
            .
     50 CONTINUE
     40 CONTINUE
```

and use of the same index for nested DO-loops:

```
        DO 100 I = 1,M
            .
            .
            .
            DO 50 I = 1,N
                .
                .
                .
     50         CONTINUE
            .
            .
            .
    100 CONTINUE
        DO 200 I = 1,K
            .
            .
            .
    200 CONTINUE
```

Indexes for nested loops must be different to avoid error.

OK to use same index following its use elsewhere.

Additional Exercises

23. Define or explain the following terms:

    compound logical IF statement
    relational expression
    relational operator
    logical operator
    logical expression
    arithmetic IF statement
    computed GO TO statement

    DO-loop
    DO statement
    CONTINUE statement
    body or range of DO-loop
    index
    nested DO-loops

24. Solve one of the following problems from the end of Chapter 6 using new statements learned in this chapter:
    a. Exercise 28. Use DO-loops.
    b. Exercise 30. Use compound logical IF and DO-loop.
    c. Exercise 31. Use compound logical IF.
    d. Exercise 32. Use compound logical IF and DO-loop.
    e. Exercise 33. Use compound logical IF and DO-loops.
    f. Exercise 34. Use computed GO TO and DO-loop.

25. **Mailing List.** A professional group of management scientists is planning a regional meeting in New Orleans. A subgroup of information system specialists within this professional group is having a well-known computer scientist as a guest speaker. The chairperson of this subgroup plans to send meeting notices to members in two regions—southeast (code 3) and southwest (code 5)—who have an interest in information systems (code 15) or computer science (code 18).

    a. Design a flowchart and write a program that prepares mailing labels for members of the organization that satisfy the location and area of interest criteria.
        The organization maintains the following data on each member:

        (1) Last name (12 characters)
        (2) First name (8 characters)
        (3) Address (15 characters)
        (4) City (10 characters)
        (5) State (2 characters)
        (6) Zip (5 characters)
        (7) Region code (1 digit; there are 9 regions overall)
        (8) Interest code (2 digits; there are 20 interest areas overall)

        Sample Input Data

(1)	(2)	(3)	(4)	(5)	(6)	(7)	(8)
Fastcode	Frank	11 Flower	Dallas	TX	75215	5	15
Burden	Kathy	193 West St	Warwick	RI	02886	1	18
Peripheral	Leslie	18 Grande	Slidell	LA	70808	5	20
Crowley	M.I.S.	1 Hope Rd	Atlanta	GA	30901	3	15
Deff	Doris	111 High St	Hartford	CT	06518	7	12
Aides	Clyde	963 Main St	Orlando	FL	32407	3	18
Frick	Ford	2 Rose Way	Boston	MA	01906	9	18

Sample Output (First Mailing Label)

FRANK FASTCODE
11 FLOWER
DALLAS, TX 75215

b. Generalize your program so mailing labels can be prepared for any region and/or area of interest criteria. Specifically, design your program to provide the following options:

Option Code	Criteria
1	Specific region only
2	Specific interest area only
3	Specific region or interest area
4	Specific region and interest area

This version is more general than part a but requires more computer runs to print labels for multiple regions and interest areas. For example, the run in part a requires four separate runs for option 4: region 3 and interest area 15; region 3 and interest area 18; region 5 and interest area 15; region 5 and interest area 18.

26. **Sales Pay Report.** The Beachview Surfboard Company pays its salespeople 4.5 percent of monthly *net* sales plus $200. Net sales are equal to sales minus returns. If net sales are $15,000 or greater but less than $20,000, and sales expenses for the month are under $1,000, then the company pays 6.5 percent of net sales plus $200. If net sales are $15,000 or more and less than $20,000, and sales expenses are $1,000 or more, then the company pays 5.5 percent of net sales plus $200. If net sales are $20,000 or more and sales expenses for the month are under $2,500, then the company pays 8 percent of net sales plus $200. If net sales are $20,000 or more and sales expenses are $2,500 or above, then the pay is 7 percent of net sales plus $200.
    a. Design a flowchart and write a program that prints a sales pay report for N salespeople. use the following data input to test your program.

Name (up to 16 characters)	Sales ($)	Returns ($)	Sales Expenses ($)
Murph the Surf	22,000.00	1000.00	2499.99
Big Bertha	25,000.00	3000.00	3100.75
Little Bertha	16,000.00	100.00	850.00
Willy Wipeout	17,500.00	4200.00	600.00
Ridem High	18,700.50	375.20	1020.00

Output for each person includes the following: name, sales, returns, net sales, sales expenses, and pay. Output should be in the form of a table with nicely labeled column headings.
    b. At the bottom of the table include a row labeled "totals." This row shows sums for each column in the table, that is, total sales, total returns, and so on.

27. **Student Fee Bill.** The bursar's office at State University would like you to:
    a. Design a flowchart and write a program that prepares student fee bills for N students each term. The fee structure is outlined by the following chart:

	Undergraduate		Graduate	
	In-State	Out-of-State	In-State	Out-of-State
Full time				
Tuition ($)	715	1715	770	1500
Fees ($)	250	250	200	200
Part time*				
Tuition ($)	66/credit	160/credit	90/credit	150/credit
Fees ($)	10	10	25	25

* Less than 12 credits for an undergraduate student; less than 9 credits for a graduate student.

In addition, students living on campus pay room rent of $375 and/or board of $400 per term.

The following data are stored in the student file:

(1)   Student ID number (4 digits)
(2)   Last name (12 characters)
(3)   First name (10 characters)
(4)   Class code (1 = undergraduate; 2 = graduate)
(5)   Residence (1 = in-state; 2 = out-of-state)
(6)   Campus housing (1 = yes; 2 = no)
(7)   Board contract (1 = yes; 2 = no)
(8)   Credits (to one decimal place)

Sample Output

```
        FEE BILL—STATE UNIVERSITY
    student  name
    student  ID
            TUITION
            FEES
            ROOM
            BOARD_____
            TOTAL
```

Sample Input Data

(1)	(2)	(3)	(4)	(5)	(6)	(7)	(8)
6391	BOLLES	FRAN	1	1	1	1	14.0
8242	CARSON	JIMMY	1	2	2	2	8.0
8577	DALE	ROBERT	2	1	1	2	10.0
8699	HEALY	HEATHER	2	2	2	1	9.0
8811	LUCKY	SONIA	1	2	2	1	12.0
make these up.			2	2	2	2	12.0
make these up.			1	2	1	1	15.5
make these up.			2	2	1	1	11.0

b.   After all fee bills have been printed, print summary totals for tuition, fees, room, board, and overall total.

c. Print a summary which categorizes total amount billed by

(1) Full time versus part time
(2) Undergraduate versus graduate
(3) In-state versus out-of-state

28. **Electric Bill.** Gotham City Electric Company wishes to redesign the computerized bills that it sends to commercial and residential customers. It has announced a city-wide contest to determine the best flowchart and FORTRAN program for this purpose. Data input include the following:

Initialization Data

1. Month (3 letters) and day (2 digits) for beginning date of monthly billing cycle
2. Month and day for ending date of monthly billing cycle
3. Year (2 digits)
4. Number of customers to be billed (up to 4 digits)

Customer Data

5. Previous meter reading in kilowatt hours (up to 7 digits)
6. New meter reading in kilowatt hours
7. Customer rate code (1 digit)
8. Past due amount (dollars and cents)
9. Name of customer (up to 20 characters)
10. Street address of customer (up to 20 characters)
11. City, state, and zip (up to 24 characters)
12. Account number of customer (up to 8 digits)

Use the following sample data input for the computer run:

| Billing Cycle | | | Number of |
From	To	Year	Customers
SEP 19	OCT 18	1980	5

Use the following sample data input per customer:

Previous Reading	New Reading	Rate Code	Past Due Amount	Name	Street Address	City, State, ZIP	Account Number
27648	28648	1	0.	make these up . . . .
42615	45115	2	45.20	.	. . . .
314625	354625	3	0.	.	. . . .
615700	695700	3	0.	.	. . . .
800500	1025500	3	3000.00	.	. . . .

Rate codes and their corresponding rates per kilowatt hour (KWH) are explained by the following table:

Rate Code	Rate (¢) per KWH	Comment
1	5.25	Residential, partly electric home
2	4.85	Residential, all electric home
3	8.50	Commercial, usage under 50,000 KWH
3	7.50	Commercial, usage between 50,000 KWH and 100,000 KWH
3	6.50	Commercial, usage above 100,000 KWH

If a customer has a past due balance above zero, then a 1 percent per month charge on the past due balance is added to the customer's bill. For example, the last customer in the input data is commercial and used 225,000 KWH (1,025,500 − 800,500). Thus the customer is charged at 6.5 cents per KWH, which amounts to a current bill of $14,625.00. This customer, however, has a $3,000 past due account. At an interest rate of 1 percent per month, the interest charge is $30; hence, the total now due from this customer is $17,655.00.

Output from your program should include the following:

1. Name of customer
2. Street address of customer
3. City, state, and zip
4. Account number
5. Billing cycle: from (month,day) to (month,day), (year)
6. Kilowatt hours used
7. Current amount owed
8. Past due amount
9. Interest charge
10. Total amount due

Label your output and design it to fit within a 3 × 5 inch image, since these statements must fit in a standard sized envelope. By the way, the winner of the contest gets to ride the Batmobile, which recently was retrofitted with an all-electric power plant.

29. **Installment Loan.** When a consumer purchases a capital good such as an automobile, stereo, or refrigerator, more often than not credit is arranged in the form of an installment loan. This means that the consumer makes a down payment (D) on the purchase price (P) and finances (borrows) the rest, with a signed agreement to pay installments (or fixed amounts of money) each month until the loan and interest are paid off. The amount of money which must be paid each month (A) is determined from

$$A = \frac{P - D}{F}.$$

Note that the amount borrowed is given by $P - D$. The interest factor (F) is calculated from

$$F = \frac{1}{(1 + R/12)} + \frac{1}{(1 + R/12)^2} + \frac{1}{(1 + R/12)^3} + \cdots + \frac{1}{(1 + R/12)^N}$$

where R is the annual interest rate and N is the number of months it takes to pay off the loan.

These same formulas, by the way, also are used by banks to determine monthly mortgage payments for homes.

a. Prepare a flowchart and write a program which inputs P, D, R, and N; calculates A; and outputs $(P - D)$, R, N, and A with appropriate labels. Process the following data:

ITEM	PURCHASE PRICE ($)	DOWN PAYMENT ($)	ANNUAL INTEREST RATE	NUMBER OF MONTHS	
1. Debug	50	20	12.*	4	(A = 32)
2. Stereo	3,000	300	0.18	24	(A = 134.80)
3. Car	6,500	1,000	0.12	36	
4. Car	6,500	3,000	0.12	36	
5. Car	6,500	1,000	0.13	48	
6. Home	60,000	12,000	0.09	300	
7. Home	60,000	18,000	0.09	300	
8. Home	60,000	12,000	0.08	300	

*This figure is 1200%, not 12%. It's unrealistic in actual practice, but serves nicely to debug the program. You should confirm $A = 32$ by hand to make sure you understand the calculations.

Design your program such that the first item of Input is the number of times you wish to calculate A (eight for the above data). Draw conclusions for each of the following comparisons:

Item 3 versus item 4.
Item 3 versus item 5.
Item 6 versus item 7.
Item 6 versus item 8.

b. Modify your program to include the calculation and output of the total interest paid over the life of the loan.

**c. Incorporate the option of printing a table as follows, where the sample calculations are based on item 1 in part a.

```
                  AMORTIZATION TABLE

         BEGINNING              PRINCIPAL    ENDING
MONTH    BALANCE      INTEREST  REPAYMENT    BALANCE

  1      30.00        30.00       2.00       28.00
  2      28.00        28.00       4.00       24.00
  3      24.00        24.00       8.00       16.00
  4      16.00        16.00      16.00        0.

     TOTAL INTEREST  98.00

     RATIO OF TOTAL INTEREST TO LOAN = 3.27
```

(1) The first beginning balance is $P - D$. Subsequent beginning balances are simply the preceding month's ending balance.

(2) Interest for any month is calculated as the monthly interest rate times the

beginning balance for that month. In the example, the annual interest rate is 12 (1200%), which must be divided by 12 to convert to a monthly interest rate. The interest in month 1, therefore, is (1.) · (30.00), or $30.00; in month 2, it is (1.) · (28.00), or $28.00.

(3) Principal repayment for any month is the monthly installment less the interest for that month. Thus the principal repayment in month 3 is (32.00 − 24.00), or $8.

(4) The ending balance is the beginning balance less the principal repayment. For month 3, it is (24.00 − 8.00), or $16.00.

Note that the ending balance should be exactly zero, except perhaps for rounding error. Also note that this table is an option in the program; that is, it should not be printed automatically for each item. In your computer run, print this table for items 1, 2, and 4.

d. Input the name of the item (up to 16 characters) and print the main heading as
AMORTIZATION TABLE FOR name of item
beginning in column 5.

30. **Police Car Replacement.** A police administrator would like to estimate the mileage at which a police cruiser should be replaced. Data analyses show that the *cost of operation* (gasoline, maintenance, and so on) is approximated by

$$c = f + v \cdot m + s \cdot m^2$$

where f, v, and s are called parameters, and m is the mileage reading (in thousands) on the odometer. For example, a cruiser which is driven for 30,000 miles and is characterized by $f = 1,000$, $v = 200$, and $s = 2$ incurs an operating cost of approximately

$$c = 1,000 + (200) \cdot (30) + (2) \cdot (30)^2$$
$$= \$8,800.$$

The police department has an arrangement with the automaker for trade-ins of used police cruisers. The automaker has agreed to reduce the price of a new cruiser by the following amount:

$$r = pd^m$$

where r is the trade-in (salvage) value of a used cruiser, p is the original (new) car price, d is some depreciation factor, and m is defined as before. For example, if $p = \$10,000$, $d = 0.95$, and $m = 30$, then

$$r = (10,000) \cdot (0.95)^{30}$$
$$= \$2,146.$$

This means that the police department pays $10,000 for a new cruiser, drives it for 30,000 miles, and gets $2,146 on a trade-in. The *depreciation cost* in this case is $7,854, or the difference between the new car price and the salvage price.

Thus, a cruiser which is driven for 30,000 miles costs $8,800 to operate and $7,854 in depreciation cost, for a total cost of $16,654. If this type of cruiser is replaced by a new cruiser of the same type at 30,000 mile intervals, then the total cost per 1,000 miles is approximately $555 (that is, $16,654 ÷ 30)

a. Prepare a flowchart and write a program which determines the mileage (to the nearest thousand) at which cruisers should be replaced. Input should include the following:

1.   Number of analyses to be performed;

2.   *f, v, s, p, d.*

Note that input of item 1 implies that you should have an outer loop in your program. Output should appear as follows:

m	*c*	$c \div m$	Depreciation Cost	Depreciation Cost $\div m$	Total Cost per 1,000 Miles
(1)	(2)	(3) = (2)/(1)	(4)	(5) = (4)/(1)	(6) = (3) + (5)
1					
2					
3					
.					
.					
100					

Thus, the best mileage at which to replace a cruiser is that which gives the smallest value in column (6). Note that 100,000 miles is the maximum replacement mileage that the police administrator is willing to consider. The police administrator is evaluating several types of cruisers, one of which must be selected. Their characteristics follow:

Cruiser Type	*f*	*v*	*s*	*p*	*d*
1	1,000	200	2·0	10,000	0.95
2	800	300	2·5	8,000	0.93
3	1,200	225	1·6	13,000	0.98

At what mileage should each type be replaced and what is the total cost per 1,000 miles? Which cruiser is the cheapest on a total cost per 1,000 mile basis?

**b.   As you go down column (6) in this type of table, costs typically begin high, decrease to a minimum, and begin increasing again. Design your program to exit from the table loop once total cost begins to increase.

**c.   Design your program such that the program itself determines and outputs the best cruiser type and its associated total cost per 1,000 miles.

31.   **Personnel Selection: A Combination Problem.   An oceanographic food firm is planning extensive underwater experiments in aquaculture (sea farming). These experiments require people to live together in an isolated underwater environment for extended periods of time. To avoid problems associated with incompatibility, the firm has decided to run isolation tests for the purpose of judging compatibility. These tests require individuals to live together for two weeks under monitored conditions in an aboveground capsule which is cut off from the outside world.

As an example, suppose that four people are available for the experiments, but only two are required to live together underwater. How many subgroups of two persons are possible from among four? If we let P1 represent the first person, P2 the second person, and so on, then we have the following six distinct subgroups of two persons each: (P1, P2), (P1, P3), (P1, P4), (P2, P3), (P2, P4), (P3, P4). Right? This means that six separate isolation tests would have to be conducted in the capsule so as to select the most compatible two persons.

This approach of listing groups works fine when we are dealing with small numbers, but becomes impractical when the numbers get large. For instance, if ten people are available and we need four for the experiments, then we have 210 distinct groups of four each. If you have had a course in statistics, then most likely you have realized that this is a so-called **combination problem.**

Given that n people are available and k are needed, then the number of combinations of n taken k at a time is given by the formula

$$C = \frac{n \cdot (n-1) \cdot (n-2) \cdot \ldots \cdot 2 \cdot 1}{[(n-k) \cdot (n-k-1) \cdot \ldots \cdot 2 \cdot 1] \cdot [k \cdot (k-1) \cdot \ldots \cdot 2 \cdot 1]}$$

For the first example above, $n = 4$ and $k = 2$, so that

$$C = \frac{4 \cdot 3 \cdot 2 \cdot 1}{(2 \cdot 1) \cdot (2 \cdot 1)} = 6$$

For the second example, $n = 10$ and $k = 4$, so that

$$C = \frac{10 \cdot 9 \cdot 8 \cdot 7 \cdot 6 \cdot 5 \cdot 4 \cdot 3 \cdot 2 \cdot 1}{(6 \cdot 5 \cdot 4 \cdot 3 \cdot 2 \cdot 1) \cdot (4 \cdot 3 \cdot 2 \cdot 1)} = 210$$

a. Prepare a flowchart and write a program which calculates C given n and k. Output should include n, k, C, and the total number of days required for all isolation experiments given that each experiment takes 14 days. Run the following data through your program:

n	k
6	2
10	4
10	6
10	10
20	4
40	4
40	6
60	6

Design your program such that the first item of input is the number of times you wish to calculate combinations (eight for the above data). *Hint:* Calculate the products (multiplications) in C using a loop.

**b. Did you have numeric overflow when $n = 60$ and $k = 6$? Certain efficiencies can be realized in the calculation of C by dividing terms in the numerator by terms in the denominator. For example, for $n = 60$ and $k = 6$, we can write

$$C = \frac{60 \cdot 59 \cdot 58 \cdot 57 \cdot 56 \cdot 55}{6 \cdot 5 \cdot 4 \cdot 3 \cdot 2 \cdot 1}.$$

Design your program to take advantage of this efficiency.

CHAPTER 8

One-Dimensional Arrays

Most of the programs you've written or studied up to this point have had this structure:

1. Reading in data for one record
2. Processing the data
3. Printing the results
4. Returning to step 1 if more data are available.

In some problems you may want to read and store data for all records before you begin any computations. This was not possible in many earlier programs because reading in a new record automatically erased the values stored from the previous record, thus preventing access to the stored data of the previous record, that is, unless you reentered the data.

226

8.1
MOTIVATION

An **array** is a group of consecutive memory locations that have the same name. The use of arrays

1. Permits access to any data item that has been read previously
2. Provides simple yet powerful capabilities to name and manipulate a large number of storage locations

To help you visualize this concept, the illustration below shows three storage locations for an array named DEPOS:

DEPOS

Just how we specify and manipulate arrays will become clear in the next two sections. First, however, we motivate their use through the following example.

EXAMPLE 8.1   Analysis of Bank Deposits

The Vice President of Marketing for a small branch bank wants to compare the percent of deposits that each branch contributes to the bank's total deposits. The number of deposits for each of the three branches is given below:

Bank	Number of Deposits
1	3500
2	5000
3	4000

Let's first try to solve this problem using the approach used in previous chapters. A program such as the following might be written:

```
1 FORMAT(F6.0)
2 FORMAT(1X,2F6.0)
  TOT = 0.
  DO 10 I = 1,3
      READ(5,1) DEPOS
      TOT = TOT + DEPOS
10 CONTINUE
  DO 20 I = 1,3
      READ(5,1) DEPOS
      PER = DEPOS/TOT*100.
      WRITE(6,2) DEPOS,PER
20 CONTINUE
  STOP
  END
```

This program would not work if we use the following input data:

Test Input Data

12 3 4 5 6 7 . . .

3500

5000

4000

In the first loop, the three data items are read in and total deposits are accumulated for the bank; however, a problem occurs in the second loop when we try to *reenter* the data by executing the READ statement again, assuming we had only provided three input records. The data already have been read in and an "OUT OF DATA" error message occurs when you attempt to reenter the data. This program would work only if we were to provide six input records, where the last three records are identical to the

Test Input Data

12 3 4 5 6 7 . . .

3500

5000

4000

3500

5000

4000

first three records. This approach is not only conceptually unappealing but also inefficient, particularly if the program is used for a bank having many branches.

Now, consider the following program.

Test Input Data

12 3 4 5 6 7 . . .

3500

5000

4000

Output

	1	2	3	4	5	6	7	8	9	1 0	1 1	1 2	1 3	1 4	1 5	1 6	1 7	1 8	1 9	2 0
1	3	5	0	0	.					2	8	.								
2	5	0	0	0	.					4	0	.								
3	4	0	0	0	.					3	2	.								
4																				

```
1 FORMAT(F6.0)
2 FORMAT(1X,2F6.0)
  READ(5,1)DEPOS1
  READ(5,1)DEPOS2
  READ(5,1)DEPOS3
  TOT = DEPOS1 + DEPOS2 + DEPOS3
  PER = DEPOS1/TOT*100.
  WRITE(6,2) DEPOS1,PER
  PER = DEPOS2/TOT*100.
  WRITE(6,2) DEPOS2,PER
  PER = DEPOS3/TOT*100.
  WRITE(6,2) DEPOS3,PER
  STOP
  END
```

This program works but . . . it's very rigid and inefficient. It works for three branches, but if you wish to add a fourth branch, the program would have to be rewritten. Worse yet, visualize this program written for the hundreds of Chase Manhattan branch banks in New York City. What a long and tedious program it would be for such a simple problem!

A simpler solution to this problem is to use an array, as follows:

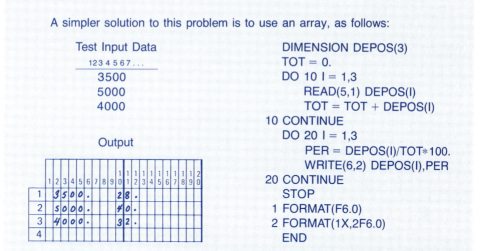

Test Input Data

12 3 4 5 6 7 . . .

```
     3500
     5000
     4000
```

Output

```
DIMENSION DEPOS(3)
TOT = 0.
DO 10 I = 1,3
     READ(5,1) DEPOS(I)
     TOT = TOT + DEPOS(I)
10 CONTINUE
DO 20 I = 1,3
     PER = DEPOS(I)/TOT*100.
     WRITE(6,2) DEPOS(I),PER
20 CONTINUE
STOP
1 FORMAT(F6.0)
2 FORMAT(1X,2F6.0)
END
```

In this program the first loop reads the number of deposits for each branch bank, storing them in an array called DEPOS, and accumulates the total deposits for all branches in TOT. The second loop references each element in the array DEPOS, divides the number of deposits for each branch by the total deposits, multiplies the fraction by 100 to give a percentage, and prints the number of deposits and the relative percent of total deposits for each branch bank. At this point, don't worry about the exact nature of the array or about the DIMENSION statement. We discuss these topics next.

8.2
SUBSCRIPTS

When programming with arrays, a number of unique memory locations "belong" to the same variable name; each memory location in the array is referred to as an **array element,** which can be referenced by its relative position in the array through the use of a **subscript.**

Array Elements   Relative Position

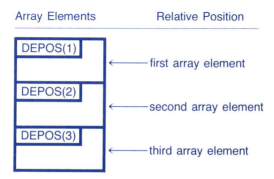

A subscript acts as an *index* or *pointer* to locate a specific array element. In FORTRAN, subscripts are written within parentheses following the array name. For example, the first array element in our sample program can be identified as

DEPOS(1)

When each array element is referenced by only one subscript, the array is called a **one-dimensional array**.

The elements of an array are sometimes called **subscripted variables,** since each element in the array is identified by a variable name followed by a subscript enclosed in parentheses. The same rules which apply to naming simple (unsubscripted) variables also apply to naming subscripted variables: there can be up to six characters in the name where the first character must be a letter which identifies mode.

The use of subscripted variables in FORTRAN gives the language great ease and flexibility in naming and manipulating a large number of *related* variables. This feature is "borrowed" from algebra, as the following illustrates:

Stock Number	Price of Stock ($)	Subscripted Variables in Algebra	Subscripted Variables in FORTRAN
1	75	x_1	X(1)
2	42	x_2	X(2)
3	24	x_3	X(3)
⋮	⋮	⋮	⋮
500	105	x_{500}	X(500)

For example, if we are dealing with a series of 500 numbers, where each number represents the price of a stock at the end of a given day on the New York Stock Exchange, then the algebraic notation x_3 refers to the price of the third stock and x_{75} refers to the price of the seventy-fifth stock. Similarly, in FORTRAN, X(3) refers to the storage location for the price of the third stock and X(75) identifies the storage location for the price of the seventy-fifth stock. Naming this many related variables would be quite tedious and impractical without the use of subscripts. For example, you wouldn't recommend a scheme such as A, B, C, . . . to name 500 variables, would you? These names not only are cumbersome but also cause difficulty in remembering exactly what is referenced by a specific name.

You should keep in mind the following additional points when working with subscripted variables:

1. Typically subscripts are *positive integer constants* or *integer variables* which store positive (nonzero) integer values. For example,

   COST(K)

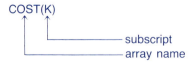

uses an *integer variable* (K) as a subscript. When you use a variable as a subscript you may reference any element in the array based upon the value you assign that variable. For example, the program segment

```
K = 3
SALE(K) = 500.
```

results in the storage of 500. in the third location of the array SALE:

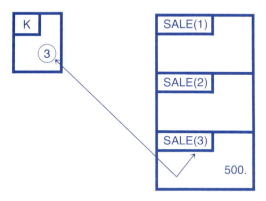

In Example 8.1, storage is accomplished as follows:

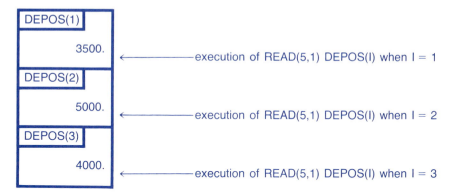

2. You can use a single variable name as a subscript to reference corresponding elements in different arrays. For example, the program segment

    ```
    K = 2
    PROFIT(K) = SALE(K) − COST(K)
    ```

    subtracts the second array element in COST from the second array element in SALE and stores the result in the second array element of PROFIT.
3. Subscripts are not part of the array name; thus TAB(J) and TAB(I) both reference the array TAB. In addition, if I and J are equal, then TAB(J) and TAB(I) reference the same element in TAB.
4. Although normally you will use a constant or a variable as a subscript, you may have need of one or more of the allowable forms shown in Table 8.1.

TABLE 8.1 *Allowable Subscript Forms**

GENERAL FORM (INTEGER EXPRESSION)	EXAMPLE
a. Constant	SALE(3)
b. Variable	COST(NUM)
c. Variable + constant	VALUE(K + 3)
d. Variable − constant	SALE(I − 1)
e. Constant*variable	PROF(2*M)
f. Constant*variable + constant	PROF(2*M + 1)
g. Constant*variable − constant	PROF(2*M − 1)

*Some compilers (for example, WATFIV and FORTRAN 77) allow any integer expression as a subscript form.

8.3
DIMENSION STATEMENT

Because an array occupies more than one memory location, these locations must be reserved for the array through the use of a **DIMENSION statement**. The general form of the DIMENSION statement for one-dimensional arrays is:

$$\textbf{DIMENSION}\ \begin{matrix} variable \\ name \end{matrix} \begin{pmatrix} integer \\ constant \end{pmatrix},\ \begin{matrix} variable \\ name \end{matrix} \begin{pmatrix} integer \\ constant \end{pmatrix}, \ldots$$

This statement declares to the compiler which variables in your program represent arrays and defines the maximum size of each array (total number of locations reserved) as specified by the value of the integer constant.[1] In Example 8.1, the statement

DIMENSION DEPOS(3)

reserves three memory locations for the array named DEPOS, which can be depicted in the usual way:

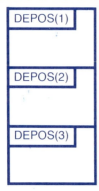

[1] FORTRAN 77 increases the flexibility of declaring the size of an array, as described in Section 11.7.

Note that the contents (stored values) of these locations are left blank; they are filled in with the appropriate values when the READ statement is executed three times in DO-loop 10. If we had used

DIMENSION DEPOS(5)

then five memory locations would have been reserved for DEPOS:

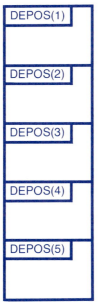

Loops 10 and 20, however, still would utilize only the first three of these locations.

More than one array can be dimensioned in a single DIMENSION statement by using commas to separate each array specification. For example,

DIMENSION COST(80),REV(50),PROFIT(50)

reserves 80 locations for an array named COST, another 50 locations for array REV, and 50 more locations for PROFIT.

Here are some additional points to keep in mind when working with arrays.

1. The DIMENSION statement is a nonexecutable statement which normally is placed at the beginning of a program, but may appear anywhere in the program before the array is used.
2. The integer constant which specifies the size of the array *must* be a constant. For example,

    DIMENSION SALE(N)

    would yield a syntax error, since a variable is *not* permitted within parentheses in the DIMENSION statement.[2]

[2]An exception to this rule is discussed in Section 10.5.

3. You can reserve more locations for an array than are actually used in a particular program; however, the opposite is not true. If you reserve only five locations for an array and you need seven, an error message may occur during the execution of your program when the value of your subscript exceeds five or, in some complex programs, a logic error may occur.

4. The **REAL** and **INTEGER** statements first discussed in Section 2.8 can be used to declare not only the mode of an array but also its size. For example,

    REAL KNOB(500)

declares that KNOB is to be a real array with 500 storage locations. The statement

    INTEGER COST(80),REV(50),PROFIT(50)

is equivalent to the two statements

    INTEGER COST,REV,PROFIT
    DIMENSION COST(80),REV(50),PROFIT(50)

Follow-up Exercises

1. With respect to the third program (the one using array DEPOS) in Example 8.1:
   a. Change the program to process 100 branch banks. How many more statements would be needed in the *second* program to accomplish the same task? How about the length of the statement that calculates TOT? Do you now see why arrays give us a simple yet powerful means to name and manipulate a large number of storage locations?
   b. Generalize the program so it can handle any number of branch banks up to 500.
2. Can you reason why an integer variable is not permitted in place of the integer constant in the DIMENSION statement?
3. Indicate what is wrong with each of the following program segments.

   a.   READ(5,*) K,X(K)
         DIMENSION X(K)
         :
         :

   b.   DIMENSION D(10),E(10)
         INTEGER D(10),E(10)
         DO 30 I = 1,20
      30 D(I) = I**2
         DO 40 I = 1,19
      40 E(I+1) = D(I)*D(I + 1)
         :
         :

   What would be stored in E(3), once the program is corrected?
4. Indicate the storage contents of specific array elements for the following, where a value of 4 is input for N.

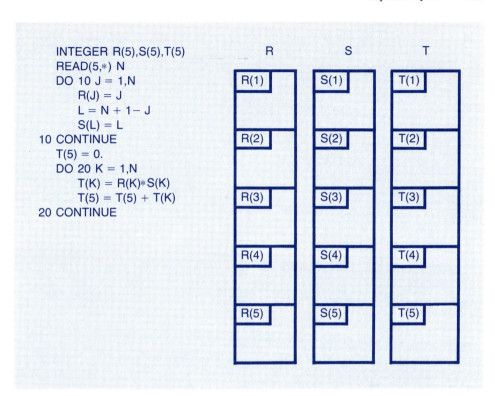

```
        INTEGER R(5),S(5),T(5)
        READ(5,*) N
        DO 10 J = 1,N
            R(J) = J
            L = N + 1 - J
            S(L) = L
10  CONTINUE
        T(5) = 0.
        DO 20 K = 1,N
            T(K) = R(K)*S(K)
            T(5) = T(5) + T(K)
20  CONTINUE
```

8.4
INPUT/OUTPUT

Essentially, we have three basic procedures for the efficient I/O of arrays. In the discussions which follow, assume that we wish to read or print every element in the array, beginning with the first element and moving sequentially through the array until the last element.

Using the DO Statement

The DO statement is a convenient device for performing I/O of arrays. In this case the *index* or *counter* of the DO may be used as a subscript which takes on values that coincide with each element in the array.

EXAMPLE 8.2   I/O with the DO Statement

The program segment

```
        DIMENSION DEPOS(3)
    1 FORMAT(F6.0)
        DO 10 I = 1,3
            READ(5,1) DEPOS(I)
10  CONTINUE
```
:
:

reads data found in columns 1–6 of three records and stores them in the array DEPOS, according to the following procedure. Initially, I is set equal to 1 (from the DO statement) and the first data item is read into DEPOS(1):

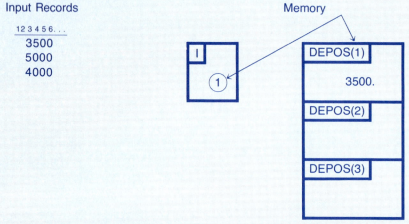

Input Records

1 2 3 4 5 6 . . .
3500
5000
4000

Memory

Then, I is incremented to 2, the READ statement is executed a second time, the second input record is processed, and 5000. is stored in DEPOS(2):

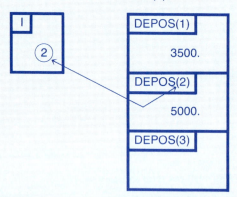

Finally, I is incremented to 3, and the third memory location for DEPOS is filled:

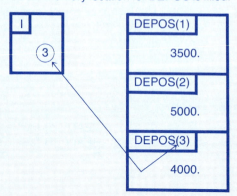

Note that a new input record is processed each time the READ statement in the DO-loop is executed.

In essence, DO-loop 10 is equivalent to the following:

```
READ(5,1) DEPOS(1)
READ(5,1) DEPOS(2)
READ(5,1) DEPOS(3)
```

In other words, identical results would be obtained if loop 10 were replaced with the above three statements. If we were reading in deposits for 200 banks, then you should readily appreciate the power of the DO-loop approach.

This looping technique using the DO statement also can be used for output. For example, the following statements result in the printout of the contents of array DEPOS:

```
    :
    :
 3 FORMAT(1X,F9.0)
   DO 30 I = 1,3
       WRITE(6,3) DEPOS(I)
30 CONTINUE
    :
    :
```

Print Column

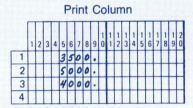

Note that a new output line is written each time the WRITE statement is executed. In effect, DO-loop 30 is equivalent to the following:

```
WRITE(6,3) DEPOS(1)
WRITE(6,3) DEPOS(2)
WRITE(6,3) DEPOS(3)
```

Follow-up Exercises

5. Consider the following program segment for reading 50 values into an array named MONEY:

```
        DIMENSION MONEY(50)
      1 FORMAT(I3)
        READ(5,1) MONEY(1)
        READ(5,1) MONEY(2)
        READ(5,1) MONEY(3)
        READ(5,1) MONEY(4)
        :
        :
        READ(5,1) MONEY(50)
```

Rewrite this segment using the DO statement. In general, which approach is more efficient?

6. Describe the output for the following program segment:

```
3 FORMAT(5X,3F6.0)
  DO 30 I = 1,3
      WRITE(6,3) DEPOS(I)
30 CONTINUE
```

7. Given the following data:

Cost	Sales
40	100
20	125
75	95

write an efficient program segment to read these data into the arrays COST and SALES. How would you place your data on the input record?

Using the Implied DO Statement

The combination of the DO statement with the READ or WRITE statement causes the processing of a new record (line) with each execution of the READ or WRITE statement. Thus, only one data item per record can be stored or output whenever the list of the READ or WRITE statement contains only one variable. Often you want to store several values on a record or print a number of values on a line of output. For example, if the bank deposit data were stored on a single record in the following manner:

```
1 2 3 4 5 6 7 8 9 10 11 12 13 14 15 16 17 18 19 20 21 22 23 24 25 ...
3500.       5000.        4000.
```

then the program segment

```
1 FORMAT(F10.0)
  DO 10 I = 1,3
      READ(5,1) DEPOS(I)
10 CONTINUE
```

would store the value 3500. in DEPOS(1), after which an "OUT OF DATA" error message would be printed.

A more flexible statement to read or print arrays combines certain features of I/O commands and DO statements in an instruction known as the ***implied DO statement.*** The implied DO statement for one-dimensional arrays is found immediately to the right of a READ or WRITE statement:

$$\text{READ }(-,-) \atop \text{or} \atop \text{WRITE}(-,-) \left(\begin{array}{l} \textit{array} \\ \textit{name} \\ \textit{list} \quad \textit{(index), index = value, value, value} \end{array} \quad \textit{initial terminal incremental} \right)$$

Immediately following the READ or WRITE statement we have the usual designation for the I/O unit number and the FORMAT statement number. The implied DO portion of the READ or WRITE statement is enclosed entirely within the second set of parentheses. Within these parentheses we usually have a list of one or more array names with subscripts corresponding to the index; a comma follows the last array name, and finally indexing information similar to the DO statement is specified.

EXAMPLE 8.3   I/O with the Implied DO Statement

In the statement

READ(5,1) (DEPOS(I), I = 1,3,1)

the indexing information I = 1,3,1 of the implied DO specifies the number of times to repeat the variables found within the implied DO. In this example, we have the following effect:

READ(5,1) DEPOS(1),DEPOS(2),DEPOS(3)

The index variable I receives an initial value of 1 and is incremented by 1 until I is equal to the terminal value. In effect, *the implied DO serves to place more than one array element in the list of a READ or WRITE statement.* As in the DO statement, the increment may be omitted, in which case it is assumed to be 1.

When you use the implied DO, how the data are read or printed depends on how you code your FORMAT statement. For example,

    READ(5,1) (DEPOS(I), I = 1,3)
1 FORMAT(3F6.0)

Input Record

1 2 3 4 5 6 7 8 9 10 11 12 13 14 15 16 17 18 . . .

3500   5 0 0 0   4 0 0 0

stores three values from one record; however, if we change the FORMAT to

1 FORMAT(F6.0)

Input Records

1 2 3 4 5 6 7 8 . . .

3500
5000
4000

then three values would be read into the array DEPOS, but from three records (one value per record). This occurs because of *imbalance* between list and specifications; that is, the input list has more variables (three) than the FORMAT statement has specifications (one). If you're fuzzy about the imbalance rule, then review Section 6.4 on pages 167–169.

The implied DO also can be used to output data stored in arrays. For example,

WRITE(6,*) (DEPOS(I), I = 1,3)

prints three values from the array DEPOS on one line:

3500.   5000.   4000.

The following statements also print the three values on one line:

WRITE(6,3) (DEPOS(I), I = 1,3)
3 FORMAT(1X,3F6.0)

However, if you change the FORMAT statement to

3 FORMAT(1X,F6.0)

then the imbalance rule causes the output to appear on three lines:

Print Column

	1	2	3	4	5	6	7	8	9	10	11	12	13	14	15	16	17	18	19	20
1		3	5	0	0	.														
2		5	0	0	0	.														
3		4	0	0	0	.														
4																				

Follow-up Exercises

8. We wish to store the values 10, 20, 30, and 40 in the first four storage locations of the array MONEY. Indicate where you would place the data for each case.

Input Records

1 2 3 4 5 6 7 8 9 10 11 12 13 14 15 16 17 18 19 20 . . .

a.   READ(5,1) (MONEY(K), K = 1,4)
1 FORMAT(4I3)
b.   READ(5,1) (MONEY(K), K = 1,4)
1 FORMAT(I3)
c.   READ(5,1) (MONEY(K), K = 1,4)
1 FORMAT(2I3)
d.   READ(5,1) (MONEY(K), K = 1,4)
1 FORMAT(8I3)
e.   1 FORMAT(I3)
DO 10 K = 1,4
READ(5,1) MONEY(K)
10 CONTINUE
f.   READ(5,*) (MONEY(K), K = 1,4)

9. Suppose we wish to output the contents of MONEY as defined in the preceding exercise. Indicate how output would appear for each case.

a. WRITE(6,15) (MONEY(J), J = 1,4)
    15 FORMAT(1X,4I5)

b. WRITE(6,15) (MONEY(J), J = 1,4)
    15 FORMAT(1X,I5)

c. WRITE(6,15) (MONEY(J), J = 1,4)
    15 FORMAT(1X,2I5)

d. 15 FORMAT(1X,I1,I5)
    DO   20 J = 1,4
        WRITE(6,15) J,MONEY(J)
    20 CONTINUE

e. WRITE(6,15) (J,MONEY(J), J = 1,4)
    15 FORMAT(1X,I1,I5)

f. WRITE(6,*) (MONEY(J), J = 1,4)

g. WRITE(6,*) (J,MONEY(J), J = 1,4)

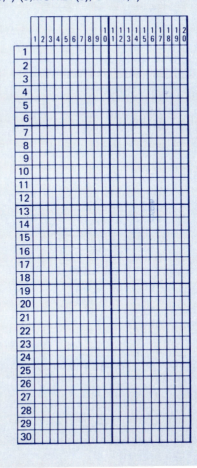

10. Code a more efficient way of handling each of the following statements.

  a. READ(5,3) X(1),X(2),X(3),X(4),X(5),X(6),X(7),X(8)
  b. WRITE(6,3) X(1),X(2),X(3),X(4),X(5),X(6),X(7),X(8)
  c. READ(5,3) X(1),X(3),X(5),X(7),X(9),X(11)
  d. WRITE(6,3) A(1),B(1),A(2),B(2),A(3),B(3)
  e. WRITE(6,3) A(1),A(2),A(3),B(1),B(2),B(3),B(4),B(5)

*11. Consider the following memory, where I represents the index for array JAG
and N represents the terminal value of the index:

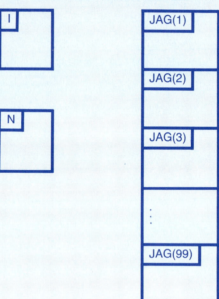

  a. Write a complete program which inputs the single record given by

Input Record

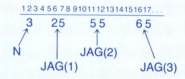

and outputs as follows:

Print Column

	1	2	3	4	5	6	7	8	9	10	11	12	13	14	15	16	17	18	19	20
1	1				2	5														
2	2				5	5														
3	3				6	5														
4																				

b. Write a complete program which inputs the single record given in part a and outputs as follows:

Print Column

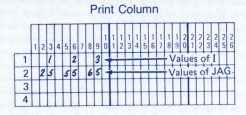

Using the Short-List Technique

Entire arrays may be read or written by placing the array name without subscripts in the input or output command. This is sometimes referred to as the **short-list technique.** For example, in the program segment

```
DIMENSION DEPOS(3)
READ(5,1) DEPOS    ←Equivalent to READ(5,1) (DEPOS(I), I = 1,3)
1 FORMAT (3F6.0)
```

the computer reads in three values from *one* record, storing the first value in DEPOS(1), the second value in DEPOS(2), and the third value in DEPOS(3).

The presence of the array name without a subscript indicates that the values for *all the elements* in the array, *as specified in the DIMENSION statement,* are to be read or written. Accordingly, this technique only can be used to read or write an *entire* array (as specified in the DIMENSION); if only part of the array is to be processed, then the DO statement or implied DO must be used. To illustrate what we mean, the program segment

```
DIMENSION SALE (10)
READ(5,*) SALE
WRITE(6,*) SALE
```

reads 10 values on one record and prints 10 values on one line. If you wish to input or output only five values of the array, but SALE has been dimensioned to 10, then the short-list technique cannot be used.

Follow-up Exercise

12. Describe I/O records for the following, where we wish to store 10 for N, the numbers 1, 2, . . . , 8 for the array KIN, and the fractions 0.1, 0.2, . . . , 1.5 for the array FRAC:

a.
```
        DIMENSION KIN(8),FRAC(15)
      1 FORMAT(I2)
      2 FORMAT(8I1)
      3 FORMAT(15F4.2)
        READ(5,1) N
        READ(5,2) KIN
        READ(5,3) FRAC
```

How would your output appear for each of the following?

b.
```
        WRITE(6,4) KIN,(FRAC(J), J = 1,N)
      4 FORMAT(1X,8I2,15F5.2)
```

c.
```
        WRITE(6,4) KIN,(FRAC(J), J = 1,N)
      4 FORMAT(1X,8I2/1X,10F5.2)
```

**d.
```
        WRITE(6,4) KIN,(FRAC(J), J = 1,N)
      4 FORMAT(1X,8(I2/1X)/(1X,F5.2))
```

8.5
MANIPULATING ARRAYS

This section presents three examples that illustrate techniques of manipulation for one-dimensional arrays.

EXAMPLE 8.4   Initialization

Often it is necessary to set each element in an array to some initial value. For example, to initialize all values in a 100-element array to zero, you could write the following instructions:

```
      DO 10 I = 1,100
         SUM(I) = 0.
   10 CONTINUE
```

As the value of I changes from 1 to 100, each of the 100 locations in the array SUM is set to zero. After this segment of the program is complete, array SUM appears as follows:

The above procedure initializes the array during execution of the program. Alternatively, we can initialize the array during compilation using the **DATA statement** first discussed in Section 2.8:

DATA SUM/100∗0./

Use of the DATA statement is efficient if we only need to initialize the array once. If the array needs to be reinitialized during execution, then you must use the DO-loop approach, since the DATA statement is nonexecutable.

EXAMPLE 8.5 Simple Arithmetic Operations

Quite often it is necessary to perform arithmetic operations on all the elements in an array. The following segment from Example 8.1 illustrates this process:

```
    DO 20 I = 1,3
        PER = DEPOS(I)/TOT∗100.
        WRITE(6,2) DEPOS(I),PER
20 CONTINUE
```

As the value of I changes from 1 to 3, each element of the array DEPOS is divided by the cumulative number of deposits (TOT) and multiplied by 100.

EXAMPLE 8.6 Correspondence Among Arrays

Sometimes we need to perform operations among corresponding elements of different arrays. For example, assume that a banking program has stored the current month's total dollar deposits in array DEPA and the total dollar withdrawals in array WITA. A third array can be used to accumulate the new balance (BAL), as follows:

```
    DO 30 I = 1,N
        BAL(I) = BAL(I) + DEPA(I) − WITA(I)
30 CONTINUE
```

where N represents the number of customers to be processed. Note that the appearance of BAL(I) on the right side reflects the previous value of BAL(I), that is, last month's balance for the Ith account.

Follow-up Exercises

13. Suppose that before running the program segment in Example 8.6, memory appears as follows:

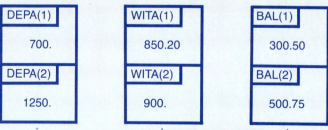

DEPA(1)	WITA(1)	BAL(1)
700.	850.20	300.50

DEPA(2)	WITA(2)	BAL(2)
1250.	900.	500.75

What changes would occur for the first two customer accounts following execution of the program segment in Example 8.6?

14. Sometimes, beginning programmers will try to use the implied DO statement for arithmetic operations. This is not possible. Correct the following attempt at summing the K elements in array REVEN:

    SUM = (SUM + REVEN(I), I = 1,K)

15. A student, wishing to initialize an array with 10 elements to zero, wrote the following:

    TOTAL (K) = 0.

    On seeing this, his girlfriend (who also takes FORTRAN programming) says the above doesn't make sense because K is undefined. Perhaps, she reasons, we can try a short-list approach:

    TOTAL = 0.

    Explain why each approach would provoke an error. Correct this segment of the program.

8.6 APPLICATIONS

This section illustrates three common applications of one-dimensional arrays.

EXAMPLE 8.7   Table Look-Up: Life Insurance Premium

The term **table look-up** refers to procedures for accessing data that are stored in a table. These procedures satisfy a very common need across a wide variety of professional fields and occupational areas. In this example we work with one-dimensional "tables"; in the next chapter, we discuss two-dimensional tables.

Suppose that a life insurance company uses the following premium schedule to bill its customers. In this case, the annual premium is based on the age of the policyholder. For example, a policyholder who is 47 years old would pay a premium of $327 per year.

Premium Schedule

Upper Age Limit	Annual Premium ($)
25	277
35	287
45	307
55	327
65	357

When looking up information in a table, three basic elements are required. First, there is the "search key," which is the item of information that helps you to locate the right place within the table. In the case of the life insurance company, each policyholder's age is the search key.

The table that is to be searched usually makes up the other two sets of elements needed for the search: (1) the set of "keys" used to access the proper location, and (2) the set of "function values." In the premium schedule the set of keys is the limits on the various age classes, and the corresponding premiums are the function values.

Figure 8.1 illustrates the flowchart for the program below, which determines the appropriate premium for each of N customers.

Program	Comments
| ```
      INTEGER AGELIM,PREM,AGE
      DIMENSION AGELIM(5),PREM(5),NAME(6)
      DO 10 I = 1,5
          READ(5,1) AGELIM(I),PREM(I)
   10 CONTINUE
      READ(5,2) N

      DO 25 J = 1,N
          READ (5,3) AGE, NAME



          DO 15 I = 1,5
              IF (AGE .LE. AGELIM(I)) GO TO 20
   15     CONTINUE
   20     WRITE(6,4) NAME,PREM(I)
   25 CONTINUE
      STOP
    1 FORMAT(I2,I4)
    2 FORMAT(I2)
    3 FORMAT(I2,6A4)
    4 FORMAT('0',6A4,' $',I3)
      END
``` | AGELIM, PREM, and AGE are to store integer values. DO-loop 10 reads the premium schedule row by row.<br><br>N is the number of customers to be processed. DO-loop 25 reads age and name for each customer and prints name and appropriate premium. DO-loop 15 searches age limits to determine location of appropriate premium. This represents the table look-up logic. |
```

FIGURE 8.1   *Flowchart for Table Look-up Problem*

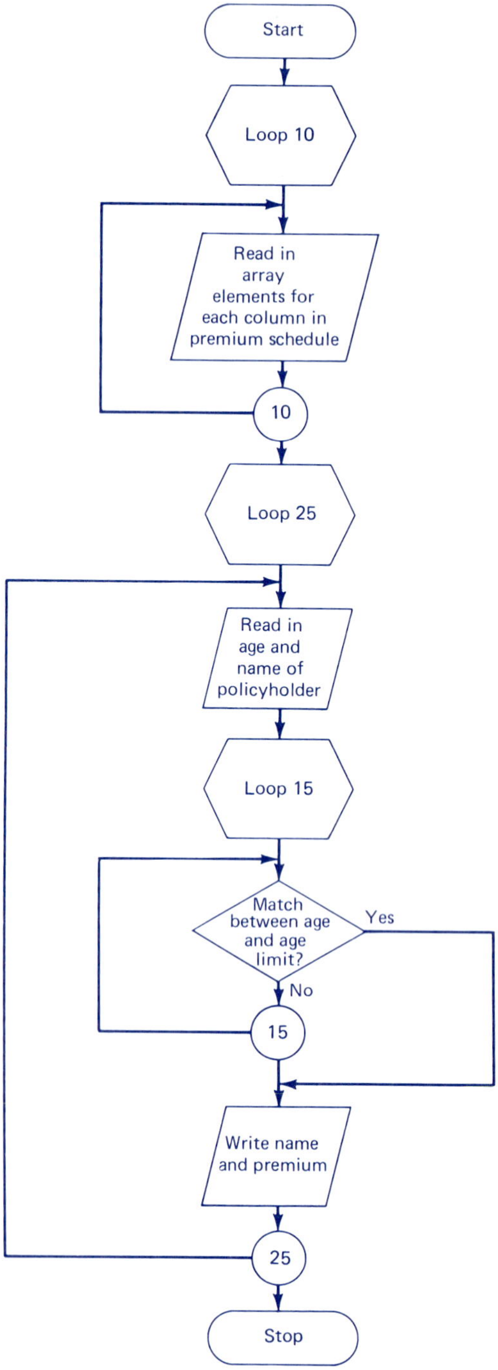

Input data for the premium schedule and two customers are described below.

Input Records

```
1 2 3  4  5  6  7  8  9 1011121314151617181920212223242526272829 30
25  277
35  287
45  307
55  327
65  357
 2
42CLARK  S.  KENT
28LOIS  S.  LANE
```

The premium schedule is read into two one-dimensional arrays: AGELIM and PREM. Memory locations for these arrays appear as follows *after* loop 10 is completed:

AGELIM(1)		PREM(1)
25		277

AGELIM(2)		PREM(2)
35		287

AGELIM(3)		PREM(3)
45		307

AGELIM(4)		PREM(4)
55		327

AGELIM(5)		PREM(5)
65		357

Next, the number of customers which need to be processed (N) is read in, after which we enter loop 25. The first statement in loop 25 reads in the policyholder's age and name. Note that *NAME is a six-element array which contains alphanumeric data.* Also note that the READ statement uses the short-list technique to read NAME. If we assume a computer that stores four alphanumeric characters per storage location, then the data for a policyholder named Clark S. Kent, age 42, would be stored as follows:

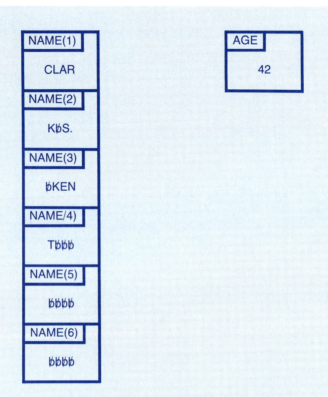

Thus, you should realize that the I/O of alphanumeric data is best designed by using an array coupled with the short-list technique.

Loop 15 contains the table look-up logic for this problem. In this case, the "search key" is the value stored in AGE and the "set of keys" is given by the array elements in AGELIM. The loop scans each element of AGELIM until the proper age class is found, that is, until the age of the policyholder (the search key) is less than or equal to an age limit value in the array AGELIM. When this condition is satisfied, the appropriate premium (function value) is identified as the array element of PREM which corresponds to the matching age class. For example, when 42 is stored in AGE, loop 15 operates as follows:

I	Is AGE Less than or Equal to AGELIM(I)?	Result
1	No; 42 is not less than or equal to 25	Continue
2	No; 42 is not less than or equal to 35	Continue
3	Yes; 42 is less than or equal to 45	Go to statement 20

Thus, when statement 20 is executed, the correct value of 3 in I (age class) is used as the subscript of PREM. In this case, the contents of PREM(3) are printed, which gives a premium of $307 for someone aged 42.

Sample output for the given input data is shown below.

Print Column

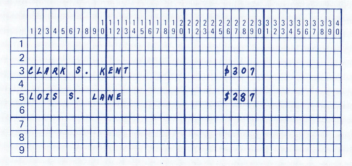

Follow-up Exercises

16. With respect to Example 8.7:
    a. What would the output look like if the last input record were as follows:

        99 RIP VAN WINKLE

    *b. Modify the program to print the message

        OVER 65 - - UNINSURABLE

        beginning in column 25 of the same line as the person's name for any person over 65 years of age.
17. What changes would be required in the program if we were to use the FORMAT below:

        3 FORMAT(12,24A1)

    Describe memory for the array NAME. How would the name Clark S. Kent appear in storage? Comment on this approach versus the approach in the example.
18. Sometimes beginning programmers will insert a READ statement in loop 15 of Example 8.7 as follows:

        :
        :
        DO 15 I = 1,5
        READ(5,1) AGELIM(I),PREM(I)
        :
        :

    Explain why this approach will not work.

EXAMPLE 8.8   Direct Access to Array Element

A more efficient method of utilizing arrays in some applications is to access or process values *directly* from one array location without moving sequentially through an entire array.

To illustrate the direct access concept, consider the problem in Example 7.8 on page 199, where we accumulated the total number of freshmen, sophomores, juniors, and seniors enrolled at State College. Figure 8.2 and the program below illustrate a new, more efficient solution to that problem.

```
DIMENSION COUNT(4),TOT(4),AVG(4)
DO 10 I = 1,4
    COUNT(I) = 0.
    TOT(I) = 0.
10 CONTINUE
READ(5,*) NOS
DO 20 J = 1, NOS
    READ(5,*) ICLASS,SATVER,SATMTH
    TOTSAT = SATVER + SATMTH
    COUNT(ICLASS) = COUNT(ICLASS) + 1.
    TOT(ICLASS) = TOT(ICLASS) + TOTSAT
20 CONTINUE
DO 30 I = 1,4
    AVG(I) = TOT(I)/COUNT(I)
30 CONTINUE
WRITE(6,*) AVG
STOP
END
```

Note 1.   As before, NOS represents "number of students" and ICLASS represents "class code." The variable ICLASS stores coded values 1 through 4, which represent 1 for freshmen, 2 for sophomore, 3 for junior, and 4 for senior. The array COUNT is used to store the accumulated count of students in each class. For example, COUNT(1) represents number of freshmen, COUNT(2) represents number of sophomores, and so forth. The array TOT stores the sum of combined SAT scores by class. For example, TOT(1) will contain the sum of combined (math and verbal) SAT scores for all freshmen. The array AVG is used to store the average combined SAT score by class.

Note 2.   If a student has a class standing of 2, then the statement

COUNT(ICLASS) = COUNT(ICLASS) + 1.

increments by 1 the second storage location in COUNT. In other words, the equivalent statement given by

COUNT(2) = COUNT(2) + 1.

is executed. Thus, ICLASS acts as a "pointer" (subscript) to the specific location in COUNT that is to be manipulated. The same approach is used to manipulate or update the array TOT.

Note 3.   Notice that both COUNT(I) and COUNT(ICLASS) are used in this program to access specific elements in COUNT. Our use of I rather than ICLASS as the subscript of COUNT outside of loop 20 illustrates the fact that one should focus on the *value* taken on by the subscript rather than the *variable name* of the

FIGURE 8.2   *Flowchart for Example 8.8*

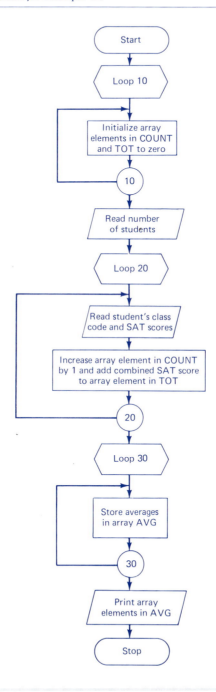

subscript. We have no need to use ICLASS as a subscript outside of loop 20; hence, we use the simpler I.

Note 4.   In this particular example, the concept of "direct access" is illustrated by the fact that we need not loop through the entire array each time we wish to update (increment or sum) the contents of a specific location in COUNT or TOT. The pointer ICLASS conveniently serves to locate specific elements in COUNT and TOT.

Follow-up Exercises

19. For the program in Example 8.8:
     a. Assuming a snapshot of memory is taken just before the execution of CONTINUE, indicate how the storage locations of COUNT and TOT change as the program processes the following data in loop 20:

J	ICLASS	SATVER	SATMTH	TOTSAT	COUNT(1)	COUNT(2)	COUNT(3)	COUNT(4)	TOT(1)	TOT(2)	TOT(3)	TOT(4)
—	—				0.	0.	0.	0.	0.	0.	0.	0.
1	2	580.	640.									
2	3	720.	680.									
3	2	610.	560.									
4	1	560.	590.									
5	2	580.	420.									

     b. Indicate how the output would appear.

20. Modify Example 8.8 as follows:
     a. Use a DATA statement to initialize COUNT and TOT.
     b. Eliminate the use of AVG by utilizing one of the existing arrays.
     Why is this version more efficient?

EXAMPLE 8.9   Sorting

One of the most common operations performed in data processing, called **sorting,** is arranging data either numerically or alphabetically into sequential order according to some criterion. For example, a student file contains a number of records, one for each student. Each record contains student name and identification number in addition to other data. We could sort the file either by ID number in ascending or descending order or we could arrange the file alphabetically using the student names. In either case, the item in the record which is used to sort the file is known as the "sort key".

Let's assume we want a listing of students in ascending numeric order according to their ID number. For simplicity, let's further assume we have only four students. The one-dimensional array called LIST is used to store and sort ID numbers, as shown below:

ID Number	Array LIST
8321	LIST(1)
	8321
3076	LIST(2)
	3076
2501	LIST(3)
	2501
7771	LIST(4)
	7771

For this problem, we use the **exchange method** of sorting. On each pass through the array, the first element is compared with the second: the smaller number is stored in the first position and the larger number is stored in the second position. Then, the second element of the array is compared with the third: the smaller number is placed in the second position and the larger number is placed in the third position. This process of comparison and rearranging continues throughout the entire array. When this first pass through the array is complete, the array is processed again, from beginning to end. This procedure continues until no exchanges take place in a pass through the entire array. The exchange method is also called a **bubble sort** since items which are below their correct positions in the array tend to move upward to their proper places, like bubbles in a carbonated drink.

Figure 8.3 illustrates the flowchart for the sorting program below.

```
      INTEGER LIST(1000),TEMP,SWITCH
      READ(5,1) N,(LIST(I), I = 1,N)
   20 SWITCH = 0
      DO 30 I = 2,N
         IF (LIST(I) .GE. LIST(I − 1)) GO TO 30
         TEMP = LIST(I)
         LIST(I) = LIST (I − 1)
         LIST (I − 1) = TEMP
         SWITCH = 1
   30 CONTINUE
      IF (SWITCH .EQ. 1) GO TO 20
      WRITE(6,2) (LIST(I), I = 1,N)
      STOP
    1 FORMAT(16I5)
    2 FORMAT('1SORT COMPLETED'/('0',16I5))
      END
```

FIGURE 8.3   Flowchart for Sorting Program

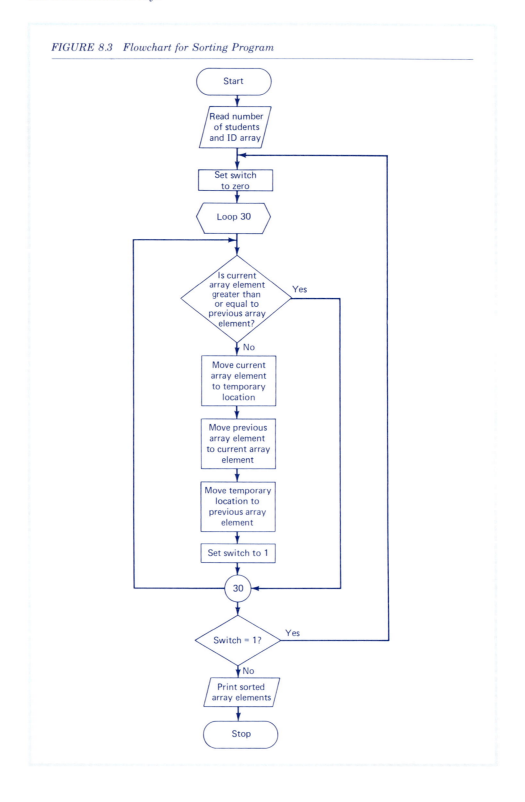

For the input record given by

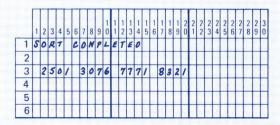

```
1234 5 6 7 8 9 101112131415161718192021222324 25  ...
  4 8321  3076  2501  7771
```

we would get the following output:

	1	2	3	4	5	6	7	8	9	1 0	1 1	1 2	1 3	1 4	1 5	1 6	1 7	1 8	1 9	2 0	2 1	2 2	2 3	2 4	2 5	2 6	2 7	2 8	2 9	3 0
1	S	O	R	T		C	O	N	P	L	E	T	E	D																
2																														
3	2	5	0	1		3	0	7	6		7	7	7	1		8	3	2	1											
4																														
5																														
6																														

The logic within loop 30 illustrates the bubble sort. The subscripts I and I − 1 are used to compare values stored in adjacent array elements. When an exchange takes place between two adjacent elements, a separate memory location (TEMP) serves as a temporary location to hold one of the values while the exchange takes place. To understand exactly what's happening, follow the diagram and steps below for the case I = 2 in loop 30.

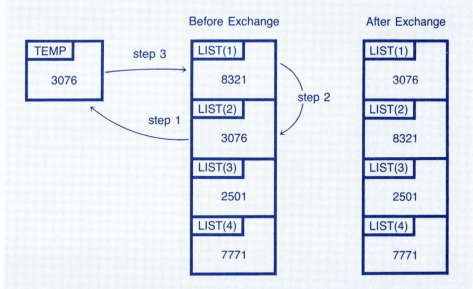

The variable SWITCH acts as a switch by storing either 0 or 1. If the value in SWITCH is 1 after a complete pass through the array LIST, then the sort is not complete and the entire array must be scanned again for numbers out of sequence. If the value in SWITCH is 0 after a complete pass through the array LIST, then the sort is complete.

Follow-up Exercises

21. Fill in the following table based on the data in the example:

			Contents When Control Is at 30 CONTINUE			
I	TEMP	LIST(1)	LIST(2)	LIST(3)	LIST(4)	SWITCH
2	3076	3076	8321	2501	7771	1
3						
4						
2						
3						
4						
2						
3						
4						

How many passes through the entire array does it take to sort the array? How many passes does it take to terminate execution?

22. Make appropriate changes in the program for a numeric sort in descending order. Test your program by tracing through the given data.

23. Is it possible to sort alphabetic data using the program in Example 8.9?

8.7
COMMON ERRORS

Arrays are great for giving a lot of practice in debugging. Often one "small" error will result in an "avalanche" of error messages. Pay attention to the following and you might avoid apoplexy.

1. *Declaration of Array.* Don't forget to declare your array by using the DIMENSION, REAL, or INTEGER statement. If you forget to dimension an array, then you will get a *syntax* error message for *each* line containing a subscripted variable. So, if you get an error message such as "UNDE-FINED ARRAY" or "UNDEFINED FUNCTION" for each line where the subscripted variable appears, then check whether or not you dimensioned the array.

Also, don't forget to declare arrays before their use in the program. To be safe, place your DIMENSION, REAL, or INTEGER statement before all other executable statements in the program.

Finally, you must use an integer constant to declare the size of your array. Don't try the following:

```
DIMENSION X(N)
```

unless you like to see syntax errors. A variable number of locations is not permitted, except for the material discussed in section 10.5.

2. *Subscripts.* If you get an *execution* error message such as "SUBSCRIPT OUT OF BOUNDS" or "SUBSCRIPT OUT OF RANGE," then a subscript is negative, zero, or greater than the number of storage locations reserved for the array.[3] Two kinds of mistakes are possible here: either you reserved too few locations for your array or you made a logic error in assigning values to subscripts. In the latter case, you might want to diagnose the error by using a trace to print subscript values, as illustrated by the following simple example:

```
        :
        :
        DO 10 J = 1,5
            K = 5 − J
            WRITE(6,*) J,K
            X(K) = J**3
     10 CONTINUE
        :
        :
```

```
     Output
       1   4
       2   3
       3   2
       4   1
       5   0
     SUBSCRIPT OUT OF BOUNDS
```

The error message is the result of a zero in the subscript K. If we wish K to take on the successive values 5, 4, 3, 2, 1, then the statement that defines K should read

```
     K = 6 − J
```

Other common subscripting errors include the following: using a real variable or constant for a subscript; entirely forgetting the subscript for a variable that has been declared an array.

3. *Array Names.* A common point of confusion among beginning programmers is just what portion of a subscripted variable represents the array name. For example, are B(J) and B(I) one and the same array? Yes. In this case, the array name is B, not B(J) or B(I). B(J) and B(I) simply reference specific elements in array B.

   A related problem is the following: Many students, thinking that the parentheses are part of the array name, believe it is all right to also use B as a simple (unsubscripted) variable that is different from the array B. Not so. Once B is dimensioned, the variable B is treated as an array throughout the program, as the following illustrates:

---

[3]FORTRAN 77 allows negative or zero values for subscripts, as illustrated in Section 11.7.

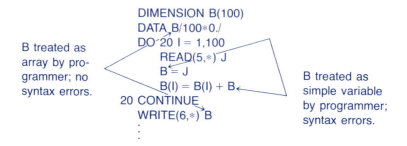

B treated as array by programmer; no syntax errors.

```
DIMENSION B(100)
DATA B/100*0./
DO 20 I = 1,100
    READ(5,*) J
    B = J
    B(I) = B(I) + B
20 CONTINUE
WRITE(6,*) B
    :
    :
```

B treated as simple variable by programmer; syntax errors.

4. *Initialization.* If an array is to act as a summer or counter, then don't forget to initialize its contents to whatever values are required. (See Example 8.4.) Some compilers automatically initialize all storage locations to zero, but others don't. If yours does not, then you will get an execution error the first time your program attempts to use an uninitialized counter or summer. Sometimes during the same computer run you need to reinitialize your array. If so, don't use a DATA statement, as illustrated below for a 500-element array:

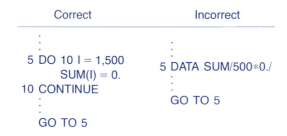

Correct	Incorrect
⋮	⋮
5 DO 10 I = 1,500	5 DATA SUM/500*0./
SUM(I) = 0.	⋮
10 CONTINUE	
⋮	GO TO 5
GO TO 5	

A DATA statement is nonexecutable, so it would not be possible to reinitialize an array by this method once the program begins executing.

5. *I/O.* Don't forget to coordinate the placement of data on the input record with the design of your input loop, as the following illustrates:

Input Record	Program Segment
1 2 3 4 5 6 7 8 9 ...	
10 2 5	1 FORMAT(3I2)
	DO 10 I = 1,3
	READ(5,1) LOAD(I)
	10 CONTINUE

An "OUT OF DATA" execution error message would occur here, since loop 10 attempts to read three records. Don't forget that a new input record is processed each time a READ statement is executed. Also, the list in the above READ statement contains only one array element, so the fact that 3I2 appears in the FORMAT is irrelevant according to the imbalance rules. For the given input record, we need to use an implied DO.

Finally, unless you use the short-list technique, don't forget to use a loop to output an array. We often see the following approach in an attempt to output the entire contents of an array:

```
WRITE(6,15) ARR(I)
```

This statement either prints one element (if a positive integer within the bounds of the array is stored for I) or results in an execution error.

Additional Exercises

24. Define or explain each of the following:

array	DIMENSION statement	DATA statement
array element	REAL statement	table look-up
subscript	INTEGER statement	sorting
one-dimensional array	implied DO statement	exchange method
subscripted variables	short-list technique	bubble sort

25. **Mopups Revisited.** Rewrite the program in Example 4.10 on page 115 as follows:
    a. Use one-dimensional arrays to store the rate schedule. Treat the number of rows in the rate schedule as an input variable. Use DO-loops for your loops. Nicely label your output. *Hint:* Let the numbers 10, 20, and 30 represent the "set of keys."
    b. After all dealers have been processed, print the total number of bikes ordered, the sum of total prices, and the average price per bike.
    **c. Design your program such that the program itself calculates and stores the values 2250, 4650, and 6900.

26. **Property Tax Assessment Revisited.** Solve Exercise 40 in Chapter 4 on page 122 as follows:
    a. Store the tax schedule, lot numbers, property values, and tax charges in one-dimensional arrays. Treat the number of rows in the rate schedule as an input variable. Use DO-loops for your loops. Nicely label your output. Following the output table print the sum of property values and the total tax charge. *Hint:* Let the numbers 10,000 and 30,000 represent the "set of keys."
    **b. Following the output in part a, print a second table that shows tax charges (together with corresponding lot numbers and property values) in descending order.

27. **Alphanumeric Distribution Revisited.** Solve both parts of Exercise 27 in Chapter 6 on page 178 as follows:
    a. Store the five states in a five-element array, the tabulated frequencies by complaint code in a three-element array, and the tabulated frequencies by state in a five-element array. Use DO-loops to tabulate frequencies.
    **b. Design your program to handle all 50 states.

28. **Crime Data Summary.** The data below represent the number of arrests for felony crimes in a state over a three-year period:

Arrest Data by Year

	1	2	3
Homicide	1,000	1,000	1,000
Robbery	10,000	9,000	11,000
Burglary	27,000	24,000	28,000
Assault	13,000	15,000	16,000
Theft	19,000	20,000	23,000
Forgery	10,000	9,000	10,000

a. Write a flowchart and program to read the data into several one-dimensional arrays. Print out the data in a table format which includes a new row for total arrests in each year and a new column for average arrests for each crime over the past three years. No need to label rows and columns here.

b. In the output of part a, label your columns 1, 2, 3, and "AVERAGE." Label your rows according to the felony names in the above table, the last row being "TOTALS." Preferably, the output of felony names should be handled through the use of arrays.

c. Print a second table which gives the percent of arrests for each crime to the total number of arrests in that year.

29. **Revenue-Sharing.** Consider the allocation program whereby the federal government. apportions certain federal funds to the states on the basis of each state's population to the total U.S. population. The table below provides population figures for all 50 states according to a recent census:

Population by State (in thousands)

State	Population	State	Population
ME	1,059	NC	5,451
NH	808	SC	2,818
VT	468	GA	4,926
MA	5,199	FL	8,327
RI	938	KY	3,396
CT	3,080	TN	4,188
NY	18,101	AL	3,614
NJ	7,322	MS	2,364
PA	11,841	AR	2,068
OH	10,745	LA	3,762
IN	5,313	OK	2,681
IL	11,160	TX	12,017
MI	9,117	MT	748
WI	4,566	ID	820
MN	3,905	WY	374
IA	2,857	CO	2,534
MO	4,772	NM	1,147
ND	636	AZ	2,224

SD	681	UT	1,206
NB	1,541	NV	592
KS	2,266	WA	3,544
DE	577	OR	2,288
MD	4,089	CA	20,876
VA	4,967	AK	341
WV	1,803	HI	854

a. Write a program which uses one array for the names of the states and another array for the population figures. Input these arrays, calculate how much revenue should go to each state if $380 million is available for allocation, and output a table with appropriate labels which lists each state and its allocated amount. Include a flowchart.

b. Modify the preceding program to include a loop which processes more than one allocation. For example, if three allocation programs are to be run, then the output should appear as follows:

DOLLAR AMOUNTS ALLOCATED UNDER
EACH PROGRAM

STATE	1	2	3	TOTALS
ME	XXXXXXX.	XXXXXXX.	XXXXXXX.	XXXXXXXX.
NH	XXXXXXX.	XXXXXXX.	XXXXXXX.	XXXXXXXX.

The number of allocations to be made (three in the above example) should be a variable. Note that the total amount which is to be allocated to each state is given by row sums and output under the column labeled "TOTALS." Test your program by processing the following funds available for allocation under three programs: $380M, $800M, $500M.

**c. Modify your output in either part a or part b such that the states are listed in alphabetical order. *Hint:* The bubble sort can be used for alphabetic data.

**d. Modify your output in part a, b, or c such that the entire state name is listed instead of the state abbreviation. *Hint:* A direct access can be used to find the appropriate state name. To store up to 12 characters for state name, you need three 50-element one-dimensional arrays (assuming a computer that stores four characters per array element).

30. **Exam Grading.** Consider an N-question multiple choice exam, where only one answer is correct for each question.

a. Write a flowchart and program to grade the exam and print the student's Social Security number, the number right, the number wrong, and the final grade. The final grade is the percent number right. The input data consist of

(1) One record for N
(2) One record containing N integers representing the N correct answers (answer key)
(3) One record indicating the number of students in the class who took the exam (M)
(4) M records, one for each student, containing the student's Social Security number and N answers

Use one-dimensional arrays for both the answer key and a student's answers. Test your program with the following test data:

```
20
13544112355123445321
5
266619724   13444112335123445111
291658412   13543212343223335121
035642185   13544112355123444321
456123890   12544223312133355311
356765431   23544113354154445213
```

b. Input and output a name (of your choice) for each student. Allow up to 20 characters for each name. Use a one-dimensional array to store a student's name.

**c. Print a frequency distribution of final grades for the exam, as follows:

90 OR ABOVE	XX
80 BUT UNDER 90	XX
70 BUT UNDER 80	XX
60 BUT UNDER 70	XX
50 BUT UNDER 60	XX
BELOW 50	XX
	XXX

AVERAGE GRADE FOR EXAM = XX.X

31. **Text Processing. A typing textbook contains numerous exercises consisting of paragraphs for students to type. These exercises vary in their level of difficulty according to the following criteria:

1. *Number of strokes* in the exercise. A stroke is any keyboard act, such as typing a letter, typing a space, and returning the carriage to the next line (except for the last line in the exercise), and so on.
2. *Number of words* in the exercise. Words can include a single letter. For example, the phrase "I love computers" has three words.
3. *Average word length* in the exercise. This is defined as the number of strokes divided by the number of words.

The usual approach to developing these exercises is for someone to manually count strokes, words, and word length for each proposed exercise, to ensure that exercises having various levels of difficulty are selected—a tedious task. This is where you come in: You are to computerize this task.

The three criteria discussed earlier are to be calculated by a computer program for each of the following two exercises.

Exercise 1.

Jack and Jill went up the hill
To fetch a pail of water;
Jack fell down and broke his crown,
And Jill came tumbling after.

Exercise 2.

Among other duties, a regional office of the Environmental Protection Agency (EPA) is charged with investigating complaints regarding industrial pollution, when "warranted." A complaint is investigated by sending a panel of three experts, collectively called the "proboscis patrol," to the site of the alleged offender. By consensus, the proboscis patrol then renders one of three opinions: low level, medium level, or high level of pollution. (We might note that the human nose has yet to find an electronic "equal" in detecting offending odors.) Following an opinion, the regional director of the EPA then has the option of issuing or not issuing a citation to the offender. Alternatively, the EPA may choose not to investigate the complaint and then make a decision regarding issuance of a citation.

Design your program as follows:

1. Treat the number of exercises to be processed as an input variable.
2. Treat the number of lines in an exercise as an input variable.
3. Each line of the exercise is to be placed on a single input record. Place an asterisk immediately after the last character in a line to signify the end of that line on the input record.
4. Each input record is 80 columns. Use an 80-element one-dimensional array to store a line at a time. Each element of this array is read in using A1 as the FORMAT specification. Thus, the number of strokes and words are counted one line at a time.
5. Strokes on a line are counted until the asterisk at the end of that line is encountered. The asterisk itself does not count as a stroke. For example, the first line of Exercise 1 has 31 strokes, including the carriage return at the end of the line.
6. To count words, count the number of times a blank character is succeeded by a nonblank character. For example, line 3 of Exercise 2 has 8 words. At the very end of a line, add a word to the count if the asterisk is preceded by any character other than a hyphen. *Hint:* Use a logical IF to test each element of the array against an unsubscripted variable that stores a blank character. Use a DATA statement to initialize this unsubscripted variable. Be careful when the first word in a line is indented.
7. Output each line of the exercise followed by a count of the number of strokes and words for that line. For example, the first two lines of Exercise 1 should be printed as follows:

	STROKES	WORDS
JACK AND JILL WENT UP THE HILL	31	7
TO FETCH A PAIL OF WATER;	28	6

At the end of the exercise print summary values for the three criteria discussed earlier.

CHAPTER 9

Two-Dimensional Arrays

In many situations it is convenient to store data in arrays with more than one dimension. Some computer systems allow up to seven dimensions, but we will focus here on the more common two-dimensional arrays.

9.1 MOTIVATION

Generally, it is desirable to use two-dimensional arrays whenever we wish to store and manipulate data that are characterized by two attributes. For example, the Premium Schedule of Example 8.7 on page 247 incorporates the attributes "upper age limit" and "annual premium." Other examples include the following:

266

Occupied beds in a hospital are tabulated by day of the week and by ward.
Deposits for a major bank are recorded for all branch banks on a quarterly or monthly basis.
Enrollments at a college are tabulated by major and class standing.
Exam scores for a course are recorded for all students.
Ten financial ratios from the Fortune 500 list of major U.S. corporations are recorded for all 500 corporations.

9.2
SUBSCRIPTS

You will more easily understand **two-dimensional arrays** (those with two subscripts) if you visualize a group of memory locations as a grid of boxes (table) arranged in rows and columns:

An element within a two-dimensional array is referenced by specifying two subscripts: row number and column number. For example, in the three-row by four-column array below, the memory location that is marked with an X is found by looking at row 2, column 3; the memory location marked with XX is found in row 3, column 2:

As you can see, two subscripts are needed when you use two-dimensional arrays. In FORTRAN, the subscripts must be enclosed in parentheses and separated by a comma. For example, if the above array is named DEPOS, then the location where the X is found would be referenced as DEPOS(2,3) and the location where the XX is found would be referenced as DEPOS(3,2). Notice that, in accordance with mathematical convention, the subscripts are always given in the order:

$$\text{array name} \left(\substack{\text{row} \\ \text{subscript,}} \quad \substack{\text{column} \\ \text{subscript}} \right)$$

Other than the use of two subscripts according to the above convention, subscripts for two-dimensional arrays are treated in the same manner as for one-dimensional arrays.

Storage of two-dimensional arrays is best conceptualized as a table. For example, the twelve-element array named DEPOS can be visualized as a three-row by four-column table in memory, as follows:

DEPOS(1,1)	DEPOS(1,2)	DEPOS(1,3)	DEPOS(1,4)
DEPOS(2,1)	DEPOS(2,2)	DEPOS(2,3)	DEPOS(2,4)
DEPOS(3,1)	DEPOS(3,2)	DEPOS(3,3)	DEPOS(3,4)

In actual practice, storage locations for two-dimensional arrays do not "look" like a table in memory, but that need not concern us since the FORTRAN convention treats it like a table.

9.3
DIMENSION STATEMENT

Just as with one-dimensional arrays, two-dimensional arrays must be dimensioned in order to reserve memory locations for the array. In addition to identifying one-dimensional variables, the DIMENSION statement can indicate which variables are two-dimensional, and establishes the number of rows and columns that will be reserved in memory for the array.

The general form of the DIMENSION statement for use with two-dimensional arrays is

$$\textbf{DIMENSION} \; \text{variable name} \left(\substack{\text{row} \\ \text{constant,}} \quad \substack{\text{column} \\ \text{constant}} \right), \; \text{variable name} \left(\substack{\text{row} \\ \text{constant,}} \quad \substack{\text{column} \\ \text{constant}} \right), \; \ldots$$

For example, we might store the number of deposits for three branch banks in each of four quarters in a three-row by four-column two-dimensional array named DEPOS, where each row stores the quarterly data for one branch. The DIMENSION statement would be specified as

DIMENSION DEPOS(3,4)

If you wanted DEPOS to store branch deposits for each month of the year, then you could set up an array with 3 rows and 12 columns. In this case, the DIMENSION statement would be given by

DIMENSION DEPOS(3,12)

In the first case DEPOS has 12 elements in memory, whereas in the second case, 36 locations are reserved in memory.

Both one- and two-dimensional arrays can be dimensioned in a single DIMENSION statement by using commas to separate each array specification. For example,

DIMENSION SALE(5,10),EXP(8,10),TOT(5)

This results in the reservation of 50 locations for the two-dimensional array SALE, 80 locations for the two-dimensional array EXP, and 5 locations for the one-dimensional array TOT.[1]

As with one-dimensional arrays, the REAL and INTEGER statements can be used to declare both mode and size of two-dimensional arrays. For example, if the 5 by 10 array SALE and the 5-element array TOT are to store integer values, then we can use

INTEGER SALE(5,10),TOT(5)

instead of

INTEGER SALE,TOT
DIMENSION SALE(5,10),TOT(5)

Likewise, if the 100 by 50 array LOAD is to store real values, then we can use

REAL LOAD(100,50)

9.4
INPUT/OUTPUT

The same three methods for I/O that we illustrated for one-dimensional arrays can be used for two-dimensional arrays. For the examples that follow, we will illustrate I/O for the two-dimensional array DEPOS, which is to store the following data on the number of deposits by branch and by quarter:

Branch	Quarter 1	2	3	4
1	1000	800	500	1200
2	500	2000	2000	500
3	1500	300	700	1500

---

[1]FORTRAN 77 is more flexible in declaring arrays, as described in Section 11.7.

Using DO Statements

I/O of two-dimensional arrays with DO statements requires the use of two DO statements, one "nested" within the other, as illustrated in the next example.

EXAMPLE 9.1   I/O with Nested DO Loops

Consider the following program segment for reading DEPOS:

```
              2 FORMAT(F5.0)
inner    ┌    DO 20 IROW = 1,3
loop     │   ┌DO 10 ICOL = 1,4
outer    │   │    READ(5,2) DEPOS(IROW,ICOL)
loop     10  └CONTINUE
         └20 CONTINUE
```

The flowchart in Figure 9.1 should help you visualize how the nesting of DO-loops works. The key concept that you need to understand here is the exact manner in which the subscripts change values. Carefully look at the program and the flowchart to confirm that the subscripts of DEPOS change values as follows:

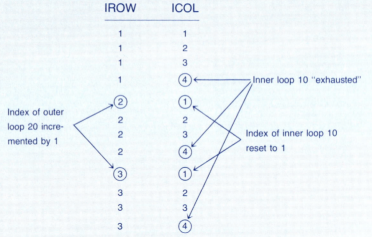

Suppose we have placed our data on input records as follows:

```
        12 3 4 56 . . .
        1000
         800
         500
        1200
         500
        2000
        2000
         500
        1500
         300
         700
        1500
```

FIGURE 9.1   Nested DO Loops for Input

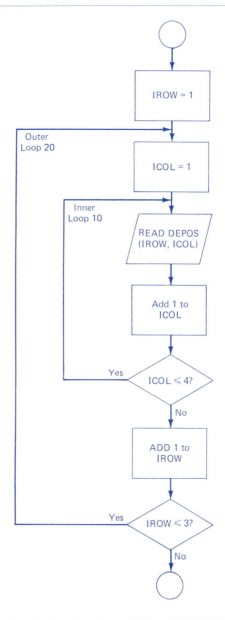

The first time through the loops, IROW = 1 and ICOL = 1, so the first data item is read into DEPOS(1,1):

DEPOS(1,1)	DEPOS(1,2)	DEPOS(1,3)	DEPOS(1,4)
1000.			
DEPOS(2,1)	DEPOS(2,2)	DEPOS(2,3)	DEPOS(2,4)
DEPOS(3,1)	DEPOS(3,2)	DEPOS(3,3)	DEPOS(3,4)

The second time through the inner loop, IROW = 1 and ICOL = 2, so the second item is read into DEPOS(1,2):

DEPOS(1,1)	DEPOS(1,2)	DEPOS(1,3)	DEPOS(1,4)
1000.	800.		
DEPOS(2,1)	DEPOS(2,2)	DEPOS(2,3)	DEPOS(2,4)
DEPOS(3,1)	DEPOS(3,2)	DEPOS(3,3)	DEPOS(3,4)

The third time through the inner loop, IROW = 1 and ICOL = 3, so the third item is read into DEPOS(1,3):

DEPOS(1,1)	DEPOS(1,2)	DEPOS(1,3)	DEPOS(1,4)
1000.	800.	500.	
DEPOS(2,1)	DEPOS(2,2)	DEPOS(2,3)	DEPOS(2,4)
DEPOS(3,1)	DEPOS(3,2)	DEPOS(3,3)	DEPOS(3,4)

The fourth time through the inner loop, IROW = 1 and ICOL = 4, so the fourth item is read into DEPOS(1,4):

DEPOS(1,1)	DEPOS(1,2)	DEPOS(1,3)	DEPOS(1,4)
1000.	800.	500.	1200.
DEPOS(2,1)	DEPOS(2,2)	DEPOS(2,3)	DEPOS(2,4)
DEPOS(3,1)	DEPOS(3,2)	DEPOS(3,3)	DEPOS(3,4)

Then, IROW is incremented to 2 and again the inner loop (ICOL) varies from 1 to 4. This results in the following sequence:

IROW	ICOL	
2	1	READ(5,2) DEPOS(2,1)
2	2	READ(5,2) DEPOS(2,2)
2	3	READ(5,2) DEPOS(2,3)
2	4	READ(5,2) DEPOS(2,4)

Now the array appears as follows in memory:

DEPOS(1,1)	DEPOS(1,2)	DEPOS(1,3)	DEPOS(1,4)
1000.	800.	500.	1200.
DEPOS(2,1)	DEPOS(2,2)	DEPOS(2,3)	DEPOS(2,4)
500.	2000.	2000.	500.
DEPOS(3,1)	DEPOS(3,2)	DEPOS(3,3)	DEPOS(3,4)

Finally, IROW is set equal to 3 and the inner index, ICOL, varies from 1 to 4. This results in the sequence:

IROW	ICOL	
3	1	READ(5,2) DEPOS(3,1)
3	2	READ(5,2) DEPOS(3,2)
3	3	READ(5,2) DEPOS(3,3)
3	4	READ(5,2) DEPOS(3,4)

At this point, read-in of the array is complete, yielding the following configuration in memory:

DEPOS(1,1)	DEPOS(1,2)	DEPOS(1,3)	DEPOS(1,4)
1000.	800.	500.	1200.
DEPOS(2,1)	DEPOS(2,2)	DEPOS(2,3)	DEPOS(2,4)
500.	2000.	2000.	500.
DEPOS(3,1)	DEPOS(3,2)	DEPOS(3,3)	DEPOS(3,4)
1500.	300.	700.	1500.

Note that the READ statement is executed exactly 12 times. *Since there is only one variable in the list of the READ statement, this means that 12 input records are required, each with a single value.*

Finally, we cannot overemphasize the need for you to concentrate on the manner in which the subscripts change values. Again, *the inner loop must be exhausted (the index must exceed its terminal value) for each iteration (loop) of the outer loop. Once the inner loop is exhausted, then the index of the outer loop is incremented and the index of the inner loop is reset to its initial value.*

Follow-up Exercises

1. Write a program segment which utilizes nested DO loops to output the contents of DEPOS. Use

   ```
   4   FORMAT(1X,F10.0)
   ```

   and indicate how the printout would appear.

2. Suppose the following program segment is executed using the same input records as the example:

   ```
     2 FORMAT(F5.0)
       DO 20 J = 1,4
          DO 10 I = 1,3
             READ(5,2) DEPOS(I,J)
    10      CONTINUE
    20 CONTINUE
   ```

   How would DEPOS appear in memory? Does the array in memory get filled in row by row or column by column? How should we place data on the input records so as to store the proper values in DEPOS using this program segment?

3. The array LOT is to be stored in memory as follows:

LOT(1,1)	LOT(1,2)
10	50
LOT(2,1)	LOT(2,2)
4	320
LOT(3,1)	LOT(3,2)
15	8

a. Prepare a program segment that could be used to read in these six values into the array LOT. Indicate how the data would be placed on input records.

Given the following program segment, indicate how the output would appear with each FORMAT statement:

```
        DO 50 I = 1,3
        DO 40 J = 1,2
        WRITE(6,2) LOT(I,J)
   40 CONTINUE
   50 CONTINUE
```

b. 2 FORMAT('0',I5)
c. 2 FORMAT('0',2I5)
d. 2 FORMAT('0','LOT SIZES'//(1X,I5))

4. The program segment in the preceding exercise can be written more concisely by using only one CONTINUE:

```
        DO 50 I = 1,3
        DO 50 J = 1,2
            WRITE(6,2) LOT(I,J)
   50 CONTINUE
```

Right? Can you think of a change that would make these loops even more concise?

Using the Nested Implied DO Statement

The implied DO is used with two-dimensional arrays for more flexible control of I/O than is possible with the nesting of DO loops. A common form of the implied DO with two-dimensional arrays is given by

READ(-,-)
or
WRITE(-,-) $\left(\left(\begin{array}{c} array \\ name \end{array}\left(\begin{array}{cc} row & column \\ index, & index \end{array}\right), \begin{array}{c} inner \\ index \end{array} = \begin{array}{ccc} initial & terminal & incremental \\ value, & value, & value \end{array}\right),\right.$

$\left.\begin{array}{c} outer \\ index \end{array} = \begin{array}{ccc} initial & terminal & incremental \\ value, & value, & value \end{array}\right)$

The entire specification of the implied DO is enclosed within nested parentheses, hence the term **nested implied DO.** Within the nested parentheses is the array name, followed by the two subscripts enclosed in parentheses, followed by a comma, and then the indexing information for each subscript. As in the one-dimensional array case, each index of the nested implied DO also serves as a subscript.

EXAMPLE 9.2   Unformatted I/O with the Nested Implied DO

To illustrate the nested implied DO, consider the following statement:

Inner Loop⌐   ⌐Outer Loop

READ(5,*) ((X(I,J), J = 1,3), I = 1,2)

As you can see, the implied DO statement is nested, and functions in a way similar to the nesting of DO statements. The inner loop (with the index variable closest to the array) is enclosed within the outer loop. As before, *the inner loop must be satisfied for each iteration of the outer loop.* In the above example, this is equivalent to the following FORTRAN statement:

READ(5,*) X(1,1),X(1,2),X(1,3),X(2,1),X(2,2),X(2,3)

In effect, *the READ statement contains a list of six variables, which allows us to input all six values for X on one input record.*

Did you pay attention to the manner in which the I and J subscripts varied? The index of the inner loop (J subscript) varies from 1 to 3 while the index of the outer loop (I subscript) is held constant at 1. Then, the I subscript is incremented to 2 and the inner loop varies from 1 to 3 once more.

If we wish to store the following in X

X(1,1)	X(1,2)	X(1,3)
10.	8.	6.
X(2,1)	X(2,2)	X(2,3)
4.	2.	0.

then the following input record can be used with the above READ statement:

10.,8.,6.,4.,2.,0.

However, suppose we wish to read values row by row into the array X. In other words, the input records are to be set up in a manner which is conceptually compatible with the table nature of a two-dimensional array, as follows:

10.,8.,6.
4.,2.,0.

Then, the following *combination of the DO statement and the implied DO* can be used to store these values into a two-dimensional array:

```
        DO 10 I = 1,2
            READ(5,*) (X(I,J), J = 1,3)
    10 CONTINUE
```

In this case, *the implied DO is the inner loop and the DO/CONTINUE statements define the outer loop.* You should carefully note that the READ statement is executed twice, once for each value of I (two input records are provided). Also, note that the list of the READ statement contains three variables (which is why we have three values for each line of input). This is equivalent to the following statements:

```
READ(5,*) X(1,1),X(1,2),X(1,3)
READ(5,*) X(2,1),X(2,2),X(2,3)
```

Follow-up Exercise

5. Write the appropriate statement(s) such that X is printed out without FORMATs as follows:
    a. The entire array is printed on one line.
    b. The first row of the array appears on one line and the second row on the next line.
    c. The first column of the array appears on one line, the second column on the next line, and the third column on the third line.

EXAMPLE 9.3   Formatted I/O with the Nested Implied DO

Getting back to the banking problem in Example 9.1, suppose that the data are recorded on three input records as follows:

```
123 4 5 6789 101112131415161718192021222324 25
   1000    800     500     1200
    500  2000    2000      500
   1500    300     700     1500
```

Then the execution of

READ(5,1) ((DEPOS(I,J), J = 1,4),I = 1,3)
1 FORMAT(4F6.0)

results in the following storage for DEPOS:

DEPOS(1,1)	DEPOS(1,2)	DEPOS(1,3)	DEPOS(1,4)
1000.	800.	500.	1200.
DEPOS(2,1)	DEPOS(2,2)	DEPOS(2,3)	DEPOS(2,4)
500.	2000.	2000.	500.
DEPOS(3,1)	DEPOS(3,2)	DEPOS(3,3)	DEPOS(3,4)
1500.	300.	700.	1500.

Carefully note that there is *imbalance* between the number of variables (12) in the list of the READ statement and the number of specifications (4) in the FORMAT. Thus, according to the procedure outlined in Section 6.4 on page 168, *the computer resets to the beginning of this FORMAT (and reads a new input record) after reading in each group of four values.* Do you realize why we selected a repeat factor of 4 in the FORMAT? Because we wish to input four values per line, which is consistent with the number of values found in each row of this table.

This array can be printed in table form using

WRITE(6,9) ((DEPOS(I,J), J = 1,4),I = 1,3)
9 FORMAT('0', 4F6.0)

which gives the following output:

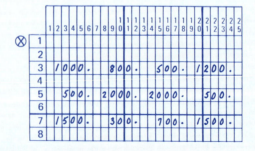

If we were to change the FORMAT to

9 FORMAT(1X,F6.0)

then the following would be printed:

Finally, if the FORMAT is given by

9 FORMAT(1X,12F6.0)

then we would have

Follow-up Exercises

6. Specify the exact appearance of input records if DEPOS is read in using the nested implied DO in the example and

   a. 1 FORMAT(F6.0)
   b. 1 FORMAT(16F5.0)

7. Write the appropriate READ and FORMAT statements if the data for DEPOS are recorded as follows:

   ```
   1 2 3 4 5 6 7 8 9 1011121314 1516
     1000    500   1500
      800   2000    300
      500   2000    700
     1200    500   1500
   ```

   Note that input records contain column entries rather than row entries in this case; however, we still wish to store the data as in Example 9.3.

8. Specify the exact appearance of output records for the program segment

   ```
      DO 70 I = 1,3
   70 WRITE(6,2) (DEPOS(I,J), J = 1,4)
   ```

using each of the following FORMAT statements:

a. 2 FORMAT(1X,F6.0)
b. 2 FORMAT(1X,4F6.0)
c. 2 FORMAT(1X,12F6.0)
d. 2 FORMAT('0', 'BANK DEPOSITS'//('0',4F6.0))
e. What must you do to the FORMAT in part d such that the label BANK DEPOSITS is printed once rather than three times?

Using the Short-List Technique

The short-list technique can be used with two-dimensional arrays to input or output entire arrays. In other words, the array name without subscripts can appear in a READ or WRITE statement:

```
DIMENSION DEPOS(3,4)
READ(5,*) DEPOS
```

The number of elements read in is equal to the number of rows times the number of columns that have been specified in the DIMENSION statement. In this case, there are 12 variables in the list of the READ statement.

One word of caution: *this technique requires that the data be arranged by column.* In other words, the above READ statement is equivalent to the following:

```
READ(5,*) DEPOS(1,1),DEPOS(2,1),DEPOS(3,1),DEPOS(1,2),DEPOS(2,2),
          DEPOS(3,2), . . . ,DEPOS(2,4),DEPOS(3,4)
```

The data would appear as follows on the input record:

```
1000.,500.,1500.,800.,2000.,300.,500.,2000.,700.,1200.,500.,1500.
```

Also, the short-list technique can be applied only if the entire array, as specified in the DIMENSION, is to be read or written. If only part of the array is to be used, then you must use the DO or implied DO statement.

Follow-up Exercises

9. Specify the appearance of input records for each of the following:

```
        DIMENSION DEPOS(3,4)
        READ(5,1) DEPOS
```
a. 1 FORMAT(F5.0)
b. 1 FORMAT(12F5.0)
c. 1 FORMAT(3F5.0)

10. Are the following statements equivalent?

```
        DIMENSION Y(5,8)
        WRITE(6,*) Y
        WRITE(6,*) ((Y(I,J), J = 1,8), I = 1,5)
```

Alphanumeric Arrays

Two-dimensional arrays are a convenient vehicle for processing textual data such as entire stories, articles, reports, letters, and other documents that need to be stored in primary memory, as we illustrate next.

EXAMPLE 9.4   Humpty Dumpty Sat . . .

How long has it been since you've read this nursery rhyme?

Input Records

```
1 2 3 4 5 6 7 8 9 10 11 12 13 14 15 16 17 18 19 20 21 22 23 24 25 26 27 28 29 30 31 32 33 34 35 36 37 38 39 40
    5  10   1

HUMPTY DUMPTY SAT ON A WALL,
HUMPTY DUMPTY HAD A GREAT FALL.
   ALL THE KING'S HORSES,
    AND ALL THE KING'S MEN,
COULDN'T PUT HUMPTY TOGETHER AGAIN.
```

The program below processes the above input records, stores the nursery rhyme in a two-dimensional array named NR, and prints as many copies of the nursery rhyme as desired. Variables are defined as follows:

```
  M = number of lines in the nursery rhyme
  N = number of columns to be used in the array
NUM = number of copies to be printed
```

```
    DIMENSION NR(50,20)
    READ(5,2) M,N,NUM
    DO 20 I = 1,M
        READ(5,4) (NR(I,J), J = 1,N)
 20 CONTINUE
    DO 40 K = 1,NUM
        WRITE(6,6)
        DO 30 I = 1,M
            WRITE(6,8) (NR(I,J), J = 1,N)
 30     CONTINUE
 40 CONTINUE
    STOP
  2 FORMAT(3I3)
  4 FORMAT(20A4)
  6 FORMAT('1'//20X,'NURSERY RHYME'/1X,13('*'))
  8 FORMAT('0',19X,20A4)
    END
```

Assuming a computer that stores four characters per storage location, NR would contain the following in memory after loop 20 is executed.

	NR(_,1)	NR(_,2)	NR(_,3)	NR(_,4)	NR(_,5)	NR(_,6)	NR(_,7)	NR(_,8)	NR(_,9)	NR(_,10)	…	NR(_,20)
NR(1,_)	HUMP	TYƀD	UMPT	YƀSA	TƀON	ƀAƀW	ALL,	ƀƀƀƀ	ƀƀƀƀ	ƀƀƀƀ	⋮	
NR(2,_)	HUMP	TYƀD	UMPT	YƀHA	DƀAƀ	GREA	TƀFA	LL.ƀ	ƀƀƀƀ	ƀƀƀƀ		
NR(3,_)	ƀƀAL	LƀTH	EƀKI	NG'S	ƀHOR	SES,	ƀƀƀƀ	ƀƀƀƀ	ƀƀƀƀ	ƀƀƀƀ		
NR(4,_)	ƀƀAN	DƀAL	LƀTH	EƀKI	NG'S	ƀMEN	.ƀƀƀ	ƀƀƀƀ	ƀƀƀƀ	ƀƀƀƀ		
NR(5,_)	COUL	DN'T	ƀPUT	ƀHUM	PTYƀ	TOGE	THER	ƀAGA	IN.ƀ	ƀƀƀƀ	⋰	
NR(50,_)	…										⋮	

After loops 30 and 40 are executed, we end up with the following printout:

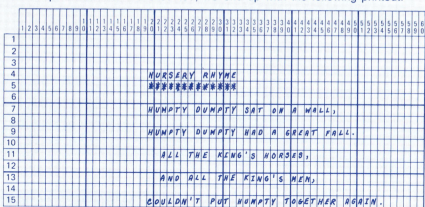

Follow-up Exercises

11. Make sure you really understand this program by roleplaying the computer. In particular, confirm how the input records are processed, how the nursery rhyme appears in memory, and the exact placement of output.

12. Answer the following short questions:
    a. Up to how many characters of text can this program handle per line?
    b. Up to how many lines of text can this program handle?
    c. Why would it be unwise to read in the nursery rhyme using the short-list technique?
    d. In loop 20 why would it be unwise to read in the nursery rhyme using two nested DO loops?
    e. What is the purpose of loop 40?
    f. Suppose that the input value of N is the number of characters of text per line that this particular run is to handle. How would you modify the program?

9.5
MANIPULATING ARRAYS

Processing data stored in two-dimensional arrays normally involves nesting of DO statements. The next example illustrates some common manipulations of two-dimensional arrays.

EXAMPLE 9.5   Row and Column Totals

One of the more common processing tasks is finding totals of each row or column in an array. The row or column totals can be stored either in one-dimensional arrays or in an extra row or column of the two-dimensional array. For example, to find the annual bank deposits in each branch for the data given on page 274, we need to sum the entries in each row. The following program segment would determine row sums:

```
        DO 30 I = 1,3
            SUM(I) = 0.
            DO 25 J = 1,4
                SUM(I) = SUM(I) + DEPOS(I,J)
    25      CONTINUE
    30  CONTINUE
```

When I = 1, SUM(1) is initialized to zero; then the inner loop 25 sums the values in the first row given by DEPOS(1,1), DEPOS(1,2), DEPOS(1,3), and DEPOS(1,4), and stores this sum in the first element of the array SUM.

SUM(1)	DEPOS(1,1)	DEPOS(1,2)	DEPOS(1,3)	DEPOS(1,4)
3500.	1000.	800.	500.	1200.

SUM(2)	DEPOS(2,1)	DEPOS(2,2)	DEPOS(2,3)	DEPOS(2,4)
	500.	2000.	2000.	500.

SUM(3)	DEPOS(3,1)	DEPOS(3,2)	DEPOS(3,3)	DEPOS(3,4)
	1500.	300.	700.	1500.

When the outer loop is incremented (I = 2), SUM(2) is initialized to zero, and the values in row 2 are accumulated and stored in the second element of array SUM.

SUM(1)	DEPOS(1,1)	DEPOS(1,2)	DEPOS(1,3)	DEPOS(1,4)
3500.	1000.	800.	500.	1200.

SUM(2)	DEPOS(2,1)	DEPOS(2,2)	DEPOS(2,3)	DEPOS(2,4)
5000.	500.	2000.	2000.	500.

SUM(3)	DEPOS(3,1)	DEPOS(3,2)	DEPOS(3,3)	DEPOS(3,4)
	1500.	300.	700.	1500.

Finally the outer loop is incremented (I = 3) and the values of the third row are added to the third element in the array SUM.

SUM(1)	DEPOS(1,1)	DEPOS(1,2)	DEPOS(1,3)	DEPOS(1,4)
3500.	1000.	800.	500.	1200.
SUM(2)	DEPOS(2,1)	DEPOS(2,2)	DEPOS(2,3)	DEPOS(2,4)
5000.	500.	2000.	2000.	500.
SUM(3)	DEPOS(3,1)	DEPOS(3,2)	DEPOS(3,3)	DEPOS(3,4)
4000.	1500.	300.	700.	1500.

Follow-up Exercises

13. Write a program segment which accumulates the bank's total deposits for each quarter. Store these totals in a one-dimensional array called TOT.

*14. Assume that DEPOS has been dimensioned to four rows and five columns. Instead of using SUM as in the example and TOT as in the preceding exercise, use the fourth row of DEPOS to store column totals and the fifth column to store row totals. Write program segments which accomplish this. Don't forget to initialize your summers to zero.

15. Write a program segment which calculates the percentage of each quarter's deposit to the annual number of deposits for each branch. Store these percentages in the two-dimensional array PER. After processing, PER should have the stored values below. Can you fill in the third row? Note that, except for possible rounding error, rows of PER sum to 100.

PER(1,1)	PER(1,2)	PER(1,3)	PER(1,4)
28.57143	22.85714	14.28571	34.28571
PER(2,1)	PER(2,2)	PER(2,3)	PER(2,4)
10.00000	40.00000	40.00000	10.00000
PER(3,1)	PER(3,2)	PER(3,3)	PER(3,4)

16. Suppose the following array has been dimensioned as follows:

    DIMENSION WEIGHT(100,50)

    Write a program segment that initializes each element in WEIGHT to 100 using
    a. Two nested DO-loops.
    b. A DATA statement.
    Under what circumstances should you not use the approach in part b?

9.6
APPLICATIONS

This section illustrates two applications using two-dimensional arrays.

EXAMPLE 9.6 Financial Report

The sales revenue and cost data for each region and model line of the Effete Automotive Corporation have been collected. The controller needs a report that presents sales, cost, and profit with totals for each region and model line.

The program on pages 287–288 prepares the desired report, where the variables are defined as follows:

NREG = number of regions
NMOD = number of models
REV   = two-dimensional array for sales revenue, where rows represent regions and columns represent models
COST = two-dimensional array for costs, where rows represent regions and columns represent models
PROF = two-dimensional array for profits, where rows represent regions and columns represent models

Note that the sums for each region and model line are stored within each of the two-dimensional arrays (REV,COST,PROF). For example, the statement

REV(I,NMOD + 1) = REV(I,NMOD + 1) + REV(I,J)

stores a row total (region total) in the column immediately after the last model-line column. The statement

REV(NREG + 1,J) = REV(NREG + 1,J) + REV(I,J)

stores column totals (model-line totals) in the row immediately following the last row which stores revenues.

For the test input records given by

1 2 3 4 5 6 7 8 9 10 11 12 13 14 15 16 17 18 19 20 21 22 23 24 25 26 27 28 29 30 31 32 33 34 35 36 37 38 39 40 41 42 43 44 45 46 47 48

3 2					
100	150	60	40	30	70
50	100	40	10	25	75

we would get the output shown on page 289.

Follow-up Exercises

17. Roleplay the computer by processing the given input data. In particular, notice how the program stores row and column sums. Confirm the output, paying close attention to output FORMATs.

**18. The program does not accumulate overall totals for revenue, cost, and profit. (Did you notice the zero in the fourth row and third column of each table?) Modify the program so these totals are accumulated.

**19. Modify the program so one additional row and one additional column is used with each array. The new row contains each model's contribution to overall revenue, cost, and profit (each column total as a percentage of the overall total). The new column contains each region's contribution to overall revenue, cost, and profit (each row total as a percentage of the overall total).

Program

```
DIMENSION REV(10,10),COST(10,10),PROF(10,10)

READ(5,1) NREG,NMOD
READ(5,2) ((REV(I,J), J = 1,NMOD), I = 1, NREG)
READ(5,2) ((COST(I,J), J = 1,NMOD), I = 1,NREG)

DO 15 I = 1,NREG
    DO 10 J = 1,NMOD
        PROF(I,J) = REV(I,J) − COST(I,J)
10    CONTINUE
15 CONTINUE

DO 25 I = 1,NREG
    REV  (I,NMOD + 1) = 0.
    COST(I,NMOD + 1) = 0.
    PROF(I,NMOD + 1) = 0.
    DO 20 J = 1,NMOD
        REV  (I,NMOD + 1) = REV(I,NMOD + 1) + REV(I,J)
        COST(I,NMOD + 1) = COST(I,NMOD + 1) + COST(I,J)
        PROF(I,NMOD + 1) = PROF(I,NMOD + 1) + PROF(I,J)
20    CONTINUE
25 CONTINUE

DO 35 J = 1,NMOD
    REV  (NREG + 1,J) = 0.
    COST(NREG + 1,J) = 0.
    PROF(NREG + 1,J) = 0.
    DO 30 I = 1,NREG
        REV  (NREG + 1,J) = REV(NREG + 1,J) + REV(I,J)
        COST(NREG + 1,J) = COST(NREG + 1,J) + COST(I,J)
        PROF(NREG + 1,J) = PROF(NREG + 1,J) + PROF(I,J)
30    CONTINUE
35 CONTINUE
```

Comments

Dimension arrays.

Read number of regions, number of models, revenue data, and cost data. Note repeated use of FORMAT number 2.

Determine profit by region and model.

Find row (region) sums for each array. Store these in the *first unused column* of each array. Note initialization of this column.

Find column (model) sums for each array. Store these in the *first unused row* of each array. Note initialization of this row.

```
        NR = NREG + 1
        NM = NMOD + 1

        REV (NR,NM) = 0.
        COST(NR,NM) = 0.
        PROF(NR,NM) = 0.

        WRITE(6,3) (J,J = 1,NM)
        DO 40 I = 1,NR
40      WRITE(6,4) I,(REV(I,J), J = 1,NM)

        WRITE(6,5) (J,J = 1,NM)
        DO 45 I = 1,NR
45      WRITE(6,4) I,(COST(I,J), J = 1,NM)

        WRITE(6,6) (J,J = 1,NM)
        DO 50 I = 1,NR
50      WRITE(6,4) I,(PROF(I,J), J = 1,NM)

        STOP

1 FORMAT(2I2)
2 FORMAT(10F8.2)
3 FORMAT('1','REVENUES'//1X,10I10)
4 FORMAT('0',I2,10F10.2)
5 FORMAT(//'0','COSTS'//1X,10I10)
6 FORMAT(//'0','PROFITS'//1X,10I10)

        END
```

Print revenue array. Note how columns (print J) and rows (print I) are numbered.

Print cost array. Note how columns (print J) and rows (print I) are numbered.

Print profit array. Note how columns (print J) and rows (print I) are numbered.

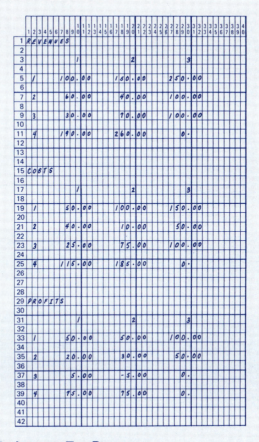

EXAMPLE 9.7 Income Tax Program

After taking a tax course, you decide to earn some extra money (so that you can pay more taxes) by opening a computerized tax service for local accountants and individual taxpayers.

Given a taxpayer's wages (WAGES) from Form W-2, dividends (DIV), interest income (INTINC), income other than wages (OTHER), and adjustments (ADJ) such as moving expenses, the adjusted gross income (AGI) is given by

$$AGI = WAGES + DIV + INTINC + OTHER - ADJ$$

Taxable income (TI) is determined as adjusted gross income less excess itemized deductions (EXDED) less the product of number of exemptions (EXEM) and the allowance per exemption (APE):

$$TI = AGI - EXDED - EXEM*APE$$

EXDED is set equal to zero if a single taxpayer's itemized deductions (DED) are less than \$2,200; however, if DED is greater than \$2,200, then EXDED = DED − 2,200. The income tax for single (unmarried) taxpayers is based on the taxable income according to the schedule on page 290.

Tax Schedule for Single Taxpayers
Column

(1) Over—	(2) But not over—	(3) (4) Income Tax	(5) of the amount over—
$ 0	$ 2,200	$ 0 + 0%	—
$ 2,200	$ 2,700	$ 0 + 14%	$ 2,200
$ 2,700	$ 3,200	$ 70 + 15%	$ 2,700
$ 3,200	$ 3,700	$ 145 + 16%	$ 3,200
$ 3,700	$ 4,200	$ 225 + 17%	$ 3,700
$ 4,200	$ 6,200	$ 310 + 19%	$ 4,200
$ 6,200	$ 8,200	$ 690 + 21%	$ 6,200
$ 8,200	$ 10,200	$ 1,110 + 24%	$ 8,200
$ 10,200	$ 12,200	$ 1,590 + 25%	$ 10,200
$ 12,200	$ 14,200	$ 2,090 + 27%	$ 12,200
$ 14,200	$ 16,200	$ 2,630 + 29%	$ 14,200
$ 16,200	$ 18,200	$ 3,210 + 31%	$ 16,200
$ 18,200	$ 20,200	$ 3,830 + 34%	$ 18,200
$ 20,200	$ 22,200	$ 4,510 + 36%	$ 20,200
$ 22,200	$ 24,200	$ 5,230 + 38%	$ 22,200
$ 24,200	$ 28,200	$ 5,990 + 40%	$ 24,200
$ 28,200	$ 34,200	$ 7,590 + 45%	$ 28,200
$ 34,200	$ 40,200	$10,290 + 50%	$ 34,200
$ 40,200	$ 46,200	$13,290 + 55%	$ 40,200
$ 46,200	$ 52,200	$16,590 + 60%	$ 46,200
$ 52,200	$ 62,200	$20,190 + 62%	$ 52,200
$ 62,200	$ 72,200	$26,390 + 64%	$ 62,200
$ 72,200	$ 82,200	$32,790 + 66%	$ 72,200
$ 82,200	$ 92,200	$39,390 + 68%	$ 82,200
$ 92,200	$102,200	$46,190 + 69%	$ 92,200
$102,200	—	$53,090 + 70%	$102,200

To illustrate the computations, consider an individual who declares $19,700 in wages, $225 in dividends, $305.20 in interest income, $3,200 in income other than wages, and no adjustments. This gives an AGI of $23,430.20. If itemized deductions amount to $4,230 and one exemption is claimed at a $750 allowance per exemption, then EXDED is $2,030 and TI is $20,650.20. From the above tax schedule, the income tax (TAX) is determined as $4510 + (.36) × (20,650.20 − 20,200), or $4,672.07. If the taxpayer had paid taxes during the year which amounted to more than TAX, then the taxpayer would receive a welcome refund from the IRS; otherwise, a not-so-welcome balance due the IRS would have to be paid.

This is another example of a table look-up, this time using a two-dimensional array to store the table. To solve this problem the data in columns 2, 3, and 4 of the tax schedule are stored in a two-dimensional array named TAXTAB. The "search key" is the taxpayer's taxable income (TI); the "set of keys" is the upper limits of each income class (column 1 of TAXTAB, which is column 2 of the tax schedule) and the "function values" are in columns 3 and 4 of the tax schedule (columns 2 and 3 of TAXTAB).

Program	Comments
REAL INTINC, TAXTAB(26,3)	
READ(5,1) TAXTAB	Remember that columns 1, 2, and 3 of TAXTAB are columns 2, 3, and 4 of the tax schedule.
READ(5,2) NUM	Read number of taxpayers to be processed.
DO 25 K = 1,NUM	
READ(5,3) WAGES,DIV,INTINC,OTHER,ADJ,DED,EXEM,APE,TAXPAY	Input data for individual taxpayer.
AGI = WAGES + DIV + INTINC + OTHER − ADJ	Calculate adjusted gross income.
EXDED = 0.	Logic for calculating EXDED.
IF (DED .GT. 2200.) EXDED = DED − 2200.	
TI = AGI − EXDED − EXEM*APE	Calculate taxable income.
DO 10 I = 1,26	Table look-up logic. Unnatural exit from loop 10
IF (TI .LT. TAXTAB(I,1)) GO TO 15	gives us correct row (value of I) in tax table.
10 CONTINUE	
15 TAX = TAXTAB(I,2) + (TI − TAXTAB(I − I,1))*TAXTAB(I,3)/100.	Income tax calculation.
WRITE(6,4) AGI,TI,TAX	
IF (TAX .LT. TAXPAY) GO TO 20	
BALDUE = TAX − TAXPAY	
WRITE(6,5) BALDUE	
GO TO 25	
20 REFUND = TAXPAY − TAX	
WRITE(6,6) REFUND	
25 CONTINUE	
STOP	
1 FORMAT(13F6.0)	
2 FORMAT(I2)	
3 FORMAT(9F8.2)	
4 FORMAT('1', 'ADJUSTED GROSS INCOME = $',F8.2/'0',7X,	
'TAXABLE INCOME = $',F8.2/'0',11X,	
'INCOME TAX = $',F8.2)	
5 FORMAT('0',PANIC. PAY THE IRS $',F8.2)	
6 FORMAT('0','GREAT. THE IRS OWES YOU $',F8.2)	
END	

Follow-up Exercises

20. Identify what the following variables represent in the program:
    a. NUM
    b. TAXPAY
    c. REFUND
    d. BALDUE
    e. TAXTAB(I,1)
    f. TAXTAB(I,2)
    g. TAXTAB(I,3)
    h. TAXTAB(I − 1,1)

21. Describe how the tax schedule is to be input. How many input records are required to input the table? What entry would you use for the last item in column 1 of TAXTAB?

22. Describe printed output and the contents of memory locations given the following input records:

```
  1 2 3 4 5 6 7 8 9 101112131415161718192021222324252627282930313233343536373839 40
1    2200    2700      3200      3700      4200      6200      82
2  22200  24200     28200    3 4200     40200     46200    522
3      0       0        70       145       225       310       6
4   4510    5230      5990      7590     10290     13290     165
5      0      14        15        16        17        19
6     36      38        40        45        50        55
7  2
8  19700          225           3 0520     3200                 0
9  12100            0                0         0                 0
```

```
 4142434445464748495051525354555657585960 61626364656667686970717273747576777879 80
00  10200   12200    14200     16200     18200    20200
00  62200   72200    82200    92200102200999999
90   1110    1590     2090      2630      3210     3830
90  20190   26390    32790     39390     46190    53090
21     24       25        27        29        31       34
60     62       64        66        68        69       70

        4230          1         7 50      4100
        1900          1         7 50      2530
```

*23. As the program stands, it has a bug whenever TI is less than $2,200. Can you identify the problem? Modify the program to eliminate this bug.

*24. TAXTAB has 26 rows and 3 columns. The last entry in the first column needs to be a very large number to account for taxable incomes that exceed $102,200. Our input FORMAT for the table limits this number to $999,999. Thus, the program will not handle taxable incomes of $1 million or more. (Not much to be concerned about, actually.) Incorporate a new statement that calculates TAX for someone who exceeds a taxable income of $102,200.

9.7
COMMON ERRORS

Errors associated with two-dimensional arrays are as likely to occur as errors associated with one-dimensional arrays. So, review once more the common errors discussed on pages 258 to 261.

Errors associated with the I/O of two-dimensional arrays are perhaps the most common. If you use the short-list technique, then remember that I/O is column by column, not row by row (see Example 9.7). Otherwise, you must use nested loops for the I/O of two-dimensional arrays.

When using nested loops, keep in mind that the inner loop index varies faster than the outer loop index. Typically, we let the inner loop index represent the column subscript and the outer loop index the row subscript. This gives us row-by-row I/O, which is conceptually consistent with the usual way we treat tables.

If you want input records or printout to "look" like a table, then you must use an implied DO. In this case, the usual approach is to use the DO/CONTINUE pair for the outer loop (row index) and an implied DO for the inner loop (column index). Alternatively, a nested implied DO can be used, but this requires a FORMAT statement that sets the number of specifications equal to the number of columns.

Case A

Input Record	Program Segment	Result
123456789...		

```
            1 FORMAT(3I3)
               DO 20 I = 1,2
                  DO 10 J = 1,3
                     READ(5,1) KAT(I,J)
            10       CONTINUE
            20 CONTINUE
```
Input Record: `10 20 30` / `40 50 60`

Result: "OUT OF DATA ERROR" condition during execution.

```
            1 FORMAT(3I3)
               DO 20 I = 1,2
                  READ(5,1) (KAT(I,J), J = 1,3)
            20 CONTINUE
```

Note: Repeat factor in the FORMAT must be 3 or greater.

Result: KAT

10	20	30
40	50	60

```
            1 FORMAT(3I3)
               READ(5,1) ((KAT(I,J), J = 1,3),I = 1,2)
```

Note: Repeat factor in the FORMAT must be exactly 3.

Result: KAT

10	20	30
40	50	60

Case B

| Array KAT in Memory | Program Segment | Expected Output | Actual Output |

Array KAT in Memory:

10	20	30
40	50	60

Program Segment 1

```
2 FORMAT(1X,3I3)
  DO 40 I = 1,2
    DO 30 J = 1,3
      WRITE(6,2) KAT(I,J)
30  CONTINUE
40  CONTINUE
```

Expected Output (columns 1234567890):

```
1
2  10 20 30
3  40 50 60
4
```

Actual Output (columns 1234567890):

```
1
2  10
3  20
4  30
5  40
6  50
7  60
```

Program Segment 2

```
2 FORMAT(1X,3I3)
  DO 40 I = 1,2
    WRITE(6,2) (KAT(I,J), J = 1,3)
40  CONTINUE
```

Note: Repeat factor in the FORMAT must
be 3 or greater.

Actual Output (columns 1234567890):

```
1
2  10 20 30
3  40 50 60
4
```

Program Segment 3

```
2 FORMAT(1X,3I3)
  WRITE(6,2) ((KAT(I,J), J = 1,3),I = 1,2)
```

Note: Repeat factor in the FORMAT must
be exactly 3.

Actual Output (columns 1234567890):

```
1
2  10 20 30
3  40 50 60
4
```

Additional Exercises

25. **Mailing List Revisited.** Rewrite the program in part b of Exercise 25 in Chapter 7 on page 217 by storing the input data file in a two-dimensional array. Design your program to include a DO-loop for processing multiple regions and interest areas. Thus, one run can handle the four separate runs required by the old version.

26. **Computerized Matching.** Rewrite the program in part b of Exercise 31 in Chapter 6 on page 183 by incorporating a loop to handle the different inquiries. Store the placement office file in one or more arrays. Store name, ID, and address in a two-dimensional array.

27. **Questionnaire Analysis.** A university is conducting a survey to determine its under-graduates' "attitudes toward and experiences with the consumption of alcoholic beverages." The following questionnaire has been designed for this survey:

_____ 1. What is your sex? 1. male _____ 2. female _____

_____ 2. Where do you live? 1. on campus _____ 2. off campus with parents _____ 3. off campus alone/with roommates _____

_____ 3. What is your class standing? 1. freshman _____ 2. sopho-more _____ 3. junior _____ 4. senior _____ 5. other _____

_____ 4. How often on the average do you drink alcoholic beverages? 1. never _____ 2. less than once a week _____ 3. 1–3 times per week _____ 4. 4–5 times per week _____ 5. more than 5 times per week _____

_____ 5. Do you feel other people's drinking has any adverse effects on your life? 1. frequently _____ 2. occasionally _____ 3. rarely _____ 4. never _____

_____ 6. Do your drinking habits affect your academic life? 1. frequently _____ 2. occasionally _____ 3. rarely _____ 4. never _____

_____ 7. Do you ever feel guilty about your drinking? 1. frequently _____ 2. occasionally _____ 3. rarely _____ 4. never _____

_____ 8. Do you feel you drink primarily because of 1. boredom _____ 2. peer pressure _____ 3. tension _____ 4. other _____ (specify)

Before conducting the full survey, it has been decided to pretest the questionnaire on ten students. The results are shown below:

Student	Answer to Question Number							
	1	2	3	4	5	6	7	8
1	1	1	3	3	4	4	2	3
2	1	1	3	1	2	2	1	1
3	2	2	2	2	1	3	3	2
4	2	3	1	4	3	1	3	3
5	1	1	4	4	1	1	2	3
6	1	2	2	2	1	1	2	3
7	2	3	4	1	3	2	1	2
8	2	1	1	2	4	4	2	1
9	1	2	3	3	1	1	1	1
10	2	2	1	4	2	3	2	1

a. Prepare a flowchart and write a program that inputs questionnaire data into a two-dimensional array and outputs a frequency distribution for each question.

For example, the frequency distribution for the first question and the above data would be:

	Responses	
Question	1	2
1	5	5

For the second question, we have:

	Responses		
Question	1	2	3
2	4	4	2

Label your output and try to make it as efficient as possible.

**b. Modify your program to provide cross tabulation of responses for any two questions which are specified by the user. For example, if we wish to assess differences between the drinking frequencies of men and women, then your output might appear as follows:

	Question 1	
Question 4	1	2
1	1	1
2	1	2
3	2	0
4	1	2
5	0	0

To make sure you understand this cross tabulation, confirm the numbers based on the data.

28. **Personnel Salary Budget.** The personnel office for a state government agency is in the process of developing a salary budget for the next fiscal year. The personnel file contains the following information on each employee:

Field Information	Columns
Employee name	1–16
Social Security number	17–25
Current annual salary	28–32
Union code (1 = clerical, 2 = teachers, 3 = electrical)	35
Current step in pay schedule (1 through 5)	38
Year hired	41–42

The state agency deals with three labor unions: clerical, teachers, and electrical. Each union has negotiated a separate salary schedule which entitles each employee to an annual step increase. The salary schedules are listed in the table below. Each employee is hired at the lowest step in the salary schedule for their union and moves up one step each year. The field "current step in pay schedule" indicates the employee's step before the new salary for the coming year; that is, "current annual salary" is consistent with this step. The salary for the upcoming year is to be based on the next highest step.

In addition to the salary step increase, employees who have been employed by the state for 10 years or more are entitled to a longevity increase. A longevity increase represents a 5-percent increment added to the employee's *new* step salary.

Salary Schedules ($)

Step	Clerical	Teachers	Electrical
1	10,176	9,133	12,170
2	10,592	10,433	14,260
3	10,956	11,833	16,668
4	11,320	13,333	19,501
5	11,921	14,893	22,801

Personnel File

SMYTHIE SMILE	032166789	10956	1	3	71
ALFRED ALFREDO	123454321	13333	2	4	68
MENDAL MICKEY	987654345	22801	3	5	67
FIELD FLORA	543297541	12170	3	1	76
CURRAN CURRENT	045811222	10176	1	1	76
HANDEL HALO	315791123	11320	1	4	70
UNKIND CORA	129834765	9133	2	1	75

a. Prepare a flowchart and write a program that prints a budget report for the personnel office. Output from the report includes employee's name, current salary, increase in salary due to step, increase in salary due to longevity, and new salary. Following the output table, print totals for the four numeric columns. Treat the salary schedules as a two-dimensional (5 by 3) array called SALARY, which is to be input. Data in the personnel file and in the output table need not be treated as arrays, except perhaps for employee name. Use an appropriate end-of-file test to terminate file input.

b. Print a table which summarizes the salary budgets as follows:

SALARY BUDGETS

```
CLERICAL   $ xxxxxxx.
TEACHERS   $ xxxxxxx.
ELECTRICAL $ xxxxxxx.
           $xxxxxxxx.
```

**c. Print the table of part b *before* the output in part a. *Hint:* Unlike part a, now you must subscript both the variables in the personnel file and the output in the report of part a. Do you see why? Use two-dimensional arrays.

29. **Interactive Airline Reservation System.** All major airlines have automated their systems for handling seat reservations. A central computer keeps a record in storage of all relevant information describing the services being sold: flight numbers, flight schedules, seats available, prices, and other data.

A reservation clerk can request information on seat availability, can sell seats to passengers (providing they are available), can cancel reservations (which increases available seats), and if a flight is full, can put individuals on a waiting list.

a. Develop a flowchart and an interactive program to update the table shown below. For example, if a customer requests one tourist reservation on flight number 4, then the program should check for available tourist seats. Since one is available, it should then adjust the available tourist seats to zero and print a message such as

'RESERVATION ALLOWED'. If the passenger had requested two seats, however, the program should print 'RESERVATION DISALLOWED. SORRY, OUR HIGH ETHICAL STANDARDS PREVENT OVERBOOKING.' Note that, first, you need to input the current array of flight information.

Current Table of Flight Information

Flight Number	Departing Airport	Arriving Airport	Time of Departure	Time of Arrival	Available Seats First Class	Available Seats Tourist	Seats Sold First Class	Seats Sold Tourist
1	BOS	CHI	0730	0855	20	8	10	75
2	BOS	CHI	1200	1357	20	20	10	50
3	BOS	DEN	0810	1111	30	10	0	120
4	ATL	SF	1145	1604	15	1	25	129
5	CHI	BOS	0645	0948	30	25	5	90
6	CHI	NY	0945	1237	30	8	0	120
7	CHI	LA	1530	1851	20	10	30	60
8	CHI	DEN	1955	2114	5	5	25	85
9	DEN	PIT	1025	1611	10	6	60	60
10	DEN	SF	1435	1556	20	10	10	89

Process the following requests in your computer run:

Flight Number	Seat Type	Number	Request
4	Tourist	1	Reserve
6	Tourist	4	Reserve
9	Tourist	2	Cancel
9	1stClass	4	Cancel
4	Tourist	2	Reserve

Next, enter code 100 for flight number, which results in a print of the entire array. After that, enter code 203, which results in the printing of row 3 in the array. Thus the program is capable of printing out either the entire array or any row in the array. Finally, enter code zero for flight number, which terminates the run.

**b. Besides the features in part a, give your program the capability to retrieve and print flight information on all flights between two specified airports. Test your program for flights Boston to Chicago and Chicago to Los Angeles. In the first case, you should get a printout of the first two rows; in the second case, the seventh row should be printed. This feature of the program should be accessed with code 300 when entering the flight number.

30. **Fortune 500 Sort.** The Fortune 500 list is a listing compiled by *Fortune Magazine* of the top 500 corporations according to sales. The table below provides selected data for the top 20 corporations in 1977.[2]

[2]Reprinted by permission from the Fortune Directory; © 1978 Time Inc.

Rank	Corporation	Sales (millions)	Assets (millions)	Profits (millions)	Employees (thousands)
1	General Motors	54961	26658	3338	797
2	Exxon	54126	38453	2423	127
3	Ford Motor	37842	19241	1673	479
4	Mobil	32126	20576	1005	201
5	Texaco	27920	18926	930	71
6	Standard Oil (CA)	20917	14822	1016	38
7	IBM	18133	18978	2719	310
8	Gulf Oil	17840	14225	752	59
9	General Electric	17519	13697	1088	384
10	Chrysler	16708	7668	163	251
11	ITT	13146	12286	551	375
12	Standard Oil (IN)	13020	12884	1012	47
13	Atlantic Richfield	10969	11119	702	52
14	Shell Oil	10112	8877	735	34
15	US Steel	9610	9914	138	166
16	DuPont	9435	7431	545	131
17	Continental Oil	8700	6625	381	43
18	Western Electric	8135	5876	490	162
19	Tenneco	7440	8278	427	93
20	Procter & Gamble	7284	4487	461	54

a. Prepare a flowchart and write a program which sorts the data from high to low according to assets, profits, or employees (as specified by the user). Your output simply would be the above two-dimensional array rearranged according to the requested sort. In your I/O use the numeric code (rank) for the corporation instead of the name. Conduct three runs for three separate sorts: by assets, by profits, and by employees. *Hint:* You might try a sort by the **pointer method,** which avoids the large number of exchanges required by the bubble sort when dealing with a two-dimensional array.

In this procedure you store your data file in a two-dimensional array and also create a separate one-dimensional array to indicate the relative order of the data in the two-dimensional array. Initially, the sequence in the one-dimensional array is 1, 2, 3, . . . , N where each value points to a row number of the data in the two-dimensional array (look at the example below). When you find two items in the two-dimensional array out of order, you interchange the row numbers in the one-dimensional array. When the sort is complete, the relative order of the file is indicated in the one-dimensional array. The data in the two-dimensional array remain undisturbed.

Sample Two-dimensional Array

ID	SALARY
1012	15000
1007	12500
1003	10000
1011	14000

Initial and final arrangement of data

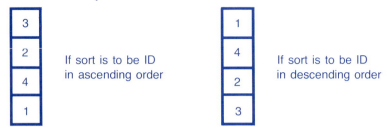

Initial One-dimensional Array

Final One-dimensional Array

b. As part of your output in part a, include the name of the corporation. Names should be stored in a two-dimensional array.

c. Include two new columns in the output to part a: profit as a percentage of sales and profit as a percentage of assets.

**d. Include the option of rearranging the output in alphabetic order according to the names. Alphabetic comparisons can be treated in the same manner as numeric comparisons. Use only the first column of your name array to make comparisons. Do you see a shortcoming in using only the first column?

31. **Cross Tabulations.** Read the problem described in Exercise 43 of Chapter 4 on page 125.

a. Prepare a flowchart and write a program that enters the personnel file into a two-dimensional array in memory and performs cross tabulations on *average salary* between any two variables specified by the user (Age versus Sex, Age versus Marital Status, Age versus Education, Sex versus Marital Status, Sex versus Education, and Marital Status versus Education). For example, the output for Age versus Sex might look like this:

	Sex	
Age	1	2
21–30	24000.	17250.
31–40	22750.	0.
41–50	27000.	25000.

For Marital Status versus Education, the output would appear as:

Marital Status	Education			
	1	2	3	4
1	0.	13500.	0.	22500.
2	0.	0.	25500.	23500.
3	0.	0.	0.	21500.

To make sure you understand the concept of cross tabulation, you should confirm the above cross tabulations by hand.

**b. Design the program such that the number of classes and their upper limits for the Age variable are specified by the user. For example, in part a above, three classes were used for the Age variable, with the following limits:

Class	Limits
1	21–30
2	31–40
3	41–50

You should let the user choose the number of classes and the specific limits.

CHAPTER 10

Subprograms

A **subprogram** is a set of statements for a specialized purpose that can be "called" or utilized by another program termed the **calling program.** The calling program itself can be either another subprogram or a program of the type you have been writing, which we now label a **main program.**

Subprograms are the last major feature of the FORTRAN language that we will discuss. Strictly speaking, subprograms are not essential to writing complex programs for problems which otherwise would go unsolved. Rather, subprogramming capability is a sophisticated refinement of the FORTRAN language with certain advantages: their use can reduce programming effort, save primary memory, and permit a "building-block" approach to programming.

The FORTRAN language allows different classes of subprograms, each with specialized advantages for particular tasks. We present four different types of subprograms in the next four sections.

10.1
FORTRAN-SUPPLIED FUNCTIONS

Suppose we wish to determine the square root of the arithmetic expression

$$b^2 - 4 \cdot a \cdot c$$

and to store it in the address labeled Y. As you know, we simply could use the assignment statement

    Y = (B**2 − 4.*A*C)**.5

An alternative approach in this case is to use the following:

    Y = SQRT(B**2 − 4.*A*C)

The right-hand side of this statement is called a **FORTRAN-supplied function**,[1] which is of the following general type:

> *function name (argument list)*

The **argument list** is either a single arithmetic expression or a list of arithmetic expressions separated by commas. As before, an arithmetic expression can include either a single constant or a single variable. In the above example, SQRT is the function name and B**2 − 4.*A*C is the single argument. The purpose of this function, of course, is to determine the square root of the argument.

Other FORTRAN-supplied functions which are used commonly in management applications are listed in Table 10.1. Study these examples and note the following points:

1. The function is called by using its name in an arithmetic expression. When this expression is compiled, the machine language instructions for performing the function are provided by the compiler. For example, to find the logarithm of a number as in Example 3 of Table 10.1, the compiler utilizes a set of instructions (a subprogram) which calculates logarithms. This saves us the trouble of having to "reinvent the wheel" (write these instructions ourselves) each time we wish to evaluate a logarithm.
2. The **argument** is any arithmetic expression, including either a single constant or a single variable. Commas must be used to separate multiple arguments. In all cases, arguments must be enclosed in parentheses following the name of the function.

---

[1]Other commonly used terms are **built-in function** and **library function.** In actual practice there are technical distinctions between these two terms, but we need not be concerned for our purposes.

TABLE 10.1   Selected* FORTRAN-Supplied Functions

FUNCTION NAME	PURPOSE	NUMBER OF ARGUMENTS	MODE OF ARGUMENT(S)	MODE OF RESULT	EXAMPLE NUMBER	ALGEBRAIC EXAMPLES	CORRESPONDING FORTRAN EXAMPLES
ABS	Absolute value of argument	1	Real	Real	1.	$z = \lvert x - y \rvert$	Z = ABS(X − Y)
IABS		1	Integer	Integer	2.	$k = j \cdot \lvert 1 - m/n \rvert$	K = J*IABS(1 − M/N)
ALOG	Base e log of argument	1	Real	Real	3.	$p = q \cdot \ln 5$	P = Q*ALOG(5.)
ALOG10	Base 10 log of argument	1	Real	Real	4.	$t = \log(a + 2 \cdot b)$	T = ALOG10(A + 2.*B)
EXP	Exponentiation; base e raised to the argument	1	Real	Real	5.	$y = ae^{-2t}$	Y = A*EXP(−2.*T)
FLOAT	Real version of integer argument	1	Integer	Real	6.	$\bar{x} = s/n$	XBAR = S/FLOAT(N)
INT	Integer version of real argument	1	Real	Integer	7.	$m = k \cdot p$	M = K*INT(P)
AMIN0	Smallest value in argument list	2+	Integer	Real	8.	$s = \min(i,j,k)$	S = AMIN0(I,J,K)
AMIN1		2+	Real	Real	9.	$s = \min(7,x)$	S = AMIN1(7.,X)
MIN0		2+	Integer	Integer	10.	$m = \min(i,j)$	M = MIN0(I,J)
MIN1		2+	Real	Integer	11.	$m = \min(p,r,q,s)$	M = MIN1(P,R,Q,S)
AMAX0	Largest value in argument list	2+	Integer	Real	12.	$b = \max(50,n)$	B = AMAX0(50,N)
AMAX1		2+	Real	Real	13.	$b = \max(5x,y,z)$	B = AMAX1(5.*X,Y,Z)
MAX0		2+	Integer	Integer	14.	$l = \max(2i,j,k)$	L = MAX0(2*I,J,K)
MAX1		2+	Real	Integer	15.	$l = \max(y,p)$	L = MAX1(Y,P)
SQRT	Square root of argument	1	Real	Real	16.	$r = \sqrt{s}$	R = SQRT(S)

*These functions represent a subset from among roughly 50 functions which are available on many FORTRAN compilers.

3. Functions can be used within functions; that is, a function can call another function. For example, the statement

    Y = SQRT(ABS(A − B))

    is legitimate. In this case, the main program calls the function SQRT; the function SQRT then calls the function ABS. Thus if 6. is stored in A and 10. is stored in B, then A − B is evaluated, giving −4.; next, the absolute value is taken giving +4.; finally, the square root is taken, giving 2., and this result is stored under Y.

4. Note *that the first letter in the name of a function identifies the mode of the function* according to the usual convention for variable names. Thus, AMIN0 yields a real result and MIN0 yields an integer result. Also note the restrictions on the mode of the argument. For example, the "0" suffix on AMIN, MIN, AMAX, and MAX refers to *integer arguments;* the "1" suffix refers to real arguments; and the logarithm and square root functions require *real arguments* in all cases.

Follow-up Exercises

1. In Table 10.1, look at the column headed "Corresponding FORTRAN Examples" and answer the following:
    a. Examples 1,2. What is stored in Z if 5.4 is in X and 6.0 is in Y? Suppose 7.0 is in X and 5.2 is in Y? What value is stored in K if 10 is stored in J, 7 in M, and 2 in N?
    b. Examples 3,4. What value is stored in P if 0.1 is stored in Q? What is stored in T if −4. is in A and 3. is in B?
    c. Example 5. What value is stored in Y if 50.1 is in A and 4.0 is in T?
    d. Examples 6,7. What would you say is the purpose of "floating" N? Of treating P as an integer in the arithmetic expression?
    e. Example 9. What is stored in S if 10.2 is in X?
    f. Example 14. What is stored in L if 5 is in I, 10 is in J, and 7 is in K?
2. Modify the following program to include the use of the ABS function:
```
READ(5,*) X,Y
P = X − .5*Y
IF(P .LT. 0.) P = −P
WRITE(6,*) P
STOP
END
```

10.2
USER-SUPPLIED STATEMENT FUNCTIONS

At times a certain arithmetic expression needs to be evaluated within different segments of a program. For such situations it is often more efficient to use the approach illustrated in the next example.

EXAMPLE 10.1   Affirmative Action Statistics

The Affirmative Action officer of a large corporation needs to determine the percentage of employees within each of the following categories:

Category Designation (CAT)	Category Description
1	American Indian, Alaskan Native
2	Asian, Pacific Islander
3	Black
4	Hispanic
5	White
6	Other

The programs on page 307 accomplish this task, where NAI is number of American Indians, NA is number of Asians, and so on; PAI is percentage of American Indians, PA is percentage of Asians, and so on. Study Program A to make sure that you understand it; then observe the similarities and differences between Programs A and B.

Program B in the example includes a **user-supplied statement function** (also called an **arithmetic statement function**) of the following general type:

function name (dummy argument list) = arithmetic expression

In the example, the function name is PER, the dummy arguments are N and D, and the arithmetic expression is

FLOAT(N)/D*100.

The **dummy argument list** is a list of variables separated by commas; these variables are used in the arithmetic expression which appears to the right of the equal sign. In this case, PER can be viewed as a subprogram which calculates a percentage given the values of the numerator (N) and the denominator (D). The following points should help you understand how this works.

1. The arithmetic statement function must precede its use; otherwise it will not be defined when first used by another statement. Typically, these functions are placed in a program before all other *executable* statements. In Program B of the example, the arithmetic statement function is the third line in the program.
2. The *name* of the function is selected by the programmer according to the rules for naming FORTRAN variables. As before, the first letter of the name determines its *mode*. Thus, the name PER defines a function in real mode.

Program A

```
INTEGER CAT
DATA NAI,NA,NB,NH,NW,NO/6*0/        ← Equivalent to 0,0,0,0,0,0

10 READ(5,*) ID,CAT
   IF (ID .LT. 0) GO TO 20
   IF (CAT .EQ. 1) NAI = NAI + 1
   IF (CAT .EQ. 2) NA = NA + 1
   IF (CAT .EQ. 3) NB = NB + 1
   IF (CAT .EQ. 4) NH = NH + 1
   IF (CAT .EQ. 5) NW = NW + 1
   IF (CAT .EQ. 6) NO = NO + 1
   GO TO 10
20 TN = NAI + NA + NB + NH + NW + NO

   PAI = FLOAT(NAI)/TN*100.
   PA = FLOAT(NA)/TN*100.
   PB = FLOAT(NB)/TN*100.
   PH = FLOAT(NH)/TN*100.
   PW = FLOAT(NW)/TN*100.
   PO = FLOAT(NO)/TN*100.
   WRITE(6,*) PAI,PA,PB,PH,PW,PO
   STOP
   END
```

Program B

```
INTEGER CAT

DATA NAI,NA,NB,NH,NW,NO/6*0/

   PER(N,D) = FLOAT(N)/D*100.        ← User-supplied
                                        statement
                                        function

10 READ(5,*) ID,CAT
   IF (ID .LT. 0) GO TO 20
   IF (CAT .EQ. 1) NAI = NAI + 1
   IF (CAT .EQ. 2) NA = NA + 1
   IF (CAT .EQ. 3) NB = NB + 1
   IF (CAT .EQ. 4) NH = NH + 1
   IF (CAT .EQ. 5) NW = NW + 1
   IF (CAT .EQ. 6) NO = NO + 1
   GO TO 10
20 TN = NAI + NA + NB + NH + NW + NO

   PAI = PER(NAI,TN)
   PA = PER(NA,TN)
   PB = PER(NB,TN)
   PH = PER(NH,TN)
   PW = PER(NW,TN)
   PO = PER(NO,TN)
   WRITE(6,*) PAI,PA,PB,PH,PW,PO
   STOP
   END
```

3. The function is called by using its name and actual arguments in the arithmetic expression of an assignment statement. In Program B, the first call or use of the function is in the assignment statement:

PAI = PER(NAI,TN)

In this case, NAI and TN represent the **actual argument list.** When this assignment statement is executed, control of the program goes to the arithmetic statement function, where the arithmetic expression is evaluated *using the actual argument in place of the dummy argument.* For example, if 5 is stored in NAI and 20000. is stored in TN, then the arithmetic expression in the statement function is evaluated using 5 for N and 20000. for D. The result 0.025 is then returned to the statement which made the call. In this case, 0.025 is stored in PAI.

4. The actual argument list must agree with the dummy argument list in *number, order, and mode.* In the example, the dummy argument list consists of two variables: the integer variable N followed by the real variable D; hence, the actual argument list also consists of two variables, where NAI (or NA, or NB, or NH, or NW, or NO) corresponds to N and TN corresponds to D. *Dummy argument lists are restricted to nonsubscripted variables. Actual argument lists, however, may include the use of constants, subscripted or nonsubscripted variables, arithmetic expressions, and other functions.*

5. Are you confused about the use or need for a dummy argument list which has differently named variables from the actual argument list? This is simply a device which generalizes the use of the arithmetic statement function for greater flexibility. For example, in Program B the function is called six separate times. In each case, the variable in the actual argument list which represents the numerator must be different; that is, NAI, NA, NB, NH, NW, and NO are different variables each of which is to serve as the numerator of the fraction for calculating percent. In the function itself, N represents each of these variables. Without loss of convenience, however, TN rather than D could have been used in the function. Do you see why?

In general, the use of a user-supplied statement function is recommended as a convenient device which can save main storage for instructions whenever a complicated arithmetic expression recurs at many points in a program (which is not all that often). You should confirm that Program B requires 11 characters less code than Program A. Of course, this is nothing to brag about, but then the arithmetic expression in the function was not exactly complicated. Besides, you have to admit that Program B is more exciting than Program A.

Follow-up Exercises

*3. Modify Program B to output the value of the range (R), which is defined as the difference between the maximum and minimum percentages. Determine R using an arithmetic statement function named RANGE. Use X1, X2, etc., for dummy arguments. Also, make use of appropriate FORTRAN-supplied functions from Table 10.1 in your statement function. Would it be better programming to omit the use of an arithmetic statement function in this case? Support your answer.

*4. Rewrite Program B using the one-dimensional subscripted variables NUM in place of NAI, NA, NB, NH, NW, and NO and PERC in place of PAI, PA, PB, PH, PW, and PO. Which program is more efficient with respect to lines of code?

5. Indicate what is wrong, if anything, with each of the following:

Statement Function	Calling Statement
a. JOY(K,L,M) = (K + L + M)/3	J = K − JOY(I,J,K)
b. JOY(K,L,M) = (K + L + M)/3	J = K − JOY(X,Y,Z)
c. GRIEF(P,Q) = P**Q	R = 10.*GRIEF(P,Q)
d. GRIEF(P,Q) = P**Q	R = SQRT(GRIEF(P))
e. GRIEF(P,Q) = X**Y	R = GRIEF(X,Y)

10.3
FUNCTION SUBPROGRAMS

A **function subprogram** is a separate and complete program that accomplishes a particular task; it is placed immediately following the main program. If additional subprograms are required, then they are placed one after another following the main program. The arrangement of main program and function subprogram(s) is shown below:

```
        ⎧  :
        ⎪  :
Main    ⎨ variable name = . . . function name (actual argument list) . . .
Program ⎪  :
        ⎪  :
        ⎩ END


           ⎧ FUNCTION function name (dummy argument list)
           ⎪  :
           ⎪  :
           ⎪ function name = . . .
Function   ⎨  :
Subprogram ⎪  :
           ⎪ RETURN
           ⎪  :
           ⎪  :
           ⎩ END

Additional   ⎧
Subprograms  ⎨  :
as Required  ⎩
```

EXAMPLE 10.2   Student Billing Program

A variation of the student billing program is shown below, this time to illustrate how a function subprogram can be used to compute the balance due. New variables include cost per credit hour (CPCH) and student fee (FEE).

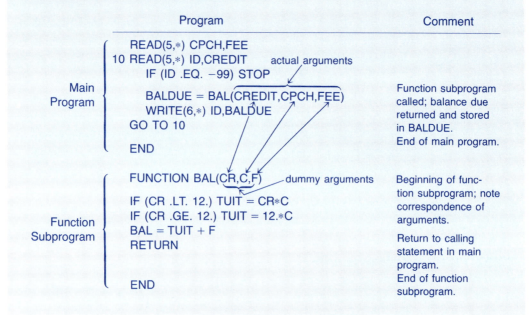

Program	Comment
READ(5,*) CPCH,FEE	
10 READ(5,*) ID,CREDIT actual arguments	
IF (ID .EQ. −99) STOP	
BALDUE = BAL(CREDIT,CPCH,FEE)	Function subprogram called; balance due returned and stored in BALDUE.
WRITE(6,*) ID,BALDUE	
GO TO 10	
END	End of main program.
FUNCTION BAL(CR,C,F) ← dummy arguments	Beginning of function subprogram; note correspondence of arguments.
IF (CR .LT. 12.) TUIT = CR*C	
IF (CR .GE. 12.) TUIT = 12.*C	
BAL = TUIT + F	
RETURN	Return to calling statement in main program.
END	End of function subprogram.

At this time, don't worry about completely understanding this program. Just read on.

Calling the Function Subprogram

A function subprogram is executed by referencing the function through another program referred to as a calling program. Any reference to a function in a calling program causes control to be transferred to the function subprogram. The function **reference** (or **call**) consists of the **function name** followed by the **actual argument list** enclosed in parentheses. Actual arguments generally consist of variables whose values are transferred to the function subprogram from the calling program.

In all cases the function subprogram is called by using its name and actual arguments in the arithmetic expression of an assignment statement. In Example 10.2 the assignment statement

    BALDUE = BAL(CREDIT,CPCH,FEE)
            ↑   ↑   ↑   ↑ ── actual arguments
            └──────────────────── function name

contains the reference to the function subprogram. When this statement is executed, control is transferred to the function subprogram named BAL and the function subprogram is executed.

In general, the calling program can be the main program or another subprogram. The effect of calling the subprogram is identical to placing the set of statements in the subprogram at the point of call in the calling program.

Structure of the Function Subprogram

Function subprograms are capable of handling most of the language features associated with main programs. For example, they can perform I/O, stop, carry out calculations, and so forth; however, they may not include other subprograms within, although they can call other subprograms.

Special FORTRAN statements are required to identify a sequence of instructions as a function subprogram, as discussed next.

FUNCTION Statement.   The **FUNCTION statement** must be the first statement in the function subprogram. The general form of this instruction is

> **FUNCTION** *function name (dummy argument list)*

Naming a function subprogram follows the same rules as naming FORTRAN variables. This means that *the first character of the function name determines the mode of the function (real or integer)*. The **dummy argument list** consists of variables whose values are received from the calling program and used in the subprogram.

In Example 10.2,

```
FUNCTION BAL(CR,C,F)
```

represents the FUNCTION statement. In this case, BAL is the name of a real function and CR, C, and F represent dummy arguments. When the function is called in the main program and control is transferred to the subprogram, *actual arguments are used in place of corresponding dummy arguments*. Thus CR utilizes the value stored in CREDIT, C utilizes the contents of CPCH, and F uses the value of FEE.

Body of the Function.   The body of the function follows the FUNCTION statement and may include any FORTRAN instruction (except another FUNCTION statement). Within the body of the subprogram the name of the function must be defined (assigned a value), since the function name is the vehicle by which the result is transmitted back to the calling program. Normally this is accomplished by placing the function name on the left side of an assignment statement.

In Example 10.2, we used the statement

```
BAL = TUIT + F
```

in the function subprogram. Notice that the name of the function, BAL, appears to the left of an equal sign. This ensures that the balance due is made available to the calling program, as discussed next.

RETURN Statement. The following statement is used in the subprogram of Example 10.2:

> **RETURN**

The execution of the RETURN statement signals the conclusion of calculations in the subprogram. At this time, control returns to the point within the calling program where the function reference appears. Thus, after the function subprogram in Example 10.2 is completed, control returns to the statement

    BALDUE = BAL(CREDIT,CPCH,FEE)

and the value stored in BAL is assigned to the variable named BALDUE.

   Finally, note that the END statement must be the last line in the function subprogram.[2]

Additional Considerations

   1. A function subprogram is compiled independently from the main program and other subprograms. Thus *you need not be concerned about repeating variable names or statement numbers*. For example, the variable TUIT can be used in both the main program and the subprogram without syntax violation. Likewise, statement number 10 can be used in both the main program and the subprogram.

   2. Arguments in the subprogram are called dummy arguments (variables) because these arguments assume the values provided by corresponding actual arguments listed in the calling program. This idea can be depicted as follows:

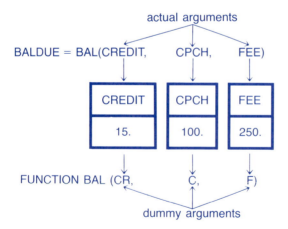

Thus, when the assignment statement for BALDUE is executed, the value stored in CREDIT (15.) is "transferred" to (or utilized by) the variable CR in the subprogram. Similarly, 100. is used for C and 250. is used for F.

   3. Actual arguments are not limited to simple variables. Constants, ex-

---

[2]The END statement in FORTRAN 77 is executable; in a subprogram it has the same effect as a RETURN statement. Thus, the RETURN statement can be eliminated in Example 10.2.

pressions, and subscripted variables (either specific elements or the entire array) also may be transmitted from a calling program to a function subprogram. Dummy argument lists, however, may include only nonsubscripted variables and array names.

4. The actual arguments must agree with the dummy arguments in number, order, and mode. In the example, the actual argument list is made up of three variables: CREDIT, CPCH, and FEE; hence, the dummy argument list must contain three variables. Since the three actual arguments are real, it follows that the dummy arguments also must be real. Finally, the ordering CR, C, and F in the dummy argument list results in the pairings CREDIT with CR, CPCH with C, and FEE with F. Note that the two variables within each pair agree in mode.

5. The use of dummy arguments generalizes the subprogram for greater flexibility; that is, the same subprogram can be used by many different programs without the need to match up identical variable names. Note in the program of Example 10.2 that the variables used within arithmetic expressions of the subprogram are dummy variables, not actual variables from the main program.

Since this subprogram is unique to this main program, however, greater flexibility is not necessary; hence, just as well, we could have used the same variable names for dummy arguments as for actual arguments. For example, the subprogram could be written as follows:

```
FUNCTION BAL(CREDIT,CPCH,FEE)
IF (CREDIT .LT. 12.) TUIT = CREDIT*CPCH
IF (CREDIT .GE. 12.) TUIT = 12.*CPCH
BAL = TUIT + FEE
RETURN
END
```

6. Here's a shocker: On many systems, *dummy variables which correspond to actual variables do not take up storage space in memory;* that is, they are not assigned addresses by the compiler. The contents of an actual variable in the argument list are used by its corresponding dummy argument in the subprogram as if the dummy argument shared the same storage location as the actual argument. Thus, rather than a transfer of values or contents between actual and corresponding dummy arguments, *we have a transfer of addresses,* so that the dummy variable can utilize the same storage location as its "sister" actual variable. In the example, CR, C, and F correspondingly utilize the storage locations defined by CREDIT, CPCH, and FEE. Note, however, that the newly defined variable TUIT in the subprogram does take up a storage location, since it is not part of the dummy argument list. On other systems, however, simple (unsubscripted) dummy variables are assigned storage locations that are separate from corresponding actual variables. In this case, values are transferred or passed during the call and return. This brings us to a word of caution: *if a dummy variable is assigned a new value in the subprogram, then the value of the corresponding actual variable is changed also.*

Follow-up Exercises

6. Modify the program in Example 10.2 so that the function subprogram returns an integer value.
7. Modify the program in Example 10.2 such that the value of CREDIT is read in by the subprogram. In the main program, read ID, CPCH, and FEE for *each* student.
*8. Modify the program in Example 10.2 so TUIT is calculated in one function subprogram and the balance due is calculated in a second function subprogram. Both subprograms are called from the main program.
*9. Modify the program in Example 10.2 so TUIT is calculated in a function subprogram called by the main program and balance due is calculated by a second function called by the first function.
**10. Modify the program in Example 10.2 such that ID and CREDIT are read in by the subprogram; the last-record-test is located in the subprogram; the subprogram prints the values of ID and the balance due; the loop is located within the subprogram; the balance due is summed within the subprogram as the variable SUM; the value of SUM is returned to the calling program as the value of the function after the last student is processed; and SUM is printed by the calling program.

10.4
SUBROUTINE SUBPROGRAMS

A **subroutine subprogram** (also called a **subroutine**) is a separate and complete program that accomplishes some particular task and may include such operations as input, output, arithmetic, and logic. The subroutine is placed immediately following the main program. If additional subprograms are required, then they are placed one after another following the main program. This arrangement of main program and subroutine subprogram is shown below:

```
                     ⎧ :
        Main         ⎪ CALL subroutine name (actual argument list)
        Program      ⎨ :
                     ⎪ :
                     ⎩ END

                     ⎧ SUBROUTINE subroutine name (dummy argument list)
                     ⎪ :
        Subroutine   ⎨ RETURN
                     ⎪ :
                     ⎪ :
                     ⎩ END

        Additional   ⎧
        Subprograms  ⎨ :
        as Required  ⎩
```

Subroutine subprograms represent the most powerful class of the subprograms. To illustrate their use, we first present a new problem scenario.

EXAMPLE 10.3   Automobile Rental Decision

Hartz Rent-Some-Wheels, the largest and most progressive car rental company, has decided to improve customer service by designing a time-shared computer program which would be used by its agents to quote projected rental fees. Basically, the program computes projected total cost for each of its two rental plans: the daily plan and the weekly plan. A customer who rents a car under the daily plan pays a fixed cost per day plus a charge per mile, but does not pay for gasoline expenses. Under the weekly plan, the customer pays both a fixed cost per week and buys gasoline, but does not pay a mileage charge. Which plan is cheaper for a customer depends on factors such as the various costs for the specific type of automobile, the projected number of miles to be driven, the number of days that the car is to be rented, the price of gasoline, the efficiency of the automobile, and (of course) the driving habits of the customer.

The table below defines the required variables and illustrates sample data:

VARIABLE	DESCRIPTION	SAMPLE VALUES	
		CASE I	CASE II
Input			
DFC	Daily fixed cost	$17.00	$17.00
CPM	Charge per mile	$0.15	$0.15
WFC	Weekly fixed cost	$145.00	$145.00
PG	Price per gallon (gasoline)	$0.75	$0.75
MG	Miles per gallon EPA rating	20	20
M	Projected miles of driving	800	300
D	Number of days	12	5
Output			
TCDP	Total cost of daily plan	$324.00	$130.00
TCWP	Total cost of weekly plan	$320.00	$156.25
DIFF	Cost difference (TCDP − TCWP)	$4.00	$−26.25

Thus, for the given data, a 12-day rental with 800 projected miles of driving is best under the weekly plan ($4.00 cheaper); however, for 5 days and 300 miles, all other things equal, the daily plan is best by $26.25. Before going on, you should confirm these calculations for TCDP and TCWP. Note that the fixed charge under the weekly plan is incurred for any part of a week; that is, the fixed charge for 12 days is the same as for 2 weeks, or $290.00 (2 × 145); the fixed charge for 5 days is the same as for 1 week, or $145.00.

The program on page 316 illustrates one way of programming this problem. In this case, the total cost of the weekly plan (TCWP) and the total cost of the daily plan (TCDP) are determined by a subroutine subprogram called COST.

	Program	Comments

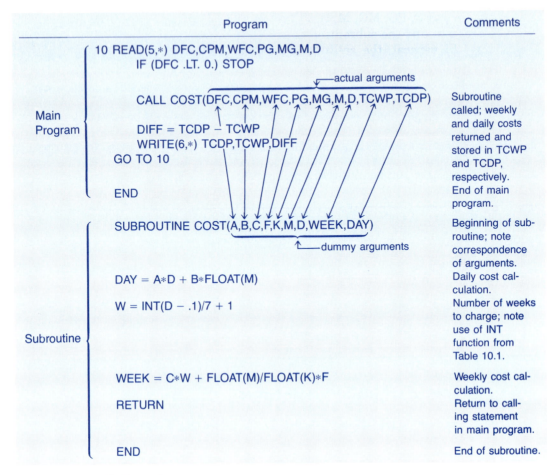

Program	Comments
Main Program	Subroutine called; weekly and daily costs returned and stored in TCWP and TCDP, respectively. End of main program.
Subroutine	Beginning of subroutine; note correspondence of arguments. Daily cost calculation. Number of weeks to charge; note use of INT function from Table 10.1. Weekly cost calculation. Return to calling statement in main program. End of subroutine.

10 READ(5,*) DFC,CPM,WFC,PG,MG,M,D
IF (DFC .LT. 0.) STOP

actual arguments

CALL COST(DFC,CPM,WFC,PG,MG,M,D,TCWP,TCDP)

DIFF = TCDP − TCWP
WRITE(6,*) TCDP,TCWP,DIFF
GO TO 10

END

SUBROUTINE COST(A,B,C,F,K,M,D,WEEK,DAY)

dummy arguments

DAY = A*D + B*FLOAT(M)

W = INT(D − .1)/7 + 1

WEEK = C*W + FLOAT(M)/FLOAT(K)*F

RETURN

END

Calling the Subroutine

The execution of a subroutine is initiated from another program (referred to as the calling program) by using the **CALL statement.** The general form of this statement is

CALL *subroutine name (actual argument list)*

The subroutine name indicates the particular subroutine to be executed. Naming a subroutine follows the same rules as naming FORTRAN variables. In this case, however, the first letter in the name does not determine mode, since subroutines return computational results via the argument list. The **actual argument list** is used in the CALL statement to pass values between the calling program and the subroutine.

For example, the statement

CALL COST (DFC,CPM,WFC,PG,MG,M,D,TCWP,TCDP)

is used to call the subroutine COST, and the contents of the variables DFC,

CPM, WFC, PG, MG, M, D, TCWP, and TCDP are passed between the calling program and the subroutine.

In general, the calling program can be the main program or another subprogram. The effect of calling the subroutine is identical to placing the set of statements in the subroutine at the point of call in the calling program.

Structure of the Subroutine

Subroutines are capable of performing most of the language features associated with main programs. For example, they can perform I/O, stop, carry out calculations, and so forth; however, they may not include other subprograms within, although they can call other subprograms. A typical form of the subroutine is shown below:

> SUBROUTINE *subroutine name (dummy argument list)*
>
> $\vdots \left\{ \right.$ body of subroutine
>
> RETURN
> END

A subroutine subprogram always begins with the **SUBROUTINE statement.** This statement identifies both the name of the subroutine and the variables in the argument list whose values are to be passed between the calling program and the subroutine.

In Example 10.3,

SUBROUTINE COST(A,B,C,F,K,M,D,WEEK,DAY)

represents the SUBROUTINE statement. In this case, COST is the name of the subroutine and A, B, C, F, K, M, D, WEEK, and DAY represent the **dummy arguments.** When the subroutine is called by the main program and control is transferred to the subroutine, *actual arguments are used in place of corresponding dummy arguments.* Thus, A utilizes the contents stored in DFC, B utilizes the contents of CPM, and so forth.

The "body" of the subroutine follows the SUBROUTINE statement and can include any FORTRAN statement (except a FUNCTION or SUBROUTINE statement). In Example 10.3, the statements

DAY = A∗D + B∗FLOAT(M)
W = INT(D − .1)/7 + 1
WEEK = C∗W + FLOAT(M)/FLOAT(K)∗F

represent the body of the subroutine.

Now, you should carefully note the following. After the execution of the assignment statements for DAY, W, and WEEK, the following statement is executed:

RETURN

At this time we can visualize the following: the computational result for DAY is returned to the storage location TCDP, since the actual variable TCDP is paired with the dummy variable DAY; likewise, the result for WEEK is stored in TCWP. Thus *computational results in the subroutine are "returned" to the calling program via the argument lists.*

A typical subprogram has at least one RETURN statement (usually, but not necessarily, placed immediately before the END statement). When the RETURN statement is executed, the computer returns control to the program that called the subroutine. Transfer of control is to the first executable statement following the CALL statement.

In Example 10.3, after the RETURN statement is executed, control returns to the main program and the instruction

    DIFF = TCDP − TCWP

is executed. Note that the value in TCDP and the value in TCWP have been calculated in (or have been "returned" from) the subroutine through the dummy variables DAY and WEEK, respectively.

Finally, since a subprogram is a complete program, you need to place an END statement as the last instruction of each subroutine.[3]

Additional Considerations

1. A subroutine is compiled independently from the main program and other subprograms. Thus *you need not be concerned about repeating variable names or statement numbers.* For example, the variable W in the subroutine of Example 10.3 also could be used in the main program without syntax violation. Likewise, statement number 10 can be used in each the main program and the subroutine.

2. The actual argument list must agree with the dummy argument list in number of arguments, their order, and their mode. You should verify that this is so in Example 10.3.

3. The actual argument list may include variable names, array names, subscripted array elements, constants, and expressions. The dummy argument list can include only variable names and array names.

4. The corresponding variable names in the actual argument list do not have to have the same names as in the dummy argument list. In fact, the ability to use different names in the two argument lists generalizes the subprogram for greater flexibility; that is, the same subprogram can be used by many different programs without the need to match up identical variable names.

Since the subroutine in Example 10.3 is unique to that main program, greater flexibility is not of much interest here. Just as well, the two argument lists could have been identical. In fact, note that M and D are identical in both lists.

---

[3]The END statement in FORTRAN 77 is executable; in a subprogram it has the same effect as a RETURN statement. Thus, the RETURN statement in Example 10.3 can be eliminated.

5. As discussed earlier, values are passed between a calling program and its subroutine by means of the argument lists. This idea can be visualized as follows.

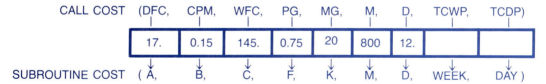

When the CALL statement is executed, for practical purposes we have a transfer of the values 17., 0.15, 145., 0.75, 20, 800, and 12. to the subroutine. In the body of the subroutine, these values are used to calculate 324. for DAY and 320. for WEEK. When the RETURN statement is executed, the following transfers can be visualized:

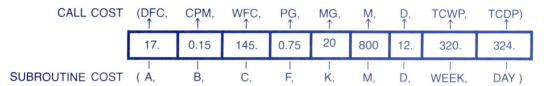

Note that the value 320. is now stored in TCWP and the value 324. is stored in TCDP. If the values of A, B, C, F, K, M, and D had been changed in the subroutine, then the corresponding values used in the main program would store the new values. This brings us to a word of caution: *if a dummy variable is assigned a new value in the subroutine, then the value of the corresponding actual variable is changed also.*

6. On many systems, *dummy variables which correspond to actual variables do not take up storage space in memory,* that is, they are not assigned addresses by the compiler. The contents of an actual variable in the argument list are used by its corresponding dummy argument in the subprogram as if the dummy argument shares the same storage location as the actual argument. Thus, rather than a transfer of values or contents between actual and corresponding dummy arguments, *we have a transfer of addresses,* so that the dummy variable can utilize the same storage location as its "sister" actual variable. For example, when WEEK is calculated as 320. in the subroutine, 320. is stored directly in TCWP. On other systems, however, simple (unsubscripted) dummy variables are assigned storage locations that are separate from corresponding actual variables. In this case, values are transferred or passed during the call and return.

Note, however, that the newly defined variable W in the subprogram does take up a storage location, since it is not part of the dummy argument list. Variables that are used only within subprograms are referred to as **local variables.**

Follow-up Exercises

11. Look at the subroutine in Example 10.3. Do you see why we subtracted 0.1 from D in the calculation of W? Does it have to be 0.1, or can we just subtract any fraction?

12. Modify the program in Example 10.3 such that the subroutine also calculates the cost difference and prints the three costs. Do we need to transfer the three costs via arguments in this case?

*13. Modify the program in Example 10.3 such that TCDP is calculated in subroutine DAILY and TCWP is calculated in subroutine WEEKLY. Each subroutine inputs data that are specific to its cost calculation and prints its cost result. The main program inputs data that are common to both subroutines and prints the cost difference. Sample output for the two cases should conform to the following:

```
TOTAL COST OF DAILY PLAN   : ￼￼ $ 324.00
TOTAL COST OF WEEKLY PLAN: ￼￼ $ 320.00

WEEKLY PLAN BEST BY  $     4.00


TOTAL COST OF DAILY PLAN   : ￼￼ $ 130.00
TOTAL COST OF WEEKLY PLAN: ￼￼ $ 156.25

DAILY PLAN BEST BY  $  26.25
```

14. Rewrite Example 10.2 using a subroutine subprogram.

15. What is the primary advantage of a subroutine over a function subprogram?

10.5
ADDITIONAL TOPICS

In this section we cover some further topics on subprograms: the use of flowcharts, the transfer of subscripted variables, and the option of omitting arguments.

Flowcharts

Figure 10.1 illustrates the flowcharts for the main program and subprogram of Example 10.3. Note the following:

1. Each subprogram has a separate flowchart. Thus a program with one main program and four subprograms would have five distinct flowcharts.

2. No distinction is made between a function subprogram and a subroutine subprogram. The flowcharts in Figure 10.1 apply equally to a function subprogram.

3. The **predefined process symbol** can be used to indicate the call of the subprogram, as illustrated in Figure 10.1a. The exact nature of the writing within the symbol is a matter of personal preference.

4. The Start-Stop symbol is used to indicate entry and exit points in the subprogram. The entry point is labeled with the name of the subprogram and the exit point is labeled with the word return. Between these two symbols, the logic of the subprogram is illustrated using any of the legitimate symbols for main programs.

Subscripted Variables

Up to now we have avoided the use of subscripted variables, in order for you to concentrate on the essentials of subprograms. Most analytical and statistical programming packages which are available commercially make use of subpro-

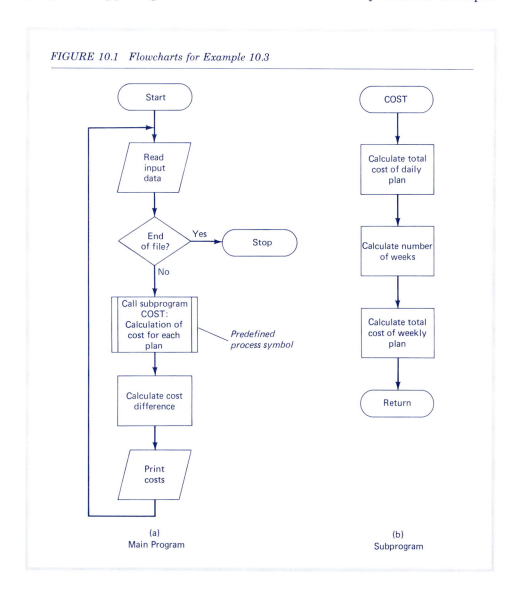

FIGURE 10.1   Flowcharts for Example 10.3

(a)
Main Program

(b)
Subprogram

grams which transfer subscripted variables. So, now that you're "off and running" on the fundamentals of subprograms, you should be ready to include subscripted variables in your subprograms.

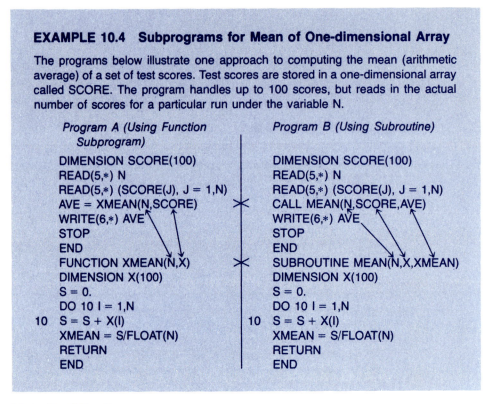

EXAMPLE 10.4   Subprograms for Mean of One-dimensional Array

The programs below illustrate one approach to computing the mean (arithmetic average) of a set of test scores. Test scores are stored in a one-dimensional array called SCORE. The program handles up to 100 scores, but reads in the actual number of scores for a particular run under the variable N.

Program A (Using Function Subprogram)

```
DIMENSION SCORE(100)
READ(5,*) N
READ(5,*) (SCORE(J), J = 1,N)
AVE = XMEAN(N,SCORE)
WRITE(6,*) AVE
STOP
END
FUNCTION XMEAN(N,X)
DIMENSION X(100)
S = 0.
DO 10 I = 1,N
10   S = S + X(I)
XMEAN = S/FLOAT(N)
RETURN
END
```

Program B (Using Subroutine)

```
DIMENSION SCORE(100)
READ(5,*) N
READ(5,*) (SCORE(J), J = 1,N)
CALL MEAN(N,SCORE,AVE)
WRITE(6,*) AVE
STOP
END
SUBROUTINE MEAN(N,X,XMEAN)
DIMENSION X(100)
S = 0.
DO 10 I = 1,N
10   S = S + X(I)
XMEAN = S/FLOAT(N)
RETURN
END
```

Note the following:

1. The two programs differ only in the usual distinctions between a function subprogram and a subroutine subprogram, as indicated by the two cross marks (✕). We named the subroutine MEAN, rather than XMEAN, out of convenience, since this name need not be concerned with mode. Just as well, it could have been named XMEAN.
2. The actual argument list passes to the subprogram the number of storage locations (N, total number of exam scores) which are used in the array and the array itself (SCORE).
3. The dummy argument list pairs N with N and X with SCORE. The dummy array X merely utilizes the storage locations for the real array SCORE; however, X *must be dimensioned in the subprogram*. Otherwise, the compiler has no way of knowing that X is a subscripted variable.
4. Many subprograms are commonly used as modules by different programs. An apparent shortcoming of the above subprograms is their apparent dependence on the explicit dimensioning of 100 elements in the main program. In other words, if this subprogram were to be used with a main

program having, say, 500 elements in the array, then it seems reasonable to expect X to be dimensioned to 500. On some systems, however, *any integer value can be used to dimension the dummy array,* since separate storage is not allocated to a dummy array. On other systems, *execution errors may result if the dimensioning of the dummy array differs from the dimensioning of the actual array.* To avoid potential problems, many programmers prefer to use **adjustable dimensions** for dummy arrays when using compilers that allow this feature. In our example, we would simply change the DIMENSION statement in the subprogram to

```
DIMENSION X(N)
```

Now, the same subprogram can be paired with calling programs having varying array sizes, without concern about the size of the dummy array. In doing so, however, certain procedures should be kept in mind:

a.   The variable used to indicate the size of a one-dimensional dummy array (N in the above example) must be an integer, must be a dummy argument, and must take on a value that is less than or equal to the number of elements in the actual array. Also, *its value may not be changed in the subprogram,* since this would imply a change in the length of the actual array.

b.   When using adjustable dimensions for arrays of two or more dimensions, the value of each *adjustable* dimension should equal exactly the corresponding *actual* dimension; otherwise, the conceptual relations of array elements (for example, a table of numbers) would not be maintained. Thus, the CALL statement in

```
   :
   :
DIMENSION A(10,5)
   :
   :
CALL TABLE(10,5,A)
   :
   :
END
SUBROUTINE TABLE(M,N,T)
   :
   :
DIMENSION T(M,N)
   :
   :
RETURN
END
```

ensures that the arrays A and T are conceptually identical (that is, the first row of elements in T is the same as the first row in A, etc.). This is because the number of rows and columns in T (given by M and N, respectively) is identical to the number of rows and columns reserved for A in the DIMENSION statement (10 and 5, respectively); however, the statement

```
CALL TABLE(4,3,A)
```

would not preserve this row-by-row conceptual relationship.

Follow-up Exercises

16. Modify Program B such that sum, the sum of the scores, is output in the main program along with AVE. Why can't this be done in Program A?
17. Modify Program B such that N and the array are input and AVE is output by the subprogram. Under what conditions can we input N through the subprogram?
*18. Add a second subroutine to Program B called SORT, which rearranges and outputs the scores in ascending order. Use an adjustable dimension, if allowed by your compiler. *Hint:* See Example 8.9 on page 255.
19. What does a compiler assume if we forget to dimension a subscripted variable? Would we get a syntax error or an execution error?
*20. **Data Editing.** Modify Program A or B by adding a new subroutine which edits scores for input errors right after the score array is read in by the main program. Specifically, if all scores are in the range 0 to 100, control is returned to the main program. Otherwise, execution stops after printing each score outside this range together with its position in the array.

**COMMON Statement*

As discussed earlier, the main program and associated subprograms are independent programming units in the sense that they are compiled separately. For this reason, statement numbers and variable names can be repeated among main program and subprograms without violating syntax rules.

Up to now, the only means of communicating between the calling program and the subprogram has been through their arguments. An alternative procedure, especially useful when a program is passing many similar variables in many subprograms, is the COMMON statement, as illustrated next.

EXAMPLE 10.5

The program of Example 10.3 can be changed as follows:

Program	Comment
COMMON DFC,CPM,WFC,PG,MG,M,D,TCWP,TCDP	*New statement.*
10 READ(5,*) DFC,CPM,WFC,PG,MG,M,D	*No change.*
⋮	⋮
CALL COST	*Argument list eliminated.*
⋮	⋮
END	*No change.*
SUBROUTINE COST	*Argument list eliminated.*
COMMON A,B,C,F,K,M,D,WEEK,DAY	*New statement.*
DAY = A*D + B*FLOAT(M)	*No change.*
⋮	⋮
END	*No change.*

The only differences between this program and the program on page 316 are the insertions of the two COMMON statements and the elimination of argument lists.

EXAMPLE 10.6

Now, study the modification of Program B in Example 10.4:

Program	Comment
DIMENSION SCORE(100)	No change.
COMMON N,SCORE,AVE	*New statement.*
READ(5,*) N	No change.
.	.
.	.
.	.
CALL MEAN	*Argument list eliminated.*
.	.
.	.
.	.
END	No change.
SUBROUTINE MEAN	*Argument list eliminated.*
DIMENSION X(100)	No change.
COMMON N,X,XMEAN	*New statement.*
.	.
.	.
.	.
END	No change.

Again, you should note the same two differences. Just how this works is explained next.

1. These examples use a statement called **blank COMMON,**[4] more frequently referred to as COMMON, which has the following general form:

> **COMMON** *list of variables*

The blank COMMON statement causes the compiler to establish a "block" or specialized area of main storage that is made up of storage locations which are to be "shared in common" by the calling program and subprograms using COMMON. For example, in the programs above, storage is shared as follows:

[4]Some versions of FORTRAN also include a statement called labeled COMMON, which we do not cover.

Common Block for Example 10.5   Common Block for Example 10.6

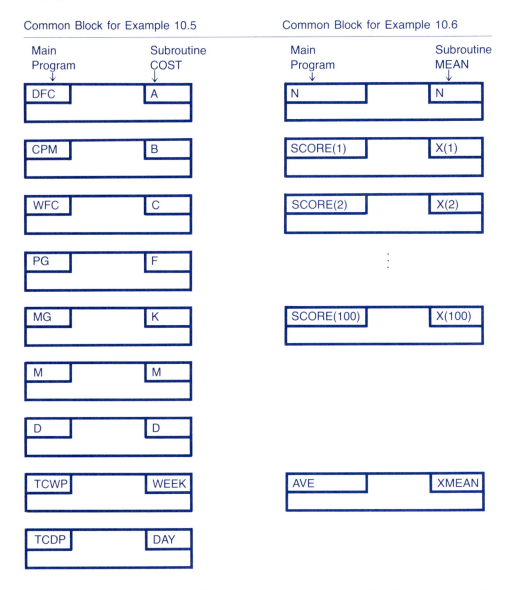

Thus, in effect, DFC and A refer to the same storage location in memory, as do CPM and B, WFC and C, and so on. In the second program, note that the arrays SCORE and X are treated as if they were one and the same.

Out of convenience and efficiency, many programmers prefer the use of COMMON to argument lists whenever many of the same variables are to be passed between the main program and several subprograms.

2. Are you confused about how the use of COMMON differs from the use of argument lists with respect to the methods of storage and data "transfers"? When using argument lists, the compiler must supply a special set of instructions in machine code which specifies the correspondence between actual and dummy argument lists. Each time a subprogram is called, these instructions

must be executed. When using COMMON, however, no special instructions are needed for "passing" values, since passing is eliminated due to the direct sharing of storage locations. To put it another way, the use of COMMON results in the *explicit sharing* of storage locations between dummy variables and corresponding actual variables, whereas the use of argument lists results in *implicit sharing*. Thus, the use of COMMON promotes less machine code instructions (which is storage-efficient) and faster execution times (since there are fewer instructions to execute).

3. Make sure that corresponding variable names among COMMON statements are consistent with respect to mode; that is, don't pair up a real variable with an integer variable, and vice versa.

4. Many compilers allow you to dimension a subscripted variable within the COMMON statement itself. For example, in the main program of Example 10.6 we could eliminate

```
DIMENSION SCORE(100)
COMMON N,SCORE,AVE
```

and insert

```
COMMON N,SCORE(100),AVE
```

Similarly, the subprogram could be changed by using

```
COMMON N,X(100),MEAN
```

instead of

```
DIMENSION X(100)
COMMON N,X,MEAN
```

5. Notice that the COMMON statement is a nonexecutable statement which serves to declare certain information about the storage of variables; hence, it must appear in the program before instructions which use common variables. Generally, the COMMON statement is placed at the beginning of programs and subprograms before executable instructions.

Follow-up Exercises

21. For each of the following, identify what is wrong (if anything):

Calling Program	Subprogram
a. COMMON M,N,Y(1),Q	COMMON R,J,P,K
b. COMMON L,S(50),T	COMMON K,R(30)A
c. COMMON A,B,C	COMMON D,E
	↙ first subprogram (D,E,F are to be paired with A,B,C)
d. COMMON A,B,C,I,J	COMMON D,E,F
	COMMON M,N
	↖ second subprogram (M,N are to be paired with I,J)

22. Use COMMON statements in each of the following programs:
    a. Exercise 14
    *b. Exercise 13

10.6
ADVANTAGES OF SUBPROGRAMS

Some of the advantages of using function and subroutine subprograms include the following:

1. *They save main storage* for instructions whenever the same set of statements is to be repeated at different points in the main program.
2. Many programs are so common that they can be used by many other types of programs. These common programs are best written as subprograms, so that they can be linked readily to programs which utilize them. For example, many statistical programs (as in Example 10.4) and sorting programs (as in Example 8.9) are standardized subprograms in the software libraries of computer systems. Their use reduces programming effort (thereby saving money), since the "wheel doesn't have to be reinvented" each time it is needed.
3. Subprograms allow a **modular approach** to writing long, complicated programs. For example, a team of programmers can write different logical segments of a long program by each writing a subprogram. The subprograms then can be linked together as a series of "blocks" or "modules." This is a very common approach in actual practice. In the next chapter we discuss this topic in more detail.

10.7
COMMON ERRORS

Certain errors regarding subprograms seem to occur more commonly than others. Make note of these.

1. *Forgetting END.* Don't forget the END statement following the main program and each subprogram or a syntax error may result. Many beginning programmers figure they only need one END statement at the very end of the last subprogram. Not so. Since the main program and each subprogram are treated as independent programming units, the END statement at the end of each programming unit signals the compiler that the current programming unit is over.

2. *Mode of a Function.* Logic and/or mixed mode errors can result if you forget that the first letter of a function name determines the mode of the value returned by that function.

3. *Mismatches in Argument Lists.* Pay close attention to the number, order, and mode of actual and dummy argument lists. In many cases, mismatches of this type may not result in syntax or execution error messages. Instead, you may get unpredictable results (wrong answers) that are system dependent, as the following chart illustrates.

Actual Argument	Corresponding Dummy Argument	Comment
IN	ON	Inconsistent mode.
X	J	Inconsistent mode.
2	COST	Inconsistent mode.
2.	COST	OK, as long as the value of COST is not changed within the subprogram.
COST	2.	Not allowed. Dummy arguments must be variables.
M	N	OK, but if the subprogram redefines the value of N, then M changes accordingly. If you're not aware of this, you've committed a logic error.
A(3)	B(1)	OK when A and B are declared arrays.
A(3)	C	OK when A is declared an array.
6*K + 3	JOB	OK, as long as the value of JOB is not changed within the subprogram.

4. *Forgetting to Dimension Arrays.* If you fail to dimension a subscripted variable, then the compiler assumes that you are calling either an arithmetic statement function or a function subprogram. In the first case you get a syntax error since it cannot find an arithmetic statement function in the main program. In the second case you get an execution error since it cannot find the subprogram which it assumes you have provided. Worse yet, the result may be unpredictable if the array you forgot to dimension is part of the dummy argument list.

5. *Mismatch in Size Between Actual Array and Corresponding Dummy Array.* Reread item 4 on page 322. Many systems allow this mismatch, but not others. For example, consider the following program:

```
      DIMENSION X(5)
      DO 10 I = 1,5
   10 X(I) = I
      CALL TRY(X)
      STOP
      END
      SUBROUTINE TRY(A)
      DIMENSION A(10)
      WRITE(6,1)(A(I), I = 1,5)
      RETURN
    1 FORMAT(1X,5F10.1)
      END
```

In this case, the size of the dummy array A (10 elements) exceeds the size of the actual array X (5 elements). We ran this program on an ITEL computer using the WATFIV compiler and got the following execution error message when subroutine TRY was called: DECLARED SIZE OF ARRAY A EXCEEDS SPACE PROVIDED BY CALLING ARGUMENT. However, when the manufacturer's ANSI compiler was used, the same program executed without error.

Next, we changed the size of the dummy array to something less than the size of the actual array by using

DIMENSION A(1)

in the subroutine. As before, the program that had been translated by the ANSI compiler ran without error, but the program using the WATFIV compiler gave an execution error as soon as the subscript I equaled 2 in

WRITE(6,1) (A(I), I = 1,5)

Moral of the story? To be safe, specify the same sizes for actual and dummy arrays. Better yet, use the option of adjustable dimensions.

Additional Exercises

23. Define or explain the following:

subprogram	subroutine subprogram
calling program	subroutine
main program	CALL statement
FORTRAN-supplied function	dummy argument list
built-in function	actual argument list
library function	SUBROUTINE statement
argument list	local variables
user-supplied statement function	predefined process symbol
arithmetic statement function	adjustable dimensions
function subprogram	blank COMMON statement
FUNCTION statement	modular approach
RETURN statement	

24. **Automobile Rental Decision Revisited.** Modify the program in Example 10.3 as follows:
    a. The main program inputs data that are common to all subroutines and calls the subroutines. It also includes a DO-loop for processing different sets of data.
    b. Subroutine DAILY calculates and prints total cost of the daily plan. It also inputs data that are specific to the daily plan.
    c. Subroutine WEEKLY calculates and prints total cost of the weekly plan. It also inputs data that are specific to the WEEKLY plan.
    d. Subroutine HYBRID calculates and prints total cost of the following new plan: The customer pays $18.95 per day, pays for gasoline expenses, and pays a charge of 25¢ for each mile over an allotment given by 100 times the number of days in the rental. It also inputs data that are specific to the new plan.
    e. Each subroutine has a nested DO-loop, where M (projected miles of driving) is the index of the outer loop and MG (miles per gallon) is the index of the inner loop. Use the same data as in the example, except let M = 100, 200, . . . , 1000 and MG = 16, 18, . . . , 36. *Note:* DAILY need not have a loop for MG.

f. Each subroutine prints a cost table, where rows represent projected miles of driving and columns represent miles per gallon. Do a nice job of labeling your output.

Conduct four runs so as to vary the number of days in the rental as follows: 2, 5, 12, 23. What factors favor each plan?

25. **Mopups Revisited.** Modify Example 4.10 on page 112 or Exercise 25 in Chapter 8 on page 261 as follows:
    a. The main program reads N, NUM, SIZE and outputs NUM, SIZE, TP. Use a DO-loop for processing number of dealers. Appropriately label your output.
    b. Develop a subprogram that determines total price (TP).
    c. Store TP values for each dealer in a one-dimensional array which is specified in the main program. Following the last dealer, call subprogram MEAN (Example 10.4), and output the sum of total prices and the mean total price.
    d. Call subroutine SORT (Example 8.9) to sort and print TP values in descending order.

    Debug your program using the test data in the example. Include flowcharts.

26. **Property Tax Assessment Revisited.** Modify Exercise 40 of Chapter 4 on page 122 or Exercise 26 of Chapter 8 on page 261 as follows:
    a. Main program reads N, lot number, property value and outputs lot number, property value, and tax charge with appropriate labels. Use a DO-loop for processing the N property values.
    b. Develop a subprogram that determines the tax charge.
    c. Store property values and tax charges in two one-dimensional arrays (or one two-dimensional array) which are specified in the main program. Following the last property, call subprogram MEAN (Example 10.4), and output the sum and mean of property values and tax charges.
    d. Use another subroutine to sort and print tax charges in descending order. Include corresponding lot numbers and property values in your output table.

27. **Telephone Company Billing Revisited.** Modify Exercise 41 of Chapter 4 on page 123 as follows:
    a. Main program reads number of customers to be processed, phone number, code, and number of extensions; outputs phone number and charge with appropriate labels.
    b. Develop a subprogram that edits the input data for errors. Specifically, it ensures that:

    (1) Phone numbers are greater than 4,000,000 but less than 9,000,000
    (2) Codes are 1, 2, 3, or 4
    (3) Number of extensions is greater than zero but less than

    > 5 for code 1
    > 10 for code 2
    > 100 for code 3
    > 1000 for code 4

    If a phone number error is encountered, allow the program to calculate charge, but print an appropriate error message to the right of the printed charge. If an error is detected in either the code or the number of extensions, bypass the charge calculation and print an appropriate error message that identifies the phone number and error. Add new customers to the input data to debug the program's edit logic for each possible error.

    c.   Develop a second subprogram that determines and outputs (with labels) total number and percent number of customers by code category.

    d.   Develop a third subprogram that computes and outputs (with labels) total charges and percent charges by code category, as well as overall total charges. *Hint:* Use arrays to store code and number of extensions.

28. **Personnel Benefits Budget Revisited.** Modify Exercise 42 of Chapter 4 on page 124 as follows:

    a.   The main program reads input data and prints output data with labels.

    b.   A subprogram edits the input data for errors. Specifically, it ensures that:

        (1)   Social Security number is greater than 100,000,000 and less than 1,000,000,000

        (2)   Annual salary is greater than $5000 and less than $50,000

        (3)   Retirement code is 1, 2, or 3

        If a Social Security number error is detected, allow the program to calculate contributions, but print an appropriate error message to the right of the printed charges. If an error is detected in either the salary or the code, bypass the calculations of contributions and print an appropriate error message that identifies the Social Security number and the error. Add new employees to the input data to debug your error logic for each possible error.

    c.   A second subprogram calculates Social Security, retirement, group life insurance, and total contributions.

  **d.   Store all contributions in a two-dimensional array in the main program, where rows represent employees and the four columns represent the contributions. Call a subprogram that calculates and prints column totals and averages.

29. **Depreciation Methods Revisited.** Modify Exercise 29 of Chapter 6 on page 180 as follows:

    a.   Use a separate subprogram for each method of depreciation. Each subprogram outputs its schedule, but headings are output by the main program. The main program inputs all data.

  **b.   Strictly use arrays for the schedules.

  **c.   Look up the "sum-of-the-years digit" method of depreciation in an accounting textbook. Add a third subprogram for this method, and compare results.

30. **Aging Retail Customer Accounts Revisited.** Modify Exercise 30 of Chapter 6 on page 181 as follows:

    a.   Use a subprogram that calculates and outputs the table of aged customer accounts.

  **b.   Use a second subprogram for part d of that exercise.

31. **Credit Billing Revisited.** Modify Exercise 32 of Chapter 6 on page 184 as follows:

    a.   The main program inputs all data.

    b.   A subprogram edits the input data for errors. Specifically, it ensures that:

        (1)   Credit limit is $800 or above and $1500 or less

        (2)   Payment is greater than zero

        (3)   New purchase amount is greater than zero

        If an error is encountered, then print an appropriate error message that includes the customer's name and address, bypass the calculation and printout for this customer, and go on to the next customer. Add new customers to your input records to test each of these three possible input errors.

    c.   A second subprogram calculates the new balance.

    d.   A third subprogram prints the bill, including the minimum payment due and any warning message. It calls a fourth subprogram that calculates the minimum payment due.

32.   **Checking Account Report Revisited.** Modify Exercise 33 of Chapter 6 on page 186 as follows:

    a.   The main program inputs all data.

    b.   A subprogram edits the input data for errors. Specifically, it ensures that:

        (1)   The bank account number is greater than 100,000 and less than 900,000

        (2)   The number of transactions is above zero but less than 100

        (3)   The beginning balance is positive

        If an error is encountered, then print an appropriate error message that includes the customer's name and account number, bypass the calculations and printout for this customer, and go on to the next customer. Add new customers to your input records to test each of these three possible input errors.

    c.   A second subprogram performs all calculations.

    d.   A third subprogram prints the report.

33.   **Payroll Revisited.** Modify Exercise 34 of Chapter 6 on page 188 as follows:

    a.   The main program inputs all data.

    b.   A subprogram edits the input data for errors. Specifically it ensures that:

        (1)   Number of dependents is greater than zero and less than 15

        (2)   Rate of pay is greater than $2.50 and less than $10.00

        (3)   Number of hours worked is greater than zero and less than 65

        (4)   Total earnings thus far this year is zero or greater and less than $40,000

        If an error is detected, then print an appropriate error message that includes the employee's name and number, bypass the calculations and printout for this employee, and go on to the next employee. Add new input data to test each of these four possible input errors.

    c.   A second subprogram calculates gross pay and net pay. This subprogram calls a third subprogram that calculates all deductions.

    d.   A fourth subprogram prints the report.

  **e.   Store data in arrays and use a fifth subprogram to calculate and print totals and means for gross pay, each deduction, and net pay.

34.   **Student Fee Bill Revisited.** Modify Exercise 27 of Chapter 7 on page 218 as follows:

    a.   The main program inputs all data.

    b.   A subprogram edits the input data for errors. Specifically, it ensures that:

        (1)   All codes are either 1 or 2

        (2)   The number of credits is 3 or greater and less than 22

        If an error is encountered, then print an appropriate error message that includes the student's ID and name, bypass the calculations and printout for this student, and go on to the next student. Add new input data to test each of the possible input errors.

    c.   A second subprogram performs all calculations.

    d.   A third subprogram prints the fee bill.

    e.   A fourth subprogram prints the summary totals.

35.   **Electric Bill Revisited.** Modify Exercise 28 of Chapter 7 on page 220 as follows:

    a.   The main program inputs all data.

b. A subprogram edits customer data for input errors. Specifically, it ensures that:

(1) The new meter reading is greater than the previous meter reading
(2) The rate code is 1, 2, or 3

If an error is encountered, then print an appropriate error message that includes the customer's name, complete address, and account number; bypass the calculations and printout for this customer; and go on to the next customer. Add new input data to test each of the possible input errors.
c. A second subprogram performs all calculations.
d. A third subprogram prints the bill.

36. **Installment Loan Revisited.** Modify Exercise 29 of Chapter 7 on page 221 as follows:
a. The main program inputs all data.
b. A subprogram calculates A and the total interest paid over the life of the loan.
c. A second subprogram calculates and prints the amortization table.

37. **Crime Data Summary Revisited.** Modify Exercise 28 of Chapter 8 on page 261 as follows:
a. The main program inputs all data.
b. A subprogram performs necessary calculations and prints the augmented table.
c. A second subprogram calculates and prints the second table described in part c.

38. **Exam Grading Revisited.** Modify Exercise 30 on Chapter 8 on page 263 as follows:
a. The main program inputs and outputs all data.
b. A subprogram grades the exam.
c. A second subprogram sorts and outputs final grades in descending order. *Hint:* As the first subprogram returns each final grade, the main program stores it in a one-dimensional array. Once this array is filled, the sort program can be called.
**d. A third subprogram determines and prints the frequency distribution of final grades. This subprogram calls a fourth subprogram that calculates the mean grade.

39. **Questionnaire Analysis Revisited.** Modify Exercise 27 of Chapter 9 on page 295 as follows:
a. The main program inputs all data.
b. A subprogram calculates and outputs frequency distributions.
**c. Another subprogram performs cross tabulations.

40. **Personnel Salary Budget Revisited.** Modify Exercise 28 of Chapter 9 on page 296 as follows:
a. The main program inputs all data.
b. A subprogram edits employee data for input errors. Specifically, it ensures that:

(1) The current annual salary is below $30,000
(2) The union code is 1, 2, or 3
(3) The step code is 1, 2, 3, 4, or 5
(4) The year hired is less than or equal to the current year

If an error is encountered, then print an appropriate error message that includes the employee's name and Social Security number, bypass the calculations and print line for this employee, and go on to the next employee. Add new input data to test each of the possible input errors.
c. A second subprogram performs all calculations.
d. A third subprogram prints the report.
e. A fourth subprogram prints totals.
f. A fifth subprogram summarizes the salary budgets by union.

CHAPTER 11

Finishing School

By now you have studied and put into practice the key features of the FORTRAN language. As you probably realize, the act of writing good programs for solving specific problems requires not only knowledge of FORTRAN and an understanding of the problem, but also practice, skill, judgment, thought, and art.

In this chapter we take you to "finishing school," which means that we're going to complete your FORTRAN education by illustrating some principles and techniques for improving the design of programs.

11.1
ON DESIGNING BETTER PROGRAMS

Most computer applications in business, government, education, and other organizations require complex programs. For instance, an application such as a company's payroll may include dozens of programs with hundreds of instructions within each program.

A programmer's ability to organize and develop a program becomes considerably more important as the complexity of the task increases. Unfortunately, many applications programs have been planned inadequately, which makes them difficult to follow, hard to debug, and time consuming to modify.

In recent years, a number of guidelines and new techniques have evolved for improving the design of programs. In all cases their aim is to produce readable, well-organized, easy-to-debug, reliable, easy-to-update programs. These guidelines and techniques include the following, many of which you will recognize:

1. *Indentation.* The indentation of statements within loops improves the readability of programs by clearly identifying loops.

2. *Selecting Variable Names.* The effective selection of variable names requires paying attention to meaning and structure. If names reflect what they represent, then a programmer can follow programming logic without constantly referring to a key that defines variables. For example, the variable COST has more meaning than the variable X if we wish to represent the cost of an item. The structure which the variable is to represent also should be considered. For example, a table of numbers is best represented by a two-dimensional subscripted variable than by a series of one-dimensional subscripted variables or by an "army" of unsubscripted variables. In other situations, the use of subscripted variables promotes shorter programs. For instance, compare Example 8.8 (page 252) to Example 7.8 (page 199).

3. *Use of GO TO Statements.* For better readability GO TO statements should be used sparingly. For example, the statement

        IF (COST1 .GT. COST2) STOP

    is preferred to the statements

         IF (COST1 .GT. COST2) GO TO 100
          :
          :
        100 STOP

    For the same reasons, loops are best designed with DO statements than with IFs paired with GO TO statements, as the following illustrates:

```
      I = 1                            DO 50 I = 1,N
  50 SUM(I) = 0.                           SUM(I) = 0
        J = 1                              DO 30 J = 1,M
  30      SUM(I) = SUM(I) + A(I,J)             SUM(I) = SUM(I) = A(I,J)
            J = J + 1                 30       CONTINUE
          IF (J .LE. M) GO TO 30              WRITE (6,*) SUM(I)
          WRITE(6,*) SUM(I)          50 CONTINUE
          I = I + 1
        IF (I .LE. N) GO TO 50
```

See what we mean? The segment on the left has a "jumbled" appearance which is more difficult to follow than the segment on the right.

In general, it is desirable to design programs that simplify transfers of control. In fact, some would go so far as to eliminate the use of the GO TO statement altogether. New statements in FORTRAN which are consistent with this philosophy are introduced in Section 11.6.

4. *General versus Specific Programs.* A general program requires less upkeep than a specific program for applications where certain data items may change. To illustrate what we mean, consider a program that calculates the mean (average) of a set of numbers or items. A general program would treat the number of items as an input variable (say, N), whereas a specific program would calculate the mean for, say, 100 items. Thus, the general program can calculate the mean for any number of items, whereas the specific program is restricted to 100 items. If the number of items is likely to change from one application to the next, then the general program is best since the specific program would require frequent changes.

Some estimates now place the cost of designing and maintaining software above the cost of purchasing or leasing hardware. Thus *it is good programming practice to treat all required data as variables rather than constants*. This practice reduces the cost of updating programs in situations where data may change.

5. *Documentation.* Programs that are to be used over long periods of time should be carefully documented. This facilitates the evolutionary process of updating (changing) programs to reflect improvements or new circumstances. In other words, well-documented programs are easier to understand and change than poorly documented programs. Documentation aids include flowcharts and the use of comment lines within programs. Comment lines should be used liberally (1) to incorporate elements of Step I in our four-step procedure (brief program description and definition of variables); (2) to explain computations and program logic at appropriate locations in the program; and (3) to otherwise facilitate the appearance and readability of programs. See the payroll program in Section 11.8 beginning on page 359 for an illustration of a well-documented program using comment lines.

6. *Efficiency.* A good program, in addition to being readable, is one that accomplishes its objective efficiently with respect to computer time. Here are a few suggestions to help you write more efficient programs: Integer arithmetic is faster than real arithmetic. On some machines 25 or more integer computations can be performed in the time it takes to execute one real computation. Thus, *if a numeric variable is to store strictly whole numbers and is not used in real arithmetic expressions, then it should be named as an integer variable.* For example, the instruction

    KOUNT = KOUNT + 1

is more efficient than

    COUNT = COUNT + 1.

Similarly, if N and XN store the same whole number, then the expression P**N is computed faster than P**XN, since the latter requires the computer to use logarithmic routines.

   Another common inefficiency is to use

    SUM = 0

instead of

    SUM = 0.

The former requires the compiler to provide additional machine instructions for converting integer zero to real zero for storage in a real variable. If you mix mode in an arithmetic expression (when allowed by the compiler), then the compiler must provide additional machine instructions to convert integer values to real values. For example, the instruction

    SALES = QTY*UNITPR

is more efficient than

    SALES = NUMBER*UNITPR

since the contents of NUMBER must be converted to real mode before multiplication.

7. *Reliability.* A program should reliably operate as intended once it is implemented on an on-going basis. This means that the design of a program should anticipate "unforeseen circumstances" as much as feasible. For example, good commercial programs anticipate errors in the input data through programmed error routines, as emphasized in the last chapter. Generally programmers should anticipate what might go wrong operationally, thereby designing their programs to react accordingly. At the same time the temptation to make programs "over-reliable" must be tempered by judgments regarding the benefits versus the costs. In other words, reliable program design requires assessments regarding the nature of potential operational difficulties, their likelihood of occurrences, the

costs of incorporating programmed reactions to these difficulties, and the benefits (or cost savings) realized when these difficulties are avoided through program design.

8. *Other Techniques.*   Recent trends point to a growing use of certain approaches, techniques, and new statements for improving the documentation, readability, design, and reliability of programs. Among these, we discuss top down design, modular programming, pseudocode, and structured FORTRAN in the next several sections.

11.2
TOP DOWN DESIGN

The term **top down design** refers to a process for simplifying and systematizing the design and development of complex programs. Strictly speaking, it is not a specific technique, but rather a philosophy which translates into a personalized process for writing programs. As such, the manner of implementing top down design will vary from programmer to programmer.

Top down design first requires an overall "look" at the entire problem, that is, a look from the "top." This first step is essentially an elaboration of part 1 of "Step I, Analyzing the Problem," in our four-step procedure for documenting and developing programs, first introduced in Chapter 2. Once the nature of the problem is fully defined in words, then the process can be refined further by working "down" through successive levels of greater detail. For example, in parts 2 (specification of inputs), 3 (specification of outputs), and 4 (computations and logical processes) of Step I, the problem is expressed at a greater level of detail than in part 1.

The preparation of the flowchart in Step II of the procedure is one way of representing the next level of detail, which then can be followed by the final level of detail, the program itself (Step III); however, relatively complex programs may require an additional level of detail between that of Step I and flowcharting: the specification of modules, which we discuss next.

11.3
MODULAR PROGRAMMING

Another approach to the organization and development of complex programs is **modular programming**. This approach divides a program into groups of related instructions called **modules**. Each module within a program typically performs one function related to the overall purpose of the program. For example, in a telephone billing program separate modules may be developed for the following purposes:

1. Data input
2. Calculation of bills
3. Printing of bills
4. Management report which includes statistical summaries of billing information, for example, sums, averages, frequency distributions (Exercise 30c

in Chapter 8), aging of accounts receivables (Exercise 30 in Chapter 6)
5. Bills sorted by ZIP codes (for the purpose of simplifying mailings)

You might recall from the end of Chapter 10 that modules in FORTRAN are written as subroutines. Typically a main program, called the **control module,** directs the entire program by calling each module (subroutine) as required.

A **hierarchy chart** represents a useful way to express the relationships among modules. This chart is similar in appearance to an organization chart, with each box representing a module. For example, the telephone billing modules might be related as shown in Figure 11.1.

In this case, the control module (main program) not only calls modules (subroutines) 1, 2, and 3 as required, but also might perform certain "house-keeping" chores such as documentation (features of programs, definition of variables, and so forth) and initializations. Notice that module 2 successively calls modules 4 and 5.

The use of modular programming concepts results in several advantages when writing long, complicated programs:

1. *Facilitates design and improves readability and comprehension of programs.*   For example, the hierarchy chart in Figure 11.1 gives the "big picture" and shows interrelationships among programming tasks. As mentioned in Section 11.2, this breaking down of the problem is consistent with top down design.
2. *Provides flexibility in a dynamic environment.*   Most applications programs evolve over time, which means that they are changed either to reflect new conditions or to incorporate improvements. The use of modules simplifies

FIGURE 11.1   *Hierarchy Chart For Telephone Billing Program*

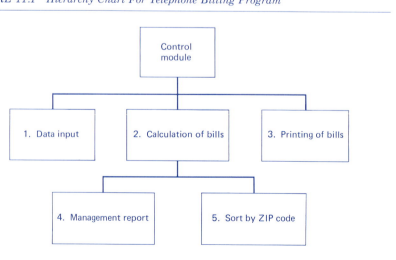

this evolutionary process by minimizing the required effort in making changes; that is, modules can be changed, added, or deleted with greater independence and ease.

3. *Allows specialization and division of labor.* Specific modules can be assigned to specific programmers, which can promote greater productivity and more effective programs. For example, Programmer A might be better at designing I/0 features than Programmer B, but the latter is better at designing efficient calculating procedures. The assignment of modules, therefore, should reflect these specializations.

11.4
PSEUDOCODE

A flowchart is one way of diagramming the logic of a program. Many professional programmers and systems analysts use them regularly; others do not. One reason for their not using flowcharts is the difficulty in revising the flowchart once a program has been modified.

In the past few years, a program design tool called **pseudocode** has been gaining acceptance among professional programmers. A key reason for the growing acceptance of pseudocode is its compatibility with the thinking processes of the programmer. Unfortunately, pseudocode has not been standardized, because there are many variations. The example which follows, however, should give you some idea of its syntax and structure.

EXAMPLE 11.1   Student Billing Program: Pseudocode and FORTRAN Versions

Before writing a FORTRAN program, a programmer might map out the structure of the program using a "false" (pseudo) code, as follows:

```
READ STUDENT DATA
IF # OF CREDITS ≥ 12 THEN
    TUITION = $1200
ELSE
    TUITION = # OF CREDITS X $100
END IF
BALANCE DUE = TUITION + $250
PRINT BALANCE DUE
END
```

Given the above structure, the FORTRAN version follows readily:

```
READ(5,*) ID,CREDIT
IF (CREDIT .GE. 12.) TUIT = 1200.
IF (CREDIT .LT. 12.) TUIT = CREDIT*100.
BALDUE = TUIT + 250.
WRITE(6,*) ID,BALDUE
STOP
END
```

In general, a program written in pseudocode is similar to a program written in a higher-level language such as FORTRAN. The major difference is the emphasis placed on structure versus syntax. Pseudocode primarily concentrates on mapping out the structure of a program, with little regard for the syntax of the actual programming language to be used.

Like a flowchart, a program in pseudocode represents a blueprint of the actual program. Unlike a flowchart, however, this blueprint is expressed by the written word in the manner of a program, rather than by the written word using diagrams.

11.5
CONTROL STRUCTURES

Structured programming is an approach to organizing and writing programs. Compared to unstructured programs, structured programs have easier-to-follow logic, code that is more readable, and a greater likelihood of reliable execution.

FIGURE 11.2   *Sample Sequence Structure*

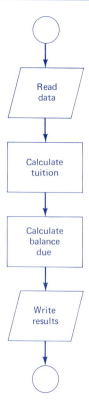

The basic foundation of structured programming consists of three types of structures:

1. Sequence structure
2. Decision structure
3. Loop structure

These so-called **control structures** can be used to describe the logic of any program completely.

Sequence Structure

The **sequence structure** consists of a sequence of instructions that occur one after the other without any transfer of control statements. The flowchart in Figure 11.2 illustrates the concept of the sequence structure for the student billing program.

Decision Structure

The **decision structure** consists of a choice between two or more alternatives. In the two-alternative case, either a sequence of one or more statements is to be executed if the condition is true, or a sequence of one or more statements is to be executed if the condition is false. The flowchart in Figure 11.3 illustrates this structure.

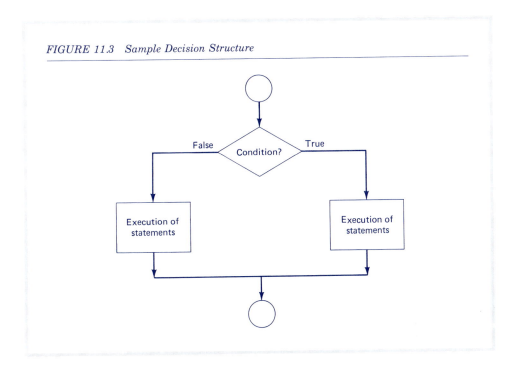

FIGURE 11.3   *Sample Decision Structure*

FIGURE 11.4   *Decision Structure for Student Billing Problem*

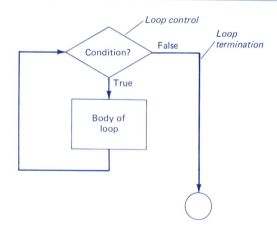

FIGURE 11.5   *DO WHILE Structure*

One familiar example of the decision structure is the calculation of tuition based on part-time versus full-time student status, as illustrated in Figure 11.4.

Loop Structure

The **loop structure** refers to the repeated execution of a sequence of instructions. This structure consists of two parts:

1. A *loop body,* which represents the sequence of steps that are to be repeated
2. A *loop control,* which specifies either the number of times a loop must be executed or the condition under which the loop is to be terminated

The flowchart in Figure 11.5 represents the logic of the loop structure. This loop structure specifically represents the **DO WHILE structure**. In this structure, the first action is to test whether or not the loop is to be executed. If the loop is to be executed, then control passes to the body of the loop. After the statements within the body have been executed, control goes back to the test statement preceding the loop body. When the test indicates that looping is finished, control passes to a statement outside the loop.

A variation of the DO WHILE structure is the **DO UNTIL structure**. This structure ensures that the body of the loop is executed at least once. In this case, the test for the end of the loop is made after the loop body is executed. The flowchart in Figure 11.6 illustrates the DO UNTIL structure, and the flowcharts in Figure 11.7 depict both loop structures for the student billing problem.

FIGURE 11.6   DO UNTIL Structure

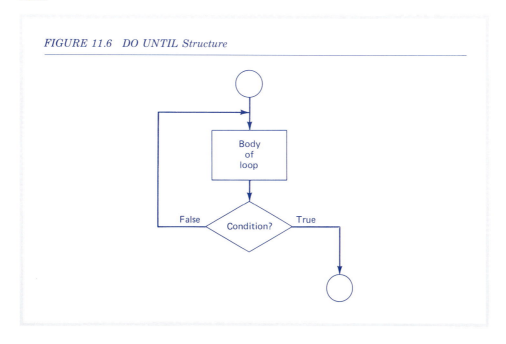

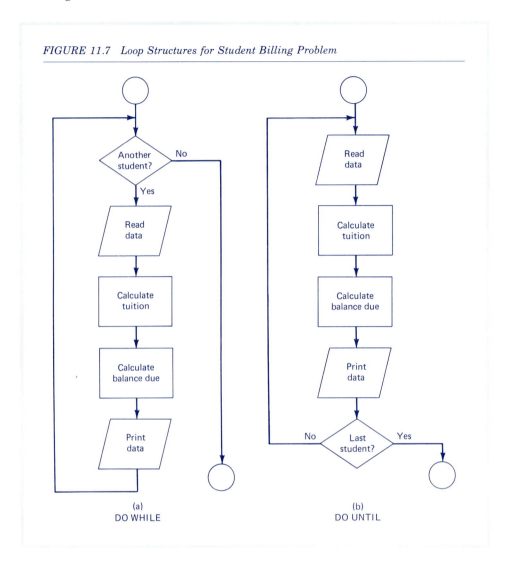

FIGURE 11.7   *Loop Structures for Student Billing Problem*

A subtle difference between the DO WHILE and DO UNTIL structures is that the former gives a loop exit when the condition is false, whereas the latter results in a loop exit when the condition is true. What type of loop structure is the DO statement similar to?[1]

11.6
STRUCTURED FORTRAN COMMANDS

The decision and loop structures which we identified in the preceding section were not new to you. We represented these structures by using logical IF, GO TO, and DO statements. In recent years, new FORTRAN commands have been

---

[1] The DO loop is similar to the DO UNTIL structure in that the loop body precedes the test for loop exit. In FORTRAN 77, however, the DO loop has a DO WHILE structure, as noted in Section 11.7.

developed which facilitate the use of structured programs in FORTRAN. These new commands, called **structured** (or **enhanced**) **FORTRAN commands,** directly incorporate specific control structures.

In this section we discuss three structured FORTRAN commands:

1. IF THEN ELSE
2. WHILE DO
3. DO CASE

These commands are not available on many FORTRAN compilers; however, a new version of WATFIV called WATFIV-S supports these and other structured FORTRAN commands.[2]

IF THEN ELSE

The structured FORTRAN statement that represents the two-choice decision structure is the IF THEN ELSE. This statement is an extension of the logical IF statement. Its general form is

```
IF (logical expression) THEN DO
     :  ⎫ group of statements
     :  ⎬ executed if condition is "true"
ELSE DO
     :  ⎫ group of statements
     :  ⎬ executed if condition is "false"
END IF
```

First, the condition indicated by the logical expression is evaluated. If the condition is true, then the block of statements following the THEN DO is executed, after which control passes to the statement following the END IF. If the condition is false, however, then the block of statements following the ELSE DO is executed, after which control passes to the statement following the END IF.

EXAMPLE 11.2

The tuition calculation based on part-time versus full-time status can be written as follows:

```
IF (CREDIT .GE. 12.) THEN DO
    TUIT = 1200.
    IFULL = IFULL + 1
ELSE DO
    TUIT = CREDIT*100.
    IPART = IPART + 1
END IF
```

---

[2] The latest version of FORTRAN also supports certain structured commands, as discussed in Section 11.7.

If the value stored in CREDIT is greater than or equal to 12., then 1200. is stored in TUIT, the full-time student counter (IFULL) is incremented, and control passes to the statements following END IF. If the value stored in CREDIT is less than 12., then the value in TUIT is the product of the value stored in CREDIT multiplied by 100., the part-time student counter (IPART) is incremented and control passes to the statement following END IF.

The ELSE DO segment of this statement is optional, as the following variation indicates:

IF *(logical expression)* **THEN DO**

$\left.\begin{matrix} \vdots \\ \vdots \end{matrix}\right\}$ true condition

END IF

EXAMPLE 11.3

The use of this option is illustrated by the following revision of the sort program (Example 8.9, p. 255):

```
IF (LIST(I) .LT. LIST(I − 1)) THEN DO
    TEMP = LIST(I)
    LIST(I) = LIST (I − 1)
    LIST(I − 1) = TEMP
    SWITCH = 1
END IF
```

If the value in LIST(I) is less than the value in LIST(I − 1), then the three statements following the THEN DO are executed, after which control passes to the statement following END IF. Otherwise, control passes directly to the statement following the END IF.

Follow-up Exercises

1. Did you notice that the pseudocode in Example 11.1 is consistent with the IF THEN ELSE statement? Why is the FORTRAN program of Example 11.1 not exactly consistent with the IF THEN ELSE statement and the two-choice decision structure of Figure 11.4? Make the FORTRAN program consistent by using the logical IF paired with the GO TO statement. Of the three approaches (that in Example 11.1, use of IF THEN ELSE, and use of logical IF paired with GO TO), which do you prefer and why?
2. Modify Example 11.2 by using the logical IF paired with the GO TO in place of the IF THEN ELSE. Which approach do you prefer and why? Why can't you use the approach of Example 11.1 here? Or can you?
3. Draw a flowchart for the type of decision structure reflected in Example 11.3.

WHILE DO

The structured FORTRAN statement that represents the loop structure is the WHILE DO statement. This statement is similar to the DO statement, although a number of differences exist. The general form of the WHILE DO is

WHILE*(logical expression)* **DO**

$\left. \begin{array}{c} \vdots \\ \vdots \end{array} \right\}$ loop body

END WHILE

The condition given by the logical expression is tested before entry into the body of the loop. If the condition is false, then control passes to the statement following the END WHILE statement. If the condition is true, then the body of the loop is executed. When the END WHILE statement is reached, the condition in the WHILE statement is tested again, and if false, control passes to the statement following the END WHILE; if true, the loop body is executed again. Thus, the WHILE DO statement represents the loop structure exhibited in Figure 11.5.

EXAMPLE 11.4   Student Billing Program

The student billing program is rewritten using the WHILE DO statement as follows:

```
READ(5,*) N
I = 1
WHILE (I .LE. N) DO
     READ(5,*) ID,CREDIT
     BALDUE = TUIT*100. + 250.
     WRITE(6,*) ID,BALDUE
     I = I + 1
END WHILE
STOP
END
```

In this case, the counter variable I must be initialized before the loop and needs to be incremented within the loop body. This differs from the DO statement, where the counter variable is automatically initialized and incremented.

For straightforward looping of this type, the WHILE DO statement is less efficient than the DO statement. In general, however, the WHILE DO statement provides added flexibility and power over the DO statement, as illustrated by the following example.

EXAMPLE 11.5   Predicting Future Population Levels

```
C
C  POPULATION GROWTH PROGRAM
C
C  INPUTS:
C       CY = CURRENT YEAR
C        N = NUMBER OF YEARS INTO FUTURE
C      CPL = CURRENT POPULATION LEVEL
C      BMD = BIRTH RATE MINUS DEATH RATE
C  OUTPUTS:
C     YEAR = YEAR
C      FPL = FUTURE POPULATION LEVEL
C
    5 FORMAT('0','YEAR',5X,'POPULATION'/)
   10 FORMAT(1X,I4,F14.4)
C
      INTEGER CY,YEAR
C
      READ(5,*) CY,N,CPL,BMD
      WRITE(6,5)
      FPL = CPL
      YEAR = CY
      I = 1
      WHILE(I .LE. N .OR. FPL .LT. 2.*CPL) DO
         FPL = FPL*(1. + BMD)
         YEAR = YEAR + 1
         WRITE(6,10) YEAR,FPL
         I = I + 1
      END WHILE
      STOP
      END
```

First, make sure that you understand the calculating logic. For example, if the world population level was 4 billion in 1976 with birth and death rates of 0.03 and 0.01, respectively, then CPL = 4 and BMD = 0.02. For the first year into the future (noticing that FPL is initialized to CPL before the loop), we have

$$FPL = (4.) \cdot (1. + .02) = 4.08$$

For the second year into the future (I = 2), the result is

$$FPL = (4.08) \cdot (1.02) = 4.1616$$

According to the WHILE DO statement, looping will continue as long as I is less than or equal to its maximum value (N) *or* as long as the future level of population is less than double its current level. For example, if N = 20, then the following output would be obtained for the input data given above:

	YEAR	POPULATION
I = 1 ⟶	1977	4.0800
I = 2 ⟶	1978	4.1616
⋮		
I = 20 ⟶	1996	5.9438
⋮		
I = 35 ⟶	2011	7.9996
I = 36 ⟶	2012	8.1595

Thus, output continues until the year 2012, since at this point population first exceeds double its initial level and I already has exceeded its maximum value. In this case, output does not stop at I = 20 because population is still below 8 billion; however, if N = 40 had been input, then output would continue until the year 2016. Do you see why? It would not stop at I = 36 because I is still less than N. It would stop at I = 40 because I has reached its terminal value and population already has more than doubled.

Finally, notice that, compared to the DO statement, the WHILE DO statement has the added flexibility and power to (1) directly test complicated conditions by using logical expressions; (2) work with real indices and fractional increments; (3) test a computational result within the loop; and (4) test more than one looping condition through the use of compound logical expressions.

Follow-up Exercise

*4. Modify Example 11.5 as follows:
   a. Input initial, terminal, and incremental birth minus death rates (BMDINI, BMDTER,BMDINC) instead of BMD.
   b. Nest the existing WHILE DO loop within a new WHILE DO loop which tests the index BMD against its terminal value BMDTER. In other words, we now want a population table for each desired value of the birth minus death rate. For example, if BMDINI = 0.005, BMDTER = 0.030, and BMDINC = 0.001, then BMD will take on the values 0.005, 0.006, 0.007, . . . 0.030.

DO CASE

The DO CASE statement is a variation of the computed GO TO statement and is best used when control is passed to one of a group of statements based on the value of the index variable.

The general form of this statement is

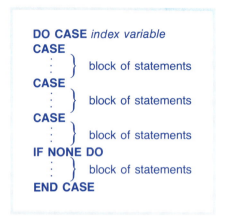

Each alternative block of statements is preceded by the word CASE. The value of the index variable, *which must be an integer variable,* determines which alternative CASE is to be executed. The index variable must store integer values (1,2,3, . . .) that fall within the range of 1 and the total number of cases. If the value of the index is 1, then the statements in the block following the first case are executed, after which control passes to the statement following the END CASE statement. If the value of the index is 2, then the second case is executed, and so on. The IF NONE DO segment is executed only if the value of the index variable is negative, zero, or greater than the number of cases provided.

EXAMPLE 11.6

The following program segment sums grade point averages (GPA) and counts the number of freshmen, sophomores, juniors, and seniors, where ICLASS contains one of the coded values 1 through 4.

```
      DO CASE ICLASS
      CASE
         SFR = SFR + GPA
         IFR = IFR + 1
      CASE
         SSO = SSO + GPA
         ISO = ISO + 1
      CASE
         SJR = SJR + GPA
         IJR = IJR + 1
      CASE
         SSR = SSR + GPA
         ISR = ISR + 1
      IF NONE DO
         WRITE(6,2) ICLASS
    2    FORMAT(1X,'ERROR IN CLASS',I4)
      END CASE
```

Whenever ICLASS has the value 1, the program branches to the first CASE and executes the statements SFR = SFR + GPA and IFR = IFR + 1, after which control passes to the statement following END CASE. Whenever ICLASS has the value 2, the program branches to the second CASE, sums GPAs for sophomores, and increments the sophomore counter. Similarly, when ICLASS is 3, the program branches to the third CASE, and so on. If ICLASS is negative, zero, or greater than 4, then the program executes the IF NONE DO branch and prints an error message.

Follow-up Exercises

5. What are the advantages of using the DO CASE instead of the computed GO TO?
6. Draw a flowchart for the program segment in Example 11.6.

11.7
FORTRAN 77

In 1978 ANSI finalized its latest version of FORTRAN in a document labeled ANSI X3.9-1978. This version of the language, called **FORTRAN 77,** is a significant revision of the 1966 version.

In general, FORTRAN 77 has greater scope, power, and flexibility than its predecessor. In particular, it has incorporated unformatted input/output, it includes certain elements of control structures, it is more flexible in the treatment of real and integer variables, and it has enhanced alphanumeric capabilities.

In the remainder of this section we briefly summarize some highlights of FORTRAN 77, many of which you are already familiar with.

Unformatted (List-Directed) I/O

Input/output without formats is now allowed by using the asterisk in place of the format label in a READ or WRITE statement, as we have illustrated throughout this text. Additionally, the list in a WRITE or PRINT statement need not be restricted to variables; it can include a literal, a numeric constant, and any arithmetic expression. For example, the execution of

    WRITE(6,*)'COST = $',50 + 4*M

would print

    COST= $ 90

if 10 is stored in M.

Use of Apostrophe

The apostrophe can be used to represent a literal (alphanumeric constant) in an output list (as in the above WRITE statement), in a FORMAT statement (as we have shown throughout), in DATA statements, and in character expressions (see next page).

END Statement

The END statement is now an executable statement. In a main program it has the effect of a STOP statement and in a subprogram it has the effect of a RETURN statement.

Mixed-Mode Arithmetic

Real and integer variables and constants can be mixed in an arithmetic expression. For example, the expression

    SUM/N

is treated the same as

    SUM/REAL(N)

which is to say that the value obtained from N is converted to real mode when the expression is evaluated. The mode of the result is real.

Alphanumeric Data

The length of alphanumeric (character) variables can be specified by the CHARACTER statement, as illustrated in Exercise 6 of Chapter 6 (page 159).

Additionally, FORTRAN 77 has enhanced alphanumeric capabilities, including character substring manipulations (the ability to access portions of an alphanumeric data item), character expressions, and character assignment statements. For example, the execution of

    MONTH = 'JUNE'

stores the character data item JUNE in the location MONTH.

Array Declarations

The method of declaring arrays and their bounds is more flexible. For example, the statement

    DIMENSION A(100),B(-10:50),C(20,-5:5)

specifies that A is a one-dimensional array of 100 elements (lower subscript bound of 1 and upper subscript bound of 100 as before), B is a one-dimensional array of 60 elements (lower subscript bound of -10 and upper subscript bound of 50), and C is a two-dimensional array of 20 rows and 10 columns (rows have subscript bounds of 1 to 20 and columns have subscript bounds of -5 to 5).

DO Statement

FORTRAN 77 allows a real variable for the index; negative values for parameters (initial, terminal, and incremental values); and real or integer arithmetic expressions for parameters. Additionally, the DO-loop remains inactive (is not processed at all) if the initial value exceeds the terminal value, which is consistent with a DO WHILE structure.

Structured Commands

Four new statements reflect the two-choice decision structure: **Block IF, ELSE, END IF,** and **ELSE IF.** The program segment in Example 11.2 on page 347 would require a minor rewrite (the DO is dropped) as follows:

```
IF (CREDIT .GE. 12.) THEN
   TUIT = 1200.
   IFULL = IFULL + 1
ELSE
   TUIT = CREDIT*100.
   IPART = IPART + 1
END IF
```

This segment uses the block IF, ELSE, and END IF statements. The ELSE IF statement can be nested within the block IF statement to establish another "block" of statements whose execution is contingent on the result of another logical test. For example, suppose we wish to account for graduate students, where all graduate students are restricted to less than 12 credits and pay a tuition of $1000. If the variable KODE stores a 1 for undergraduate students and a 2 for graduate students, then the program segment can be written as follows:

```
IF (CREDIT .GE. 12.) THEN
   TUIT = 1200.
   IFULL = IFULL + 1
ELSE IF(KODE .EQ. 1) THEN
   TUIT = CREDIT*100.
   IPART = IPART + 1
ELSE
   TUIT = 1000.
   IGRAD = IGRAD + 1
END IF
```

11.8
PAYROLL APPLICATION

We conclude this chapter by presenting a simplified payroll application which incorporates many of the concepts and techniques which we have discussed.

Step I   Analyzing the Problem
1. *Problem Statement*
    Payroll program in FORTRAN which processes hourly employees. Program calculates and outputs gross pay, deductions, and net pay based on number of dependents, rate of pay, number of hours worked, and total earnings for the year. Deductions include Social Security (FICA) tax, income tax, and contribution to group health insurance.

2. *Data Input*
    a. Name of employee (NAME)
    b. Employee number (NUM)
    c. Number of dependents (NODEP)
    d. Hourly rate of pay (RATE)
    e. Number of hours worked (HOURS)
    f. Total gross earnings thus far this year (TOTERN)
3. *Data Output*
    a. Employee name
    b. Employee number
    c. Gross pay (GPAY)
    d. Total deduction (TOTDED)
    e. Net pay (PAYNET)
    f. Updated cumulative gross earnings (CUMPAY)
4. *Computations and Logical Processes*
    a. Gross pay is RATE times HOURS when HOURS is 40 or less; otherwise, GPAY is RATE times 40 plus 1.5 times RATE for each hour above 40.
    b. Social Security tax is 6.13 percent of gross pay. The deduction is made until the employee's cumulative earnings are above $22,900, after which there is no deduction.
    c. Deductions for income tax and group health insurance plan are tied to the number of dependents as follows:

Dependents	Income Tax (% of gross pay)	Group Health ($/wk)
1	22	2.50
2	20	3.60
3	18	5.10
4	16	6.00
5 or more	13	6.50

    d. Total deduction is given by the sum of FICA tax (SSTAX), income withholding tax (WTHTAX), and health insurance contribution (HEALTH).
    e. Net pay is gross pay less total deductions.

Step II   Flowchart and/or Pseudocode and/or Modules.   Here we specify the modules, show the hierarchy chart, and develop each module in pseudocode. Our main intent is to demonstrate the top down design/modular programming principle of breaking up an overall problem into simpler functional components which we call modules. As mentioned previously, an actual payroll program would incorporate more features by using either a greater number of modules or longer modules (or both). In the interest of sanity, we omit the flowcharts.

1. *Description of Modules*
    a. Control module—inputs data and calls modules b, c, d, e.
    b. Gross pay module—calculates gross pay.
    c. Deductions module—calls modules f and g and calculates total deductions.

    d. Net pay module—calculates net pay.

    e. Output module—outputs table headings and output data.

    f. FICA tax module—calculates Social Security tax.

    g. Health and income tax module—calculates health insurance contribution and income withholding tax.

2. *Hierarchy Chart*
    See Figure 11.8

3. *Pseudocode*

```
START: CONTROL MODULE
  READ EMPLOYEE RECORD
  CALL OUTPUT MODULE
  START LOOP
    CALL GROSS PAY MODULE
    CALL DEDUCTIONS MODULE
    CALL NET PAY MODULE
    CALL OUTPUT MODULE
    READ EMPLOYEE RECORD
  END LOOP
END: MODULE

START: GROSS PAY MODULE
  IF HOURS WORKED > 40 THEN
    GROSS PAY = (RATE OF PAY × 40) + (HOURS WORKED − 40) ×
    (RATE OF PAY × 1.5)
  ELSE
    GROSS PAY = RATE OF PAY × HOURS WORKED
  END IF
END: MODULE
```

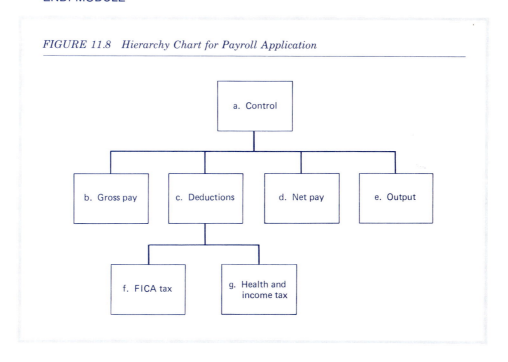

FIGURE 11.8 *Hierarchy Chart for Payroll Application*

```
START:  DEDUCTIONS MODULE
   CALL FICA TAX MODULE
   CALL HEALTH AND INCOME TAX MODULE
   TOTAL DEDUCTIONS = SOCIAL SECURITY TAX + INCOME
                    WITHHOLDING TAX + HEALTH INSURANCE
                    CONTRIBUTION
END: MODULE


START: FICA TAX MODULE
   IF TOTAL EARNINGS > 22900 THEN
      SOCIAL SECURITY TAX = 0
   ELSE
     IF TOTAL EARNINGS + GROSS PAY > 22900 THEN
        SOCIAL SECURITY TAX = (22900 − TOTAL EARNINGS) × 6.13%
     ELSE
        SOCIAL SECURITY TAX = GROSS PAY × 6.13%.
     END IF
END: MODULE


START: HEALTH AND INCOME TAX MODULE
      IF # DEPENDENTS = 1 THEN
            WITHHOLDING TAX = GROSS PAY × 22%
            HEALTH DEDUCTION = $2.50
      IF # DEPENDENTS = 2 THEN
            WITHHOLDING TAX = GROSS PAY × 20%
            HEALTH DEDUCTION = $3.60
      IF # DEPENDENTS = 3 THEN
            WITHHOLDING TAX = GROSS PAY × 18%
            HEALTH DEDUCTION = $5.10
      IF # DEPENDENTS = 4 THEN
            WITHHOLDING TAX = GROSS PAY × 16%
            HEALTH DEDUCTION = $6.00
      IF # DEPENDENTS ⩾5 THEN
            WITHHOLDING TAX = GROSS PAY × 13%
            HEALTH DEDUCTION = $6.50
      END IF
END: MODULE


START: NET PAY MODULE
   NET PAY = GROSS PAY − TOTAL DEDUCTIONS
END: MODULE

START: OUTPUT MODULE
   IF OPTION CODE = 1 THEN
     PRINT HEADINGS
   IF OPTION CODE = 2 THEN
     PRINT EMPLOYEE RESULTS
   IF OPTION CODE = 3 THEN
     PRINT END-OF-TABLE HEADINGS
   END IF
END: MODULE
```

Step III Coding the Problem

```
        C                                                      00000140
        C****************                                      00000150
        C PROBLEM STATEMENT                                    00000160
        C****************                                      00000170
        C                                                      00000180
        C                                                      00000190
        C      PAYROLL PROGRAM IN FORTRAN WHICH PROCESSES HOURLY EMPLOYEES.   00000200
        C      PROGRAM CALCULATES AND OUTPUTS GROSS PAY,DEDUCTIONS,AND NET    00000210
        C      PAY BASED ON NUMBER OF DEPENDENTS, RATE OF PAY, NUMBER OF      00000220
        C      HOURS WORKED, AND TOTAL EARNINGS FOR THE YEAR.  DEDUCTIONS     00000230
        C      INCLUDE SOCIAL SECURITY (FICA) TAX, INCOME TAX AND            00000240
        C      CONTRIBUTIONS TO GROUP HEALTH INSURANCE                        00000250
        C                                                      00000260
        C****************                                      00000270
        C                                                      00000280
        C****************                                      00000290
        C DATA INPUT--VARIABLES USED                           00000300
        C****************                                      00000310
        C                                                      00000320
        C      NAME OF EMPLOYEE (NAME)                          00000330
        C      EMPLOYEE NUMBER (NUM)                            00000340
        C      NUMBER OF DEPENDENTS (NODEP)                     00000350
        C      HOURLY RATE OF PAY  (RATE)                       00000360
        C      NUMBER OF HOURS WORKED (HOURS)                   00000370
        C      TOTAL GROSS  EARNINGS THUS FAR THIS YEAR (TOTERN)   00000380
        C****************                                      00000390
        C                                                      00000400
        C****************                                      00000410
        C DATA OUTPUT--VARIABLES USED                          00000420
        C****************                                      00000430
        C                                                      00000440
        C      EMPLOYEE NAME                                    00000450
        C      EMPLOYEE NUMBER                                  00000460
        C      GROSS PAY (GPAY)                                 00000470
        C      TOTAL DEDUCTIONS (TOTDED)                        00000480
        C      NET PAY (PAYNET)                                 00000490
        C      UPDATED CUMULATIVE GROSS EARNINGS (CUMPAY)       00000500
        C                                                      00000510
        C****************                                      00000520
        C                                                      00000530
        C****************                                      00000540
        C CONTROL MODULE--READS INPUT DATA.  CALLS SUBROUTINES TO   00000550
        C                 PROCESS PAYROLL.                     00000560
        C****************                                      00000570
        C                                                      00000580
   1        2   FORMAT(5A4,I5,I2,F3.2,F4.0,F10.2)              00000590
        C                                                      00000600
   2          DIMENSION NAME(5)                                00000610
   3          READ(5,2) NAME,NUM,NODEP,RATE,HOURS,TOTERN       00000620
   4          CALL OUT (1,NAME,NUM,GPAY,TOTDED,PAYNET,TOTERN)  00000630
   5          WHILE(NUM.GT.0) DO                               00000640
   6            CALL GROSS (RATE,HOURS,GPAY)                   00000650
   7            CALL DEDUCT(TOTERN,GPAY,NODEP,TOTDED)          00000660
   8            CALL NET (GPAY,TOTDED,PAYNET)                  00000670
   9            CALL OUT (2,NAME,NUM,GPAY,TOTDED,PAYNET,TOTERN)   00000680
  10            READ(5,2) NAME,NUM,NODEP,RATE,HOURS,TOTERN     00000690
  11          END WHILE                                        00000700
  12          CALL OUT(3,NAME,NUM,GPAY,TOTDED,PAYNET,TOTERN)   00000710
  13          STOP                                             00000720
  14          END                                              00000730

        C                                                      00000740
        C****************                                      00000750
        C GROSS PAY MODULE--CALCULATES AND RETURNS TO MAIN PROGRAM EMPLOYEE'S   00000760
        C                 GROSS PAY(GPAY).                     00000770
        C****************                                      00000780
        C                                                      00000790
  15          SUBROUTINE GROSS(RATE,HOURS,GPAY)                00000800
  16          IF(HOURS.GT.40.)THEN DO                          00000810
  17            GPAY=RATE*40.+(HOURS-40.)*RATE*1.5             00000820
  18          ELSE DO                                          00000830
  19            GPAY=RATE*HOURS                                00000840
  20          END IF                                           00000850
  21          RETURN                                           00000860
  22          END                                              00000870
```

```
      C                                                                00000880
      C**************                                                   00000890
      C DEDUCTIONS MODULE--CALLS SUBROUTINES TO CALCULATE EMPLOYEE'S    00000900
      C                    DEDUCTIONS FOR FICA AND HEALTH. RETURNS TOTAL 00000910
      C                    DEDUCTIONS(TOTDED) TO MAIN PROGRAM.           00000920
      C**************                                                   00000930
      C                                                                00000940

23          SUBROUTINE DEDUCT(TOTERN,GPAY,NODEP,TOTDED)                00000950
24          CALL FICA(TOTERN,GPAY,SSTAX)                               00000960
25          CALL HEALWT(NODEP,GPAY,WTHTAX,HEALTH)                      00000970
26          TOTDED=SSTAX+WTHTAX+HEALTH                                 00000980
27          RETURN                                                     00000990
28          END                                                       00001000
      C                                                                00001010
      C**************                                                   00001020
      C FICA TAX MODULE--DETERMINES AND RETURNS TO DEDUCTIONS MODULE    00001030
      C                  AMOUNT OF SOCIAL SECURITY TAX TO BE WITHHELD   00001040
      C                  FROM GROSS PAY(SSTAX).                         00001050
      C**************                                                   00001060
      C                                                                00001070

29          SUBROUTINE FICA(TOTERN,GPAY,SSTAX)                         00001080
30          IF(TOTERN.GT.22900.)THEN DO                                00001090
31              SSTAX=0.                                               00001100
32          ELSE DO                                                    00001110
33              IF(TOTERN+GPAY.GT.22900.)THEN DO                       00001120
34                  SSTAX=(22900.-TOTERN)*.0613                        00001130
35              ELSE DO                                                00001140
36                  SSTAX=GPAY*.0613                                   00001150
37              END IF                                                 00001160
38          END IF                                                     00001170
39          RETURN                                                     00001180
40          END                                                       00001190
      C                                                                00001200
      C**************                                                   00001210
      C HEALTH AND INCOME TAX MODULE--DETERMINES HEALTH AND INCOME TAX  00001220
      C                              (WTHTAX) DEDUCTIONS AND RETURNS    00001230
      C                              THESE TO DEDUCTIONS MODULE.        00001240
      C**************                                                   00001250
      C                                                                00001260

41          SUBROUTINE HEALWT(NODEP,GPAY,WTHTAX,HEALTH)                00001270
42          DO CASE NODEP                                              00001280
43          CASE                                                       00001290
44              WTHTAX=GPAY*.22                                        00001300
45              HEALTH=2.50                                            00001310
46          CASE                                                       00001320
47              WTHTAX=GPAY*.20                                        00001330
48              HEALTH=3.60                                            00001340
49          CASE                                                       00001350
50              WTHTAX=GPAY*.18                                        00001360
51              HEALTH=5.10                                            00001370
52          CASE                                                       00001380
53              WTHTAX=GPAY*.16                                        00001390
54              HEALTH=6.00                                            00001400
55          CASE                                                       00001410
56              WTHTAX=GPAY*.13                                        00001420
57              HEALTH=6.50                                            00001430
58          IF NONE DO                                                 00001440
59              WTHTAX=GPAY*.13                                        00001450
60              HEALTH=6.50                                            00001460
61          END CASE                                                   00001470
62          RETURN                                                     00001480
63          END                                                       00001490
      C                                                                00001500
      C**************                                                   00001510
      C NET PAY MODULE--CALCULATES AND RETURNS TO MAIN PROGRAM EMPLOYEE'S 00001520
      C                 NET SALARY(PAYNET) BY SUBTRACTING TOTAL DEDUCTIONS 00001530
      C                 FROM GROSS PAY.                                 00001540
      C**************                                                   00001550
      C                                                                00001560

64          SUBROUTINE NET(GPAY,TOTDED,PAYNET)                         00001570
65          PAYNET=GPAY-TOTDED                                         00001580
66          RETURN                                                     00001590
67          END                                                       00001600
```

```
      C                                                                      00001610
      C**************                                                        00001620
      C OUTPUT MODULE--PRINTS OUTPUT HEADER, CALCULATES CUMULATIVE PAY        00001630
      C               (CUMPAY), AND PRINTS PAYROLL TABLE.                     00001640
      C**************                                                         00001650
      C                                                                       00001660
  68        SUBROUTINE OUT(IOPT,NAME,NUM,GPAY,TOTDED,PAYNET,TOTERN)           00001670
  69        DIMENSION NAME(5)                                                 00001680
  70        DO CASE IOPT                                                      00001690
  71        CASE                                                              00001700
  72           WRITE(6,1)                                                     00001710
  73        CASE                                                              00001720
  74           CUMPAY=TOTERN+GPAY                                             00001730
  75           WRITE(6,2) NAME,NUM,GPAY,TOTDED,PAYNET,CUMPAY                  00001740
  76        CASE                                                              00001750
  77           WRITE(6,3)                                                     00001760
  78        END CASE                                                          00001770
  79        RETURN                                                            00001780
      C                                                                       00001790
  80      1 FORMAT('1',26X,'*** PAYROLL REPORT ***',///1X,73('-'),/1X,31X,    00001800
           *'GROSS PAY   DEDUCTIONS    NET PAY   CUM. PAY',/1X,               00001810
           *'EMPLOYEE NAME',9X,'NUMBER',6X,'($)',9X,'($)',9X,'($)',7X,'($)',  00001820
           */1X,73('-'))                                                      00001825
  81      2 FORMAT(1X,5A4,I7,F11.2,2F12.2,F11.2)                              00001830
  82      3 FORMAT(1X,73('-'),///1X,26X,'*** END PAYROLL REPORT ***')         00001840
  83        END                                                              00001850
```

Step IV   Debugging the Computer Program

For the given test data, the output should appear as illustrated below:

Test Data

Record	Name	Number	Dependents	Rate	Hours	Total Earnings
1	Al Della Bitta	1940	4	2.50	60	1500.00
2	Frank Budnick	1942	4	8.25	40	24000.00
3	Diane Marcotte	2001	1	6.00	45	12300.00
4	Arun Sanghvi	1776	3	8.00	35	22850.00
5						

Output Data

```
                        *** PAYROLL REPORT ***

-----------------------------------------------------------------------
                              GROSS PAY   DEDUCTIONS    NET PAY   CUM. PAY
EMPLOYEE NAME       NUMBER      ($)          ($)         ($)        ($)
-----------------------------------------------------------------------
AL DELLA BITTA       1940      175.00       44.73       130.27    1675.00
FRANK BUDNICK        1942      330.00       58.80       271.20   24330.00
DIANE MARCOTTE       2001      285.00       82.67       202.33   12585.00
ARUN SANGHVI         1776      280.00       58.56       221.44   23130.00
-----------------------------------------------------------------------

                      *** END PAYROLL REPORT ***
```

Follow-up Exercises

7. Describe how the payroll program stops execution.
8. Describe the contents of NAME, NUM, NODEP, RATE, HOURS, TOTERN, GPAY, SSTAX, WTHTAX, HEALTH, TOTDED, PAYNET, and CUMPAY just before the processing of the second input record.

*9. Modify the program to eliminate all arguments in favor of COMMON statements. Which approach do you prefer and why?

Additional Exercises

10. Describe how top down design is part of our four-step procedure.
11. How is modular programming related to top down design?
12. Where would you place pseudocode in our four-step procedure?
13. **Data Edit Module.** Add a data edit module to the payroll program in Section 11.7. This subprogram edits the input data for errors. Specifically, it ensures that

    (1) Number of dependents is greater than zero and less than 15.
    (2) Rate of pay is greater than $2.50 and less than $10.00.
    (3) Number of hours worked is greater than zero and less than 65.
    (4) Total earnings thus far this year is zero or greater and less than $40,000.

    If an error is detected, then print an appropriate error message that includes the employee's name and number, bypass the calculations and printout for this employee, and go on to the next employee. Add new employees to your input records to test each of these four possible input errors.

14. **Simulating Structured Commands.** Standard FORTRAN instructions can be used to reproduce functionally (simulate) the mechanics of structured commands. This has the advantage of creating structured programs for processing on standard FORTRAN compilers that do not support structured commands. Clarity and efficiency are somewhat sacrificed, however, since it takes some "gymnastics" to force standard commands into a structured framework. To illustrate what we mean, consider the following:

Actual Structured Version	Simulated Version
WHILE (logical expression) DO	998 IF (.NOT. (logical expression)) GO TO 999
⋮ } body	⋮ } body
END WHILE	GO TO 998
⋮	999 ⋯

    You should convince yourself that the version on the right exactly reproduces the mechanics of the version on the left. Thus the use of GO TOs, the logical IF, and the .NOT. operator can be used to simulate the DO WHILE loop structure.
    a. Revise the payroll program in Section 11.8 by simulating all structured commands using standard FORTRAN instructions. Run the program for the given input data.
    b. Include the feature described in Exercise 13.

15. **Bracket Search Algorithm Revisited.** Solve Exercise 44 in Chapter 4 on page 126 using structured FORTRAN commands. Try to eliminate all GO TO statements. Terminate the algorithm by testing the increment in R using a WHILE DO statement.

16. **Personnel Selection Revisited.** Solve Exercise 31 in Chapter 7 on page 224 by using structured FORTRAN commands. Try to eliminate all GO TO statements.

17. Select one of the following exercises from Chapter 10. In each case, specify Steps I–IV, draw a hierarchy chart, include flowcharts, give pseudocode a try (improvise when you need to), and eliminate all GO TO statements (if possible) by using structured FORTRAN commands.

a.	Exercise 24	i.	Exercise 32
b.	Exercise 25	j.	Exercise 34
c.	Exercise 26	k.	Exercise 35
d.	Exercise 27	l.	Exercise 36
e.	Exercise 28	m.	Exercise 37
f.	Exercise 29	n.	Exercise 38
g.	Exercise 30	o.	Exercise 39
h.	Exercise 31	p.	Exercise 40

CHAPTER 12

Other Programming Languages

In this chapter we present material which serves to broaden your orientation with respect to programming languages. After studying this chapter you will *not* have the capability to program in these languages. You should, however, gain an appreciation for the structural characteristics, similarities, richness, advantages, and disadvantages of various programming languages.

12.1 INTRODUCTION

As you might recall, three levels of programming languages were discussed briefly in Chapter 1:

1. Machine language
2. Assembly language
3. Higher-level language

364

Machine Languages

The first level, machine language, is the form the computer "understands." The control unit of the computer is designed to activate electronic circuits that cause the machine to carry out operations such as addition, subtraction, comparison, branching, I/O, and so on. Each operation (instruction) is represented as a series of binary (0–1) digits. The set of binary instructions makes up the computer's **machine language.** As you might expect, this set of instructions is different for each model of a computer, since each model differs from other models in hardware design.

Coding (writing the program) in machine language is an exceedingly tedious and time-consuming task because

1. Instructions must be in binary notation (a sequence of 0s and 1s), base 8 notation (called octal), or base 16 notation (called hexadecimal)
2. The programmer must assign specific numeric address locations for data and instructions

The program segment below illustrates machine language code.

FORTRAN Segment	Machine Language Segment*	Comments on Machine Language Segment
NUM1 = 11	5820C012	Load (58) the constant 11 in register 2.†
NUM2 = 5	5B20C016	Subtract (5B) the constant 5 from the constant 11 and store result in register 2.
NUM3 = 14	5A20C01A	Add (5A) the constant 14 to register 2 and store result in register 2.
ANS = NUM1 − NUM2 + NUM3	5020E01E	Store (50) contents of register 2 in memory address reserved for ANS.
	$\vdots$ }	Other instructions to make this a complete program
	0000000B	Constant 11.
	00000005	Constant 5.
	0000000E	Constant 14.

*This program is written in hexadecimal (base 16) notation, a "shorthand" notation for binary machine language instructions. For example, the hexadecimal digit 5 is equivalent to the binary digits 0101; the hexadecimal character B is equivalent to the binary digits 1011.
†A register is a memory location within the arithmetic-logic unit.

Assembly Languages

The difficulty of programming in machine languages promoted the development of a second level of languages called **assembly languages.** Assembly languages substitute a symbolic, easy-to-remember code for the binary code of a machine language; however, the format of an assembly language still closely reflects the format of the machine language.

A program written in an assembly-level language must be converted into machine language by a computer language translator called an **assembler.** The assembler

1. Translates each assembly instruction into one or more machine instructions
2. Allocates data and instructions to computer memory so the programmer does not have to keep track of where everything is located

Assembly-level languages are machine oriented in that each language is designed for a specific machine. Thus, an assembly language program written in BAL (Basic Assembly Language) for the IBM 370 type computers could not be run on Univac, Burroughs, or Control Data machines.

The program segment below illustrates the BAL assembly language.

FORTRAN Segment	Assembler Segment	Comments on Assembler Segment
	Operands(locations) ‾‾	
	Op code ⟶	Load (L) value from NUM1 into regis-
NUM1 = 11	(instructions) L 2,NUM1	ter 2.
NUM2 = 5	S 2,NUM2	Subtract (S) contents of NUM2 from value in register 2. Result stored in register 2.
NUM3 = 14	A 2,NUM3	Add (A) contents of NUM3 to value in register 2. Result stored in register 2.
ANS = NUM1 − NUM2 + NUM3	ST 2,ANS	Store (ST) contents of register 2 in ANS.
	⋮ }	Other instructions to make this a complete program
	NUM1 DC F'11' ⎫	
	NUM2 DC F '5' ⎬	Initialize memory locations.
	NUM3 DC F'14' ⎪	
	ANS DS F ⎭	

Higher-Level Languages

The shortcomings of assembly languages encouraged the development of a third level of languages referred to as higher-level languages. FORTRAN, BASIC, COBOL, and PL/1 are all examples of higher-level languages.

Higher-level languages are user oriented, that is, they permit instructions to be expressed in terms that are similar to the way the user approaches a problem. For this reason, they also are referred to as **procedure-oriented languages.** Higher-level languages are widely used because they are:

1. Easier to learn than lower-level languages
2. Quicker to code
3. Easier to debug and modify
4. Theoretically machine independent, that is, once a program is written it can be processed on any computer that can handle that language, for example, you may have run your programs on IBM computers, but you could have run them with no or only slight modifications on CDC, Univac, and Burroughs machines

Since the computer requires machine language, higher-level languages must be converted (translated) to machine language by a program called a **compiler.** Necessarily, each computer manufacturer must develop a separate compiler for each high-level language available for use on a particular computer.

12.2
HIGHER-LEVEL LANGUAGES

In this section we present a brief overview of four popular high-level languages: FORTRAN, BASIC, COBOL, and PL/1.[1] In addition, we code the student billing program in each of these languages, so you can observe their similarities and differences.

FORTRAN

The FORTRAN language was developed by IBM in the late 1950s as an aid to mathematicians, engineers, and other scientists. Over the years, improved versions have evolved, each of which is overseen by a group called the **American National Standards Institute (ANSI).** This institute has the primary mission of establishing standards for higher-level languages, which allows computer manufacturers to design compatible compilers.

Advantages of FORTRAN include the following:

1. Easy to learn. It's a compact language, having a relatively small body of instructions for solving a wide variety of problems. For this reason, it has become a popular language in the management and social sciences.
2. Excellent mathematical capability. Statements can be written in a manner similar to algebraic equations. In addition, mathematical functions such as square root, trigonometric functions, and logarithmic operations are built into the language.

Some of the disadvantages are

1. Processing nonnumeric data is awkward, which makes for cumbersome solutions to data processing problems.

---

[1]Other commonly used, high-level languages exist: APL, RPG, and ALGOL.

2. Editing management reports is difficult because dollar signs, commas, and other business data processing symbols are not easily inserted.

Because of its strong mathematical capabilities, FORTRAN is the premier language among scientific disciplines. Interestingly, FORTRAN also has become a popular language within the management and social sciences, for the same two reasons: it is easy to learn and it is mathematical. As discussed in Chapter 1, this latter advantage has become important in recent years due to the increasing use of mathematical and statistical techniques by social scientists and managers.

In Example 12.1 we restate the FORTRAN version of the student billing program. In the next few pages you will see this program rewritten in BASIC, COBOL, and PL/1.

EXAMPLE 12.1   FORTRAN Version of Student Billing Program

```
      READ(5,*) N
      DO 30 J = 1,N
         READ(5,*) ID,CREDIT
         IF (CREDIT .LT. 12.) TUIT = CREDIT*100.
         IF (CREDIT .GE. 12.) TUIT = 1200.
         BALDUE = TUIT + 250.
         WRITE(6,*) ID, CREDIT,BALDUE
30    CONTINUE
      STOP
      END
```

BASIC

BASIC (Beginners All-purpose Symbolic Instruction Code) was developed at Dartmouth College in the mid-1960s to simplify the learning of computer programming in a time-sharing environment.

The BASIC language is primarily suited for mathematical and statistical computations. The language is used extensively on time-sharing systems by engineering firms, educational institutions, and others with a quantitative orientation.

Some of the advantages of BASIC are

1. Easy to learn. Most versions of the language have less than 20 instructions, and its unformatted I/O makes programming easier.
2. Easy to code. For example, BASIC has no rules for column placement of instructions or for punctuation.
3. Excellent mathematical capability. In addition to an algebraic orientation and built-in functions, the language has matrix manipulation commands that are not available with other languages.

4. Small compiler. "Stripped-down" versions of BASIC utilize compilers which take up little storage in memory. As a result, BASIC is increasingly available on minicomputers and microcomputers.

Some of the disadvantages of BASIC are

1. Restricted variable names. Variable names consist of only one or two characters, which provides little or no clue as to their meaning.
2. Processing of alphabetic data is limited compared to business-oriented languages.
3. Restricted input of data. Because BASIC is used primarily on time-sharing systems, data must be keyed in at the terminal. Thus data stored on cards or magnetic tape can not be read in directly.
4. Limited batch capability. Batch BASIC compilers are available, but not universally. Also, the language itself is not as well suited to batch processing as is FORTRAN. Thus, advantages associated with batch processing (such as fast I/O and large amounts of calculation) are restricted.
5. ANSI standards do not yet exist for BASIC. Thus a BASIC program written for one computer may have to be modified for another computer.[2]

EXAMPLE 12.2   BASIC Version of Student Billing Program

```
10 READ N
20 FOR J = 1 TO N
30    READ I,C
40    IF C > = 12 THEN 70
50    LET T = C*100
60    GO TO 80
70    LET T = 1200
80    LET B = T + 250
90    PRINT I,C,B
100 NEXT J
110 DATA 2
111 DATA 5142,16
112 DATA 6245,18
200 END
```

1. *Input.*   The statement

    READ *list of variables*

is used in BASIC to input data that are incorporated in the program within DATA statements, which are nonexecutable statements of the following form:

    DATA *list of data items*

[2]A proposed standard for ANSI BASIC is currently under review.

Thus, when the statement

    READ N

is executed, the value 2 is placed in the storage location for N, since 2 is the first item of data in the first DATA statement on line 110. The first time

    READ I,C

is executed, 5142 is stored in I and 16 is stored in C; the second time this READ statement is executed, 6245 is placed in I and 18 is placed in C.

An alternative input statement in BASIC is

    INPUT *list of variables*

which, when executed, causes the terminal to print a question mark for the purpose of accepting data input that is directly typed by the user during execution of the program.

Did you notice that the variable names illustrated in this program are only one character in length? In the BASIC language, variable names for numeric data are restricted either to a letter followed by a one-digit number or to a letter alone.

2. *Loops.* Repeating a series of instructions is best accomplished in BASIC by combining two statements: **FOR** and **NEXT.** The FOR statement is placed at the beginning of the loop (like the DO statement in FORTRAN) and the NEXT statement appears as the last instruction in the loop (similar to the CONTINUE statement in FORTRAN). For example, the two statements

    20 FOR J = 1 TO N
      .
      .
      .
    100 NEXT J

indicate a loop which is processed N times.

3. *Transfer of Control.* An example of the conditional branching statement in BASIC is

    IF C > = 12 THEN 70

This statement on line 40 is similar to the logical IF statement in FORTRAN. If the value stored in C is 12 or more, then a "true" condition exists and the program branches to line 70; however, if C stores a value under 12, then a "false" condition is indicated, and the next instruction following the IF statement is executed (line 50).

The unconditional GO TO statement in BASIC is identical to that in FORTRAN, as you can see in line 60 of Example 12.2. BASIC also has a computed GO TO statement which is similar to its FORTRAN counterpart.

4. *Assignment Statements.* The assignment statement in BASIC is

    LET *variable name = arithmetic expression*

Lines 50, 70, and 80 illustrate three such statements in Example 12.2.
Some BASIC compilers allow an alternative assignment statement that is identical to that in FORTRAN:

variable name = arithmetic expression

For example, line 50 could be rewritten as

T = C*100

By the way, BASIC does not distinguish mode in arithmetic expressions; that is, variables and constants do not have mode.

5. *Output.* Output in BASIC is accomplished through the statement

PRINT list of variables

which is similar to the unformatted WRITE statement in FORTRAN. The statement

90   PRINT I,C,B

causes the contents of I, C, and B to be printed on one line according to predefined rules built into the BASIC compiler.
BASIC also has the capability of output according to formats which are specified by the programmer.

6. *Termination.* The **END** statement on line 200 is identical to its FORTRAN counterpart. Unlike its FORTRAN equivalent, however, it also causes execution to terminate.
BASIC also has a **STOP** statement for halting execution, which is used whenever it makes sense to terminate execution at points in the program other than at the physical end.

COBOL

COBOL (COmmon Business Oriented Language) was developed as a result of pressure by the federal government for a standardized language which processed business-oriented activities such as payroll, inventory, accounts receivable, and so on. Today, COBOL is the major language used to solve business data processing problems. In 1959 the Conference On Data System Languages (CODASYL) developed a set of specifications for the COBOL language. Since then many versions of COBOL have been developed. ANSI set standards for the COBOL language in 1968 and again in 1974.
Some of the advantages of COBOL are

1. Self-documenting language. The language is divided into divisions, sections, paragraphs, sentences, and clauses which make it easy to follow.
2. Alphanumeric processing capability. The language is designed to process business-type data, which include large amounts of nonnumeric data such as names, addresses, and descriptions.

3. Editing of output for report preparation. Commands are available for the insertion of the dollar sign, commas, asterisks, and other business data processing symbols.

Disadvantages include the following:

1. Wordy. The self-documenting features make for long programs. For example, a 20-line FORTRAN program might take 100 lines in COBOL.
2. Rigid structure. The placement of instructions, punctuation, and spacing must be carefully followed.
3. Fair mathematical capability. Mathematical manipulations lack the power of those in FORTRAN, BASIC, or PL/1.
4. Memory requirements. COBOL compilers require a large amount of primary memory; therefore, the language is not available for use with smaller computers.

EXAMPLE 12.3 COBOL Version of Student Billing Program

```
IDENTIFICATION DIVISION.
PROGRAM-ID. BILLING.
DATE-WRITTEN. DECEMBER 1, 1978.
REMARKS. STUDENT BILLING PROGRAM.

ENVIRONMENT DIVISION.
CONFIGURATION SECTION.
SOURCE-COMPUTER. IBM-370.
OBJECT-COMPUTER. IBM-370.
INPUT-OUTPUT SECTION.
FILE CONTROL.
   SELECT STUDENT-FILE ASSIGN TO CARD-READER.
   SELECT OUTPUT-FILE ASSIGN TO PRINTER.

DATA DIVISION.
FILE  SECTION.
FD    STUDENT-FILE LABEL RECORDS OMITTED.
01    STUDENT-RECORD.
      02 STUDENT-ID      PICTURE 9(6).
      02 CREDIT          PICTURE 9(2).
      02 FILLER          PICTURE X(72).
FD    OUTPUT-FILE LABEL RECORDS OMITTED.
01    OUTPUT-LINE.
      02 ID-OUT          PICTURE ZZZZZ9.
      02 FILLER          PICTURE X.
      02 CREDIT-OUT      PICTURE Z9.
      02 FILLER          PICTURE X.
      02 BALANCE-DUE     PICTURE $ZZ,ZZ9.
      02 FILLER          PICTURE X(115).
```

```
        WORKING-STORAGE SECTION.
        77 TUITION PICTURE 9(5).

        PROCEDURE DIVISION.
        OPEN FILES.
                OPEN INPUT STUDENT-FILE
                    OUTPUT OUTPUT-FILE.
        NEXT-STUDENT.
                MOVE SPACES TO OUTPUT-LINE.
                READ STUDENT-FILE AT END GO TO EOJ.
                MOVE STUDENT-ID TO ID-OUT.
                MOVE CREDIT TO CREDIT-OUT.
                IF CREDIT IS LESS THAN 12
                   MULTIPLY CREDIT BY 100 GIVING TUITION
                ELSE
                   MOVE 1200 TO TUITION.
                ADD 250 TUITION GIVING BALANCE-DUE.
                WRITE OUTPUT-LINE.
                GO TO NEXT-STUDENT.
        EOJ.
                CLOSE STUDENT-FILE OUTPUT-FILE.
                STOP RUN.
```

A COBOL program always consists of the following four divisions:

IDENTIFICATION—General information about the program.
ENVIRONMENT—Descriptions of computers used and input and output devices.
DATA—The format of the input data, definition of all variables, description of the output.
PROCEDURE—The steps to be followed in processing the program.

The following points should be of some help in clarifying this program.

1. *Input.* The COBOL statement

```
READ STUDENT-FILE AT END GO TO EOJ.
```

reads one data record into memory locations that were defined in the DATA DIVISION.

The DATA DIVISION describes the appearance of data. In the DATA DIVISION segment

```
FD   STUDENT-FILE LABEL RECORDS OMITTED
01   STUDENT-RECORD.
        02 STUDENT-ID     PICTURE 9(6).
        02 CREDIT         PICTURE 9(2).
        02 FILLER         PICTURE X(72).
```

storage locations are established for the variables STUDENT-ID and CREDIT. Variables in COBOL can be up to 30 characters in length. The picture clause describes the type of data within that location (9 for numeric and X for alphanumeric) and the field size (6 for STUDENT-ID and 2 for CREDIT). The word FILLER is a reserved word which is used when you want to disregard certain positions in a record. In this case, 72 positions (9–80) are ignored.

2. *Assignment Statements.* Four statements in COBOL perform the following arithmetic operations: ADD, SUBTRACT, MULTIPLY, and DIVIDE. In the statement

ADD 250   TUITION GIVING BALANCE-DUE.

the constant and/or variable before the word GIVING are added together and the result is stored in the variable following the word GIVING. Thus, if the value 1200 is stored in TUITION, then 1450 is stored in BALANCE-DUE.

The main drawback with the ADD, MULTIPLY, DIVIDE, or SUBTRACT statement is that only one mathematical operation can be performed at a time. To add *and* multiply requires two instructions. An alternative statement, called the COMPUTE statement, is used when several mathematical operations must be performed on the same variables.

3. *Data Movement.* The MOVE statement transfers data from one area of memory to another. It is often used in COBOL to copy the contents of a memory location, initialize a variable with a fixed value, or move data to an output line. For example, the statement

MOVE 1200 TO TUITION.

results in the storage of 1200 in the location TUITION.

4. *Output.* The statement

WRITE OUTPUT-LINE.

results in the output of one line based on the description of OUTPUT-LINE defined in the DATA DIVISION. In the DATA DIVISION segment

```
FD   OUTPUT-FILE LABEL RECORDS OMITTED.
01   OUTPUT-LINE.
     02   ID-OUT            PICTURE ZZZZZ9.
     02   FILLER            PICTURE X.
     02   CREDIT-OUT        PICTURE Z9.
     02   FILLER            PICTURE X.
     02   BALANCE-DUE       PICTURE $ZZ,ZZ9.
     02   FILLER            PICTURE X(115).
```

storage locations are created for the output of the ID number (ID-OUT), the number of credits (CREDIT-OUT), and the amount owed (BALANCE-DUE). The information following the picture clause illustrates editing symbols. These symbols describe how the value stored within that variable should be printed.

The symbol Z means that leading zeros are suppressed. Thus an ID of 001001 is printed as 1001. The symbols $ and , indicate that these characters are to be inserted in the output as shown. For example, if the value stored in BAL-ANCE-DUE is 01450, then the value printed is $ḅ1,450.

5. *Transfer of Control.* COBOL has several variations of the conditional branching statement. The statement

```
IF   CREDIT IS LESS THAN 12
       MULTIPLY CREDIT BY 100 GIVING TUITION
ELSE
       MOVE 1200 TO TUITION.
```

is similar to the IF THEN ELSE illustrated in Chapter 11. If CREDIT stores a value less than 12, then a "true condition" exists and the statements immediately following the condition are executed; that is,

```
MULTIPLY CREDIT BY 100 GIVING TUITION
```

would be executed. If the value stored in CREDIT is 12 or more, then the statements following the ELSE clause are executed; in this case,

```
MOVE 1200 TO TUITION
```

would be executed.

6. *Loops.* The statements

```
NEXT-STUDENT
      ⋮
      ⋮
       GO TO NEXT-STUDENT.
```

establish a loop in COBOL. Within the loop, the statement

```
READ STUDENT-FILE AT END GO TO EOJ.
```

combines the reading in of data for a student with a last record check. If an "end-of-file mark" is found during input, then control is transferred out of the loop to the label EOJ; otherwise, control drops to the statement immediately below the READ.

7. *Termination.* The statement

```
STOP RUN.
```

is equivalent to the STOP statement in FORTRAN; unlike FORTRAN, there is no END statement. In COBOL, the compiler acknowledges the end of a program when an appropriate card is inserted which signals the beginning of the data cards.

PL/1

PL/1 (Programming Language/1), developed by IBM in 1963, combines many of the features of both FORTRAN and COBOL, plus some others neither language has. These features make the language suitable for both business data processing and scientific applications; however, PL/1 is not as widely used as either FORTRAN or COBOL within each of these areas of application.

Advantages of PL/1 include

1. Ease of coding. Spacing and punctuation are simple. Placement of instructions is not restricted to particular columns, and more than one instruction can be placed on a line.
2. Modular approach. The language is set up in a modular fashion, which means that the programmer does not have to learn the entire language to solve a problem.
3. Flexibility. The language is available for use in both batch and time-sharing environments. It also can be used for mathematical and data processing problems.
4. Strong mathematical and logic capability.

Some of the disadvantages of PL/1 are

1. No industry-wide standards have been established.
2. Not all computer manufacturers supply PL/1 compilers.
3. The PL/1 compiler requires a sizable amount of primary memory, so it can not be used with small computers.
4. Difficult to learn. Despite the modular approach, PL/1 contains a large number of instructions which may be difficult to master.

EXAMPLE 12.4   PL/1 Version of Student Billing Program

```
BILLING: PROCEDURE OPTIONS (MAIN);
        DECLARE N FIXED DECIMAL (2,0),
                ID FIXED DECIMAL (6,0),
                CREDIT FIXED DECIMAL (2,0);
        GET LIST (N);
        DO J = 1 TO N;
            GET LIST (ID,CREDIT);
            IF(CREDIT > = 12) THEN
                TUIT = 1200
            ELSE
                TUIT = CREDIT*100;
            BALDUE = TUIT + 250;
            PUT LIST (ID,CREDIT,BALDUE);
        END;
    END BILLING;
```

1. *Input.* The GET LIST statement is used to enter data, where the variables to be entered are enclosed within parentheses. Information about the type of data, field size, and decimal position is established in a DECLARE statement.

In the sample program, three variables are defined in the DECLARE statement: N and CREDIT are defined as fixed decimal, 2 characters in size, and 0 digits to the right of the decimal place; ID is defined as fixed decimal of 6 characters length, with 0 digits to the right of the decimal place. The term FIXED DECIMAL defines these variables as integer in the FORTRAN sense. Besides many other options, the DECLARE statement can define real variables by using the term FLOAT DECIMAL. By the way, variable names in PL/1 can be up to 31 characters in length.

2. *Loops.* A series of instructions is repeated by combining two statements: DO and END.

The DO statement is placed at the beginning of the loop, and the END statement is the last instruction in the loop. These two statements have many powerful variations that are not illustrated in this example.

3. *Transfer of Control.* There are several variations of the IF statement in PL/1. The one illustrated in this program is similar to the IF THEN ELSE statement discussed in the chapter on structured FORTRAN. In Example 12.4, if CREDIT stores a value of 12 or more, then a true condition exists, and the statements immediately following the condition are executed; in this case,

    TUIT = 1200

is executed. If the value in CREDIT is less than 12, then a false condition exists, and all the statements following the ELSE clause are executed until a semicolon (;) is encountered.

4. *Assignment Statements.* The assignment statements in PL/1 are identical to those in FORTRAN.

5. *Output.* The PUT statement transfers the contents of variables to the printer. In the student billing program, the statement

    PUT LIST (ID,CREDIT,BALDUE)

outputs the contents of ID, CREDIT, and BALDUE without formats on one line. PL/1 also has formatted output statements.

6. *Termination.* The statement

    END BILLING;

accomplishes the function of the STOP and END statements in FORTRAN. Note that the word BILLING is the name of this program, as defined by the first statement in the program.

12.3
SPECIAL-PURPOSE LANGUAGES

Some languages provide a way for the programmer to describe what is wanted without the programmer having to specify each instruction in detail. These languages, called **special-purpose languages** or **problem-oriented lan-**

guages, use commands that are specifically designed to save large amounts of programming effort. Simulation, information retrieval, and text editing are some of the more common situations for which special-purpose languages are available.

Simulation

Simulation is the process of designing and conducting experiments using a mathematical model of a real system; the usual purpose is either to better understand the behavior of the system or to evaluate various strategies for the operation of the system. This quantitative technique has been applied by many business and government managers to assist them in their decision making. For example, simulation has been used for:

Financial planning and budgeting
Production scheduling and inventory control systems
Traffic planning in airports and highway networks
Routing of emergency vehicles, such as police cars, fire units, and ambulances
Scheduling and treating patients in health care facilities

Simulation programs can be written in general-purpose languages such as FORTRAN, PL/1, and BASIC; however, the use of special-purpose simulation languages can save a great deal of programming effort. Two of the most widely used simulation languages are **GPSS** (General Purpose System Simulation), developed by IBM, and **SIMSCRIPT,** developed by the Rand Corporation. These languages simplify the programming of simulations and provide conceptual frameworks for structuring the problem.

EXAMPLE 12.5   Queuing Models

A queue is a waiting line of units requiring service from one or more servers. Common examples of the existence of queues are listed below:

Units	Servers	Queues
Automobiles	Toll booths	Automobiles waiting to pay
Patients	Hospital beds	Patients waiting to enter hospital
Airplanes	Runways	Airplanes waiting to depart or to arrive
Computer jobs	Computer	Jobs not yet begun
Burning buildings	Fire engines	Buildings waiting to be extinguished

In recent years, many studies have used simulation models to analyze the structure of the types of queuing systems illustrated above. Typically, GPSS is the simulation language that is implemented.

To illustrate the advantage of such a language, consider the following GPSS statements:

```
TABLE        P3,20,20,25
  .
  .
  .
TABULATE   3
```

The first statement identifies a variable (P3) whose values are to be tabulated in a frequency-type table. The sequence of numbers 20,20,25 specifies that the first row of the table is to represent an upper limit of 20 for the variable, the increment from one row to the next is to be 20, and the table is to have 25 rows. The TABULATE statement is an executable statement which tabulates the necessary statistics for the variable P3, as identified in the TABLE statement.

For example, if P3 is defined in the program as "property damage in dollars due to fire," then part of the GPSS output would include the illustrative table below for a simulation of, say, 1000 fires:

TABLE 3
ENTRIES IN TABLE   MEAN ARGUMENT   . . .
            1000   200.516

	UPPER LIMIT	OBSERVED FREQUENCY . . .
	20	12
	40	55
25 rows	60	105
	.	.
	.	.
	500	3

Thus, the average property damage was $200,516 per fire; 12 fires resulted in damages less than $20,000; 55 fires incurred damages of between $20,000 and $40,000; and so forth. Note that we show only a partial table here; actual output would include other statistical measures and a seven-column table.

The important point to realize is the following: The two GPSS statements shown above plus a third assignment-like statement which we do not show result in the calculation and output of the above table; in FORTRAN, BASIC, or PL/1, at least 50 statements would be required to accomplish the same task.

Query

Managers often need information either for making decisions or for responding to requests from outside agencies, customers, or other departments. Frequently, these information needs are not known in advance, and programs are not available to give immediate answers. To better handle these "special" (often called ad hoc) inquiries, **query languages** have been developed. These special-purpose languages facilitate the programming of information retrieval; in many cases, nonprogrammers can learn the commands needed to retrieve information in a matter of minutes.

Several query languages are available from commercial software vendors. One example is a query language known as **ASAP,** which we illustrate next.

EXAMPLE 12.6   Query Language Example: ASAP

The Placement Director on a college campus frequently receives calls from firms looking for students with certain backgrounds and skills. Often, because of limited time and poor files, the director may not do a thorough search of eligible students.

For instance, assume a firm is looking for a graduating senior with a major in economics, a B or better average, willingness to travel, and a proficiency in Spanish. If the placement office has a computerized pool of student applicants, then the director or an assistant could quickly write the following ASAP program:

```
FOR ALL OF THE STUDENTS WITH
        GPA  > 3.0                AND
        CLASS  = 'SENIOR'    AND
        MAJOR = 'ECN'         AND
        TRAVEL = 'HEAVY'     AND
        SKILL    = 'SPANISH'
PRINT: LAST-NAME, FIRST-NAME, ADDRESS, PHONE
```

This program searches the student file and provides a list of names, addresses, and phone numbers of all students who meet the criteria specified by the firm.

Text Editing

Text-editor languages permit a user to create, maintain, and produce final copy of English running text via the computer. Increasingly, these special-purpose languages are used by secretaries, newspaper editors, book publishers, and others to generate final copy of letters, reports, articles, stories, books, and other text.

Once the original manuscript is typed and stored by the computer, all modifications (deletions, additions, replacements, exchanges) are performed by typing instructions to the computer. In other words, subsequent drafts of the manuscript need not be typed in again in their entirety—only the changes need to be typed in. The end result is a clean, final manuscript at great savings in typing costs.

One popular text editor, developed by IBM, is known as **ATS** (Administrative Terminal System), which is specifically designed for secretarial use in offices. Another text editor, called the **ESI system,** is illustrated below:

Replace the word "run" in the fifth paragraph with "ran"
Replace ":" in the twentieth paragraph with ";"
Indent the fourth sentence in the third paragraph
Delete and close the expression "as is true in all cases"
Insert "Another example includes the following:" before the third line in the tenth paragraph
Start a new page with the paragraph ending with the expression "costs have increased"
Exchange the third paragraph with the fifth paragraph

As you can see, text-editor languages have a decided advantage over the classical "brute force" approach to editing. In addition, languages such as ATS include commands for printing multiple copies of final text, and systems such as ESI can be used to prepare final copy for systems which computerize the typesetting of newspapers, magazines, and books.

Word processing is a new development in office technology that is related to text editing. Word-processing equipment automates the production of letters, reports, and lists. These machines, in addition to other functions, provide text manipulation, revision, and formatting capabilities.

Computer technology and word processing technology are undergoing integration. Equipment is now available that allows machine-readable business data from computer files to be transferred to office documents without keying the data. Thus variable data, such as names, addresses, salutations, and dollar amounts can be merged with prerecorded standard text. Under this approach, for example, a university's admission office can generate individualized acceptance or rejection letters to thousands of applicants without the use of typists.

CHAPTER 13

Selected Cases

13.1   CASE I: REPLACEMENT CONSULTANTS, INC.
13.2   CASE II: ARMS (AUTOMATED REPAIR AND MAINTENANCE SYSTEM)
13.3   CASE III: INVENTORY SIMULATION ASSOCIATES, INC.

The **case method** of study pioneered by Harvard Business School is a widely used approach to study real problems. A **case** is a written description of a realistic problem that requires a solution. The problem scenario is usually based on actual events, although certain aspects might be fictionalized (to protect the innocent, of course).

Typically, the instructor assigns the case either to individuals or to teams of individuals. The latter is more common because large-scale, real-world management problems are usually best solved by groups or teams made up of individuals having expertise in different areas.

The solution of a case generally includes an oral presentation summarizing a typewritten report that outlines the problem, describes solutions or analyses, and recommends courses of action to be taken by management. This closely parallels the approach taken by large governmental agencies, corporations, and consultants.

In short, the case method of study gives the student an opportunity to actively participate in the creative solution of a "meaty" problem in an environment that effectively simulates real-world conditions.

13.1
CASE I: REPLACEMENT CONSULTANTS, INC.

The **replacement problem** is concerned with determining the best time period (week, month, year) in which to replace a capital asset (automobile, machine, bus, ship). As you might know from owning a car, these types of assets typically

382

are characterized by *operating costs* which increase over time and *salvage values* (resale prices) which decrease over time. As the car gets older, the increases in operating costs, which include the costs of maintenance, repair, and regular operation, tend to favor a short ownership period. As time goes on, however, the resale price of a car tends to decrease more slowly than previously. This means that the *capital* or *depreciation cost,* which is the difference between the price you paid and the price you get on resale, decreases from year to year, on the average. For example, a car that costs $5,000 when new might resell for $4,000 one year later, which gives a capital cost of $1,000 for the first year. Now, if it can be sold for $2,800 at the end of three years and for $2,400 at the end of four years, then the capital cost in the fourth year is $400. Annual capital costs, therefore, tend to decrease as the years go by, which favors a long ownership period, all other things equal (such as styling, prestige, and so on).

This dilemma now raises an interesting question: Since operating costs favor a short ownership period and capital costs favor a long ownership period, what is the best period to replace the asset? One way of resolving this tradeoff is to define total cost per time period as the sum of capital costs and operating costs divided by the number of time periods and to replace the asset in the time period for which this cost is a minimum. In the scenario which follows, we present only one replacement model of the many that are available.

Suppose that, once you get your degree, you are hired as a consultant by Replacement Consultants, Inc., one of the many management consulting firms that operate nationally. You have been assigned to advise the administrator of a very large urban hospital. Specifically, you are to recommend how many years the hospital is to keep its fleet of ambulances before replacing them.

Fortunately, detailed records have been kept on the costs of operating each ambulance. On the average, it costs $2,800 to operate an ambulance in its first year, which includes the costs of insurance, gasoline, regular maintenance, and repairs. Each year thereafter, it is estimated that the cost increases by $300 per year on the average.

A new ambulance of this type costs $15,000. Experience shows that the used ambulance price decreases by a *depreciation factor* of 20 percent each year on the average. Thus, after one year, the ambulance can be sold for $12,000 (or $0.8 \times 15,000$). This gives a capital cost in the first year of $3,000 (or $15,000 - $12,000).

It follows that the total cost in the first year is $5,800, or $2,800 for operating cost and $3,000 for capital cost. Sample calculations of total cost per year for each of the first three years are shown in Table 13.1. Note that column 3 is a running sum of column 2; each entry in column 4 is 80 percent of the preceding entry in that column; each entry in column 5 is the new ambulance price ($15,000) minus the corresponding entry in column 4; column 6 is the sum of corresponding elements in columns 3 and 5; and column 7 is column 6 divided by column 1.

As you can see from this table, it would cost $5,800 per year to replace an ambulance every year. If each ambulance were replaced every two years, then the cost per year would drop to $5,650 per ambulance. This cost further drops to

TABLE 13.1   *Cost Calculations for Ambulance Replacement Problem*

1	2	3	4	5	6	7
REPLACEMENT PERIOD (END OF YEAR)	OPERATING COST FOR PERIOD ($)	CUMULATIVE OPERATING COST ($)	SALVAGE PRICE ($)	CUMULATIVE CAPITAL COST ($)	CUMULATIVE TOTAL COST ($)	TOTAL COST PER YEAR ($)
1	2,800	2,800	12,000	3,000	5,800	5,800
2	3,100	5,900	9,600	5,400	11,300	5,650
3	3,400	9,300	7,680	7,320	16,620	5,540

$5,540 per year per ambulance when the ambulances are replaced every three years. The best replacement cycle, that which yields minimum total cost per year, is yet to be found.

In addition to the analysis of the current ambulance, called the Deluxe Model, the administrator wants you to analyze costs and replacement cycles for the Economy Model, costing $10,000. After some effort, you have located a hospital that has been using this particular model. Luckily, this hospital also is a client of Replacement Consultants, Inc., so they cooperated in providing the following estimates: $2,500 to operate the ambulance in the first year, thereafter increasing by approximately $500 per year; average decrease of 30 percent per year in the used ambulance price.

Within two weeks, the administrator would like you to present your analyses for each ambulance and to make recommendations as to which model to purchase and how long it should be kept.

Trudging home one night with your briefcase full of facts and figures, the following thoughts occurred to you: "I would be insane to analyze this problem by hand. It makes more sense to program it for our computer. In fact, if I make the program general enough, we could use it for any ambulance and hospital in the city, the country, even the world! Besides, I would not only pass myself off as an ambulance expert but also as an applications programmer of the first magnitude."

The following suggestions might be helpful in designing your program:

1. Design your program using the principles discussed in Sections 11.1 to 11.3.
2. If your compiler supports it, use structured FORTRAN commands (see Section 11.6).
3. Make sure you answer the following questions:
   a. How often should the $15,000 ambulance be replaced?
   b. On the average, how much would such a replacement policy cost per year?
   c. Compared to the best cost in part b, how much more would it cost per year to replace the ambulance every 4 years? every 10 years?

d. How would you characterize the $10,000 ambulance compared to the $15,000 ambulance?
e. How often and at what average cost per year should you replace the $10,000 ambulance?
f. Which ambulance do you recommend? Should you consider factors or criteria other than financial?
g. Which ambulance would you recommend if the administrator's policy was to replace an ambulance every eight years? Every five years?

4. Design your program to include the option of an exit from the table loop as soon as total cost per year begins to increase.
5. Design your program to print the best replacement period and its associated total cost per period.
6. The figures given for operating cost in the first year, increase in operating cost, and percent depreciation factor are *estimates* of actual values. In reality, these estimates can be in error. Design your program to perform and output **sensitivity analysis** based on ±20-percent errors as shown in Table 13.2. Three tables of this type should be printed for each model: the first for a −20-percent error in the depreciation factor; the second for the expected depreciation factor; and the third for a +20-percent error in the depreciation factor. This means that depreciation factors of 16 percent, 20 percent, and 24 percent would be considered for the $15,000 ambulance. Better yet, let the user specify through data input just what ± percent error is to be considered.
7. You might try using the same computer program to analyze replacement periods and costs for some popular automobiles. Try to get good estimates

TABLE 13.2   *Best Replacement Cycle and Associated Total Cost per Year*

	−20% ERROR IN OPERAT-ING COST INCREASE	EXPECTED OPERAT-ING COST INCREASE	+20% ERROR IN OPERAT-ING COST INCREASE
−20% ERROR IN FIRST YEAR OPERATING COST	XX YEARS $XXXXX	XX YEARS $XXXXX	XX YEARS $XXXXX
EXPECTED FIRST YEAR OPERATING COST	XX YEARS $XXXXX	XX YEARS $XXXXX	XX YEARS $XXXXX
+20% ERROR IN FIRST YEAR OPERATING COST	XX YEARS $XXXXX	XX YEARS $XXXXX	XX YEARS $XXXXX

for input data by asking around, class discussion, and personal experience. Don't forget to include the effects of differences in gas mileage. Any surprises?

13.2
CASE II: ARMS
(AUTOMATED REPAIR AND
MAINTENANCE SYSTEM)

A municipality maintains a fleet of vehicles, including automobiles, vans, trucks, buses, pay loaders, and others. Because of energy problems, rising prices, and wages, the costs of running this fleet continue to rise.

Ms. Sterlina Moss, the newly hired manager of the physical plant, has the responsibility of reviewing the condition of all assets within the municipality, including the fleet. For the fleet, she must formulate a replacement policy on these vehicles as well as evaluate lease versus buy financial alternatives.

Currently the municipality has its own maintenance and repair facility. When a vehicle needs maintenance, a work order is filled out specifying the problem. When work is completed, the parts cost and labor cost are listed on this form so the department owning the vehicle can be billed.

Unfortunately, Ms. Moss has quite a task because records to date have been maintained manually. Worse yet, these records are incomplete: an inventory of each vehicle is not available and no history of operating costs for each vehicle can be determined.

Luckily, she remembered an article in the newspaper about college students helping local businessmen find solutions to some of their business problems. So she contacted Professor Harvey Core, who teaches a systems analysis course, and arranged to have a team of students investigate the maintenance facility. Ms. Moss, however, placed two constraints on the team:

1. Although the municipality does have a computer, no funds would be available for additional hardware.
2. A minimum amount of time should be required of the maintenance supervisor in providing data for any automated system.

During the previous school term, a team of Professor Core's students studied the problem and submitted the accompanying report, entitled Automated Repair and Maintenance System (ARMS). This school term Professor Core has instructed you (or your team) to write the necessary FORTRAN program(s).

Automated Repair and Maintenance System (ARMS)

I. Objectives
    A. Produce a monthly report of vehicles owned by the municipality.
    B. Produce a cumulative record of maintenance cost incurred for each vehicle.
II. System Flowchart—The design of the new maintenance reporting system is shown pictorially in the system flowchart of Figure 13.1.

FIGURE 13.1   System Flowchart

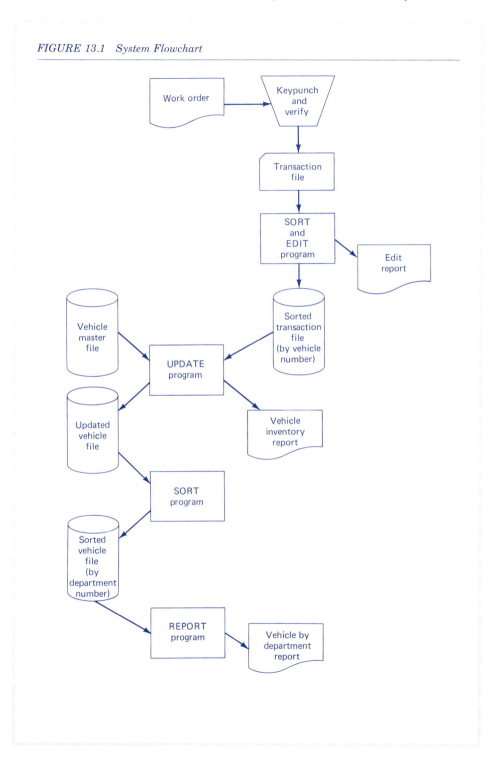

III. Reports (see print charts)
    A. Edit run—Lists all transactions to be processed within the month
    B. Vehicle inventory—Lists all vehicles within municipality
    C. Vehicle by department—Lists vehicles owned by each department
IV. Files
    A. Vehicle Master File

Column	Description
1–4	Vehicle number
5–6	Department number
7–8	Type of vehicle (code)
9–10	Manufacturer (code)
11–12	Year made
13–14	Year acquired
15–20	Purchase cost
21–25	Odometer reading at date of purchase
26–30	Odometer reading at start of year
31–35	Current odometer reading
36–39	Cumulative parts cost, previous year (including no cost from current year)
40–43	Cumulative labor cost, previous year (including no cost from current year)
44–47	Year to date part cost
48–51	Year to date labor cost
52–55	Current period, part cost
56–59	Current period, labor cost

    B. Transaction File—Monthly Maintenance Transactions

Record Type	Column	Description
New vehicle (add record to file)	1–4	Vehicle number
	5	Action code = 1
	6	Department number
	7–8	Type of vehicle (code)
	9–10	Manufacturer (code)
	11–12	Year made
	13–14	Year acquired
	15–20	Purchase cost
	21–25	Original odometer reading
	26–30	Odometer reading at start of year
	31–35	Current odometer reading
Sold vehicle (delete record from file)	1–4	Vehicle number
	5	Action code = 2
Maintained vehicle (update cost information in existing record)	1–4	Vehicle number
	5	Action code = 3
	36–40	Current odometer reading
	41–44	Current cost, parts
	45–48	Current cost, labor

V. Program Specifications

    A. Edit and Sort Phase
        Input
          Transaction file
        Process
          1. Sort record into vehicle number sequence
          2. Edit checks
             a. Vehicle number must be in ascending order sequence
             b. No vehicle number is greater than 975
             c. Valid action codes are 1, 2, and 3 only
             d. If action code = 3, the current cost of parts should not be greater than $500 nor the current cost of labor greater than $250
        Printed Output
          Edit report (see print layout)—all transactions are listed; however, place an asterisk in front of any record that has an error
        Other Output
          Valid transaction file (see layout as input file)—any record with error is not to be placed on this file

    B. Update Phase
        Input
          1. Transaction file
          2. Vehicle master file
          3. Code tables
        Process
          1. Action code 1—add record to file; set cost fields to zero
          2. Action code 2—remove entire record from vehicle file
          3. Action code 3
             a. Add current cost of parts in the transaction file to year-to-date cost of parts in the master file.
             b. Replace current cost of parts in the master file by the current cost of parts in the transaction file.
             c. Add current cost of labor in the transaction file to year-to-date cost of labor in the master file.
             d. Replace current cost of labor in the master file by the current cost of labor in the transaction file.
             e. Replace current odometer reading field in master file with current odometer reading from transaction file.
        Printed Output
          Printed vehicle inventory report (see print layout)
        Other Output
          Update master file

    C. Sort Phase
        Input
          Vehicle master file (vehicle number sequence)

Process

Sort on department number

Other Output

Vehicle master file (department number sequence)

D. Report Phase

Input

1. Vehicle master file
2. Code table

Process

1. Cost field in output report—includes total of parts and labor
2. Cost per mile—represents total costs (parts and labor) since acquisition divided by total miles since acquisition

Printed Output

Vehicle by department report (see print chart)

For all printed output, the following descriptions should be used in place of code numbers.

Type of Vehicle		*Manufacturer*		*Department*	
Code	*Description*	*Code*	*Name*	*Code*	*Name*
1	Pickup	1	Ford	1	Land and grounds
2	Sedan	2	Plymouth	2	Administration
3	Jeep	3	International	3	Recreation
4	Forklift	4	Willys		
5	Van	5	Chevrolet		
6	Trailer	6	Baker		
7	Tractor				

PROGRAM TITLE __ARMS__

PROGRAMMER OR DOCUMENTALIST _____

CHART TITLE __EDIT RUN__

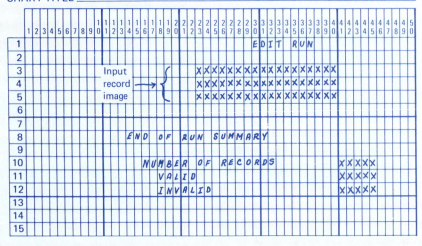

PROGRAM TITLE ____ ARMS
PROGRAMMER OR DOCUMENTALIST ____
CHART TITLE ____ VEHICLE INVENTORY

```
                                        VEHICLE INVENTORY
                                        REPORTING PERIOD
                                        XX/XX/XX TO  XX/XX/XX

 VEHICLE    VEHICLE         MANUFACTURER        DEPARTMENT              CURRENT     YEAR TO DATE   COST SINCE
 NUMBER     TYPE                                                        COSTS       COSTS          PURCHASE

 XXXX       AAAAAAAA    AAAAAAAAAAAAAA    AAAAAAAAAAAAAAAAAA            XXXX        XXXX           XXXX
 XXXX       AAAAAAAA                                                   XXXX        XXXX           XXXX
  .          .                                                          .           .              .
  .          .                                                          .           .              .
  .          .                                                          .           .              .

                                                                TOTALS  XXXXX       XXXXX          XXXXX


 END OF RUN SUMMARY

    RECORDS IN-MASTER           XXX

    TRANSACTIONS PROCESSED
       ADDS                     XXX
       DELETES                  XXX
       UPDATES  (XXX)

    RECORDS OUT-MASTER          XXX
```

PROGRAM TITLE ____ ARMS
PROGRAMMER OR DOCUMENTALIST ____
CHART TITLE ____ VEHICLE BY DEPARTMENT

Note: New page for each department

```
                        VEHICLE BY DEPARTMENT REPORT
                        PERIOD XX/XX/XX  TO  XX/XX/XX


 DEPARTMENT    AAAAAAAAAAAAAAA


                                        C   O   S   T   S
 VEHICLE       VEHICLE       CURRENT        YEAR TO        SINCE
 NUMBER        TYPE          MONTH          DATE           PURCHASE

 XXXX          AAAAAAAA      XXXX           XXXX           XXXX
 XXXX          AAAAAAAA      XXXX           XXXX           XXXX
   (             (             (              (              (
 DEPARTMENT TOTALS           XXXXX          XXXXX          XXXXX
```

MASTER FILE DATA

```
         1 2 3 4 5 6 7 8 9 10111213141516171819202122232425262728293031323334353637383940414243444546474849505152535455565758596061626364 65
0593  102017878  4000150001500015000000000000000000000000000000000   . . .
0613  307037476  1000060000600006000000000000000000000000000000000
0645  303037070  3500400004000040000000000000000000000000000000000
0659  202027979  5000000000000000000000000000000000000000000000000
0667  202057577  2500022000022000220000000000000000000000000000000
0668  302057676  4200300003000030000000000000000000000000000000000
0674  104067777  8000012000012000012000000000000000000000000000000
0676  102017878  4500150001500015000000000000000000000000000000000
0677  302057878  4500120001200012000000000000000000000000000000000
0678  306036969  6200650006500065000000000000000000000000000000000
0679  103046565  2900850008500085000000000000000000000000000000000   . . .
0688  201017075  3600450004500045000000000000000000000000000000000
0689  205057276  3000330003300033000000000000000000000000000000000
0692  301037577  3200210002100021000000000000000000000000000000000
0695  107037676  1015003100031000310000000000000000000000000000000
0696  202027979  4800000000000000000000000000000000000000000000000
0699  101056161  2600780007800078000000000000000000000000000000000   . . .
0798  103047072  2900480004800048000000000000000000000000000000000
0804  104047374  2500060000600006000000000000000000000000000000000
0805  302017575  2300520005200052000000000000000000000000000000000
0806  106067878  8000065000065000650000000000000000000000000000000
0807  202057778  3950170001700017000000000000000000000000000000000
0838  105057779  4000090000900009000000000000000000000000000000000
0841  301017679  3700260002600026000000000000000000000000000000000
```

TRANSACTION FILE DATA—MONTH 1

```
1 2 3 4 5 6 7 8 9 10 11 12 13 14 15 16 17 18 19 20 21 22 23 24 25 26 27 28 29 30 31 32 33 34 35 36 37 38 39 40 41 42 43 44 45 46 47 48 49 50 51 52 53 54 55 56 57 58 59 60 61 62 63 64 65
06992
0842120201797900500000000000000000
0844130105797900600000000000000000
06453                               42000     52    75
08063                                 775     10    10
06593                                3275    150    60
06923                               25788     40    25
06133                                6250     35    50
07983                               52000     95   125
08414                               27500     14    45
09793                               85400     37   350
06743                                1200    625   125
```

TRANSACTION FILE DATA—MONTH 2

```
1 2 3 4 5 6 7 8 9 10 11 12 13 14 15 16 17 18 19 20 21 22 23 24 25 26 27 28 29 30 31 32 33 34 35 36 37 38 39 40 41 42 43 44 45 46 47 48 49 50 51 52 53 54 55 56 57 58 59 60 61 62 63 64 65
06782
06773                               13900    150    75
06883                               48375     25    50
05933                               17275    175    70
06673                               22500     45    50
08043                                6700     15    10
```

13.3
CASE III:
INVENTORY SIMULATION
ASSOCIATES, INC.

Fresh out of college you have been hired by a dynamic management consulting firm called Inventory Simulation Associates, Inc., otherwise known as ISA. As the name of the firm suggests, it specializes in performing inventory simulations for clients in government, nonprofit institutions, industry, and other organizations willing to pay stiff consulting fees.

In your job interview with ISA you passed yourself off as an expert in inventory theory and simulation, among other things, based on the strength of a course in each area. So, in their infinite wisdom, the management of ISA has assigned you to study the inventory policies of Gotham City Hospital's (GCH) blood bank. Your first act in tackling this problem was to review your class notes on inventory theory and simulation, portions of which follow.

An **inventory** may be thought of as a stock of an item (material, machine, spare part, money, consumable product, and so on) that gets "added to" and "depleted from" over time. In retail and nonprofit environments, inventories improve the degree of customer service by absorbing variabilities in customer demands and replenishment times. For example, the inventory of blood in a hospital serves to satisfy a critical need whenever patients require (demand) blood. In manufacturing environments, inventories smooth the variability in work force levels. For example, the same number of workers can be used during slow periods of demand as during busy periods of demand by building up inventories during slow periods and depleting inventories during busy periods.

Inventories are pervasive and expensive to maintain. The U.S. business investment in physical materials inventory amounts to more than $200 billion. For General Motors Corporation alone, this investment runs over $4 billion. For the reasons mentioned, procedures to best manage inventories are topics of great interest to organizations.

In managing an inventory, two decisions need to be made: (1) When should an order be placed to replenish inventory? (2) What should be the size of this order?

In recent years, mathematical approaches to answering these questions have been very successful. One such approach, the **economic order quantity (EOQ) inventory model,** specifies the *order quantity* (Q) and *reorder point* (R, the inventory level below which a replenishment order is placed) that minimizes total inventory cost per time period.

Total inventory cost is defined as the sum of ordering cost, carrying cost, and shortage cost. *Ordering cost* is the cost associated with placing a replenishment order. It includes the clerical and administrative costs associated with processing, expediting, receiving, inspecting, and storing the order. *Carrying cost* is made up of the explicit and implicit costs of maintaining and owning the inventory. Explicit costs include the cost of storage space, handling costs, insurance, taxes, utility costs, and costs of administering inventory and maintaining records. A significant implicit component of carrying cost is called the *opportunity cost.* This cost reflects the rate of return that a company might expect to earn on the money tied up in inventory. For example, if General Motors could invest its $4 billion inventory in Treasury Notes yielding 9-percent interest per year, then it could earn $360 million in one year. This $360 million represents their opportunity cost (lost income). *Shortage cost* includes the costs of running out of stock when items are requested. These costs are difficult to estimate, but include costs relating to backorders, lost sales, ill will, and so on.

Simulation is a methodology for conducting experiments using a mathematical model of the real system. It is primarily concerned with describing or predicting the behavior of a real system. Its usual purpose is either to design a new system or to modify behavior in an existing system. Simulation is particularly useful either as a low-cost substitute for actual experimentation on the real system or as the only approach for studying the behavior of a proposed system. For example, computer programs have been designed to simulate traffic flow systems in cities for the purpose of establishing the best configuration of computer-controlled traffic signals.

A type of simulation called **Monte Carlo simulation** is used to reconstruct the behavior of phenomena that can be described according to rules of probability. For example, suppose that the number of days between the placement and receipt of an inventory order (called *lead time*) is described by the following:

Lead Time (Number of Days)	Relative Frequency (Probability)
1	0.2
2	0.5
3	0.3
	1.0

This says that the probability of receiving an order one day after placing it is 0.2, or that this occurs 20 percent of the time. Similarly, a lead time of 2 days occurs 50 percent of the time; a lead time of 3 days occurs the remaining 30 percent of the time.

One way to simulate this process is to mark 10 poker chips as follows: write the digit 1 on two chips, the digit 2 on five chips, and the digit 3 on three chips. Mix these up and select a poker chip without looking. Chances are 2 in 10 (probability = 0.2) that you select a chip marked with a 1; 5 in 10 that you select a chip marked with a 2; and 3 in 10 that you select a chip marked with a 3. Since these probabilities are identical to the probabilities describing the real process, it follows that we can use the poker chips to reconstruct or simulate the lead times.

"Poker chips" on the computer are represented by subroutines called *random number generators*. For example, when the subroutine below is called, it returns an integer random number between 1 and 100 as the dummy variable RN.

```
SUBROUTINE RANDOM (SEED,RN)
INTEGER SEED, RN
SEED = MOD(25211*SEED,32768)
X = FLOAT(SEED)/FLOAT(32768)
RN = INT(FLOAT(100)*X) + 1
RETURN
END
```

By an integer random number between 1 and 100 we mean that the likelihood (probability) that any one number is generated is the same as any other number. To illustrate the simulation of lead times by this approach, consider the following:

Lead Time	Random Number Range
1	1–20 ⟵ 20-percent probability
2	21–70 ⟵ 50-percent probability
3	71–100 ⟵ 30-percent probability

Thus, we assign 20 random numbers to a lead time of 1 day, the next 50 random numbers to a lead time of 2 days, and the last 30 random numbers to a lead time of 3 days. If subroutine RANDOM generates, say, the random number 32, then we say that a lead time of 2 days has been simulated, since the probability of getting a random number in the interval 21–70 is 50 percent, the same as the probability of a 2-day lead time. You should confirm that the five random numbers below correspond to the simulated lead times that are indicated. (It's like having 100 poker chips.)

Sample Random Numbers Generated by Subroutine RANDOM	Simulated Days of Lead Time
90	3
15	1
60	2
70	2
81	3

The dummy variable SEED must be initialized by the calling program to any 5-digit integer value. It simply represents a starting number (seed) that gets the random number generator started. *Make sure you do not reinitialize SEED in the calling program each time you call RANDOM.* Otherwise, you will get the same random number each time you call RANDOM.

After studying these notes, you made an appointment with the head administrator at GCH. After lengthy talks with the administrator and staff, you came away with the following facts:

1. The management of blood by blood banks is an important function of health care delivery systems. A *blood bank* within the hospital performs the functions of procurement, storage, processing, and distribution of blood. The hospital's blood bank places replenishment orders with a regional blood bank that serves member hospitals.

2. Inventory costs have been estimated as follows:

   Ordering cost: $50 per order
   Carrying cost: $0.10 per unit per day
   Shortage cost: $2 per unit backordered

   The shortage cost reflects a loan arrangement with the regional blood bank in Gotham City whereby if GCH incurs a temporary shortage of blood, it can *immediately* borrow units at a cost of $2.00 per unit. The agreement also specifies the replacement of the borrowed blood units when GCH receives its next replenishment supply.

3. GCH places replenishment orders with the regional blood bank for 400 units whenever its inventory level drops below 300 units. A study of the records shows that the ordered blood always arrives 2 days after the order. Thus, lead time is 2 days and, according to hospital inventory policy, R = 300 and Q = 400.

4. A study of daily demand (requirements by patients) for units of blood over a recent 200-day period shows the following:

Number of Units Demanded Daily	Mid-point Demand	Number of Days in Which Specified Demand Occurred	Corresponding Relative Frequency (Probability)	Random Number Range
0 but under 50		0		
50 but under 70	60	14	0.07	1– 7
70 but under 90	80	28	0.14	8– 21
90 but under 110	100	36	0.18	22– 39
110 but under 130	120	58	0.29	40– 68
130 but under 150	140	32	0.16	69– 84
150 but under 170	160	22	0.11	85– 95
170 but under 190	180	10	0.05	96–100
190 or over		0		
		200	1.00	

Thus 7 percent (14/200) of the days demand was between 50 and 70 units, 14 percent (28/200) of the days demand was between 70 and 90 units, and so on. For simulation purposes we can say that 7 percent is the probability of 60 units, 14 percent the probability of 80 units, 18 percent the probability of 100 units, and so on. Note that the random number ranges are consistent with these probabilities.

Based on the above information, it seemed like a good idea to get a better feel for the process by "hand" simulating a 20-day period. This is shown in Table 13.3.

Based on this 20-day simulation, certain characteristics about the process came to light:

1. To simulate Day 1, we arbitrarily set the beginning inventory level to some "reasonable" figure (500 in this case). Then we generate a random number to simulate demand for that day. The random number 17 translates into a demand of 80 units. This gives us an ending inventory of 420 for Day 1. The carrying cost of $42 is based on the physical *ending* inventory (420 × 0.10). Since ending inventory is above the reorder point given by R = 300, we do not place an order in Day 1. Thus, order cost is zero. No shortages were incurred in Day 1, so shortage cost also is zero. This gives a total cost of $42 for Day 1.

2. The beginning inventory for the next day is based on the ending inventory for the previous day; however, when the ending inventory is negative (units have been backordered), then the beginning physical inventory for the next day is zero. (See Days 9, 11, 12.)

3. An order is triggered whenever ending inventory drops below R = 300, providing no order is currently outstanding. In other words, by policy a maximum of one outstanding order is allowed at any one time. When an order is launched, a $50 cost is incurred. (See Days 3, 6, 9, 12, 16.) The order for Q = 400 is placed at the end of the day. It takes two days for the order to arrive, so it is available by the beginning of the third day following the order. For example, an order for 400 units is placed at the end of Day 3, it arrives at the end of Day 5, and can be utilized in Day 6. Thus, Day 6 has an entry of 400 in the column labeled "Units Received."

4. A shortage cost of $2 per unit is incurred whenever ending inventory is negative. (See Days 8, 10, 11.) Note that backordered units must be replaced as soon as replenishment arrives. For example, the 100 units backordered in Day 8 were "returned" to the regional blood bank in Day 9. Thus only 300 units (400 − 100) were received in Day 9.

5. Based on this short simulation, the hospital's current inventory policy of R = 300 and Q = 400 results in the following average cost estimates:

Carrying cost per day = $16.70
Ordering cost per day =   12.50
Shortage cost per day =   22.00
Total cost per day   = $51.20

At this time, certain realizations came to mind: First, to get a better cost per day estimate, I should simulate many more days than 20. This would give me more confidence that my estimates are accurate. It's kind of like estimating whether or not a coin is balanced by flipping it 20 times versus, say, 1,000 times. A simulation of 1,000 days would be preferable, so I'd better computerize

TABLE 13.3 *Inventory Hand Simulation*

DAY	UNITS OF BEGINNING INVENTORY	UNITS RECEIVED	RANDOM NUMBER FOR DEMAND	UNITS OF DEMAND	UNITS OF ENDING INVENTORY	CARRYING COST IN $	ORDERING COST IN $	SHORTAGE COST IN $	TOTAL COST IN $
1	500	0	17	80	420	42	0	0	42
2	420	0	25	100	320	32	0	0	32
3	320	0	37	100	220	22	50	0	72
4	220	0	65	120	100	10	0	0	10
5	100	0	23	100	0	0	0	0	0
6	0	400	72	140	260	26	50	0	76
7	260	0	98	180	80	8	0	0	8
8	80	0	96	180	-100	0	0	200	200
9	0	300	88	160	140	14	50	0	64
10	140	0	92	160	-20	0	0	40	40
11	0	0	30	100	-120	0	0	200	200
12	0	280	28	100	180	18	50	0	68
13	180	0	9	80	100	10	0	0	10
14	100	0	15	80	20	2	0	0	2
15	20	400	12	80	340	34	0	0	34
16	340	0	55	120	220	22	50	0	72
17	220	0	5	60	160	16	0	0	16
18	160	0	2	60	100	10	0	0	10
19	100	400	50	120	380	38	0	0	38
20	380	0	20	80	300	30	0	0	30
Total	3540	—	—	2200	—	334	250	440	1024
Average	177	—	—	110	—	16.70	12.50	22.00	51.20

this process if I don't want to be a glutton for punishment. Second, it makes sense to try different R − Q combinations. Maybe I can suggest a better inventory policy?

Further thought resulted in the following additional programming suggestions:

1. Incorporate the principles discussed in Sections 11.1–11.3.
2. Use structured FORTRAN commands if possible (Section 11.6).
3. Input the ranges and increments for R and Q.
4. Reset the random number seed for each new R − Q combination. This ensures the same set of demands for each policy, thereby isolating the effect that a new R − Q has on total cost per day.
5. Store total cost per day in a two-dimensional array, where rows represent reorder points and columns represent order quantities.
6. Output of the inventory simulation table as in Table 13.3 should be optional. It is primarily used to debug the program.
7. It might be of interest to vary the cost input data by, say, ±20 percent. This allows us to assess the sensitivity of the best inventory policy to errors in estimating the cost data.
**8. Modify the simulation to include probabilistic lead times. Use the lead time data on page 395.

Answers to Selected Follow-up Exercises

CHAPTER 2

1. (a) Acceptable. (b) Acceptable. (c) Unacceptable; begins with number. (d) Acceptable. (e) Unacceptable; special character. (f) Acceptable. (g) Unacceptable; special character. (h) Unacceptable; more than six characters. (i) Acceptable. (j) Unacceptable; special character, more than six characters. (k) Acceptable; not recommended. (l) Acceptable.

2. (a) Unacceptable constant; comma. (b) Integer constant. (c) Real constant. (d) Real constant. (e) Real constant. (f) Real constant. (g) Real constant. (h) Unacceptable; comma. (i) Integer constant.

3. (a) Real variable. (b) Integer variable. (c) Integer variable. (d) Real variable. (e) Real variable. (f) Integer variable. (g) Unacceptable variable. (h) Real variable.

4. (a) Variable must appear to left of =:

    A = B + C

   (b) Two operation symbols next to each other.
   (c) Variable must appear to left of =:

    AGE = 5.

   (d) Incorrect two assignments. Change to:

    X = 5.3
    Y = 5.3

5.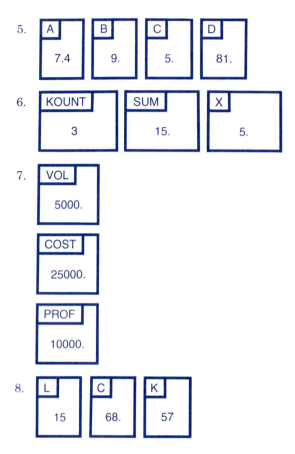

A	B	C	D
7.4	9.	5.	81.

6.

KOUNT	SUM	X
3	15.	5.

7.

VOL
5000.

COST
25000.

PROF
10000.

8.

L	C	K
15	68.	57

9. (a) CABE − 100.
   (b) 5∗K − 1
   (c) 7.∗∗Q
   (d) Undefined; execution error because base is negative. See footnote 2.
   (e) OK. Not considered mixed mode. Y∗∗2 computed faster than Y∗∗2., since the latter uses logs.

10. 85.77778

11. (a) 116.
    (b) 28.
    (c) 28.
    (d) 8.5
    (e) 4.
    (f) 4.
    (g) 10.5

12. (a) X∗∗(I + 1)
    (b) X∗∗I + 1.
    (c) S∗∗2/(P − 1.)

(d) (X − A)∗∗2/(P − 1.)
(e) (Y − 3.∗∗(X − 1.) + 2.)∗∗5
(f) (7. − X)∗∗(1./2.) Why would (7. − X)∗∗(1/2) give incorrect results?
(g) ((X − A)∗∗2/(P − 1.))∗∗.5

13.   15.
1500.
1750.

14. (a) PRINT, 'THE NUMBER OF CREDITS IS', CREDIT
     (b) PRINT, 'CREDITS =', CREDIT, 'BALANCE DUE =', BALDUE

15. (a) 0.32E 08
     (b) 0.32E 08
     (c) 0.32E 08
     (d) −0.32E 08
     (e) 0.4576E-04
     (f) $.134 \times 10^{-5}$
     (g) $-.56 \times 10^{35}$

17. READ,ID,CREDIT,CPC,FEES

18. (a)   WRITE(6,75) ID,BALDUE
            75 FORMAT(1X,I5,F13.0)
     (b)   WRITE(6,75) ID,BALDUE
            75 FORMAT(1X,I10,F10.0)
     (c)   WRITE(6,75) BALDUE,ID
            75 FORMAT(1X,F10.2,I10)

19. (a)   WRITE(6,75) ID,BALDUE,CREDIT,TUIT
            75 FORMAT(1X,I6,F9.0,F5.0,F10.0)
     (b)   WRITE(6,75) ID,BALDUE,CREDIT,TUIT
            75 FORMAT(1X,I5,F10.2,F5.0,F10.2)
     (c)   WRITE(6,75) ID,BALDUE,CREDIT,TUIT
            75 FORMAT(1X,I5,F15.2,F7.0,F12.2)

20.

	1	2	3	4	5	6	7	8	9	1 0
1										
2		7	5	8	1					
3				1	7	5	0	.		
4										
5										
6										

21.   1 2 3 4 5 6 7 8 9 10 11 12 13 14 15 16 17 18 19 20 . . .
     (a) 758115.
     (b)   7581   15 .

      (Note: 15. can be anywhere in columns 11–20.)

22. I3 allows only three digits—ID is a four-digit number. F2.0 only allows less than 10. credits.

24.   INTEGER CREDIT,TUIT,BALDUE
    DATA CREDIT/15/
    TUIT = CREDIT*100
    BALDUE = TUIT + 250
    :
    :

25. Adds flexibility to the program by giving it the ability to process different values for these variables; otherwise, the program would have to be changed each time we process a different value for P, R, or N.

26.

	1 2 3 4 5 6 7 8 9 0	1 1 1 1 1 1 1 1 1 1 2	1 2 3 4 5 6 7 8 9 0	2 2 2 2 2 2 2 2 2 2 3	1 2 3 4 5 6 7 8 9 0	3 3 3 3 3 3 3 3 3 3 4	1 2 3 4 5 6 7 8 9 0
1							
2	1000.00		0.0150		2	1030.23	
3							

CHAPTER 3

1. (a) Expected output:

ID	BALDUE
543	2050.
70105	1450.

   (b) Expected output:

P	R	N	A
1000.	.015	4	1061.36
1000.	.015	20	1346.82

2. (a) $1061.36
   (b) $1346.82

3. (a) See answers to Exercise 1a.
   (b) Expected output:

P	R	N	A
1000.	.015	4	1061.36
1000.	.015	8	1126.49
1000.	.015	12	1195.60
1000.	.015	16	1268.96
1000.	.015	20	1346.82
1000.	.015	40	1813.95

CHAPTER 4

1. 5   READ(5,*) ID,CREDIT

2. It would never be executed in this program.

3. Loop excludes the READ statement. The results for the first student would be calculated and printed over and over again:

        101   1750.
        101   1750.
        101   1750.

         ⋮   ⋮

4. (a) Correct. (b) Correct. (c) Correct, but not recommended for readability. (d) LE must be enclosed in periods. (e) Mixed mode. Q is real and J + L is integer. (f) END is not an acceptable statement.

5. (a) True. (b) False. (c) True. (d) True. **Warning:** Generally it's not a good idea to test a real expression using .EQ. as the relational operator. For example, if D is determined by an arithmetic expression, an expected computational result of exactly 33. may not be achieved due to roundoff error in real arithmetic. (e) False. (f) True.

6. (a)

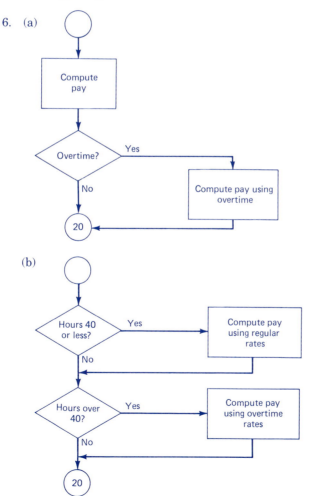

(b)

7. (a)   IF (ECA .GT. 17700.) GO TO 20
        FICA = SAL*.055
        GO TO 30
   20 FICA = 0.
   30 . . .
       :
       :

(b)   IF (ECA .GT. 17700.) FICA = 0.
        IF (ECA .LE. 17700.) FICA = SAL*.055
   30 . . .
       :
       :

(c)   FICA = 0.
        IF (ECA .LE. 17700.) FICA = SAL*.055
   30 . . .
       :

(d)   50 IF (A .GT. C) GO TO 100
        X = X + 3.
        Y = Y + 2.
        A = A + 1.
     GO TO 50
   100 . . .
       :

(e)   IF (A*C .LT. B/D) GO TO 10
        X = A + B
        D = B − A
        GO TO 75
   10 C = D/E
     F = F − 1.
   75 . . .
       :

ISAP	ISOP

9. (a)   5   5
  (b)   10   10

10. Example 4.4:

      IF (KOUNT .LE. 25) GO TO 10

    Example 4.5: Change data input for LOOPS from 3 to 25.

11. Use .LT. instead of .LE.

12. Infinite (unending) loop—KOUNT never reaches 3.

13. IF (ID .EQ. 0) STOP

14. Yes, you process data for a nonexisting student.

15. Depends on the computer system. The value in CREDIT can be any value, since the value in ID is the one being tested.

16. IF (CREDIT .LE. 0.) STOP   Any suitable test value can be used.

17. Fewer statements.
Don't have to know exact number of loops.

18. (a) No. (b) Yes. First time through BALDUE is undefined, which can result in an execution error, depending on the system. If the system initializes BALDUE to zero, then SUM would not include the last student's balance owed.

19. 101   1750.
    1750.
    102   1450.
    3200.
    103   1300.
    4500.
    4500. ⟵ Following last record check.
    ??? ⟵ "Out of data" error message on batch system; more data requested on time-sharing system.

20. After

         SUM = 0.

insert the following:

         SUMT = 0.
         SUMFEE = 0.

After

         SUM = SUM + BALDUE

insert the following:

         SUMT = SUMT + TUIT
         SUMFEE = SUMFEE + 250.

Change statement 30 to:

      30 WRITE(6,∗) SUMT,SUMFEE,SUM

Yes, for example, eliminate

         SUMFEE = 0.
         SUMFEE = SUMFEE + 250.

and make the following changes after the loop:

      30 SUMFEE = SUM − SUMT
         WRITE(6,∗) SUMT,SUMFEE,SUM

21. Before the loop insert:

         STU = 0.

Anywhere between the logical IF and the GO TO insert:

         STU = STU + 1.

After the GO TO insert:

```
30 AVE = SUM/STU
   WRITE(6,*) SUM,AVE
```

23.
```
       DATA SUM,CPC,FEE/0.,100.,250./
   10 READ(5,*) ID,CREDIT
       IF (ID .EQ. -99) GO TO 30
       TUIT = CREDIT*CPC
       BALDUE = TUIT + FEE
       .
       .
       .
```

Easy to initialize and change constants. Not recommended to initialize SUM if outer loop is inserted to process a different set of students.

24. (a) Program works, but the second IF simply could be replaced by GO TO 20.
(b) Yes, result always will be based on part-time student values.
(c) `IF (CREDIT .GE. 12.) TUIT = 1200.`
`IF (CREDIT .LT. 12.) TUIT = CREDIT*100.`
In flowchart, replace box labeled "Set tuition at $1200" with:

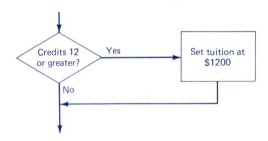

25.

```
      85.                    25.
     ↗                      ↗
 TOTMOV              TOTSTD
```

26. Yes, we need two possible *values* (such as 1 and 2) for one coded *variable,* not one possible value for two coded variables.

27. Before the initializations, insert

INTEGER TYPE

31.

Loop	N	K	NUM	SIZE	TP
1	4	1	6152	25.	6000.
2	4	2	4169	12.	2970.
3	4	3	5574	29.	6900.
4	4	4	3456	55.	12230.

33. Extra computations made with new version, but it's shorter and easier to follow.

CHAPTER 5

1. 514

2. JACK = 5
   JILL = 6
   IUP = 24
   KHILL = 19840

3.   READ(5,1) K,M,N
   1 FORMAT(I3,I4,I1)

4.   <u>1 2 3 4 5 6 7 8 9 10 11 12 13 14 ...</u>
      35 600   3

5. Place 7.553 anywhere in the first 10 columns. Change the first specification in the FORMAT to F10.3 and place 7553 in columns 7–10.

6. XJACK = 5.
   XJILL = .6
   UP = 24.
   HILL = 19.84

7. CREDIT is a real variable, so you must use an F specification to enter its value.

8.   READ(5,2) X,Y,Z
   2 FORMAT(F3.2,F4.0,F1.1)

9.   <u>1 2 3 4 5 6 7 8 9 10 11 12 13 14 15 ...</u>

   (a) 15.25   45 507.
        1525   45   507
   ―――――――――――――――

   (b) 152.5 4505070.
        1525   450 5070
   ―――――――――――――――

   (c) 1525.   50507.4
       Need field width of 6 to input
       COST without decimal point.
   ―――――――――――――――

   (d) 105.   5 300.
       105   5   300

10.   <u>1 2 3 4 5 6 ...</u>
      5142
      16
    Two input records.

11.   <u>1 2 3 4 5 6 7 8 9 10 ...</u>
      734 100
      607   3

12.   READ 2, X,Y,Z
       2 FORMAT(F3.2,F4.0,F1.1)

13.   15 FORMAT(I4,67X,F4.0)

14.   READ(5,20) AGE,ISEX,SALRY
      20 FORMAT(45X,F2.0,1X,I1,F8.2)

15.   (a) 15 FORMAT('+','HAL SPEAKS')
      (b) 15 FORMAT(' ','HAL SPEAKS')
      (c) 15 FORMAT('0','HAL SPEAKS')
      (d) 15 FORMAT('0','ƀƀƀƀƀHAL SPEAKS')
      (e) 15 FORMAT('1','HAL SPEAKS')

16.

17.   WRITE(6,1)
       1 FORMAT('0','THE ANSWER =')
         WRITE(6,2)
       2 FORMAT('+','_____')

                    ⟋—12 underscore characters

18.   10 FORMAT(1H1,30HIDENTIFICATIONƀƀƀƀƀBALANCE DUE)
      or
      10 FORMAT(31H1IDENTIFICATIONƀƀƀƀƀBALANCE DUE)

      The disadvantage of this method is that you must specify the exact number of characters, which requires you to count accurately. For particularly long string constants, this approach is tedious and error prone.

19.   Example 5.7:

         PRINT 10,J,X
      10 FORMAT('0',I5,F10.4)

      Example 5.8:

         PRINT 10
      10 FORMAT('1','IDENTIFICATIONƀƀƀƀƀBALANCE DUE')

21.

	1	2	3	4	5	6	7	8	9	0	1	2	3	4	5	6	7	8	9	0
1	M	=		7	5	6		N	=		-	4	0	1						
2																				
3				L	=		I	0												
4																				
5																				
6																				

L = 10   M = 756   N = −401

23.

	1	2	3	4	5	6	7	8	9	0
(a) 1	−	.	I	0	7	4				
(b) 2	−	0	.	I	0	7	4			
(c) 3			−	0	.	I	0	7	4	
(d) 4	0	.	I	0	7	4				
(e) 5				3	7	6	4	.	0	
(f) 6				3	7	6	4	.	2	
(g) 7				3	7	6	4	.		
(h) 8		3	7	6	4	.	I	6	0	
(i) 9	*	*	*	*	*	*				

(a) (Overflow if computer inserts leading zero.)

(j) F5.1

(k) F8.4

24.   WRITE(6,26)
    26 FORMAT(' ',7X,'NAME',18X,'WEEKLY')

    or

    26 FORMAT(8X,'NAME',18X,'WEEKLY')

CHAPTER 6

1.   READ(5,1) NAM1,NAM2,NAM3,NAM4,NAM5
    1 FORMAT(A4,A4,A4,A4,A4)

    WRITE(6,2)NAM3,NAM4,NAM5,NAM1,NAM2
    2 FORMAT(1X,A4,A4,A4,'   ',A4,A4)

2.   READ(5,1) SS1,SS2,SS3,N1,N2,N3,N4,N5,JAGE,MS,SEX,SAL
    1 FORMAT(A4,A4,A3,A4,A4,A4,A4,A4,I2,A1,A1,F7.2)

3. (a)

(b)

⊗		1	2	3	4	5	6	7	8	9	0
	1										
	2	C	A	P		N	E	M	O		
	3										

(c)

⊗		1	2	3	4	5	6	7	8	9	0
	1										
	2	C	A		N	E	M				
	3										

4.

5. Disadvantage: Inconvenient, since data have to be broken up into "words" of four (or max) characters.

6. (a)

(b)   CHARACTER SSN*11,NAME*20,MS*1,SEX*1

READ(5,1) SSN,NAME,JAGE,MS,SEX,SAL
1 FORMAT(A11,A20,I2,A1,A1,F7.2)

7.

Loop	SUMT	SUMBD	NAME1	NAME2	NAME3	ID	CREDIT	TUIT	BALDUE	SUMFEE
0	0.	0.								
1	1200.	1450.	FCƀM	EYER	ƀƀƀƀ	5142	16.	1200.	1450.	
2	2400.	2900.	RHƀM	EYER	ƀƀƀƀ	6245	18.5	1200.	1450.	
3	3300.	4050.	AAƀA	RIST	OTLE	322	9.	900.	1150.	
4	4500.	5500.	PPƀE	RUDI	TEƀƀ	3164	12.	1200.	1450.	
5	5100.	6350.	JJƀA	IDSƀ	ƀƀƀƀ	1969	6.	600.	850.	
	5100.	6350.	ƀƀƀƀ	ƀƀƀƀ	ƀƀƀƀ	−99	0.	600.	850.	1250.

8. (a) Immediately after WRITE(6,92) insert:

WRITE(6,93)   (60 underscore characters)
93 FORMAT('+','_____')

(b)   Immediately after statement 20 insert:

WRITE(6,97)   (30 underscore characters)
97 FORMAT('+',28X,'_____')

(c) 96 FORMAT('0',A4,A4,A4,I9,7X,'$',F7.2,4X,'$250.00',3X,'$',F7.2)
(d) 98 FORMAT('0',19X,'TOTALS',1X,'$',F9.2,2X,'$',F8.2,1X,'$',F9.2)

12. 25 FORMAT(3F10.2/2F5.2)

13. 30 FORMAT('1',4(F12.1,'%',I12))

14. (a)

(b)

(c)

(d)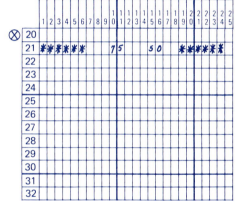

15. (a) No explicit carriage control after / /.
    (b) No explicit carriage control after / / /.
    (c) Do we mean I52,3X or I5,23X?

16.

	Columns	Variable
First record	1–5	A
	6–10	B
	11–20	L
Second record	1–5	C
	6–10	D

17. a.

	1 2 3 4 5 6 7 8 9 0 1 2 3 4 5 6 7 8 9 0
1	
2	
3	5 . 2 7 . 1
4	
5	1 0 . 4 6 . 3
6	

b.

	1 2 3 4 5 6 7 8 9 0 1 2 3 4 5 6 7 8 9 0
1	
2	5 . 2
3	7 . 1
4	1 0 . 4
5	6 . 3
6	

18. $3379.46 at 1.5 percent
    3514.96 at 2 percent
    6623.99 − 5441.92 = $1182.07

20. (a)   READ(5,1) P,R,N1,N2,IN,NAME1,NAME2,NAME3,NAME4,NAME5
           1 FORMAT(F8.2,F7.4,3I3,5A4)

    (b)   WRITE(6,2) NAME1,NAME2,NAME3,NAME4,NAME5
           2 FORMAT(/ / /'0',5A4)
           In FORMAT 3, eliminate / / /.

21. Replace N1 with N in the READ statement, and remove the statement N = N1.

22. $3379.46 at 1.5 percent
    $3514.96 at 2 percent
    $1182.07 difference (6623.99 − 5441.92)

23.   5 FORMAT(/ / 'ɓDO YOU WISH TO RUN AGAIN? 0 = NO, 1 = YES'/)

24. (a)   .
              ⋮
           100 FORMAT('0PLEASE ENTER CUSTOMER NAME')
           101 FORMAT(5A4)
            10 WRITE(6,100)
                  READ(5,101) NAME1,NAME2,NAME3,NAME4,NAME5
                  WRITE(6,2)
                  ⋮
              END

    (b) Just before WRITE(6,3) P,R insert:

           WRITE(6,103) NAME1,NAME2,NAME3,NAME4,NAME5
           103 FORMAT(/ / / '0',5A4)

    Eliminate / / / in FORMAT 3.

    (c) Replace N1 with N in the READ statement, and remove the statement N = N1.

CHAPTER 7

1. (a) Insert SIZE between .AND. and .LT.
   (b) No syntax error, but it's bad practice to use .EQ. with real expressions. For

example, A*C may never exactly equal 7.2 due to rounding error.
(c) Use .AND. not AND; IN .EQ. ON is a mixed mode comparison.

2. (a) IF (X .LT. 2. .OR. X .GT. 10.) GO TO 25
    (b) IF (A .GT. B .AND. A .GT. C) D = E − A

3. (a) K not incremented.
    (b) K is incremented, since (false) .OR. (true) gives true.
    (c) K not incremented, since (false) .AND. (true) .AND. (true) is followed by (false) .AND. (true), which is false.
    (d) K is incremented, since (true) .AND. (true) gives true.

4. (a) IF (INCOME .GT. 10000 .AND. SEX .EQ. 1.) K = K + 1
    (b) IF (INCOME .LE. 5000 .OR. AGE .GE. 65.) WRITE (6,*) ID
    (d) IF (A .GT. B .AND. C .GT. D .OR. A .GT. D) N = N + 1

5.
```
10 READ(5,*) ID,CREDIT
      IF (ID + 99) 15,20,15
15    TUIT = CREDIT*100.
      BALDUE = TUIT + 250.
      WRITE(6,*) ID,BALDUE
   GO TO 10
20 STOP
   END
```

6.
```
   K = 0
 5 READ(5,*) NUM,SIZE
      IF (NUM) 30,30,9
 9    IF (SIZE − 10.) 10,15,11
      .
      .
      .
25    WRITE(6,*)NUM,SIZE,TP
   GO TO 5
30 STOP
   END
```

7. (a) Missing comma following right parenthesis; however, FORTRAN 77 compilers allow this option. (b) ON is a real variable. (c) K has value outside of range.

8. Before the DATA statement insert:

    INTEGER CLASS

10.

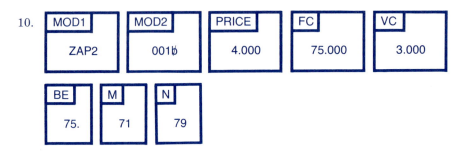

NUM	CARS	TR	TC	TP
71	71.	284.	288.	−4.
72	72.	288.	291.	−3.
73	73.	292.	294.	−2.

11. For rounding to the nearest thousand.
Because they are parameters in the DO statement.
To avoid mixing mode in the TR, TC calculations.

12.
```
      READ(5,1) MOD1,MOD2,PRICE,FC,VC,PLOW,PUP,INC
      :
      :
      :
      M = PLOW*BE + .5
      N = PUP*BE + .5
      DO 20 NUM = M,N,INC
          :
          :
   20 CONTINUE
      STOP
    1 FORMAT(2A4,3F6.3,2F4.2,I3)
      END
```

Changes are desirable because they make the program more general.

14.
```
      REAL JUN
      DATA FR,SOPH,JUN,SEN,TOTF,TOTSO,TOTJ,TOTSR/8*0./
      READ(5,*) NOS
      DO 100 K = 1,NOS
         READ(5,*) ICLASS,SATVER,SATMTH
         :
         :
  100 CONTINUE
      AVGF = TOTF/FR
      :
      :
      END
```

Note: K eliminated from
       DATA statement.

15.

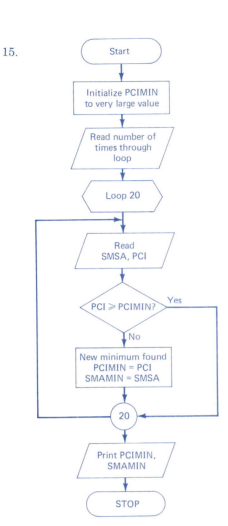

N is number of SMSAs.

J	SMSA	PCI	PCIMIN	SMAMIN
1	1472	5165.	5165.	1472
2	4165	7860.	5165.	1472
3	2134	6350.	5165.	1472
4	0415	4293.	4293.	0415
5	3147	5415.	4293.	0415

We initialize PCIMIN to a large value to assure that the first value of PCI is smaller.

17. (a)   DO 15 (X) = 1,N, (−2) ←— must be positive

    ↖ must be integer

    (15) CONTINUE

    ↖ insert

(b) Do not redefine loop parameters L and M within loop.

(c) 15   IF (I/4 .GT. K) GO TO (10) ←— 20 (Within loop, you can transfer to end of loop, not to DO.)

    GO TO (15)

    ↑
    10 (Outside loop, you can transfer to DO, but not to a point within loop.)

18. (a) 4. (b) Depends on system: 50, or 51, or error.

21. (a) Eliminate 20 CONTINUE and replace DO 20 with

    DO 40 NUM = M,N

(b) Eliminate both CONTINUE's, replace DO 20 with

    DO 40 NUM = M,N

and label the WRITE(6,5) statement as number 40.

CHAPTER 8

1. (a)   DIMENSION DEPOS (100)

    ⋮

    DO 10 I = 1,100

    ⋮

    DO 20 I = 1,100

The second program would require 291 new statements. One hundred variables would appear to the right of the equal sign in the calculation of TOT.

(b)   DIMENSION DEPOS (500)
    3 FORMAT(I3)
    READ(5,3) N

    ⋮

    DO 10 I = 1,N

    ⋮

    DO 20 I = 1,N

    ⋮

2. Compiler needs to know the number of locations to reserve for the array before execution begins.

3. (a)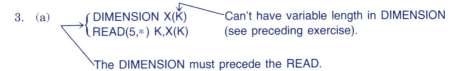

DIMENSION X(K)   Can't have variable length in DIMENSION
READ(5,*) K,X(K)   (see preceding exercise).

The DIMENSION must precede the READ.

(b) Arrays D and E have only 10 elements. As soon as I reaches 11, an execution error occurs. Also, cannot dimension D and E twice, so either eliminate the DIMENSION statement or change the INTEGER statement to INTEGER D, E. E(3) would store 36.

4.

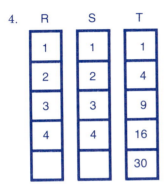

R	S	T
1	1	1
2	2	4
3	3	9
4	4	16
		30

5.
```
      DO 10 I = 1,50
          READ(5,1) MONEY(I)
  10 CONTINUE
```

6.

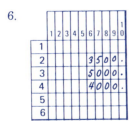

7.
```
      DIMENSION COST(3),SALES(3)
      DO 10 I = 1,3
          READ(5,1) COST(I),SALES(I)
  10 CONTINUE
   1 FORMAT (2F3.0)
```

Input Records

    1 2 3 4 5 6 . . .

    040100
    020125
    075095

8.

1 2 3 4 5 6 7 8 9 10 11 12 13 14 15 16 17 18 19 20 . . .

(a) and (d) 10 20 30 4 0

(b) and (e) 10
20
30
40

(c) 10 20
30 40

(f) 10,20,30 , 4 0

9. (a)

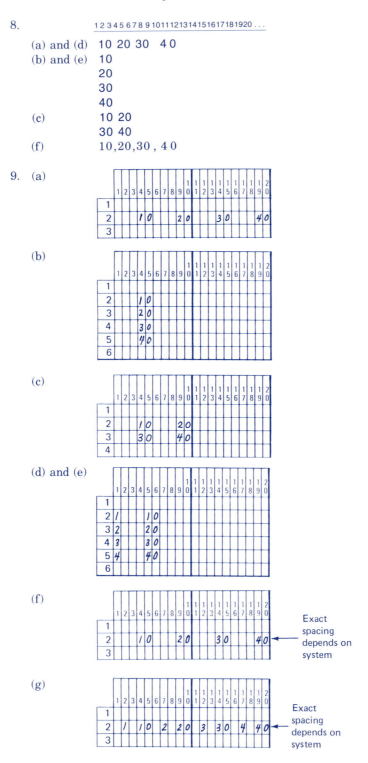

(b)

(c)

(d) and (e)

(f)

Exact spacing depends on system

(g)

Exact spacing depends on system

10. (a) READ(5,3) (X(I),I = 1,8)
     (b) WRITE(6,3) (X(I),I = 1,8)
     (c) READ(5,3) (X(I),I = 1,11,2)
     (d) WRITE(6,3) (A(I),B(I),I = 1,3)
     (e) WRITE(6,3) (A(I),I = 1,3),(B(I),I = 1,5)

12. (a) 1 2 3 4 5 6 7 8 9 10111213141516171819202122232425262728293031323334353637383940414243444546474849505152535455565758 59 60

```
10
12345678
 1      2      3      4      5      6      7      8      9     1 0    1 1    1 2    1 3    1 4    1 5
```

(b)

(c)

13.
```
┌──────────┐
│  BAL(1)  │
├──────────┤
│  150.30  │
├──────────┤
│  BAL(2)  │
├──────────┤
│  850.75  │
└──────────┘
```

14.   DO 10 I = 1,K
            SUM = SUM + REVEN(I)
      10 CONTINUE

15.   DO 100 K = 1,10
            TOTAL(K) = 0.
      100 CONTINUE

         or

      DATA TOTAL/10*0./

16. (a)

	1	2	3	4	5	6	7	8	9	0	1	2	3	4	5	6	7	8	9	0	1	2	3	4	5	6	7	8	9	0
1																														
2																														
3	R	I	P		V	A	N		W	I	N	K	L	E								$	3	5	7					
4																														
5																														

This would be incorrect output since the maximum insurable age is 65 according to the premium schedule. Some systems might give an execution error at statement 20 if I is undefined or equal to 6.

17. In the DIMENSION statement replace NAME(6) with NAME(24)

NAME

1
Cbbb

2
Lbbb

3
Abbb

4
Rbbb

5
Kbbb

6
bbbb

7
Sbbb

8
.bbb

9
bbbb

10
Kbbb

(continued on next page)

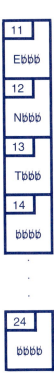

This approach wastes storage.

18. If the premium schedule had already been read through loop 10, then we would get an "out of data error" message in loop 15. If loop 10 is eliminated, then this approach requires the partial read-in of the premium schedule for each person that's processed. It doesn't work because we would not know beforehand exactly how to arrange the data.

19. (a)

TOTSAT	COUNT(1)	COUNT(2)	COUNT(3)	COUNT(4)	TOT(1)	TOT(2)	TOT(3)	TOT(4)
—	0.	0.	0.	0.	0.	0.	0.	0.
1220.	0.	1.	0.	0.	0.	1220.	0.	0.
1400.	0.	1.	1.	0.	0.	1220.	1400.	0.
1170.	0.	2.	1.	0.	0.	2390.	1400.	0.
1150.	1.	2.	1.	0.	1150.	2390.	1400.	0.
1000.	1.	3.	1.	0.	1150.	3390.	1400.	0.

(b) 1150. 1130. 1400. ****   Execution error in loop 30 when we attempt to divide by COUNT(4) = 0. Some systems allow processing to continue, giving format overflow in the output of AVG(4).

20. (a)   DATA COUNT, TOT/8*0./
    (b)   DIMENSION COUNT(4),TOT(4)
           .
           .
           .
           DO 30 I = 1,4
                TOT(I) = TOT(I)/COUNT(I)
        30 CONTINUE
           WRITE(6,*) TOT
           .
           .
           .

    Once we use a stored sum in an element of TOT we have no more need for that sum—so we use that element to store the average, thereby saving four storage locations.

21. | I | TEMP | LIST(1) | LIST(2) | LIST(3) | LIST(4) | SWITCH |
    |---|------|---------|---------|---------|---------|--------|
    | 2 | 3076 | 3076 | 8321 | 2501 | 7771 | 1 |
    | 3 | 2501 | 3076 | 2501 | 8321 | 7771 | 1 |
    | 4 | 7771 | 3076 | 2501 | 7771 | 8321 | 1 |
    | 2 | 2501 | 2501 | 3076 | 7771 | 8321 | 1 |
    | 3 | 2501 | 2501 | 3076 | 7771 | 8321 | 1 |
    | 4 | 2501 | 2501 | 3076 | 7771 | 8321 | 1 |
    | 2 | 2501 | 2501 | 3076 | 7771 | 8321 | 0 |
    | 3 | 2501 | 2501 | 3076 | 7771 | 8321 | 0 |
    | 4 | 2501 | 2501 | 3076 | 7771 | 8321 | 0 |

    Two passes; three passes.

22. Change the IF to:

    IF (LIST(I) .LT. LIST(I − 1)) GO TO 30

23. Yes, since the internal computer coding of alphabetic data is expressed in numeric code. This means, for example, that the alphabetic character A is represented by a coded value that is "numerically" less than the code for the alphabetic character B. (See Exercise 29c.)

CHAPTER 9

1.   DO 40 I = 1,3
           DO 30 J = 1,4
                WRITE(6,4) DEPOS(I,J)
        30 CONTINUE
        40 CONTINUE

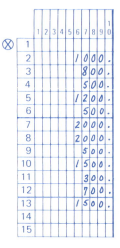

2.   DEPOS

1000.	1200.	2000.	300.
800.	500.	500.	700.
500.	2000.	1500.	1500.

Array is filled column by column. Input data should be in the following order:

1 2 3 4 5 . . .

```
1000
 500
1500
 800
2000
 300
 500
2000
 700
1200
 500
1500
```

3. (a)   DO 10 I = 1,3
               DO 10 J = 1,2
               READ(5,1) LOT(I,J)
        10 CONTINUE
         1 FORMAT(I3)

Input Data

1 2 3 . . .

```
 10
 50
  4
320
 15
  8
```

(b) and (c)

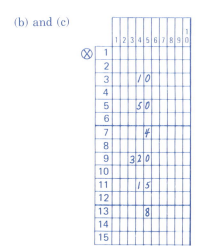

(d)

4.   DO 50 I = 1,3
         DO 50 J = 1,2
       50 WRITE(6,2) LOT(I,J)

5. (a)   WRITE(6,*) ((X(I,J),J = 1,3),I = 1,2)
    (b)   DO 20 I = 1,2
         20 WRITE(6,*) (X(I,J),J = 1,3)
    (c)   DO 20 J = 1,3
         20 WRITE(6,*) (X(I,J),I = 1,2)

6. (a) 1 2 3 4 5 6 . . .

         1000
          800
          500
           ⋮
          700
         1500

    (b) 1 2 3 4 5 67 8 9 101112 . . . 5657585960

         1000 800   . . .   1 5 0 0

7.   READ(5,1) ((DEPOS(I,J),I = 1,3),J = 1,4)
       1 FORMAT(3F5.0)

    Array in memory gets filled in column by column, ending up the same as in Example 9.3.

8. (a)

⊗	1-2-3-4	.
1		
2	1 0 0 0	.
3	8 0 0	.
4	5 0 0	.
5	1 2 0 0	.
6	5 0 0	.
7	2 0 0 0	.
8	2 0 0 0	.
9	5 0 0	.
10	1 5 0 0	.
11	3 0 0	.
12	7 0 0	.
13	1 5 0 0	.

    (b) and (c)

⊗				
1				
2	1 0 0 0 .	8 0 0 .	5 0 0 .	1 2 0 0 .
3	5 0 0 .	2 0 0 0 .	2 0 0 0 .	5 0 0 .
4	1 5 0 0 .	3 0 0 .	7 0 0 .	1 5 0 0 .
5				

(d)

```
         111111111122222222223
 123456789012345678901234567890
 1
 2
 3 BANK DEPOSITS
 4
 5
 6  1000.    800.    500.   1200.
 7
 8 BANK DEPOSITS
 9
10
11    500.   2000.   2000.    500.
12
13 BANK DEPOSITS
14
15
16  1500.    300.    700.   1500.
17
18
```

(e)   WRITE(6,2) ((DEPOS(I,J), J = 1,4), I = 1,3)
     2 FORMAT('0','BANK DEPOSITS'//3('0',4F6.0))

9. (a) 12 records, each with one item   ⎫ Remember: Data are read column by
   (b) 12 items on one record   ⎬ column in the sequence 1000,500,
   (c) 4 records, each with 3 items   ⎭ 1500,...,500,1500.

10. No. The first prints column by column and the second prints in the usual row-by-row manner.

12. (a) 80
   (b) 50
   (c) Two reasons: You don't always need the entire 50×20 array; short list would read in column by column, so the nursery rhyme would look "jumbled" on the input records.
   (d) Each input record would have only 4 characters per line.
   (e) Print as many copies as desired (NUM).
   (f)

Method 1	Method 2
Change as follows: DIMENSION NR(50,80) 4 FORMAT(80A1) 8 FORMAT('0',19X,80A1)	Immediately after N is read in, insert: N = (N + 3)/4 This assumes a computer that stores 4 characters per storage location.

13.
```
     DO 40 J = 1,4
        TOT(J) = 0.
        DO 35 I = 1,3
           TOT(J) = TOT(J) + DEPOS(I,J)
35      CONTINUE
40 CONTINUE
```

15.　　　DO 80 I = 1,3
　　　　DO 80 J = 1,4
　　　80 PER(I,J) = DEPOS(I,J)/SUM(I)*100.

Third row of PER:　37.5　7.5　17.5　37.5

16. (a)　　DO 10 I = 1,100
　　　　　DO 10 J = 1,50
　　　　10 WEIGHT(I,J) = 100.
　　(b) DATA WEIGHT/5000*100./

The alternative in b should not be used if there's need to reinitialize during execution.

20.　NUM = Number of taxpayers to be processed
　　TAXPAY = Taxes paid through withholding
　　REFUND = Amount of tax owed to taxpayer
　　BALDUE = Amount of tax taxpayer owes
　　TAXTAB(I,1) = Upper limit of taxable income (column 2 in Tax Schedule)
　　TAXTAB(I,2) = Fixed amount of tax within a class (column 3 in Tax Schedule)
　　TAXTAB(I,3) = Variable percent amount of tax within a class (column 4 in Tax Schedule)
　　TAXTAB(I − 1,1) = Upper limit of taxable income for previous class, which is the same as lower limit in class I (column 1 in Tax Schedule)

21.　Column by column.
　　Six records (12 items per record for total of 78 items; see next exercise).
　　A number that's as large as possible. Since F6.0 is used to input, enter 999999 for this number.

22.

```
1  ADJUSTED GROSS INCOME = $23430.20
2
3            TAXABLE INCOME = $20650.20
4
5            INCOME TAX = $ 4672.07
6
7  PANIC. PAY THE IRS $  572.07
8
```

```
1  ADJUSTED GROSS INCOME = $12100.00
2
3            TAXABLE INCOME = $11350.00
4
5            INCOME TAX = $ 1877.50
6
7  GREAT. THE IRS OWES YOU $  652.50
8
```

CHAPTER 10

1. (a) Z = .6   Z = 1.8   K = 20
    (b) P = .1609438   T = .3010300
    (c) 0.1680668E-01
    (d) In both cases, to avoid mixing mode in the arithmetic expressions.
    (e) S = 7.
    (f) L = 10

2. READ(5,*) X,Y
    P = ABS(X − .5*Y)
    WRITE(6,*) P
    STOP
    END

5. (a) OK, but intended ordering of arguments may be logically incorrect.
    (b) Inconsistent mode in arguments: (K,L,M) versus (X,Y,Z)
    (c) OK.
    (d) Calling statement has one argument, but statement function needs two.
    (e) Statement function should be GRIEF(P,Q) = P**Q

6. At the beginning of the main program insert:

    INTEGER BAL

    In the subprogram, use the following altered FUNCTION statement:

    INTEGER FUNCTION BAL(CR,C,F)

    Alternatively, we could have called the function IBAL, or JBAL, or any other integer name.

7. 10 READ(5,*) ID,CPCH,FEE
       IF (ID .EQ. −99) STOP
       BALDUE = BAL(CPCH,FEE)
          :
          :
       END
       FUNCTION BAL(C,F)
       READ(5,*) CREDIT
       IF (CREDIT .LT. 12.) TUIT = CREDIT*C
       IF (CREDIT .GE. 12.) TUIT = 12.*C
       BAL = TUIT + F
       RETURN
       END

11. To get correct value for number of weeks when the number of days is a multiple of 7.
    Any fraction could be used.

12.
```
10 READ(5,*) DFC,CPM,WFC,PG,MG,M,D
      IF(DFC .LT. 0.) STOP
      CALL COST(DFC,CPM,WFC,PG,MG,M,D)
   GO TO 10
   END
   SUBROUTINE COST(A,B,C,F,K,M,D)
   DAY = A*D + B*FLOAT(M)
   W = INT(D - .1)/7 + 1
   WEEK = C*W + FLOAT(M)/FLOAT(K)*F
   DIFF = DAY - WEEK
   WRITE(6,*) DAY,WEEK,DIFF
   RETURN
   END
```

No, the costs are calculated and printed in the subroutine.

14.
```
   .
   .
   .
      IF (ID .EQ. -99) STOP
      CALL BAL(CREDIT,CPCH,FEE,BALDUE)
      WRITE(6,*) ID,BALDUE
   GO TO 10
   END
   SUBROUTINE BAL(CR,C,F,BALDUE)
   IF (CR .LT. 12.) TUIT = CR*C
   IF (CR .GE. 12.) TUIT = 12.*C
   BALDUE = TUIT + F
   RETURN
   END
```

15. You can pass more than one value from the subprogram to the calling program.

16.
```
   .
   .
   .
   CALL MEAN(N,SCORE,SUM,AVE)
   WRITE(6,*) SUM,AVE
   STOP
   END
   SUBROUTINE MEAN(N,X,S,XMEAN)
   .
   .
   .
```

You can't pass more than one value from a function subprogram to the calling program.

17.
```
   CALL MEAN
   STOP
   END
   SUBROUTINE MEAN
   DIMENSION X(100)
   READ(5,*) N,(X(J),J = 1,N)
   S = 0.
```

```
      DO 10 I = 1,N
   10 S = S + X(I)
      XMEAN = S/FLOAT(N)
      WRITE(6,*) XMEAN
      RETURN
      END
```

N need only be less than 100 in this case. In general, N can be input through the subprogram if it is not used as an adjustable dimension.

19. Depends on the compiler. See item 4 in Section 10.7.

21. (a) N and J, Y(1) and P matchups OK, but integer M must not be paired with real R; real Q must not be paired with integer K.
     (b) Missing comma after R(30); dimension of S should coincide with dimension on R. Either change the 50 to 30 or the 30 to 50. If this dimension change is not made, then A will share storage with S(31).
     (c) OK. D shares with A, and E shares with B.
     (d) COMMON D,E,F is OK, but COMMON for the second subprogram should be changed to:

         COMMON A,B,C,M,N

     in order to align M with I and N with J.

22. (a) COMMON CREDIT,CPCH,FEE,BALDUE
         .
         .
         CALL BAL
         .
         .
         END
         SUBROUTINE BAL
         COMMON CR,C,F,BALDUE
         .
         .
         END

CHAPTER 11

1.   READ(5,*) ID,CREDIT
      IF (CREDIT .GE. 12.) GO TO 20
      TUIT = CREDIT*100.
      GO TO 25
   20 TUIT = 1200.
   25 BALDUE = TUIT + 250.
      WRITE(6,*) ID,BALDUE
      STOP
      END
```
```

2.   IF (CREDIT .GE. 12.) GO TO 20
          TUIT = CREDIT*100.
          IPART = IPART + 1
          GO TO 25
     20 TUIT = 1200.
          IFULL = IFULL + 1
     25 . . .
          .
          .
          .

The approach used in Example 11.1 cannot be used directly here because more than one statement needs to be executed within each branch; however, we could use the following tedious approach:

          .
          .
          .
     IF (CREDIT .GE. 12.) TUIT = 1200.
     IF (CREDIT .GE. 12.) IFULL = IFULL + 1
     IF (CREDIT .LT. 12.) TUIT = CREDIT*100.
     IF (CREDIT .LT. 12.) IPART = IPART + 1
          .
          .
          .

3.

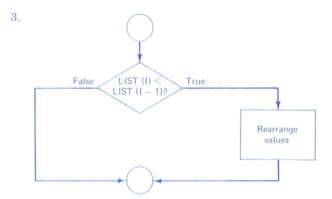

5.   The DO CASE statement highlights the alternative branches by starting each with the instruction CASE. Second, transfer to the end of all cases is automatic following the execution of a branch. This eliminates the need to have a GO TO at the end of each branch, which was required when using the computed GO TO. Third, statement numbers are not needed, which simplifies the code. Finally, the DO CASE provides an explicit test when the index is outside the range.

6.

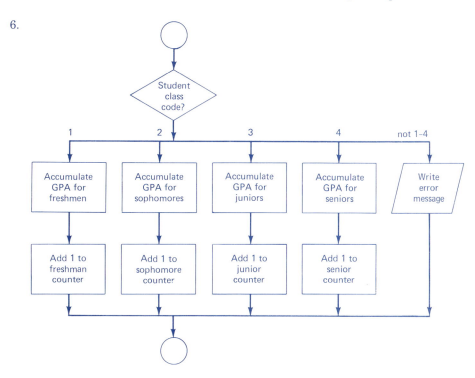

7. When the employee number (NUM) is zero or negative.

8.

NAME(1) = ALḃD	NODEP = 4	SSTAX = 10.73
NAME(2) = ELLA	RATE = 2.50	WTHTAX = 28.
NAME(3) = ḃBIT	HOURS = 60.	HEALTH = 6.
NAME(4) = TAḃḃ	TOTERN = 1500.	TOTDED = 44.73
NAME(5) = ḃḃḃḃ	GPAY = 175.	PAYNET = 130.27
NUM = 1940		CUMPAY = 1675.

Index